CHEAT CODE EXPLOSION

FOR CONSOLES

W9-BLJ-006

FLIP THIS BOOK OVER FOR HANDHELD SYSTEMS
Nintendo DS™
PlayStation® Portable

LOOK FOR CODEY
When you see Codey's face, you've found the newest and coolest codes!

SPECIAL SECTION: GUITAR HERO & ROCK BAND

GAMES LIST

BAND HERO

MOST CHARACTERS UNLOCKED

Select Input Cheats from the options and enter Blue, Yellow, Green, Yellow, Red, Green, Red, Yellow.

ELECTRIKA STEEL UNLOCKED

Select Input Cheats from the options and enter Blue, Blue, Red, Yellow, Red, Yellow, Blue, Blue.

ALL HOPO MODE

Select Input Cheats from the options and enter Red, Green, Blue, Green, Blue, Green, Red, Green.

ALWAYS SLIDE

Select Input Cheats from the options and enter Yellow, Green, Yellow, Yellow, Yellow, Red, Blue, Red.

AUTO KICK

Select Input Cheats from the options and enter Yellow, Green, Yellow, Blue, Blue, Red, Blue, Red.

FOCUS MODE

Select Input Cheats from the options and enter Yellow, Yellow, Green, Green, Red, Red, Blue, Blue.

HUD FREE MODE

Select Input Cheats from the options and enter Green, Red, Green, Red, Yellow, Blue, Green, Red.

PERFORMANCE MODE

Select Input Cheats from the options and enter Yellow, Yellow, Blue, Green, Blue, Red, Red, Red.

AIR INSTRUMENTS

Select Input Cheats from the options and enter Blue, Yellow, Blue, Red, Red, Yellow, Green, Yellow.

INVISIBLE ROCKER

Select Input Cheats from the options and enter Green, Red, Yellow, Green, Yellow, Blue, Yellow, Green.

GUITAR HERO

UNLOCK ALL

At the Main menu, press Yellow, Orange, Blue, Blue, Orange, Yellow, Yellow.

GUITAR HERO GUITAR CHEAT

At the Main menu, press Blue, Orange, Yellow, Blue, Blue.

CROWD METER CHEAT

At the Main menu, press Yellow, Blue, Orange, Orange, Blue, Blue, Yellow, Orange.

MONKEY HEAD CROWD CHEAT

At the Main menu, press Blue, Orange, Yellow, Yellow, Yellow, Blue, Orange.

SKULL HEAD CROWD CHEAT

At the Main menu, press Orange, Yellow, Blue, Blue, Orange, Yellow, Blue, Blue.

AIR GUITAR CHEAT

At the Main menu, press Orange, Orange, Blue, Yellow, Orange.

NO VENUE CHEAT

At the Main menu, press Blue, Yellow, Orange, Blue, Yellow, Orange.

GUITAR HERO II

AIR GUITAR

At the Main menu, press Yellow, Yellow, Blue, Orange, Yellow, Blue.

EYEBALL HEAD CROWD

At the Main menu, press Blue, Orange, Yellow, Orange, Yellow, Orange, Blue.

MONKEY HEAD CROWD

At the Main menu, press Orange, Blue, Yellow, Yellow, Orange, Blue, Yellow, Yellow.

FLAMING HEAD

At the Main menu, press Orange, Yellow, Orange, Orange, Yellow, Orange, Yellow, Yellow.

HORSE HEAD

At the Main menu, press Blue, Orange, Orange, Blue, Orange, Orange, Blue, Orange, Orange, Blue.

HYPER SPEED

At the Main menu, press Orange, Blue, Orange, Yellow, Orange, Blue, Orange, Yellow.

PERFORMANCE MODE

At the Main menu, press Yellow, Yellow, Blue, Yellow, Yellow, Orange, Yellow, Yellow.

GUITAR HERO III: LEGENDS OF ROCK

To enter the following cheats, strum the guitar while holding the listed buttons. For example, if the code lists Yellow + Orange, hold the Yellow and Orange buttons as you strum. Air Guitar, Precision Mode and Performance Mode can be toggled on and off from the Cheats menu. You can also change between five different levels of Hyperspeed at this menu.

UNLOCK EVERYTHING

Select Cheats from the Options. Choose Enter Cheat and enter the following (no sounds play while this code is entered):

Green + Red + Blue + Orange
Green + Red + Yellow + Blue
Green + Red + Yellow + Orange
Green + Yellow + Blue + Orange
Green + Red + Yellow + Blue
Red + Yellow + Blue + Orange
Green + Red + Yellow + Blue
Green + Yellow + Blue + Orange
Green + Red + Yellow + Blue
Green + Red + Yellow + Orange
Green + Red + Yellow + Orange
Green + Red + Yellow + Blue
Green + Red + Yellow + Orange

An easier way to illustrate this code is to represent Green as 1, progressing down the guitar neck to Orange as 5. For example, if you have 1345, you would hold Green + Yellow + Blue + Orange while strumming: 1245 + 1234 + 1235 + 1345 + 1234 + 2345 + 1234 + 1345 + 1234 + 1235 + 1235 + 1234 + 1235.

ALL SONGS

Select Cheats from the Options. Choose Enter Cheat and enter:

Yellow + Orange	Yellow + Blue
Red + Blue	Yellow + Orange
Red + Orange	Yellow + Orange
Green + Blue	Yellow + Blue
Red + Yellow	Yellow
Yellow + Orange	Red
Red + Yellow	Red + Yellow
Red + Blue	Red
Green + Yellow	Yellow
Green + Yellow	Orange
Yellow + Blue	

NO FAIL

Select Cheats from the Options. Choose Enter Cheat and enter:

Green + Red	Orange
Blue	Red + Yellow
Green + Red	Green + Yellow
Green + Yellow	Yellow
Blue	Green + Yellow
Green + Yellow	Green + Red
Red + Yellow	

AIR GUITAR

Select Cheats from the Options. Choose Enter Cheat and enter:

Blue + Yellow	Red + Yellow
Green + Yellow	Blue + Yellow
Green + Yellow	Green + Yellow
Red + Blue	Green + Yellow
Red + Blue	Red + Blue
Red + Yellow	Red + Blue

Red + Yellow	
Red + Yellow	
Green + Yellow	
Green + Yellow	
Red + Yellow	
Red + Yellow	

HYPERSPEED

Select Cheats from the Options. Choose Enter Cheat and enter:

Orange	Orange
Blue	Blue
Orange	Orange
Yellow	Yellow

PERFORMANCE MODE

Select Cheats from the Options. Choose Enter Cheat and enter:

Red + Yellow	Red + Yellow
Red + Blue	Green + Blue
Red + Orange	Red + Yellow
Red + Blue	Red + Blue

EASY EXPERT

Select Cheats from the Options. Choose Enter Cheat and enter:

Green + Red	Blue + Orange
Green + Yellow	Yellow + Orange
Yellow + Blue	Red + Yellow
Red + Blue	Red + Blue

PRECISION MODE

Select Cheats from the Options. Choose Enter Cheat and enter:

Green + Red	Green + Red
Green + Red	Green + Red
Green + Red	Green + Red
Red + Yellow	Red + Yellow
Red + Yellow	Red + Yellow
Red + Blue	Red + Blue
Red + Blue	Red + Blue
Yellow + Blue	Yellow + Blue
Yellow + Orange	Yellow + Orange
Yellow + Orange	Yellow + Orange

BRET MICHAELS SINGER

Select Cheats from the Options. Choose Enter Cheat and enter:

Green + Red	Red
Green + Red	Red + Blue
Green + Red	Red
Green + Blue	Red
Green + Blue	Red
Green + Blue	Red + Blue
Red + Blue	Red
Red	Red
Red	Red

5

GUITAR HERO 5

ALL HOPOS

Select Input Cheats from the Options menu and enter Green, Green, Blue, Green, Green, Green, Yellow, Green.

ALWAYS SLIDE

Select Input Cheats from the Options menu and enter Green, Green, Red, Red, Yellow, Blue, Yellow, Blue.

AUTO KICK

Select Input Cheats from the Options menu and enter Yellow, Green, Red, Blue, Blue, Blue, Blue, Red.

FOCUS MODE

Select Input Cheats from the Options menu and enter Yellow, Green, Red, Green, Yellow, Blue, Green, Green.

HUD FREE MODE

Select Input Cheats from the Options menu and enter Green, Red, Green, Green, Yellow, Green, Green, Green.

PERFORMANCE MODE

Select Input Cheats from the Options menu and enter Yellow, Yellow, Blue, Red, Blue, Green, Red, Red.

AIR INSTRUMENTS

Select Input Cheats from the Options menu and enter Red, Red, Blue, Yellow, Green, Green, Green, Yellow.

INVISIBLE ROCKER

Select Input Cheats from the Options menu and enter Green, Red, Yellow, Yellow, Yellow, Blue, Blue, Green.

ALL CHARACTERS

Select Input Cheats from the Options menu and enter Blue, Blue, Green, Green, Red, Green, Red, Yellow.

CONTEST WINNER 1

Select Input Cheats from the Options menu and enter Green, Green, Red, Red, Yellow, Red, Yellow, Blue.

GUITAR HERO ENCORE: ROCKS THE 80S

UNLOCK EVERYTHING

At the Main menu, press Blue, Orange, Yellow, Red, Orange, Yellow, Blue, Yellow, Red, Yellow, Blue, Yellow, Red, Yellow, Blue, Yellow.

HYPERSPEED

At the Main menu, press Yellow, Blue, Orange, Orange, Blue, Yellow, Yellow, Orange.

PERFORMANCE MODE

At the Main menu, press Blue, Blue, Orange, Yellow, Yellow, Blue, Orange, Blue.

AIR GUITAR

At the Main menu, press Yellow, Blue, Yellow, Orange, Blue, Blue.

EYEBALL HEAD CROWD

At the Main menu, press Yellow, Blue, Orange, Orange, Orange, Blue, Yellow.

MONKEY HEAD CROWD

At the Main menu, press Blue, Blue, Orange, Yellow, Blue, Blue, Orange, Yellow.

FLAME HEAD

At the Main menu, press Yellow, Orange, Yellow, Orange, Yellow, Orange, Blue, Orange.

HORSE HEAD

At the Main menu, press Blue, Orange, Orange, Blue, Yellow, Blue, Orange, Orange, Blue, Yellow.

GUITAR HERO WORLD TOUR

The following cheats can be toggled on and off at the Cheats menu.

QUICKPLAY SONGS

Select Cheats from the Options menu, choose Enter New Cheat and press Blue, Blue, Red, Green, Green, Blue, Blue, Yellow.

ALWAYS SLIDE

Select Cheats from the Options menu, choose Enter New Cheat and press Green, Green, Red, Red, Yellow, Red, Yellow, Blue.

AT&T BALLPARK

Select Cheats from the Options menu, choose Enter New Cheat and press Yellow, Green, Red, Red, Green, Blue, Red, Yellow.

AUTO KICK

Select Cheats from the Options menu, choose Enter New Cheat and press Yellow, Green, Red, Blue (x4), Red.

EXTRA LINE 6 TONES

Select Cheats from the Options menu, choose Enter New Cheat and press Green, Red, Yellow, Blue, Red, Yellow, Blue, Green.

FLAME COLOR

Select Cheats from the Options menu, choose Enter New Cheat and press Green, Red, Green, Blue, Red, Red, Yellow, Blue.

GEM COLOR

Select Cheats from the Options menu, choose Enter New Cheat and press Blue, Red, Red, Green, Red, Green, Red, Yellow.

STAR COLOR

Select Cheats from the Options menu, choose Enter New Cheat and press Red, Red, Yellow, Red, Blue, Red, Red, Blue.

AIR INSTRUMENTS

Select Cheats from the Options menu, choose Enter New Cheat and press Red, Red, Blue, Yellow, Green (x3), Yellow.

HYPERSPEED

Select Cheats from the Options menu, choose Enter New Cheat and press Green, Blue, Red, Yellow, Yellow, Red, Green, Green. These show up in the menu as HyperGuitar, HyperBass, and HyperDrums.

PERFORMANCE MODE

Select Cheats from the Options menu, choose Enter New Cheat and press Yellow, Yellow, Blue, Red, Blue, Green, Red, Red.

INVISIBLE ROCKER

Select Cheats from the Options menu, choose Enter New Cheat and press Green, Red, Yellow (x3), Blue, Blue, Green.

VOCAL FIREBALL

Select Cheats from the Options menu, choose Enter New Cheat and press Red, Green, Green, Yellow, Blue, Green, Yellow, Green.

AARON STEELE!

Select Cheats from the Options menu, choose Enter New Cheat and press Blue, Red, Yellow (x5), Green.

JONNY VIPER

Select Cheats from the Options menu, choose Enter New Cheat and press Blue, Red, Blue, Blue, Yellow (x3), Green.

NICK

Select Cheats from the Options menu, choose Enter New Cheat and press Green, Red, Blue, Green, Red, Blue, Blue, Green.

RINA

Select Cheats from the Options menu, choose Enter New Cheat and press Blue, Red, Green, Green, Yellow (x3), Green.

GUITAR HERO: AEROSMITH

To enter the following cheats, strum the guitar while holding the listed buttons. For example, if the codes lists Yellow + Orange, hold Yellow and Orange as you strum. Air Guitar, Precision Mode, and Performance Mode can be toggled on and off from the Cheats menu. You can also change between five different levels of Hyperspeed at this menu.

ALL SONGS

Red + Yellow
Green + Red
Green + Red
Red + Yellow
Red + Yellow
Green + Red
Red + Yellow
Red + Yellow
Green + Red
Green + Red
Red + Yellow
Red + Yellow
Green + Red
Red + Yellow
Red + Blue

AIR GUITAR

Red + Yellow
Green + Red
Red + Yellow
Red + Yellow
Red + Blue
Red + Blue
Red + Blue
Red + Blue
Red + Blue
Yellow + Blue
Yellow + Blue
Yellow + Orange

HYPERSPEED

Yellow + Orange
Yellow + Orange
Yellow + Orange
Yellow + Orange
Yellow + Orange
Red + Yellow
Red + Yellow
Red + Yellow
Red + Yellow
Red + Blue
Red + Blue
Red + Blue
Red + Blue
Red + Blue
Yellow + Blue
Yellow + Orange
Yellow + Orange

NO FAIL

Green + Red
Blue
Green + Red
Green + Yellow
Blue
Green + Yellow
Red + Yellow
Orange
Red + Yellow
Green + Yellow
Yellow
Green + Yellow
Green + Red

PERFORMANCE MODE

Green + Red
Green + Red
Red + Orange
Red + Blue
Green + Red
Green + Red
Red + Orange
Red + Blue

PRECISION MODE

Red + Yellow
Red + Blue
Red + Blue
Red + Yellow
Red + Yellow
Yellow + Blue
Yellow + Blue
Yellow + Blue
Red + Blue
Red + Yellow
Red + Blue
Red + Blue
Red + Yellow
Red + Yellow
Yellow + Blue
Yellow + Blue
Yellow + Blue
Red + Blue

GUITAR HERO: METALLICA

Once entered, the cheats must be activated in the Cheats menu.

METALLICA COSTUMES

Select Cheats from Settings and enter Green, Red, Yellow, Blue, Blue, Yellow, Red, Green.

HYPERSPEED

Select Cheats from Settings and enter Green, Blue, Red, Yellow, Yellow, Red, Green, Green.

PERFORMANCE MODE

Select Cheats from Settings and enter Yellow, Yellow, Blue, Red, Blue, Green, Red, Red.

INVISIBLE ROCKER

Select Cheats from Settings and enter Green, Red, Yellow (x3), Blue, Blue, Green.

AIR INSTRUMENTS

Select Cheats from Settings and enter Red, Red, Blue, Yellow, Green (x3), Yellow.

ALWAYS DRUM FILL

Select Cheats from Settings and enter Red (x3), Blue, Blue, Green, Green, Yellow.

AUTO KICK

Select Cheats from Settings and enter Yellow, Green, Red, Blue (x4), Red. With this cheat activated, the bass pedal is automatically hit.

ALWAYS SLIDE

Select Cheats from Settings and enter Green, Green, Red, Red, Yellow, Red, Yellow, Blue. All Guitar Notes Become Touch Pad Sliding Notes.

BLACK HIGHWAY

Select Cheats from Settings and enter Yellow, Red, Green, Red, Green, Red, Red, Blue.

FLAME COLOR

Select Cheats from Settings and enter Green, Red, Green, Blue, Red, Red, Yellow, Blue.

GEM COLOR

Select Cheats from Settings and enter Blue, Red, Red, Green, Red, Green, Red, Yellow.

STAR COLOR

Select Cheats from Settings and enter Press Red, Red, Yellow, Red, Blue, Red, Red, Blue.

ADDITIONAL LINE 6 TONES

Select Cheats from Settings and enter Green, Red, Yellow, Blue, Red, Yellow, Blue, Green.

VOCAL FIREBALL

Select Cheats from Settings and enter Red, Green, Green, Yellow, Blue, Green, Yellow, Green.

GUITAR HERO: SMASH HITS

Enter the following in the cheats menu which can be found in the options menu.

ALWAYS DRUM FILL
Green, Green, Red, Red, Blue, Yellow, Yellow

ALWAYS SLIDE
Blue, Yellow, Red, Green, Blue, Green, Green, Yellow

HYPERSPEED
Red, Green, Blue, Yellow, Green, Yellow, Red, Red

AIR INSTRUMENTS
Yellow, Red, Blue, Green, Yellow, Red, Red, Red

INVISIBLE ROCKER
Blue, Red, Red, Red, Red, Yellow, Blue, Green

GEM COLOR
Red, Red, Red, Blue, Blue, Blue, Yellow, Green

STAR COLOR
Green, Red, Green, Yellow, Green, Blue, Yellow, Red

LINE 6 UNLOCK
Green, Red, Yellow, Blue, Red, Yellow, Blue, Green

VOCAL FIREBALL
Green, Blue, Red, Red, Yellow, Yellow, Blue, Blue

GUITAR HERO: VAN HALEN

ALWAYS DRUM FILL
Select Input Cheats from the Options menu and enter Red, Red, Red, Blue, Blue, Green, Green, Yellow.

ALWAYS SLIDE
Select Input Cheats from the Options menu and enter Green, Green, Red, Red, Yellow, Red, Yellow, Blue.

AUTO KICK
Select Input Cheats from the Options menu and enter Yellow, Green, Red, Blue, Blue, Blue, Blue, Red.

HYPERSPEED
Select Input Cheats from the Options menu and enter Green, Blue, Red, Yellow, Yellow, Red, Green, Green. This allows you to enable Hyperguitar, Hyperbass, and Hyperdrums.

PERFORMANCE MODE
Select Input Cheats from the Options menu and enter Yellow, Yellow, Blue, Red, Blue, Green, Red, Red.

AIR INSTRUMENTS
Select Input Cheats from the Options menu and enter Red, Red, Blue, Yellow, Green, Green, Green, Yellow.

INVISIBLE ROCKER
Select Input Cheats from the Options menu and enter Green, Red, Yellow, Yellow, Yellow, Blue, Blue, Green.

BLACK HIGHWAY
Select Input Cheats from the Options menu and enter Yellow, Red, Green, Red, Green, Red, Red, Blue.

FLAME COLOR

Select Input Cheats from the Options menu and enter Green, Red, Green, Blue, Red, Red, Yellow, Blue.

GEM COLOR

Select Input Cheats from the Options menu and enter Blue, Red, Red, Green, Red, Green, Red, Yellow.

STAR COLOR

Select Input Cheats from the Options menu and enter Red, Red, Yellow, Red, Blue, Red, Red, Blue.

VOCAL FIREBALL

Select Input Cheats from the Options menu and enter Red, Green, Green, Yellow, Blue, Green, Yellow, Green.

EXTRA LINE 6 TONES

Select Input Cheats from the Options menu and enter Green, Red, Yellow, Blue, Red, Yellow, Blue, Green.

GUITAR HERO: WARRIORS OF ROCK

Select Extras from Options to toggle the following on and off. Some cheats will disable Achievements.

ALL CHARACTERS

Select Cheats from the Options menu and enter Blue, Green, Green, Red, Green, Red, Yellow, Blue.

ALL VENUES

Select Cheats from the Options menu and enter Red, Blue, Blue, Red, Red, Blue, Blue, Red.

ALWAYS SLIDE

Select Cheats from the Options menu and enter Blue, Green, Green, Red, Red, Yellow, Blue, Yellow.

ALL HOPOS

Select Cheats from the Options menu and enter Green (x3), Blue, Green (x3), Yellow. Most notes become hammer-ons or pull-offs.

INVISIBLE ROCKER

Select Cheats from the Options menu and enter Green, Green, Red, Yellow (x3), Blue, Blue.

AIR INSTRUMENTS

Select Cheats from the Options menu and enter Yellow, Red, Red, Blue, Yellow, Green (x3).

FOCUS MODE

Select Cheats from the Options menu and enter Green, Yellow, Green, Red, Green, Yellow, Blue, Green. This removes the busy background.

HUD FREE MODE

Select Cheats from the Options menu and enter Green, Green, Red, Green, Green, Yellow, Green, Green.

PERFORMANCE MODE

Select Cheats from the Options menu and enter Red, Yellow, Yellow, Blue, Red, Blue, Green, Red.

COLOR SHUFFLE

Select Cheats from the Options menu and enter Blue, Green, Blue, Red, Yellow, Green, Red, Yellow.

MIRROR GEMS

Select Cheats from the Options menu and enter Blue, Blue, Red, Blue, Green, Green, Red, Green.

RANDOM GEMS

Select Cheats from the Options menu and enter Green, Green, Red, Red, Yellow, Red, Yellow, Blue.

ROCK BAND

ALL SONGS

At the title screen, press Red, Yellow, Blue, Red, Red, Blue, Blue, Red, Yellow, Blue. Saving and all network features are disabled with this code.

TRANSPARENT INSTRUMENTS

Complete the hall of fame concert with that instrument.

GOLD INSTRUMENT

Complete the solo tour with that instrument.

SILVER INSTRUMENT

Complete the bonus tour with that instrument.

ROCK BAND 2

Most of these codes disable saving, achievements, and Xbox LIVE play.

UNLOCK ALL SONGS

Select Modify Game from the Extras menu, choose Enter Unlock Code and press Red, Yellow, Blue, Red, Red, Blue, Blue, Red, Yellow, Blue or ⓨ, Ⓑ, ⓧ, ⓨ, ⓨ, ⓧ, ⓧ, ⓨ, Ⓑ, ⓧ. Toggle this cheat on or off from the Modify Game menu.

SELECT VENUE SCREEN

Select Modify Game from the Extras menu, choose Enter Unlock Code and press Blue, Orange, Orange, Blue, Yellow, Blue, Orange, Orange, Blue, Yellow or (for Xbox 360) ⓧ, Left Bumper, Left Bumper, ⓧ, Ⓑ, ⓧ, Left Bumper, Left Bumper, ⓧ, Ⓑ. Toggle this cheat on or off from the Modify Game menu.

NEW VENUES ONLY

Select Modify Game from the Extras menu, choose Enter Unlock Code and press Red, Red, Red, Red, Yellow, Yellow, Yellow, Yellow or (for Xbox 360) ⓨ (x4), Ⓑ (x4). Toggle this cheat on or off from the Modify Game menu.

PLAY THE GAME WITHOUT A TRACK

Select Modify Game from the Extras menu, choose Enter Unlock Code and press Bl...
Red, Red, Yellow, Yellow, Blue, Blue or (for Xbox 360) ❌, ❌, ⓨ, ⓨ, Ⓑ, Ⓑ, ❌,
Toggle this cheat on or off from the Modify Game menu.

AWESOMENESS DETECTION

Select Modify Game from the Extras menu, choose Enter Unlock Code and press Yellow, Blue,
Orange, Yellow, Blue, Orange, Yellow, Blue, Orange or (for Xbox 360) Ⓑ, ❌, Left Bumper,
Ⓑ, ❌, Left Bumper, Ⓑ, ❌, Left Bumper. Toggle this cheat on or off from the Modify
Game menu.

STAGE MODE

Select Modify Game from the Extras menu, choose Enter Unlock Code and press Blue, Yellow,
Red, Blue, Yellow, Red, Blue, Yellow, Red or (for Xbox 360) ❌, Ⓑ, ⓨ, ❌, Ⓑ, ⓨ, ❌,
Ⓑ, ⓨ. Toggle this cheat on or off from the Modify Game menu.

ROCK BAND 3

GUILD X-79 GUITAR

At the main menu, press Blue, Orange, Orange, Blue, Orange, Orange, Blue, Blue.

OVATION D-2010 GUITAR

At the main menu, press Orange, Blue, Orange, Orange, Blue, Blue, Orange, Blue.

THE BEATLES: ROCK BAND

BONUS PHOTOS

At the title screen, press Blue, Yellow, Orange, Orange, Orange, Blue, Blue, Blue, Yellow,
Orange.

CONTENTS

THE BIGS

START A ROOKIE WITH HIGHER STATS

When you create a rookie, name him HOT DOG. His stats will be higher than when you normally start.

BLAZING ANGELS 2: SECRET MISSIONS OF WWII

ALL MISSIONS AND PLANES UNLOCKED

At the main menu, hold **L2** + **R2**, and press ●, **L1**, **R1**, ▲, ▲, **R1**, **L1**, ●.

GOD MODE

Pause the game, hold **L2**, and press ●, ▲, ▲, ●. Release **L2**, hold **R2** and press ▲, ●, ●, ▲. Re-enter the code to disable it.

INCREASED DAMAGE WITH ALL WEAPONS

Pause the game, hold **L2**, and press **L1**, **L1**, **R1**. Release **L2**, hold **R2**, and press **R1**, **R1**, **L1**. Re-enter the code to disable it.

BLUR

CONCEPT 1 SERIES TII CHROME

In the Multiplayer Showroom, highlight the BMW Concept 1 Series tii and press **L2**, **R2**, **L2**, **R2**.

FULLY UPGRADE FORD BRONCO

In the Multiplayer Showroom, highlight the Ford Bronco and press **L2**, **R2**, **L2**, **R2**.

BOLT

Many of the following cheats can be toggled on/off by pausing the game and selecting Cheats.

LEVEL SELECT

Select Cheats from the Extras menu and enter Right, Up, Left, Right, Up, Right.

ALL MINIGAMES

Select Cheats from the Extras menu and enter Right, Up, Right, Right.

UNLIMITED ENHANCED VISION

Select Cheats from the Extras menu and enter Left, Right, Up, Down.

UNLIMITED GROUND POUND

Select Cheats from the Extras menu and enter Right, Up, Right, Up, Left, Down.

UNLIMITED INVULNERABILITY

Select Cheats from the Extras menu and enter Down, Down, Up, Left.

UNLIMITED GAS MINES

Select Cheats from the Extras menu and enter Right, Left, Left, Up, Down, Right.

UNLIMITED LASER EYES

Select Cheats from the Extras menu and enter Left, Left, Up, Right.

UNLIMITED STEALTH CAMO

Select Cheats from the Extras menu and enter Left, Down (x3).

UNLIMITED SUPERBARK

Select Cheats from the Extras menu and enter Right, Left, Left, Up, Down, Up.

BURNOUT PARADISE

BEST BUY CAR

Pause the game and select Sponsor Product Code from the Under the Hood menu. Enter Bestbuy. Need A License to use this car offline.

CIRCUIT CITY CAR

Pause the game and select Sponsor Product Code from the Under the Hood menu. Enter Circuitcity. Need Burnout Paradise License to use this car offline.

GAMESTOP CAR

Pause the game and select Sponsor Product Code from the Under the Hood menu. Enter Gamestop. Need A License to use this car offline.

WALMART CAR

Pause the game and select Sponsor Product Code from the Under the Hood menu.. Enter Walmart. Need Burnout Paradise License to use this car offline.

"STEEL WHEELS" GT

Pause the game and select Sponsor Product Code from the Under the Hood menu. Enter G23X 5K8Q GX2V 04B1 or E60J 8Z7T MS8L 51U6.

LICENSES

LICENSE	NUMBER OF WINS NEEDED
D	2
C	7
B	16
A	26
Burnout Paradise	45
Elite License	All events

CARS MATER-NATIONAL

ALL ARCADE RACES, MINI-GAMES, AND WORLDS

Select Codes/Cheats from the options and enter PLAYALL.

ALL CARS

Select Codes/Cheats from the options and enter MATTEL07.

ALTERNATE LIGHTNING MCQUEEN COLORS

Select Codes/Cheats from the options and enter NCEDUDZ.

ALL COLORS FOR OTHERS

Select Codes/Cheats from the options and enter PAINTIT.

UNLIMITED TURBO

Select Codes/Cheats from the options and enter ZZOOOOM.

EXTREME ACCELERATION

Select Codes/Cheats from the options and enter OTO200X.

EXPERT MODE

Select Codes/Cheats from the options and enter VRYFAST.

ALL BONUS ART

Select Codes/Cheats from the options and enter BUYTALL.

DIRT 2

Win the given events to earn the following cars:

GET THIS CAR	BY WINNING THIS EVENT
Ford RS200 Evolution	Rally Cross World Tour
Toyota Stadium Truck	Landrush World Tour
Mitsubishi Pajero Dakar 1993	Raid World Tour
Dallenbach Special	Trailblazer World Tour
1995 Subaru Impreza WRX STi	Colin McRae Challenge
Colin McRae R4 [X Games]	X Games Europe
Mitsubishi Lancer Evolution X [X Games]	X Games Asia
Subaru Impreza WRX STi [X Games]	X Games America
Ford Escort MKII and MG Metro 6R4	All X Games events

DJ HERO

Select Cheats from Options and enter the following. Some codes will disable high scores and progress. Cheats cannot be used in tutorials and online.

UNLOCK ALL CONTENT
Enter tol0.

ALL CHARACTER ITEMS
Enter uNA2.

ALL VENUES
Enter Wv1u.

ALL DECKS
Enter LAuP.

ALL HEADPHONES
Enter 62Db.

ALL MIXES
Enter 82xl.

AUTO SCRATCH
Enter it6j.

AUTO EFFECTS DIAL
Enter ab1l.

AUTO FADER
Enter sl5d.

AUTO TAPPER
Enter zith.

AUTO WIN EUPHORIA
Enter r3a9.

BLANK PLINTHS
Enter ipr0.

HAMSTER SWITCH
Enter 7geo.

HYPER DECK MODE
Enter 76st.

SHORT DECK
Enter 51uc.

BLACK AND WHITE
Enter b!99.

EDGE EFFECT
Enter 2u4u.

INVISIBLE DJ
Enter oh5t.

MIDAS
Enter 4pe5.

PITCH BLACK OUT
Enter d4kr.

PLAY IN THE BEDROOM
Enter g7nh.

RAINBOW
Enter ?jy!.

ANY DJ, ANY SETLIST
Enter 0jj8.

DAFT PUNK'S CONTENT
Enter d1g?.

DJ AM'S CONTENT
Enter k07u.

DJ JAZZY JEFF'S CONTENT
Enter n1fz.

DJ SHADOW'S CONTENT
Enter omxv.

DJ Z-TRIP'S CONTENT
Enter 5rtg.

GRANDMASTER FLASH'S CONTENT
Enter ami8.

19

DJ HERO 2

ALL BONUS CONTENT
Select Cheats from the Options. Choose Retail Cheats and enter VIP Pass.

DAVID GUETTA
Select Cheats from the Options. Choose Retail Cheats and enter Guetta Blaster.

DEADMAU5
Select Cheats from the Options. Choose Retail Cheats and enter Open The Trap.

G.I. JOE: THE RISE OF COBRA

CLASSIC DUKE
At the main menu, press Left, Up, ●, Up, Right, ▲.

SHANA "SCARLETT" O'HARA
At the main menu, press Right, Up, Down, Down, ▲.

GRID

ALL DRIFT CARS
Select Bonus Codes from the Options. Then choose Enter Code and enter TUN58396.

ALL MUSCLE CARS
Select Bonus Codes from the Options. Then choose Enter Code and enter MUS59279.

BUCHBINDER EMOTIONAL ENGINEERING BMW 320SI
Select Bonus Codes from the Options. Then choose Enter Code and enter F93857372. You can use this in Race Day or in GRID World once you've started your own team.

EBAY MOTORS MUSTANG
Select Bonus Codes from the Options. Then choose Enter Code and enter DAFJ55E01473M0. You can use this in Race Day or in GRID World once you've started your own team.

GAMESTATION BMW 320SI
Select Bonus Codes from the Options. Then choose Enter Code and enter G29782655. You can use this in Race Day or in GRID World once you've started your own team.

MICROMANIA PAGANI ZONDA R
Select Bonus Codes from the Options. Then choose Enter Code and enter M38572343. You can use this in Race Day or in GRID World once you've started your own team.

PLAY.COM ASTON MARTIN DBR9
Select Bonus Codes from the Options. Then choose Enter Code and enter P47203845. You can use this in Race Day or in GRID World once you've started your own team.

IRON MAN

CLASSIC ARMOR
Clear One Man Army vs. Mercs.

EXTREMIS ARMOR
Clear One Man Army vs. Maggia.

MARK II ARMOR
Clear One Man Army vs. Ten Rings.

HULKBUSTER ARMOR
Clear One Man Army vs. AIM-X. Can also be unlocked when clear game save data from Incredible Hulk is stored on the same console.

CLASSIC MARK I ARMOR
Clear One Man Army vs. AIM.

ULTIMATE ARMOR
Clear Mission 13: Showdown.

JUICED 2: HOT IMPORT NIGHTS

ASCARI KZ1
Select Cheats and Codes from the DNA Lab menu and enter KNOX. Defeat the challenge to earn the car.

AUDI TT 1.8L QUATTRO
Select Cheats and Codes from the DNA Lab menu and enter YTHZ. Defeat the challenge to earn the car.

BMW Z4 ROADSTER
Select Cheats and Codes from the DNA Lab menu and enter GVDL. Defeat the challenge to earn the car.

FRITO-LAY INFINITI G35
Select Cheats and Codes from the DNA Lab menu and enter MNCH. Defeat the challenge to earn the car.

HOLDEN MONARO
Select Cheats and Codes from the DNA Lab menu and enter RBSG. Defeat the challenge to earn the car.

HYUNDAI COUPE 2.7L V6
Select Cheats and Codes from the DNA Lab menu and enter BSLU. Defeat the challenge to earn the car.

INFINITI G35
Select Cheats and Codes from the DNA Lab menu and enter MRHC. Defeat the challenge to earn the car.

KOENIGSEGG CCX
Select Cheats and Codes from the DNA Lab menu and enter KDTR. Defeat the challenge to earn the car.

MITSUBISHI PROTOTYPE X
Select Cheats and Codes from the DNA Lab menu and enter DOPX. Defeat the challenge to earn the car.

NISSAN 350Z
Select Cheats and Codes from the DNA Lab menu and enter PRGN. Defeat the challenge to earn the car.

NISSAN SKYLINE R34 GT-R
Select Cheats and Codes from the DNA Lab menu and enter JWRS. Defeat the challenge to earn the car.

SALEEN S7
Select Cheats and Codes from the DNA Lab menu and enter WIKF. Defeat the challenge to earn the car.

SEAT LEON CUPRA R
Select Cheats and Codes from the DNA Lab menu and enter FAMQ. Defeat the challenge to earn the car.

KUNG FU PANDA

UNLIMITED CHI
Select Cheats from the Extra menu and enter Down, Right, Left, Up, Down.

INVULNERABILITY
Select Cheats from the Extra menu and enter Down, Down, Right, Up, Left.

FULL UPGRADES
Select Cheats from the Extra menu and enter Left, Right, Down, Left, Up.

FULL AWESOME METER
Select Cheats from the Extra menu and enter Up, Down, Up, Right, Left. This gives Po 4X damage.

MULTIPLAYER CHARACTERS
Select Cheats from the Extra menu and enter Left, Down, Left, Right, Down.

OUTFITS
Select Cheats from the Extra menu and enter Right, Left, Down, Up, Right.

LARA CROFT AND THE GUARDIAN OF LIGHT

LARA CROFT HEAVY JUNGLE OUTFIT
Complete the game.

LARA CROFT JUNGLE OUTFIT
Score 1,410,000 points.

LARA CROFT BIKER OUTFIT
Score 1,900,000 points.

LARA CROFT LEGEND OUTFIT
Defeat Xolotl.

DOPPELGANGER OUTFIT
Score 2,400,000 points.

THE LEGEND OF SPYRO: DAWN OF THE DRAGON

UNLIMITED LIFE
Pause the game, hold **L1** and press Right, Right, Down, Down, Left with the Left Analog Stick.

UNLIMITED MANA
Pause the game, hold **R1** and press Up, Right, Up, Left, Down with the Left Analog Stick.

MAXIMUM XP
Pause the game, hold **R1** and press Left, Right, Right, Up, Up with the Left Analog Stick.

ALL ELEMENTAL UPGRADES
Pause the game, hold **L1** and press Left, Up, Down, Up, Right with the Left Analog Stick.

LEGO BATMAN

BATCAVE CODES

Using the computer in the Batcave, select Enter Code and enter the following codes.

CHARACTERS

CHARACTER	CODE	CHARACTER	CODE
Alfred	ZAQ637	Penguin Henchman	BJH782
Batgirl	JKR331	Penguin Minion	KJP748
Bruce Wayne	BDJ327	Poison Ivy Goon	GTB899
Catwoman (Classic)	M1AAWW	Police Marksman	HKG984
Clown Goon	HJK327	Police Officer	JRY983
Commissioner Gordon	DDP967	Riddler Goon	CRY928
Fishmonger	HGY748	Riddler Henchman	XEU824
Freeze Girl	XVK541	S.W.A.T.	HTF114
Joker Goon	UTF782	Sailor	NAV592
Joker Henchman	YUN924	Scientist	JFL786
Mad Hatter	JCA283	Security Guard	PLB946
Man-Bat	NYU942	The Joker (Tropical)	CCB199
Military Policeman	MKL382	Yeti	NJL412
Nightwing	MVY759	Zoo Sweeper	DWR243
Penguin Goon	NKA238		

VEHICLES

VEHICLE	CODE	VEHICLE	CODE
Bat-Tank	KNTT4B	Mr. Freeze's Kart	BCT229
Bruce Wayne's Private Jet	LEA664	Penguin Goon Submarine	BTN248
Catwoman's Motorcycle	HPL826	Police Bike	LJP234
Garbage Truck	DUS483	Police Boat	PLC999
Goon Helicopter	GCH328	Police Car	KJL832
Harbor Helicopter	CHP735	Police Helicopter	CWR732
Harley Quinn's Hammer Truck	RDT637	Police Van	MAC788
Mad Hatter's Glider	HS000W	Police Watercraft	VJD328
Mad Hatter's Steamboat	M4DM4N	Riddler's Jet	HAHAHA
Mr. Freeze's Iceberg	ICYICE	Robin's Submarine	TTF453
The Joker's Van	JUK657	Two-Face's Armored Truck	EFE933

CHEATS

CHEAT	CODE	CHEAT	CODE
Always Score Multiply	9LRGNB	More Batarang Targets	XWP645
Fast Batarangs	JRBDCB	Piece Detector	KHJ554
Fast Walk	ZOLM6N	Power Brick Detector	MMN786
Flame Batarang	D8NYWH	Regenerate Hearts	HJH7HJ
Freeze Batarang	XPN4NG	Score x2	N4NR3E
Extra Hearts	ML3KHP	Score x4	CX9MAT
Fast Build	EVG26J	Score x6	MLVNF2
Immune to Freeze	JXUDY6	Score x8	WCCDB9
Invincibility	WYD5CP	Score x10	18HW07
Minikit Detector	ZXGH9J		

LEGO HARRY POTTER: YEARS 1–4

RED BRICK EXTRAS

Once you have access to The Leaky Cauldron, enter Wiseacre's Wizarding Supplies from Diagon Alley. Go upstairs to enter the following. Pause the game and select Extras to toggle the cheats on/off.

CHEAT	CODE		CHEAT	CODE
Carrot Wands	AUC8EH		Invincibility	QQWC6B
Character Studs	H27KGC		Red Brick Detector	7AD7HE
Character Token Detector	HA79V8		Regenerate Hearts	89ML2W
Christmas	T7PVVN		Score x2	74YKR7
Disguise	4DMK2R		Score x4	J3WHNK
Fall Rescue	ZEX7MV		Score x6	XK9ANE
Extra Hearts	J9U6Z9		Score x8	HUFV2H
Fast Dig	Z9BFAD		Score x10	H8X69Y
Fast Magic	FA3GQA		Silhouettes	HZBVX7
Gold Brick Detector	84QNQN		Singing Mandrake	BMEU6X
Hogwarts Crest Detector	TTMC6D		Stud Magnet	67FKWZ
Ice Rink	F88VUW			

WISEACRE SPELLS

Once you have access to The Leaky Cauldron, enter Wiseacre's Wizarding Supplies from Diagon Alley. Go upstairs to enter the following. You need to learn Wingardium Leviosa before you can use these cheats.

SPELL	CODE		SPELL	CODE
Accio	VE9VV7		Incarcerous	YEB9Q9
Anteoculatia	QFB6NR		Locomotor Mortis	2M2XJ6
Calvorio	6DNR6L		Multicorfors	JK6QRM
Colovaria	9GJ442		Redactum Skullus	UW8LRH
Engorgio Skullus	CD4JLX		Rictusempra	2UCA3M
Entomorphis	MYN3NB		Slugulus Eructo	U6EE8X
Flipendo	ND2L7W		Stupefy	UWDJ4Y
Glacius	ERA9DR		Tarantallegra	KWWQ44
Herbifors	H8FTHL		Trip Jinx	YZNRF6

EEYLOPS GOLD BRICKS

Once you have access to The Leaky Cauldron, enter Wiseacre's Wizarding Supplies from Diagon Alley. Go upstairs to enter the following. To access the LEGO Builder, visit Gringott's Bank at the end of Diagon Alley.

GOLD BRICK	CODE		GOLD BRICK	CODE
1	QE4VC7		7	XY6VYZ
2	FY8H97		8	TUNC4W
3	3MQT4P		9	EJ42Q6
4	PQPM7Z		10	GFJCV9
5	ZY2CPA		11	DZCY6G
6	3GMTP6			

LEGO INDIANA JONES: THE ORIGINAL ADVENTURES

CHARACTERS

Approach the blackboard in the Classsroom and enter the following codes.

CHARACTER	CODE
Bandit	12N68W
Bandit Swordsman	1MK4RT
Barranca	04EM94
Bazooka Trooper (Crusade)	MK83R7
Bazooka Trooper (Raiders)	S93Y5R
Belloq	CHN3YU
Belloq (Jungle)	TDR197
Belloq (Robes)	VEO29L
British Commander	B73EUA
British Officer	VJ5TI9
British Soldier	DJ5I2W
Captain Katanga	VJ3TT3
Chatter Lal	ENW936
Chatter Lal (Thuggee)	CNH4RY
Chen	3NK48T
Colonel Dietrich	2K9RKS
Colonel Vogel	8EAL4H
Dancing Girl	C7EJ21
Donovan	3NFTU8
Elsa (Desert)	JSNRT9
Elsa (Officer)	VMJ5US
Enemy Boxer	8246RB
Enemy Butler	VJ48W3
Enemy Guard	VJ7R51
Enemy Guard (Mountains)	YR47WM
Enemy Officer	572E61
Enemy Officer (Desert)	2MK450
Enemy Pilot	B84ELP
Enemy Radio Operator	1MF94R
Enemy Soldier (Desert)	4NSU7Q

CHARACTER	CODE
Fedora	V75YSP
First Mate	0GIN24
Grail Knight	NE6THI
Hovitos Tribesman	H0V1SS
Indiana Jones (Desert Disguise)	4J8S4M
Indiana Jones (Officer)	VJ850S
Jungle Guide	24PF34
Kao Kan	WMO46L
Kazim	NRH23J
Kazim (Desert)	3M29TJ
Lao Che	2NK479
Maharajah	NFK5N2
Major Toht	13NS01
Masked Bandit	N48SF0
Mola Ram	FJUR31
Monkey Man	3RF6YJ
Pankot Assassin	2NKT72
Pankot Guard	VN28RH
Sherpa Brawler	VJ37WJ
Sherpa Gunner	ND762W
Slave Child	OE3ENW
Thuggee	VM683E
Thuggee Acolyte	T2R3F9
Thuggee Slave Driver	VBS7GW
Village Dignitary	KD48TN
Village Elder	4682E1
Willie (Dinner Suit)	VK93R7
Willie (Pajamas)	MEN4IP
Wu Han	3NSLT8

EXTRAS

Approach the blackboard in the Classsroom and enter the following codes. Some cheats need to be enabled by selecting Extras from the pause menu.

CHEAT	CODE
Artifact Detector	VIKED7
Beep Beep	VNF59Q
Character Treasure	VIES2R
Disarm Enemies	VKRNS9
Disguises	4ID1N6
Fast Build	V83SLO
Fast Dig	378RS6
Fast Fix	FJ59WS
Fertilizer	B1GW1F
Ice Rink	33GM7J
Parcel Detector	VUT673
Poo Treasure	WWQ1SA

CHEAT	CODE
Regenerate Hearts	MDLP69
Secret Characters	3X44AA
Silhouettes	3HE85H
Super Scream	VN3R7S
Super Slap	OP1TA5
Treasure Magnet	H86LA2
Treasure x10	VI3PS8
Treasure x2	VM4TS9
Treasure x4	VLWEN3
Treasure x6	V84RYS
Treasure x8	A72E1M

LEGO INDIANA JONES 2: THE ADVENTURE CONTINUES

Pause the game, select Enter Secret Code from the Extras menu, and enter the following.

CHARACTERS

CHARACTER	CODE
Belloq (Priest)	FTL48S
Dovchenko	WL4T6N
Enemy Boxer	7EQF47
Henry Jones	4CSAKH
Indiana Jones	PGWSEA
Indiana Jones: 2	FGLKYS
Indiana Jones (Collect)	DZFY9S
Indiana Jones (Desert)	M4C34K
Indiana Jones (Desert Disguise)	2W8QR3
Indiana Jones (Dinner Suit)	QUNZUT
Indiana Jones (Kali)	J2XS97
Indiana Jones (Officer)	3FQFKS
Interdimensional Being	PXT4UP
Lao Che	7AWX3J
Mannequin (Boy)	2UJQWC
Mannequin (Girl)	3PGSEL
Mannequin (Man)	QPWDMM
Mannequin (Woman)	U7SMVK
Mola Ram	82RMC2
Mutt	2GKS62
Salah	E88YRP
Willie	94RUAJ

EXTRAS

EFFECT	CODE
Beep Beep	UU3VSC
Disguise	Y9TE98
Fast Build	SNXC2F
Fast Dig	XYAN83
Fast Fix	3Z7PJX
Fearless	TUXNZF
Ice Rink	TY9P4U
Invincibility	6JBB65
Poo Money	SZFAAE
Score x3	PEHHPZ
Score x4	UXGTB3
Score X6	XWLJEY
Score x8	S5UZCP
Score x10	V7JYBU
Silhouettes	FQGPYH
Snake Whip	2U7YCV
Stud Magnet	EGSM5B

LEGO STAR WARS: THE COMPLETE SAGA

The following still need to be purchase after entering the codes.

CHARACTERS

ADMIRAL ACKBAR

At the bar in Mos Eisley Cantina, select Enter Code and enter ACK646.

BATTLE DROID (COMMANDER)

At the bar in Mos Eisley Cantina, select Enter Code and enter KPF958.

BOBA FETT (BOY)

At the bar in Mos Eisley Cantina, select Enter Code and enter GGF539.

BOSS NASS

At the bar in Mos Eisley Cantina, select Enter Code and enter HHY697.

CAPTAIN TARPALS

At the bar in Mos Eisley Cantina, select Enter Code and enter QRN714.

COUNT DOOKU

At the bar in Mos Eisley Cantina, select Enter Code and enter DDD748.

DARTH MAUL

At the bar in Mos Eisley Cantina, select Enter Code and enter EUK421.

EWOK

At the bar in Mos Eisley Cantina, select Enter Code and enter EWK785.

GENERAL GRIEVOUS

At the bar in Mos Eisley Cantina, select Enter Code and enter PMN576.

GREEDO

At the bar in Mos Eisley Cantina, select Enter Code and enter ZZR636.

IG-88

At the bar in Mos Eisley Cantina, select Enter Code and enter GIJ989.

IMPERIAL GUARD

At the bar in Mos Eisley Cantina, select Enter Code and enter GUA850.

JANGO FETT

At the bar in Mos Eisley Cantina, select Enter Code and enter KLJ897.

KI-ADI MUNDI

At the bar in Mos Eisley Cantina, select Enter Code and enter MUN486.

LUMINARA

At the bar in Mos Eisley Cantina, select Enter Code and enter LUM521.

PADMÉ

At the bar in Mos Eisley Cantina, select Enter Code and enter VBJ322.

R2-Q5

At the bar in Mos Eisley Cantina, select Enter Code and enter EVILR2.

STORMTROOPER

At the bar in Mos Eisley Cantina, select Enter Code and enter NBN431.

TAUN WE

At the bar in Mos Eisley Cantina, select Enter Code and enter PRX482.

VULTURE DROID

At the bar in Mos Eisley Cantina, select Enter Code and enter BDC866.

WATTO

At the bar in Mos Eisley Cantina, select Enter Code and enter PLL967.

ZAM WESELL

At the bar in Mos Eisley Cantina, select Enter Code and enter 584HJF.

SKILLS

DISGUISE

At the bar in Mos Eisley Cantina, select Enter Code and enter BRJ437.

FORCE GRAPPLE LEAP

At the bar in Mos Eisley Cantina, select Enter Code and enter CLZ738.

VEHICLES

DROID TRIFIGHTER

At the bar in Mos Eisley Cantina, select Enter Code and enter AAB123.

IMPERIAL SHUTTLE

At the bar in Mos Eisley Cantina, select Enter Code and enter HUT845.

TIE INTERCEPTOR

At the bar in Mos Eisley Cantina, select Enter Code and enter INT729.

TIE FIGHTER

At the bar in Mos Eisley Cantina, select Enter Code and enter DBH897.

ZAM'S AIRSPEEDER

At the bar in Mos Eisley Cantina, select Enter Code and enter UUU875.

LITTLEBIGPLANET

CHEAT PAST ALL THE CREATE MODE TUTORIALS
As the credits roll press Down, Up, L1, L2, R2, R1, ●, ⊗.

LUCHA LIBRE AAA: HEROES DEL RING

LITTLE ONES
At the character select, press Up, Up, Down, Down, Left, Right, Left, Right. Play with them to unlock the Little Ones Can Too Trophy.

MARVEL ULTIMATE ALLIANCE

UNLOCK ALL SKINS
At the Team Menu, press Up, Down, Left, Right, Left, Right, Start.

UNLOCKS ALL HERO POWERS
At the Team Menu, press Left, Right, Up, Down, Up, Down, Start.

ALL HEROES TO LEVEL 99
At the Team Menu, press Up, Left, Up, Left, Down, Right, Down, Right, Start.

UNLOCK ALL HEROES
At the Team Menu, press Up, Up, Down, Down, Left, Left, Left, Start.

UNLOCK DAREDEVIL
At the Team Menu, press Left, Left, Right, Right, Up, Down, Up, Down, Start.

UNLOCK SILVER SURFER
At the Team Menu, press Down, Left, Left, Up, Right, Up, Down, Left, Start.

GOD MODE
During gameplay, press Up, Down, Up, Down, Up, Left, Down, Right, Start.

TOUCH OF DEATH
During gameplay, press Left, Right, Down, Down, Right, Left, Start.

SUPER SPEED
During gameplay, press Up, Left, Up, Right, Down, Right, Start.

FILL MOMENTUM
During gameplay, press Left, Right, Right, Left, Up, Down, Down, Up, Start.

UNLOCK ALL COMICS
At the Review menu, press Left, Right, Right, Left, Up, Up, Right, Start.

UNLOCK ALL CONCEPT ART
At the Review menu, press Down, Down, Down, Right, Right, Left, Down, Start.

UNLOCK ALL CINEMATICS
At the Review menu, press Up, Left, Left, Up, Right, Right, Up, Start.

UNLOCK ALL LOAD SCREENS
At the Review menu, press Up, Down, Right, Left, Up, Up Down, Start.

UNLOCK ALL COURSES
At the Comic Missions menu, press Up, Right, Left, Down, Up, Right, Left, Down, Start.

MARVEL ULTIMATE ALLIANCE 2

These codes will disable the ability to save.

GOD MODE
During a game, press Up, Down, Up, Down, Up, Left, Down, Right, Start.

UNLIMITED FUSION
During a game, press Right, Right, Up, Down, Up, Up, Left, Start.

UNLOCK ALL POWERS
During a game, press Left, Right, Up, Down, Up, Down, Start.

UNLOCK ALL HEROES
During a game, press Up, Up, Down, Down, Left, Left, Left, Start.

UNLOCK ALL SKINS
During a game, press Up, Down, Left, Right, Left, Right, Start.

UNLOCK JEAN GREY
During a game, press Left, Left, Right, Right, Up, Down, Up, Down, Start.

UNLOCK HULK
During a game, press Down, Left, Left, Up, Right, Up, Down, Left, Start.

UNLOCK THOR
During a game, press Up, Right, Right, Down, Right, Down, Left, Right, Start.

UNLOCK ALL AUDIO LOGS
At the main menu, press Left, Right, Right, Left, Up, Up, Right, Start.

UNLOCK ALL DOSSIERS
At the main menu, press Down, Down, Down, Right, Right, Left, Down, Start.

UNLOCK ALL MOVIES
At the main menu, press Up, Left, Left, Up, Right, Right, Up, Start.

MLB 08: THE SHOW

ALL CLASSIC STADIUMS
At the main menu, press Down, Right, Circle, Square, Left, Triangle, Up, L1. The controller will vibrate if entered correctly.

MLB 10: THE SHOW

SILENCE DAVE CAMPBELL
Pause the game and press Up, Up, Down, Down, Left, Right, Left, Up.

SILENCE MATT VASGERSIAN
Pause the game and press Up, Up, Down, Down, Left, Right, Left, Right.

SILENCE REX HUDLER
Pause the game and press Up, Up, Down, Down, Left, Right, Left, Left.

MODNATION RACERS

BOOST START
Press L1 when GO appears.

MX VS. ATV REFLEX

MX VEHICLES FOR PURCHASE
Select Enter Cheat Code from the Options and enter brapbrap.

JUSTIN BRAYTON, KTM MX BIKES AND ATVS IN ARCADE MODE
Select Enter Cheat Code from the Options and enter readytorace.

ALL EVENT LOCATIONS IN ARCADE MODE
Select Enter Cheat Code from the Options and enter whereto.

ALL AI OPPONENTS
Select Enter Cheat Code from the Options and enter allai.

ATV VEHICLES FOR PURCHASE
Select Enter Cheat Code from the Options and enter couches.

ALL AVAILABLE RIDER GEAR
Select Enter Cheat Code from the Options and enter gearedup.

ALL AVAILABLE HELMETS
Select Enter Cheat Code from the Options and enter skullcap.

ALL AVAILABLE BOOTS
Select Enter Cheat Code from the Options and enter kicks.

ALL AVAILABLE GOGGLES
Select Enter Cheat Code from the Options and enter windows.

MX VS. ATV UNTAMED

ALL RIDING GEAR
Select Cheat Codes from the Options and enter crazylikea.

ALL HANDLEBARS
Select Cheat Codes from the Options and enter nohands.

NASCAR 08

ALL CHASE MODE CARS
Select cheat codes from the options menu and enter checkered flag.

EA SPORTS CAR
Select cheat codes from the options menu and enter ea sports car.

FANTASY DRIVERS
Select cheat codes from the options menu and enter race the pack.

WALMART CAR AND TRACK
Select cheat codes from the options menu and enter walmart everyday.

NASCAR 09

WAL-MART CAR & CHICAGO PIER RACETRACK
Select EA Extras from My Nascar, then choose Cheat Codes and enter WALMART EVERYDAY.

NBA 09: THE INSIDE

EASTERN ALL-STARS 09 JERSEY
Select Extras from the Progression menu. Then choose nba.com from the Jerseys menu. Press ● and enter SHPNV2K699.

WESTERN ALL-STARS 09 JERSEY
Select Extras from the Progression menu. Then choose nba.com from the Jerseys menu. Press ● and enter K8AV6YMLNF.

L.A. LAKERS LATIN NIGHT JERSEY
Select Extras from the Progression menu. Then choose nba.com from the Jerseys menu. Press ● and enter NMTWCTC84S.

MIAMI HEAT LATIN NIGHT JERSEY
Select Extras from the Progression menu. Then choose nba.com from the Jerseys menu. Press ● and enter WCTGSA8SPD.

PHOENIX SUNS LATIN NIGHT JERSEY
Select Extras from the Progression menu. Then choose nba.com from the Jerseys menu. Press ● and enter LKUTSENFJH.

SAN ANTONIO SPURS LATIN NIGHT JERSEY
Select Extras from the Progression menu. Then choose nba.com from the Jerseys menu. Press ● and enter JFHSY73MYD.

NBA 2K8

ABA BALL
Select Codes from the Features menu and enter Payrespect.

2KSPORTS TEAM
Select Codes from the Features menu and enter 2ksports.

NBA DEVELOPMENT TEAM
Select Codes from the Features menu and enter nba2k.

SUPERSTARS TEAM
Select Codes from the Features menu and enter llmohffaae.

VISUAL CONCEPTS TEAM
Select Codes from the Features menu and enter Vcteam.

2008 ALL-STAR NBA JERSEYS
Select Codes from the Features menu and enter haeitgyebs.

BOBCATS RACING JERSEY
Select Codes from the Features menu and enter agtaccsinr.

PACERS SECOND ROAD JERSEY
Select Codes from the Features menu and enter cpares.

ST. PATRICK'S DAY JERSEYS
Select Codes from the Features menu and enter uclerehanp.

VALENTINE'S DAY JERSEYS
Select Codes from the Features menu and enter amcnreo.

NBA 2K9

2K SPORTS TEAM
Select Codes from the Features menu and enter 2ksports.

NBA 2K TEAM
Select Codes from the Features menu and enter nba2k.

SUPERSTARS
Select Codes from the Features menu and enter llmohffaae.

VC TEAM
Select Codes from the Features menu and enter vcteam.

ABA BALL
Select Codes from the Features menu and enter payrespect.

NBA 2K10

ABA BALL
Select Codes from the Options menu. Then select Enter Code and enter payrespect.

2K CHINA TEAM
Select Codes from the Options menu. Then select Enter Code and enter 2kchina.

NBA 2K TEAM
Select Codes from the Options menu. Then select Enter Code and enter nba2k.

2K SPORTS TEAM
Select Codes from the Options menu. Then select Enter Code and enter 2ksports.

VISUAL CONCEPTS TEAM
Select Codes from the Options menu. Then select Enter Code and enter vcteam.

2010 ALL-STAR UNIFORMS
Select Codes from the Options menu. Then select Enter Code and enter otnresla.

HARDWOOD CLASSIC UNIFORMS
Select Codes from the Options menu. Then select Enter Code and enter wasshcicsl. This code gives Hardwood Classic Uniforms for the Cavaliers, Jazz, Magic, Raptors, timberwolves, Trail Blazers, and Warriors.

LATIN NIGHTS UNIFORMS
Select Codes from the Options menu. Then select Enter Code and enter aihinntslgt. This code gives Latin Nights jerseys for Bulls, Heat, Knicks, Lakers, Mavericks, Rockets, Spurs, and Suns.

NBA GREEN UNIFORMS
Select Codes from the Options menu. Then select Enter Code and enter nreogge. This code gives green uniforms for the Bobcats, Bulls, and Nuggets.

SECONDARY ROAD UNIFORMS
Select Codes from the Options menu. Then select Enter Code and enter eydonscar. This code gives Second Road Uniforms for the Grizzlies, Hawks, Mavericks, and Rockets.

ST. PATRICK'S DAY UNIFORMS
Select Codes from the Options menu. Then select Enter Code and enter riiasgerh. This code gives St. Patrick's Day jerseys for the Bulls, Celtics, Knicks, and Raptors.

BOBCATS RACING UNIFORM
Select Codes from the Options menu. Then select Enter Code and enter agsntrccai.

CAVALIERS CAVFANATICS UNIFORM

Select Codes from the Options menu. Then select Enter Code and enter aifnaatccv.

HORNETS MARDI GRAS UNIFORM

Select Codes from the Options menu. Then select Enter Code and enter asrdirmga.

TRAIL BLAZERS RIP CITY UNIFORM

Select Codes from the Options menu. Then select Enter Code and enter ycprtii.

NBA 2K11

MJ: CREATING A LEGEND

In Features, select Codes from the Extras menu. Choose Enter Code and enter icanbe23.

2K CHINA TEAM

In Features, select Codes from the Extras menu. Choose Enter Code and enter 2kchina.

2K SPORTS TEAM

In Features, select Codes from the Extras menu. Choose Enter Code and enter 2Ksports.

NBA 2K TEAM

In Features, select Codes from the Extras menu. Choose Enter Code and enter nba2k.

VC TEAM

In Features, select Codes from the Extras menu. Choose Enter Code and enter vcteam.

ABA BALL

In Features, select Codes from the Extras menu. Choose Enter Code and enter payrespect.

NBA LIVE 08

ADIDAS GIL-ZERO - ALL-STAR EDITION

Select NBA Codes from My NBA and enter 23DN1PPOG4.

ADIDAS TIM DUNCAN STEALTH - ALL-STAR EDITION

Select NBA Codes from My NBA and enter FE454DFJCC.

NBA LIVE 09

SUPER DUNKS MODE

Use the Sprite vending machine in the practice area and enter spriteslam.

NBA LIVE 10

CHARLOTTE BOBCATS' 2009/2010 RACE DAY ALTERNATE JERSEYS

Select Options from My NBA Live and go to Select Codes. Enter ceobdabacarstcy.

NEW ORLEANS HORNETS' 2009/2010 MARDI GRAS ALTERNATE JERSEYS

Select Options from My NBA Live and go to Select Codes. Enter nishrag1rosmad0.

ALTERNATE JERSEYS

Select Options from My NBA Live and go to Select Codes. Enter ndnba1rooaesdc0. This unlocks alternate jerseys for Atlanta Hawks, Dallas Mavericks, Houston Rockets, and Memphis Grizzlies.

MORE HARDWOOD CLASSICS NIGHTS JERSEYS

Select Options from My NBA Live and go to Select Codes. Enter hdogdrawhoticns. This unlocks Hardwood Classics Nights jerseys for Cleveland Cavaliers, Golden State Warriors, Minnesota Timberwolves, Orlando Magic, Philadelphia 76ers.

ADIDAS EQUATIONS

Select Options from My NBA Live and go to Select Codes. Enter adaodqauieints1.

ADIDAS TS CREATORS WITH ANKLE BRACES

Select Options from My NBA Live and go to Select Codes. Enter atciadsstsdhecf.

ADIDAS TS SUPERNATURAL COMMANDERS

Select Options from My NBA Live and go to Select Codes. Enter andsicdsmatdnsr.

ADIDAS TS SUPERNATURAL CREATORS

Select Options from My NBA Live and go to Select Codes. Enter ard8siscdnatstr.

AIR MAX LEBRON VII

Select Options from My NBA Live and go to Select Codes. Enter ere1nbvlaoeknii, 2ovnaebnkrielei, 3rioabeneikenvl, ri4boenanekilve, ivl5brieekaeonn, or n6ieirvalkeeobn.

KOBE V

Select Options from My NBA Live and go to Select Codes. Enter ovze1bimenkoko0, m0kveokoiebozn2, eev0nbimokk3ozo, or bmo4inozeeo0kvk.

JORDAN CP3 IIIS

Select Options from My NBA Live and go to Select Codes. Enter iaporcdian3ejis.

JORDAN MELO M6S

Select Options from My NBA Live and go to Select Codes. Enter emlarmeoo6ajdsn.

JORDAN SIXTY PLUSES

Select Options from My NBA Live and go to Select Codes. Enter aondsuilyjrspxt.

NIKE HUARACHE LEGIONS

Select Options from My NBA Live and go to Select Codes. Enter aoieuchrahelgn.

NIKE KD 2S

Select Options from My NBA Live and go to Select Codes. Enter kk2tesaosepinrd.

NIKE ZOOM FLIP'NS

Select Options from My NBA Live and go to Select Codes. Enter epfnozaeminolki.

NBA STREET HOMECOURT

ALL TEAMS

At the Main menu, hold **R1** + **L1** and press Left, Right, Left, Right.

ALL COURTS

At the Main menu, hold **R1** + **L1** and press Up, Right, Down, Left.

BLACK/RED BALL

At the Main menu, hold **R1** + **L1** and press Up, Down, Left, Right.

NEED FOR SPEED PROSTREET

$2,000
Select Career and then choose Code Entry.
Enter 1MA9X99.

$4,000
Select Career and then choose Code Entry.
Enter W2IOLL01.

$8,000
Select Career and then choose Code Entry.
Enter L1IS97A1.

$10,000
Select Career and then choose Code Entry.
Enter 1MI9K7E1.

$10,000
Select Career and then choose Code Entry.
Enter CASHMONEY.

$10,000
Select Career and then choose Code Entry.
Enter REGGAME.

AUDI TT
Select Career and then choose Code Entry.
Enter ITSABOUTYOU.

CHEVELLE SS
Select Career and then choose Code Entry.
Enter HORSEPOWER.

COKE ZERO GOLF GTI
Select Career and then choose Code Entry.
Enter COKEZERO.

DODGE VIPER
Select Career and then choose Code Entry.
Enter WORLDSLONGESTLASTING.

MITSUBISHI LANCER EVOLUTION
Select Career and then choose Code Entry.
Enter MITSUBISHIGOFAR.

UNLOCK ALL BONUSES
Select Career and then choose Code Entry.
Enter UNLOCKALLTHINGS.

5 REPAIR MARKERS
Select Career and then choose Code Entry.
Enter SAFETYNET.

ENERGIZER VINYL
Select Career and then choose Code Entry.
Enter ENERGIZERLITHIUM.

CASTROL SYNTEC VINYL
Select Career and then choose Code Entry.
Enter CASTROLSYNTEC. This also gives you
$10,000.

NEED FOR SPEED UNDERCOVER

$10,000
Select Secret Codes from the Options menu
and enter %%S3/".

DIE-CAST BMW M3 E92
Select Secret Codes from the Options menu
and enter)B7@B=.

DIE-CAST LEXUS IS F
Select Secret Codes from the Options menu
and enter 0;5M2;.

**NEEDFORSPEED.COM LOTUS
ELISE**
Select Secret Codes from the Options menu
and enter -KJ3=E.

DIE-CAST NISSAN 240SX (S13)
Select Secret Codes from the Options menu
and enter ?P:COL.

DIE-CAST PORSCHE 911 TURBO
Select Secret Codes from the Options menu
and enter >8P:I;.

SHELBY TERLINGUA
Select Secret Codes from the Options menu
and enter NeedForSpeedShelbyTerlingua.

DIE-CAST VOLKWAGEN R32
Select Secret Codes from the Options menu
and enter!2ODBJ:.

NHL 08

ALL RBK EDGE JERSEYS
At the RBK Edge Code option, enter h3oyxpwksf8ibcgt.

NHL 2K9

3RD JERSEYS
From the Features menu, enter R6y34bsH52 as a code.

NHL 10

THIRD JERSEYS

At the EA Extras screen, enter rwyhafwh6ekyjcmr

PRINCE OF PERSIA

SANDS OF TIME PRINCE/FARAH SKINS

Select Skin Manager from the Extras menu. Press ▲ and enter 52585854. This gives you the Sands of Time skin for the Prince and Farah from Sands of Time for the Princess. Access them from the Skin Manager

PRINCE ALTAIR IBN LA-AHAD SKIN

Create an Ubisoft account. Then select "Altair Skin for Prince" to unlock.

RATCHET & CLANK FUTURE: A CRACK IN TIME

DISCOUNT AT WEAPON VENDORS

Have a save game for Ratchet and Clank Future: Tools of Destruction.

PIRATE HAT SKIN

Have a save game for Ratchet and Clank Future: Quest for Booty.

BANCHO RATCHET SKIN

Pause the game and enter Up, Right, Down, Left, ▲, ■, ✕, ●, R3.

RATCHET & CLANK FUTURE: TOOLS OF DESTRUCTION

CHALLENGE MODE

After defeating the game, you can replay the game in Challenge Mode with all of Ratchet's current upgraded weapons and armor.

SKILL POINTS

Complete the following objectives to earn skill points. Each one is worth 10 to 40 points and you can use these points to unlock Cheats in the Cheats Menu. The following table lists the skill points with a location and description.

SKILL POINT	LOCATION	DESCRIPTION
Smashing Good Time	Cobalia	Destroy all crates and consumer bots in the trade port and gel factory.
I Should Have Gone Down in a Barrel	Cobalia	Jump into each of the two gel waterfall areas in Cobalia gel factory.
Giant Hunter	Cobalia	Kill several Basilisk Leviathans in the Cobalia wilderness.
Wrench Ninja 3	Stratus City	Use only the Omniwrench to get through the level to the Robo-Wings segment.
We Don't Need No Stinkin' Bridges!	Stratus City	Cross the tri-pad sequence using gel-cube bounces.
Surface-to-Air Plasma Beasts	Stratus City	Take out several flying targets using a specific weapon.
Been Around	Stratus City	Take off from every Robo-wing launch pad in Stratus City.

SKILL POINT	LOCATION	DESCRIPTION
Collector's Addition	Voron	Be very thorough in your collection of goodies.
Minesweeper	Voron	Clear out a bunch of mines.
What's That, R2?	Voron	Barrel roll multiple times.
I Think I'm Gonna Be Sick	IFF	Ride the Ferris wheel for 5 loops without getting off or taking damage.
Fast and the Fire-ious	IFF	Use the Charge Boots to cross the bridge to the arena without being burned.
One Heckuva Peephole	IFF	Return after receiving the Geo-laser and complete the Geo-laser setup.
Alphabet City	Apogee	Teleport to each of the six asteroids in alphabetical order.
Knock You Down to Size	Apogee	Wrench Slam 5 centipedes.
Dancin' with the Stars	Apogee	Make 5 enemies dance at once on an asteroid.
Taste o' Yer Own Medicine	Pirate Base	Destroy all of the Shooter Pirates with the Combuster.
Preemptive Strike	Pirate Base	Destroy all of the "sleeping bats" while they are still sleeping.
It's Mutant-E Cap'n!	Pirate Base	Change 5 pirates into penguins in one blast.
You Sunk My Battleship!	Rakar	Shoot down a large percentage of the big destroyers.
Pretty Lights	Rakar	Complete the level without destroying any of the snatchers that fire beams at Ratchet.
I've Got Places To Be	Rakar	Destroy the boss in under 2:30.
The Consumer Is Not (Always) Right	Rykan V	Destroy a bunch of consumer bots in the level.
Live Strong	Rykan V	Complete the Gryo Cycle in 1:45.
Untouchable	Rykan V	Don't take damage in the Gyro-Cycle.
It Sounded Like a Freight Train	Sargasso	Get 10 Swarmers in one tornado.
Head Examiner	Sargasso	Land on all of the dinosaur heads in Sargasso.
Extinction	Sargasso	Kill all of the Sargasso Predators.
Lombaxes Don't Like Cold	Iris	Break all the breakable icicles.
Mow Down Ho-Down	Iris	Use turrets to destroy 10 dancing pirates.
Dancin' on the Ceiling	Zordoom	Successfully use a Groovitron while on a Magboot surface.
Seared Ahi	Zordoom	Use the Pyroblaster on 3 Drophid creatures after freeing them from their robotic suits.
Shocking Ascent	Zordoom	Destroy all enemies on the elevator using just the Shock Ravager.
Expert Marksman	Borag	Kill 75% of all of the enemies.
Can't Touch This	Borag	Don't take damage before fighting the boss.
Pyoo, Pyoo!	Borag	Complete the level without secondary fire.
Dead Aim	Kerchu	Destroy several destructible towers while on the pirate barge.
Fire With Fire	Kerchu	Kill a few Kerchu Flamethrowers with the Pyro Blaster.
Rocket Jump	Kerchu	Successfully jump over a row of three rockets while on the grindrail during the boss fight in Kerchu City.
Your Friendly Neighborhood...	Slag Fleet	Destroy 5 enemies while on the grav ramp before Slag's ship.
Turret Times Two	Slag Fleet	Destroy at least 2 pirates with each turret in the level.
Six Gun Salute	Slag Fleet	Get six pirates in a row to salute Ratchet while in the Pirate Disguise.
Gotta Catch 'Em All	Cragmite Ruins	Hit all Cragmite soldiers with the Mag-Net Launcher.
Ratchet and Goliath	Cragmite Ruins	Destroy multiple walkers using just the Nano-Swarmers.
Ratchet &...Not Clank?!	Cragmite Ruins	Use Mr. Zurkon in Cragmite's Ratchet-only segment.
Stay Still So I Can Shoot You!	Meridian	Use strafe-flip 10 times while fighting the Cragmite soldiers.
Now Boarding...	Meridian	Complete the Gyro-Cycle in 55 seconds.

SKILL POINT	LOCATION	DESCRIPTION
Low Flying Howls	Meridian	Fly under an electrified barrier in the Robo-wings segment.
Extreme Alien Makeover	Fastoon2	Turn 10 Cragmites into penguins.
Empty Bag o' Tricks	Fastoon2	Complete the level without using any devices.
Nowhere to Hide	Fastoon2	Destroy every piece of breakable cover.
No, Up Your Arsenal	Global	Upgrade every weapon to the max.
Roflcopter	Global	Turn enemies into penguins, then use the Visicopter to destroy the penguins.
Stir Fry	Global	Kill 2 different enemy types using the Shock Ravager while they are trapped in a tornado.
Golden Children	Overall	Find all of the Gold Bolts.
Sacagawea	Global	Complete all of the maps 100%, leaving no area undiscovered.
Cheapskate	Global	Purchase a single Combustor round.
Everybody Dance Now	Global	Make every type of enemy in the game dance.
F5 on the Fujita Scale	Global	Pick up more than 10 enemies with one tornado.
Chorus line	Global	Get 10+ enemies to dance together.
Happy Feet	Global	Get several penguins to dance on-screen.
Disco Inferno	Global	Use the Groovitron followed by the Pyro Blaster.
Bolts in the Bank	Global	Sell a bunch of Leviathan Souls to the Smuggler.
It's Like the North Pole Here	Global	Have at least 12-15 enemies and/or citizens turned into penguins at one time.
Say Hello to My Little Friend	Global	Kill 15 enemies with one RYNO shot.
For the Hoard!	Global	Get every item.
Promoted to Inspector	Global	Get every gadget.
Global Thermonuclear War	Global	Get every weapon.
It's Even Better the Second Time!	Global	Complete Challenge Mode.
The Hardest of Core	Global	Get all skill points and everything else in the game.

RESONANCE OF FATE

Once you have reached Chapter 7, search Leanne's closet. As she speaks her first line enter the following codes to unlock more outfits.

8-BIT GIRL SHIRT
Up, Up, Down, Down, Left, Right, Left, Right, ▲, ●

CLUB FAMITSU SHIRT
▲, ▲, Up, Up, ●, ●, Left, Left, L1, R1

GEMAGA SHIRT
R2, L2, L1, R1, ▲, ▲, ▲, ●, ●, Up

HIRAKOU SHIRT
●, ▲, L1, L1, R1, R1, L3, L3, Up, Down

PLATFORM LOGO SHIRT
R2, R1, R3, L3, L1, L2, Right, Left, ●, ▲

POLITAN SUIT
R3, R3, R3, Right, Left, ▲, ●, L2, R2, L1. This requires you to have the Reindeer Suit first.

ROCK REVOLUTION

ALL CHARACTERS
At the main menu, press ●, ■, ●, ■, ●, ■, ●, ▲, ■.

ALL VENUES
At the main menu, press ■, ●, ▲, ●, ■, ●, ▲, ■, ▲.

ROCKET KNIGHT

ALL CHARACTER SKINS
At the title screen, press Up, Up, Down, Down, Left, Right, Left, Right, ●, ✕, Start.

SCOTT PILGRIM VS. THE WORLD: THE GAME

PLAY AS SAME CHARACTER
At the title screen, press Down, R1, Up, L1, ▲, ●.

HEART SWORD
At the title screen, press ●, ●, ●, ✕, ●, ✕, ▲

BLOOD MODE
At the title screen, press ✕, ●, ✕, ●, ✕, ●, ●.

BOSS RUSH MODE
Pause the game on the overworld and press Right, Right, ●, R1, Right, Right, ●, R1.

ZOMBIE MODE
At the title screen, press Down, Up, Right, Down, Up, Right, Down, Up, Right, Right, Right.

SOUND CHECK BONUS LEVEL
Pause the game on the overworld and press L1, L1, R1, R1, L1, L1, L1, R1, R1, R1, L1, R1.

CHANGE MONEY TO ANIMALS
At the title screen, press Up, Up, Down, Down, Up, Up, Up, Up.

SEGA SUPERSTARS TENNIS

UNLOCK CHARACTERS
Complete the following missions to unlock the corresponding character.

CHARACTER	MISSION TO COMPLETE
Alex Kidd	Mission 1 of Alex Kidd's World
Amy Rose	Mission 2 of Sonic the Hedgehog's World
Gilius	Mission 1 of Golden Axe's World
Gum	Mission 12 of Jet Grind Radio's World
Meemee	Mission 8 of Super Monkey Ball's World
Pudding	Mission 1 of Space Channel 5's World
Reala	Mission 2 of NiGHTs' World
Shadow The Hedgehog	Mission 14 of Sonic the Hedgehog's World

THE SIMPSONS GAME

After unlocking the following, the outfits can be changed at the downstairs closet in the Simpson's house. The Trophies can be viewed at different locations in the house: Bart's room, Lisa's room, Marge's room, and the garage.

BART'S OUTFITS AND TROPHIES (POSTER COLLECTION)
At the main menu, press Right, Left, ●, ●, ▲, R3.

HOMER'S OUTFITS AND TROPHIES (BEER BOTTLE COLLECTION)
At the main menu, press Left, Right, ▲, ▲, ●, L3.

LISA'S OUTFITS AND TROPHIES (DOLLS)
At the main menu, press ●, ▲, ●, ●, ▲, L3.

MARGE'S OUTFITS AND TROPHIES (HAIR PRODUCTS)
At the main menu, press ▲, ●, ▲, ▲, ●, R3.

THE SIMS 3

CHEATS
Load your family, press Start, and hold L1 + L2 + R1 + R2. The game prompts you to save another file before activating the cheats. Spoot the Llama is now available in Misc Décor. Place it in your lot and click it to access the cheats. This disables Trophies and challenges.

SKATE 2

BIG BLACK
Select Enter Cheat from the Extras menu and enter letsdowork.

3D MODE
Select Enter Cheat from the Extras menu and enter strangeloops. Use glasses to view in 3D.

SKATE 3

HOVERBOARD MODE
In Free Play, select Extras from the Options. Choose Enter Cheat Code and enter mcfly.

MINI SKATER MODE
In Free Play, select Extras from the Options. Choose Enter Cheat Code and enter miniskaters.

ZOMBIE MODE
In Free Play, select Extras from the Options. Choose Enter Cheat Code and enter zombie.

ISAAC CLARK FROM DEADSPACE
In Free Play, select Extras from the Options. Choose Enter Cheat Code and enter deadspacetoo.

DEM BONES
Beat most of the Hall of Meat Challenges.

MEAT MAN
Beat all Hall of Meat Challenges.

RESETS OBJECTS TO ORIGINAL POSITIONS
In Free Play, select Extras from the Options. Choose Enter Cheat Code and enter streetsweeper.

SPIDER-MAN: SHATTERED DIMENSIONS

The following can be entered after completing the tutorial. The suits can be found in the Bonus Gallery under Alternate Suits.

IRON SPIDER SUIT
At the main menu, press Up, Right, Right, Right, Left, Left, Left, Down, Up.

SCARLET SPIDER SUIT
At the main menu, press Right, Up, Left, Right, Up, Left, Right, Up, Left, Right.

NEGATIVE ZONE SUIT
At the main menu, press Left, Right, Right, Down, Right, Down, Up, Left.

SPLIT/SECOND

HANZO FX350 CX (COMPUTER SPIELE) IN QUICK PLAY
At the Options menu, press ✪, Up, ✪, Up, ✪, Up.

RYBACK COYOTE AMX IN QUICK PLAY
At the Options menu, press Left, ✪, Left, ✪, Left, ✪ Left, ✪, Left, ✪, Left, ✪, Right.

RYBACK MOHAWK XDX (DISNEY XD) IN QUICK PLAY
At the Options menu, press ✪, Down, ✪, Down, ✪, Down.

STAR WARS THE CLONE WARS: REPUBLIC HEROES

BIG HEAD MODE
Pause the game, select Shop, and enter Up, Down, Left, Right, Left, Right, Down, Up in Cheats.

MINI-GUN
Pause the game, select Shop, and enter Down, Left, Right, Up, Right, Up, Left, Down in Cheats.

ULTIMATE LIGHTSABER
Pause the game, select Shop, and enter Right, Down, Down, Up, Left, Up, Up, Down in Cheats.

LIGHTSABER THROW UPGRADE
Pause the game, select Shop, and enter Left, Left, Right, Right, Up, Down, Down, Up in Combat Upgrades.

SPIDER DROID UPGRADE
Pause the game, select Shop, and enter Up, Left, Down, Left, Right, Left, Left, Left in Droid-Jak Upgrades.

STAR WARS: THE FORCE UNLEASHED: ULTIMATE SITH EDITION

CHEAT CODES
Pause the game and select Input Code. Here you can enter the following codes. Activating any of the following cheat codes will disable some unlockables, and you will be unable to save your progress.

CHEAT	CODE
All Force Powers at Max Power	KATARN
All Force Push Ranks	EXARKUN
All Saber Throw Ranks	ADEGAN
All Repulse Ranks	DATHOMIR
All Saber Crystals	HURRIKANE
All Talents	JOCASTA
Deadly Saber	LIGHTSABER

COMBOS
Pause the game and select Input Code. Here you can enter the following codes. Activating any of the following cheat codes will disable some unlockables, and you will be unable to save your progress.

COMBO	CODE
All Combos	MOLDYCROW
Aerial Ambush	VENTRESS
Aerial Assault	EETHKOTH
Aerial Blast	YADDLE
Impale	BRUTALSTAB
Lightning Bomb	MASSASSI
Lightning Grenade	RAGNOS
Saber Slam	PLOKOON
Saber Sling	KITFISTO
Sith Saber Flurry	LUMIYA
Sith Slash	DARAGON
Sith Throw	SAZEN
New Combo	FREEDON
New Combo	MARAJADE

ALL DATABANK ENTRIES
Pause the game and select Input Code. Enter OSSUS.

MIRRORED LEVEL
Pause the game and select Input Code. Enter MINDTRICK. Re-enter the code to return level to normal.

SITH MASTER DIFFICULTY

Pause the game and select Input Code. Enter SITHSPAWN.

COSTUMES

Pause the game and select Input Code. Here you can enter the following codes.

COSTUME	CODE
All Costumes	SOHNDANN
Bail Organa	VICEROY
Ceremonial Jedi Robes	DANTOOINE
Drunken Kota	HARDBOILED
Emperor	MASTERMIND
Incinerator Trooper	PHOENIX
Jedi Adventure Robe	HOLOCRON
Kashyyyk Trooper	TK421GREEN
Kota	MANDALORE

COSTUME	CODE
Master Kento	WOOKIEE
Proxy	PROTOTYPE
Scout Trooper	FERRAL
Shadow Trooper	BLACKHOLE
Sith Stalker Armor	KORRIBAN
Snowtrooper	SNOWMAN
Stormtrooper	TK421WHITE
Stormtrooper Commander	TK421BLUE

STAR WARS: THE FORCE UNLEASHED II

BOBA FETT COSTUME

Pause the game, select Cheat Codes from the Options, and enter MANDALORE.

DARK APPRENTICE COSTUME

Pause the game, select Cheat Codes from the Options, and enter VENTRESS.

GENERAL KOTA COSTUME

Pause the game, select Cheat Codes from the Options, and enter RAHM.

NEIMOIDIAN COSTUME

Pause the game, select Cheat Codes from the Options, and enter GUNRAY.

REBEL COMMANDO COSTUME

Pause the game, select Cheat Codes from the Options, and enter SPECFORCE.

REBEL SOLDIER COSTUME

Pause the game, select Cheat Codes from the Options, and enter REBELSCUM.

SABER GUARD COSTUME

Pause the game, select Cheat Codes from the Options, and enter MORGUKAI.

SITH ACOLYTE COSTUME

Pause the game, select Cheat Codes from the Options, and enter HAAZEN.

STORMTROOPER COSTUME

Pause the game, select Cheat Codes from the Options, and enter TK421.

TERROR TROOPER COSTUME

Pause the game, select Cheat Codes from the Options, and enter SHADOW.

TRAINING DROID COSTUME

Pause the game, select Cheat Codes from the Options, and enter HOLODROID.

REPULSE FORCE POWER

Pause the game, select Cheat Codes from the Options, and enter MAREK.

SABRE THROW

Pause the game, select Cheat Codes from the Options, and enter TRAYA.

WISDOM LIGHTSABER CRYSTALS

Pause the game, select Cheat Codes from the Options, and enter SOLARI.

TRAINING GEAR

Have a save game from Star Wars: The Force Unleashed.

CEREMONIAL ROBES

Have a save game from Star Wars: The Force Unleashed with the Light Side ending.

SITH STALKER ARMOR

Have a save game from Star Wars: The Force Unleashed with the Dark Side ending.

STUNTMAN IGNITION

3 PROPS IN STUNT CREATOR MODE
Select Cheats from Extras and enter COOLPROP.

ALL ITEMS UNLOCKED FOR CONSTRUCTION MODE
Select Cheats from Extras and enter NOBLEMAN.

MVX SPARTAN
Select Cheats from Extras and enter fastride.

ALL CHEATS
Select Cheats from Extras and enter Wearefrozen. This unlocks the following cheats: Slo-mo Cool, Thrill Cam, Vision Switcher, Nitro Addiction, Freaky Fast, and Ice Wheels.

ALL CHEATS
Select Cheats from Extras and enter Kungfoopete.

ICE WHEELS CHEAT
Select Cheats from Extras and enter IceAge.

NITRO ADDICTION CHEAT
Select Cheats from Extras and enter TheDuke.

VISION SWITCHER CHEAT
Select Cheats from Extras and enter GFXMODES.

SUPER PUZZLE FIGHTER II TURBO HD REMIX

PLAY AS AKUMA
At the character select, highlight Hsien-Ko and press Down.

PLAY AS DAN
At the character select, highlight Donovan and press Down.

PLAY AS DEVILOT
At the character select, highlight Morrigan and press Down.

PLAY AS ANITA
At the character select, hold **L1** + **R1** and choose Donovan.

PLAY AS HSIEN-KO'S TALISMAN
At the character select, hold **L1** + **R1** and choose Hsien-Ko.

PLAY AS MORRIGAN AS A BAT
At the character select, hold **L1** + **R1** and choose Morrigan.

SUPER STREET FIGHTER IV

BARREL BUSTER AND CAR CRUSHER BONUS STAGES
Beat Arcade Mode in any difficulty

COLORS AND TAUNTS
Colors 1 and 2 plus the first taunt for each fighter are available from the start. For colors 11 & 12, start a game with a Street Fighter IV save game on your system. To earn the rest of the colors and taunts, you need to fight a certain number of matches with that character.

COLOR	# OF MATCHES
3	2
4	4
5	6
6	8
7	10
8	12
9	14
10	16

TAUNT	# OF MATCHES
2	1
3	3
4	5
5	7
6	9
7	11
8	13
9	15
10	16

TIGER WOODS PGA TOUR 08

ALL COURSES
Select Password from EA Sports Extras and enter greensfees.

ALL GOLFERS
Select Password from EA Sports Extras and enter allstars.

WAYNE ROONEY
Select Password from EA Sports Extras and enter playfifa08.

INFINITE MONEY
Select Password from EA Sports Extras and enter cream.

TOM CLANCY'S HAWX

A-12 AVENGER II
At the hangar, hold **L2** and press ●, **L1**, ●, **R1**, ▲, ●.

F-18 HARV
At the hangar, hold **L2** and press **L1**, ▲, **L1**, ▲, **L1**, ●.

FB-22 STRIKE RAPTOR
At the hangar, hold **L2** and press **R1**, ●, **R1**, ●, **R1**, ▲.

TONY HAWK RIDE

RYAN SHECKLER
Select Cheats from the Options menu and enter SHECKLERSIG.

QUICKSILVER 80'S LEVEL
Select Cheats from the Options menu and enter FEELINGEIGHTIES.

TONY HAWK'S PROVING GROUND

Select Cheat Codes from the Options and enter the following cheats. Some codes need to be enabled by selecting Cheats from the Options during a game.

UNLOCK	CHEAT
Unlocks Boneman	CRAZYBONEMAN
Unlocks Bosco	MOREMILK
Unlocks Cam	NOTACAMERA
Unlocks Cooper	THECOOP
Unlocks Eddie X	SKETCHY
Unlocks El Patinador	PILEDRIVER
Unlocks Eric	FLYAWAY
Unlocks Mad Dog	RABBIES
Unlocks MCA	INTERGALACTIC
Unlocks Mel	NOTADUDE
Unlocks Rube	LOOKSSMELLY
Unlocks Spence	DAPPER
Unlocks Shayne	MOVERS
Unlocks TV Producer	SHAKER
Unlock FDR	THEPREZPARK

UNLOCK	CHEAT
Unlock Lansdowne	THELOCALPARK
Unlock Air & Space Museum	THEINDOORPARK
Unlocks all Fun Items	OVERTHETOP
Unlocks all CAS items	GIVEMESTUFF
Unlocks all Decks	LETSGOSKATE
Unlock all Game Movies	WATCHTHIS
Unlock all Lounge Bling Items	SWEETSTUFF
Unlock all Lounge Themes	LAIDBACKLOUNGE
Unlock all Rigger Pieces	IMGONNABUILD
Unlock all Video Editor Effects	TRIPPY
Unlock all Video Editor Overlays	PUTEMONTOP
All specials unlocked and in player's special list	LOTSOFTRICKS
Full Stats	BEEFEDUP
Give player +50 skill points	NEEDSHELP

The following cheats lock you out of the Leaderboards:

UNLOCK	CHEAT
Unlocks Perfect Manual	STILLAINTFALLIN
Unlocks Perfect Rail	AINTFALLIN
Unlock Super Check	BOOYAH
Unlocks Unlimited Focus	MYOPIC
Unlock Unlimited Slash Grind	SUPERSLASHIN
Unlocks 100% branch completion in NTT	FOREVERNAILED
No Bails	ANDAINTFALLI

You can not use the Video Editor with the following cheats:

UNLOCK	CHEAT
Unlocks Invisible Man	THEMISSING
Mini Skater	TINYTATER
No Board	MAGICMAN

TRANSFORMERS: THE GAME

INFINITE HEALTH
At the Main menu, press Left, Left, Up, Left, Right, Down, Right.

INFINITE AMMO
At the Main menu, press Up, Down, Left, Right, Up, Up, Down.

NO MILITARY OR POLICE
At the Main menu, press Right, Left, Right, Left, Right, Left, Right.

ALL MISSIONS
At the Main menu, press Down, Up, Left, Right, Right, Right, Up, Down.

BONUS CYBERTRON MISSIONS
At the Main menu, press Right, Up, Up, Down, Right, Left, Left.

GENERATION 1 SKIN: JAZZ
At the Main menu, press Left, Up, Down, Down, Left, Up, Right.

GENERATION 1 SKIN: MEGATRON
At the Main menu, press Down, Left, Left, Down, Right, Right, Up.

GENERATION 1 SKIN: OPTIMUS PRIME
At the Main menu, press Down, Right, Left, Up, Down, Down, Left.

GENERATION 1 SKIN: ROBOVISION OPTIMUS PRIME
At the Main menu, press Down, Down, Up, Up, Right, Right, Right.

GENERATION 1 SKIN: STARSCREAM
At the Main menu, press Right, Down, Left, Left, Down, Up, Up.

TRANSFORMERS REVENGE OF THE FALLEN

LOW GRAVITY MODE
Select Cheat Code and enter ✕, ●, ▲, L3, ▲, L3.

NO WEAPON OVERHEAT
Select Cheat Code and enter L3, ●, ✕, L3, ▲, L1.

ALWAYS IN OVERDRIVE MODE
Select Cheat Code and enter L1, ●, L1, ✕, ●, R3.

UNLIMITED TURBO
Select Cheat Code and enter ●, L3, ●, R3, ✕, ▲

NO SPECIAL COOLDOWN TIME
Select Cheat Code and enter R3, ●, R3, R3, ●, ✕.

INVINCIBILITY
Select Cheat Code and enter R3, ✕, ●, L3, ●, ●.

4X ENERGON FROM DEFEATED ENEMIES
Select Cheat Code and enter ▲, ●, ●, R3, ✕, ▲.

INCREASED WEAPON DAMAGE(ROBOT FORM)
Select the Cheat Code option and enter ▲, ▲, R3, ✕, L1, ▲.

INCREASED WEAPON DAMAGE(VEHICLE FORM)
Select Cheat Code and enter ▲, ●, R1, ✕, R3, L3.

MELEE INSTANT KILLS
Select the Cheat Code option and enter R3, ✕. L1, ●, R3, L1.

LOWER ENEMY ACCURACY
Select Cheat Code and enter ✕, L3, R3, L3, R3, R1.

INCREASED ENEMY HEALTH
Select Cheat Code and enter ●, ✕, L1, ●, R3, ▲.

INCREASED ENEMY DAMAGE
Select Cheat Code and enter L1, ▲, ✕, ▲, R3, R3.

45

INCREASED ENEMY ACCURACY
Select Cheat Code and enter ▲, ▲, ◉, ✖, A, L1.

SPECIAL KILLS ONLY MODE
Select Cheat Code and enter ◉, ◉, R1, ◉, ✖, L3.

UNLOCK ALL SHANGHAI MISSIONS & ZONES
Select Cheat Code and enter ▲, L3, R3, L1, ▲, ✖.

UNLOCK ALL WEST COAST MISSIONS & ZONES
Select Cheat Code and enter L1, R1, R3, ▲, R3, ◉.

UNLOCK ALL DEEP SIX MISSIONS & ZONES
Select Cheat Code and enter ✖, R1, ▲, ◉, ✖, L1.

UNLOCK ALL EAST COAST MISSIONS & ZONES
Select Cheat Code and enter R3, L3, R1, ✖, ◉, ✖.

UNLOCK ALL CAIRO MISSIONS & ZONES
Select Cheat Code and enter R3, ▲, ✖, ▲, L3, L1.

UNLOCK & ACTIVATE ALL UPGRADES
Select Cheat Code and enter L1, ▲, L1, ◉, ✖, ✖.

UNCHARTED 2: AMONG THIEVES

In Uncharted 2: Among Thieves, upon opening the store you'll have the option to hit the Square button to check for Uncharted: Drake's Fortune save data. You'll obtain cash for having save data! This cash can be used in the single and multiplayer stores. Could be useful if you want a head start online!

$20,000
Have a saved game of Uncharted: Drake's Fortune.

$80,000
Have a saved game of Uncharted: Drake's Fortune with the story completed at least once.

VIRTUA FIGHTER 5

WATCH MODE
Select Exhibition Mode, then at the character select, hold L1 + R1 and press ✖.

WORLD OF OUTLAWS: SPRINT CARS

$5,000,000
Enter your name as CHICMCHIM.

ALL TRACKS
Enter your name as JOEYJOEJOE.

ALL DRIVERS
Enter your name as MITYMASTA.

WORLD SERIES OF POKER 2008: BATTLE FOR THE BRACELETS

PHILLIP J. HELLMUTH
Enter BEATTHEBRAT as the player name.

WWE SMACKDOWN VS. RAW 2010

THE ROCK
Select Cheat Codes from the Options and enter The Great One.

VINCE'S OFFICE AND DIRT SHEET FOR BACKSTAGE BRAWL
Select Cheat Codes from the Options menu and enter BonusBrawl.

SHAWN MICHAEL'S ALTERNATE COSTUME
Select Cheat Codes from the Options menu and enter Bow Down.

JOHN CENA'S ALTERNATE COSTUME
Select Cheat Codes from the Options menu and enter CENATION.

RANDY ORTON'S ALTERNATE COSTUME
Select Cheat Codes from the Options menu and enter ViperRKO.

SANTINO MARELLA'S ALTERNATE COSTUME
Select Cheat Codes from the Options menu and enter Milan Miracle.

TRIPLE H'S ALTERNATE COSTUME
Select Cheat Codes from the Options menu and enter Suck IT!.

WWE SMACKDOWN VS. RAW 2011

JOHN CENA (ENTRANCE/CIVILIAN)
In My WWE, select Cheat Codes from the Options and enter SLURPEE.

ALL OF RANDY ORTON'S COSTUMES
In My WWE, select Cheat Codes from the Options and enter apexpredator.

TRIBUTE TO THE TROOPS ARENA
In My WWE, select Cheat Codes from the Options and enter 8thannualtribute.

NINTENDO Wii™

CONTENTS

CHEAT CODE EXPLOSION FOR CONSOLES

NINTENDO Wii™ VIRTUAL CONSOLE GAMES

CONTENTS

2010 FIFA WORLD CUP SOUTH AFRICA

WORLD CLASSIC XI TEAM

Earn at least Bronze against each team in Kazumi's Dream Team to play the World Classic XI Team. Beat them in best of three matches to play as the team in Hit the Pitch.

ASTRO BOY: THE VIDEO GAME

INVULNERABLE

Pause the game and press Up, Down, Down, Up, 1, 2.

MAX STATS

Pause the game and press Left, Left, 2, Down, Down, 1.

INFINITE SUPERS

Pause the game and press Left, 1, Right, 1, Up, Down.

INFINITE DASHES

Pause the game and press 2, 2, 1, 2, Left, Up.

DISABLE SUPERS

Pause the game and press 1, 1, 2, 2, 1, Left.

COSTUME SWAP (ARENA AND CLASSIC COSTUMES)

Pause the game and press 2, Up, 1, Up, Down, 2.

UNLOCK LEVELS

Pause the game and press Up, 1, Right, 1, Down, 1. This allows you to travel to any level from the Story menu.

AVATAR: THE LAST AIRBENDER

UNLIMITED HEALTH

Select Code Entry from Extras and enter 94677.

UNLIMITED CHI

Select Code Entry from Extras and enter 24463.

UNLIMITED COPPER

Select Code Entry from Extras and enter 23637.

NEVERENDING STEALTH

Select Code Entry from Extras and enter 53467.

1 HIT DISHONOR

Select Code Entry from Extras and enter 54641.

DOUBLE DAMAGE

Select Code Entry from Extras and enter 34743.

ALL TREASURE MAPS

Select Code Entry from Extras and enter 37437.

THE CHARACTER CONCEPT ART GALLERY

Select Code Entry from Extras and enter 97831.

AVATAR: THE LAST AIRBENDER-THE BURNING EARTH

DOUBLE DAMAGE

Go to the code entry section and enter 90210.

INFINITE LIFE

Go to the code entry section and enter 65049.

INFINITE SPECIAL ATTACKS

Go to the code entry section and enter 66206.

MAX LEVEL

Go to the code entry section and enter 89121.

ONE-HIT DISHONOR

Go to the code entry section and enter 28260.

ALL BONUS GAMES

Go to the code entry section and enter 99801.

ALL GALLERY ITEMS

Go to the code entry section and enter 85061.

AVATAR – THE LAST AIRBENDER: INTO THE INFERNO

After you have defeated the first level, The Awakening, go to Ember Island. Walk to the left past the volleyball net to a red and yellow door. Select Game Secrets and then Code Entry. Now you can enter the following cheats.

MAX COINS
Enter 66639224.

ALL ITEMS AVAILABLE FROM SHOP
Enter 34737253.

ALL CHAPTERS
Enter 52993833.

UNLOCK CONCEPT ART IN GALLERY
Enter 27858343.

BAKUGAN BATTLE BRAWLERS

1,000 BP
Enter 33204429 as your name.

5,000 BP
Enter 42348294 as your name.

10,000 BP
Enter 46836478 as your name.

100,000 BP
Enter 18499753 as your name.

500,000 BP
Enter 26037947 as your name.

BRONZE WARIUS
Enter 44982493 as your name.

BEN 10: ALIEN FORCE VILGAX ATTACKS

LEVEL SKIP
Pause the game and enter Portal in the Cheats menu.

UNLOCK ALL SPECIAL ATTACKS FOR ALL FORMS
Pause the game and enter Everythingproof in the Cheats menu.

UNLOCK ALL ALIEN FORMS
Pause the game and enter Primus in the Cheats menu.

TOGGLE INVULNERABILITY ON AND OFF
Pause the game and enter Xlmrsmoothy in the Cheats menu.

GIVES PLAYER FULL HEALTH
Pause the game and enter Herotime in the Cheats menu.

QUICK ENERGY REGENERATION
Pause the game and enter Generator in the Cheats menu.

BEN 10: PROTECTOR OF EARTH

INVINCIBILITY
Select a game from the Continue option. Go to the Map Selection screen, press Plus and choose Extras. Select Enter Secret Code and enter XLR8, Heatblast, Wildvine, Fourarms.

ALL COMBOS
Select a game from the Continue option. Go to the Map Selection screen, press Plus and choose Extras. Select Enter Secret Code and enter Cannonblot, Heatblast, Fourarms, Heatblast.

ALL LOCATIONS

Select a game from the Continue option. Go to the Map Selection screen, press Plus and choose Extras. Select Enter Secret Code and enter Heatblast, XLR8, XLR8, Cannonblot.

DNA FORCE SKINS

Select a game from the Continue option. Go to the Map Selection screen, press Plus and choose Extras. Select Enter Secret Code and enter Wildvine, Fourarms, Heatblast, Cannonbolt.

DARK HEROES SKINS

Select a game from the Continue option. Go to the Map Selection screen, press Plus and choose Extras. Select Enter Secret Code and enter Cannonbolt, Cannonbolt, Fourarms, Heatblast.

ALL ALIEN FORMS

Select a game from the Continue option. Go to the Map Selection screen, press Plus and choose Extras. Select Enter Secret Code and enter Wildvine, Fourarms, Heatblast, Wildvine.

MASTER CONTROL

Select a game from the Continue option. Go to the Map Selection screen, press Plus and choose Extras. Select Enter Secret Code and enter Cannonbolt, Heatblast, Wildvine, Fourarms.

BEN 10 ULTIMATE ALIEN: COSMIC DESTRUCTION

To remove the cheats, you will need to start a new game.

1,000,000 DNA

Pause the game, select Cheats, and enter Cash.

REGENERATE HEALTH

Pause the game, select Cheats, and enter Health.

REGENERATE ENERGY

Pause the game, select Cheats, and enter Energy.

UPGRADE EVERYTHING

Pause the game, select Cheats, and enter Upgrade.

ALL LEVELS

Pause the game, select Cheats, and enter Levels.

ENEMIES DO DOUBLE DAMAGE/ PLAYER DOES ½ DAMAGE

Pause the game, select Cheats, and enter Hard.

BLAZING ANGELS: SQUADRONS OF WWII

ALL AIRCRAFT AND CAMPAIGNS

After you have chosen a pilot, hold Minus + Plus and press Left, Right, 1, 2, 2, 1.

GOD MODE

Pause the game, hold Minus and press 1, 2, 1, 2.

WEAPON DAMAGE INCREASED

Pause the game, hold Minus and press 2, 1, 1, 2.

BOOM BLOX

ALL TOYS IN CREATE MODE

At the title screen, press Up, Right, Down, Left to bring up a cheats menu. Enter Tool Pool.

SLOW-MO IN SINGLE PLAYER

At the title screen, press Up, Right, Down, Left to bring up a cheats menu. Enter Blox Time.

CHEERLEADERS BECOME PROFILE CHARACTER

At the title screen, press Up, Right, Down, Left to bring up a cheats menu. Enter My Team.

FLOWER EXPLOSIONS

At the title screen, press Up, Right, Down, Left to bring up a cheats menu. Enter Flower Power.

JINGLE BLOCKS

At the title screen, press Up, Right, Down, Left to bring up a cheats menu. Enter Maestro.

BOOM BLOX BASH PARTY

At the title screen, press Up, Right, Down, Left. Now you can enter the following codes:

UNLOCK EVERYTHING
Enter Nothing But Hope.

1 MILLION BOOM BUX
Enter Bailout.

TURN ON BLOX TIME
Enter Freeze Frame.

TURNS ALL SOUND EFFECTS INTO VIRUS BLOX SOUND EFFECTS
Enter Musical Fruit.

ALL COLORED BLOX
Enter Rainbow Blox.

BRATZ: MOVIE STARZ

FEELIN' PRETTY CLOTHING LINE
At the Cheat Computer enter PRETTY.

HIGH SCHOOL CLOTHING LINE
At the Cheat Computer enter SCHOOL.

HOLLYWOOD CLOTHING LINE
At the Cheat Computer enter MOVIES

PASSION FOR FASHION CLOTHING LINE
At the Cheat Computer enter ANGELZ.

PRINCESS CLOTHING LINE
At the Cheat Computer enter SPARKL.

BUILD-A-BEAR WORKSHOP: A FRIEND FUR ALL SEASONS

ALL ISLANDS, MINIGAMES, OUTFITS, AND ACCESSORIES
At the main menu, press Up, Down, Left, Right, A, B.

CARS MATER-NATIONAL

ALL ARCADE RACES, MINI-GAMES, AND WORLDS
Select Codes/Cheats from the options and enter PLAYALL.

ALL CARS
Select Codes/Cheats from the options and enter MATTEL07.

ALTERNATE LIGHTNING MCQUEEN COLORS
Select Codes/Cheats from the options and enter NCEDUDZ.

ALL COLORS FOR OTHERS
Select Codes/Cheats from the options and enter PAINTIT.

UNLIMITED TURBO
Select Codes/Cheats from the options and enter ZZOOOOM.

EXTREME ACCELERATION
Select Codes/Cheats from the options and enter OTO2OOX.

EXPERT MODE
Select Codes/Cheats from the options and enter VRYFAST.

ALL BONUS ART
Select Codes/Cheats from the options and enter BUYTALL.

CARS RACE-O-RAMA

ALL ARCADE MODE EVENTS

Select Cheats from the Options menu and enter SLVRKEY.

ALL STORY MODE EVENTS

Select Cheats from the Options menu and enter GOLDKEY.

ALL OF LIGHTNING MCQUEEN'S FRIENDS

Select Cheats from the Options menu and enter EVRYBDY.

ALL LIGHTNING MCQUEEN CUSTOM KIT PARTS

Select Cheats from the Options menu and enter GR8MODS.

ALL PAINT JOBS FOR ALL NON-LIGHTNING MCQUEEN CHARACTERS

Select Cheats from the Options menu and enter CARSHOW.

CASTLEVANIA THE ADVENTURE REBIRTH

LEVEL SELECT

Select Game Start and hold Right for a few seconds. You can play any level you have already played.

CODE LYOKO: QUEST FOR INFINITY

UNLOCK EVERYTHING

Pause the game and press 2, 1, C, Z, 2, 1.

UNLIMITED HEALTH AND POWER

Pause the game and press 2, 2, Z, Z, 1, 1.

INCREASE SPEED

Pause the game and press Z, 1, 2, 1 (x3).

INCREASE DAMAGE

Pause the game and press 1, Z, Z, C (x3).

CONFIGURATION A

Pause the game and press 2, Z, 1, Z, C, Z.

CONFIGURATION B

Pause the game and press C, C, 1, C, Z, C.

ALL ABILITIES

Pause the game and press Z, C, Z, C (x3).

ALL BONUSES

Pause the game and press 1, 2, C, 2 (x3).

ALL GOODIES

Pause the game and press C, 2, 2, Z, C, Z.

CONTRA REBIRTH

DEBUG MENU

At the title screen, press Plus + 1 + 2.

CORALINE

UNLIMITED LEVEL SKIP
Select Cheats from the Options menu and enter Beldam.

UNLIMITED HEALTH
Select Cheats from the Options menu and enter beets.

UNLIMITED FIREFLYS
Select Cheats from the Options menu and enter garden.

FREE HALL PASSES
Select Cheats from the Options menu and enter well.

BUTTON EYE CORALINE
Select Cheats from the Options menu and enter cheese.

CRASH: MIND OVER MUTANT

A cheat can be deactivated by re-entering the code.

FREEZE ENEMIES WITH TOUCH
Pause the game, hold guard and press Down, Down, Down, Up.

ENEMIES DROP X4 DAMAGE
Pause the game, hold guard and press Up, Up, Up, Left.

ENEMIES DROP PURPLE FRUIT
Pause the game, hold guard and press Up, Down, Down, Up.

ENEMIES DROP SUPER KICK
Pause the game, hold guard and press Up, Right, Down, Left.

ENIMIES DROP WUMPA FRUIT
Pause the game, hold guard and press Right, Right, Right, Up.

SHADOW CRASH
Pause the game, hold guard and press Left, Right, Left, Right.

DEFORMED CRASH
Pause the game, hold guard and press Left, Left, Left, Down.

COSTUMES
Complete all of the following character's mini-games to unlock each costume.

COSTUME	DEFEAT MINI-GAMES OF
Magmadon	Little Bear
Ratcicle	Ratcicle Kid
Skeleton	Sludge Brother
Snipe	Crunch
Spike	Uka Uka

DE BLOB

INVULNERABILITY
During a game, hold C and press 1, 1, 1, 1. Re-enter the code to disable.

LIFE UP
During a game, hold C and press 1, 1, 2, 2

TIME BONUS
During a game, hold C and press 1, 2, 1, 2. This adds 10 minutes to your time.

ALL MOODS
At the main menu, hold C and press B, B, 1, 2, 1, 2, B, B.

ALL MULTIPLAYER LEVELS
At the main menu, hold C and press 2, 2, B, B, 1, 1, B, B.

DISNEY PRINCESS: ENCHANTED JOURNEY

BELLE'S KINGDOM
Select Secrets and enter GASTON.

GOLDEN SET
Select Secrets and enter BLUEBIRD.

FLOWER WAND
Select Secrets and enter SLEEPY.

HEART WAND
Select Secrets and enter BASHFUL.

SHELL WAND
Select Secrets and enter RAJAH.

SHIELD WAND
Select Secrets and enter CHIP.

STAR WAND
Select Secrets and enter SNEEZY.

DJ HERO

Select Cheats from Options and enter the following. Some codes will disable high scores and progress. Cheats cannot be used in tutorials and online.

UNLOCK ALL CONTENT
Enter tol0.

ALL CHARACTER ITEMS
Enter uNA2.

ALL VENUES
Enter Wv1u.

ALL DECKS
Enter LAuP.

ALL HEADPHONES
Enter 62Db.

ALL MIXES
Enter 82xl.

AUTO SCRATCH
Enter lT6j.

AUTO EFFECTS DIAL
Enter ab1L.

AUTO FADER
Enter SL5d.

AUTO TAPPER
Enter ZitH.

AUTO WIN EUPHORIA
Enter r3a9.

BLANK PLINTHS
Enter ipr0.

HAMSTER SWITCH
Enter 7geo.

HYPER DECK MODE
Enter 76st.

SHORT DECK
Enter 51uC.

INVISIBLE DJ
Enter oh5T.

PITCH BLACK OUT
Enter d4kR.

PLAY IN THE BEDROOM
Enter g7nH.

ANY DJ, ANY SETLIST
Enter 0jj8.

DAFT PUNK'S CONTENT
Enter d1g?.

DJ AM'S CONTENT
Enter k07u.

DJ JAZZY JEFF'S CONTENT
Enter n1fz.

DJ SHADOW'S CONTENT
Enter oMxV.

DJ Z-TRIP'S CONTENT
Enter 5rtg.

GRANDMASTER FLASH'S CONTENT
Enter ami8.

NINJUTSU	PASSWORD
Summoning: Rashomon	Earth, Monkey, Boar, Rooster
Tunneling Fang	Wind, Dog, Boar, Horse
Water Style: Ripping Torrent	Water, Ox, Dog, Sheep

NINJUTSU	PASSWORD
Water Style: Water Fang Bomb	Water, Horse, Rat, Ox
Weapon: Flash Kunai Ball	Fire, Sheep, Boar, Ox
Wind Style: Air Bullets	Wind, Ox, Boar, Rabbit

HOKAGE NARUTO WALLPAPER

At the Tree of Mettle, select Enter Password and enter Fire, Ox, Rabbit, Horse.

NBA 2K10

ABA BALL
Select Codes from the Options menu. Then select Enter Code and enter payrespect.

2K CHINA TEAM
Select Codes from the Options menu. Then select Enter Code and enter 2kchina.

NBA 2K TEAM
Select Codes from the Options menu. Then select Enter Code and enter nba2k.

2K SPORTS TEAM
Select Codes from the Options menu. Then select Enter Code and enter 2ksports.

VISUAL CONCEPTS TEAM
Select Codes from the Options menu. Then select Enter Code and enter vcteam.

2010 ALL-STAR UNIFORMS
Select Codes from the Options menu. Then select Enter Code and enter otnresla.

HARDWOOD CLASSIC UNIFORMS
Select Codes from the Options menu. Then select Enter Code and enter wasshcicsl. This code gives Hardwood Classic Uniforms for the Cavaliers, Jazz, Magic, Raptors, timberwolves, Trail Blazers, and Warriors.

LATIN NIGHTS UNIFORMS
Select Codes from the Options menu. Then select Enter Code and enter aihinntslgt. This code gives Latin Nights jerseys for Bulls, Heat, Knicks, Lakers, Mavericks, Rockets, Spurs, and Suns.

NBA GREEN UNIFORMS
Select Codes from the Options menu. Then select Enter Code and enter nreogge. This code gives green uniforms for the Bobcats, Bulls, and Nuggets.

SECONDARY ROAD UNIFORMS
Select Codes from the Options menu. Then select Enter Code and enter eydonscar. This code gives Second Road Uniforms for the Grizzlies, Hawks, Mavericks, and Rockets.

ST. PATRICK'S DAY UNIFORMS
Select Codes from the Options menu. Then select Enter Code and enter riiasgerh. This code gives St. Patrick's Day jerseys for the Bulls, Celtics, Knicks, and Raptors.

BOBCATS RACING UNIFORM
Select Codes from the Options menu. Then select Enter Code and enter agsntrccai.

CAVALIERS CAVFANATICS UNIFORM
Select Codes from the Options menu. Then select Enter Code and enter aifnaatccv.

HORNETS MARDI GRAS UNIFORM
Select Codes from the Options menu. Then select Enter Code and enter asrdirmga.

TRAIL BLAZERS RIP CITY UNIFORM
Select Codes from the Options menu. Then select Enter Code and enter ycprtii.

NBA 2K11

2K CHINA TEAM
In Features, select Codes from the Extras menu. Choose Enter Code and enter 2kchina.

2K SPORTS TEAM
In Features, select Codes from the Extras menu. Choose Enter Code and enter 2Ksports.

NBA 2K TEAM
In Features, select Codes from the Extras menu. Choose Enter Code and enter nba2k.

VC TEAM
In Features, select Codes from the Extras menu. Choose Enter Code and enter vcteam.

ABA BALL
In Features, select Codes from the Extras menu. Choose Enter Code and enter payrespect.

NBA LIVE 10

CHARLOTTE BOBCATS' 2009/2010 RACE DAY ALTERNATE JERSEYS

Select Options from My NBA Live and go to Select Codes. Enter ceobdabacarstcy.

NEW ORLEANS HORNETS' 2009/2010 MARDI GRAS ALTERNATE JERSEYS

Select Options from My NBA Live and go to Select Codes. Enter nishrag1rosmad0.

ALTERNATE JERSEYS

Select Options from My NBA Live and go to Select Codes. Enter ndnba1rooaesdc0. This unlocks alternate jerseys for Atlanta Hawks, Dallas Mavericks, Houston Rockets, and Memphis Grizzlies.

MORE HARDWOOD CLASSICS NIGHTS JERSEYS

Select Options from My NBA Live and go to Select Codes. Enter hdogdrawhoticns. This unlocks Hardwood Classics Nights jerseys for Cleveland Cavaliers, Golden State Warriors, Minnesota Timberwolves, Orlando Magic, Philadelphia 76ers.

ADIDAS EQUATIONS

Select Options from My NBA Live and go to Select Codes. Enter adaodqauieints1.

ADIDAS TS CREATORS WITH ANKLE BRACES

Select Options from My NBA Live and go to Select Codes. Enter atciadsstsdhecf.

ADIDAS TS SUPERNATURAL COMMANDERS

Select Options from My NBA Live and go to Select Codes. Enter andsicdsmatdnsr.

ADIDAS TS SUPERNATURAL CREATORS

Select Options from My NBA Live and go to Select Codes. Enter ard8siscdnatstr.

AIR MAX LEBRON VII

Select Options from My NBA Live and go to Select Codes. Enter ere1nbvlaoeknii, 2ovnaebnkrielei, 3rioabeneikenvl, ri4boenanekilve, ivl5brieekaeonn, or n6ieirvalkeeobn.

KOBE V

Select Options from My NBA Live and go to Select Codes. Enter ovze1bimenkoko0, m0kveokoiebozn2, eev0nbimokk3ozo, or bmo4inozeeo0kvk.

JORDAN CP3 IIIS

Select Options from My NBA Live and go to Select Codes. Enter iaporcdian3ejis.

JORDAN MELO M6S

Select Options from My NBA Live and go to Select Codes. Enter emlarmeoo6ajdsn.

JORDAN SIXTY PLUSES

Select Options from My NBA Live and go to Select Codes. Enter aondsuilyjrspxt.

NIKE HUARACHE LEGIONS

Select Options from My NBA Live and go to Select Codes. Enter aoieuchrahelgn.

NIKE KD 2S

Select Options from My NBA Live and go to Select Codes. Enter kk2tesaosepinrd.

NIKE ZOOM FLIP'NS

Select Options from My NBA Live and go to Select Codes. Enter epfnozaeminolki.

DONKEY KONG COUNTRY 2: DIDDY'S KONG QUEST

SOUND TEST
Highlight Two Player and press Down (x5).

CHEAT MODE
Press Down (x5) again after getting Sound Test to access the cheat mode. Now you can enter the following:

50 LIVES
Press Y, A, Select, A, Down, Left, A, Down.

HARD MODE
Press B, A, Right, Right, A, Left, A, X. This gets rid of the barrels.

DRAGON BALL Z: BUDOKAI TENKAICHI 2

Hold Z + Minus to clear codes.

DOUBLE FIST POWER
At the Stage Select in vs mode, hold Z + Plus to start code input. Swing the Nunchuk Right, Wiimote Left, Wiimote Left + Nunchuk Right, Wiimote and Nunchuk Down.

TAIL POWER
At the Stage Select in vs mode, hold Z + Plus to start code input. Swing the Wiimote Down, Up, Left, Right.

DRAGON BALL Z: BUDOKAI TENKAICHI 3

SURVIVAL MODE
Clear 30 missions in Mission 100 mode.

EA SPORTS NBA JAM

Hold the Wii Remote vertically when entering the following. The teams can be found by pressing + at the team select.

BEASTIE BOYS
At the title screen, press Up, Up, Down, Down, Left, Right, Left, Right, B, +. This team includes Ad Rock, MCA, and Mike D.

J.COLE AND 9TH WONDER
At the title screen, press Up, Left, Down, Right, Up, Left, Down, Right, 1, 2.

DEMOCRATS TEAM
At the title screen, press Left (x13), +. This team includes Barack Obama, Joe Biden, Bill Clinton, and Hillary Clinton.

REPUBLICANS TEAM
At the title screen, press Right (x13), +. The team includes George W. Bush, Sarah Palin, and John McCain.

ESPN'S SPORTSNATION
Select Play Now. When entering the initials, enter ESP for P1 and NSN for P2. Advance to the Choose Teams screen and use + to find the team. This team includes the hosts of the show; Colin Cowherd and Michelle Beadle.

NBA MASCOTS
Select Play Now. When entering the initials, enter MAS for P1 and COT for P2. Advance to the Choose Teams screen and use + to find the team.

ORIGINAL GENERATION JAM
Select Play Now. When entering the initials, enter MJT for P1. Advance to the Choose Teams screen and use + to find the team. This team includes Mark Turmell and Tim Kitzrow.

EARTHWORM JIM

CHEAT MENU
Pause the game and press Y + Left, B, B, Y, Y + Right, B, B, Y. These are the button presses for the classic controller.

FAMILY FEUD 2010 EDITION

NEW WARDROBE

Select the lock tab from the Wardrobe screen and enter FAMILY.

FATAL FURY SPECIAL

SOUND TEST

Pause the game and press A, B, C, D, A.

FIGHTING STREET

+4 CREDITS, SIMPLIFIED SPECIAL MOVES, AND STAGE SELECT

After getting a high score, enter .SD as your initials. Then, at the title screen, hold Left + 1 + 2, and press Minus.

+4 CREDITS

After getting a high score, enter .HU as your initials. Then, at the title screen, hold Left + 1 + 2, and press Minus.

SIMPLIFIED SPECIAL MOVES

After getting a high score, enter .LK as your initials. Then, at the title screen, hold Left + 1 + 2, and press Minus.

STAGE SELECT

After getting a high score, enter .AS as your initials. Then, at the title screen, hold Left + 1 + 2, and press Minus.

GHOST SQUAD

COSTUMES

Reach the following levels in single-player to unlock the corresponding costume.

LEVEL	COSTUME	LEVEL	COSTUME
07	Desert Camouflage	30	Urban Camouflage
10	Policeman	34	Virtua Cop
15	Tough Guy	38	Future Warrior
18	Sky Camouflage	50	Ninja
20	World War II	60	Panda Suit
23	Cowboy	99	Gold Uniform

NINJA MODE

Play through Arcade Mode.

PARADISE MODE

Play through Ninja Mode.

GHOUL PATROL

PASSWORDS

LEVEL	PASSWORD
5	CP4V
9	7LBR
13	KVCY

G.I. JOE: THE RISE OF COBRA

CLASSIC DUKE

At the title screen press Left, Up, -, Up, Right, +.

CLASSIC SCARLETT

At the title screen press Right, Up, Down, Down, +.

GODZILLA UNLEASHED

UNLOCK ALL
At the main menu, press A + Up to bring up the cheat entry screen. Enter 204935.

90000 STORE POINTS
At the main menu, press A + Up to bring up the cheat entry screen. Enter 031406.

SET DAY
At the main menu, press A + Up to bring up the cheat entry screen. Enter 0829XX, where XX represents the day. Use 00 for day one.

SHOW MONSTER MOVES
At the main menu, press A + Up to bring up the cheat entry screen. Enter 411411.

VERSION NUMBER
At the main menu, press A + Up to bring up the cheat entry screen. Enter 787321.

MOTHERSHIP LEVEL
Playing as the Aliens, destroy the mothership in the Invasion level.

GRADIUS REBIRTH

4 OPTIONS
Pause the game and press Up, Up, Down, Down, Left, Right, Left, Right, Fire, Powerup. This code can be used once for each stage you have attempted.

GRAVITRONIX

VERSUS OPTIONS AND LEVEL SELECT
At the Options menu, press 1, 2, 2, 2, 1.

GREG HASTINGS PAINTBALL 2

PRO AND NEW GUN
Select Career, hold C, and press Up, Up, Down, Right, Left, Left, Right, Up.

THE GRIM ADVENTURES OF BILLY & MANDY

CONCEPT ART
At the Main menu, hold 1 and press Up, Up, Down, Down, Left, Right, Left, Right.

HARRY POTTER AND THE HALF-BLOOD PRINCE

BONUS TWO-PLAYER DUELING ARENA CASTLE GATES
At the Rewards menu, press Right, Right, Down, Down, Left, Right, Left, Right, Left, Right, +.

HASBRO FAMILY GAME NIGHT 2

SECRET PRIZE
Have a saved file from the first Hasbro Family Game Night.

ICE AGE 2: THE MELTDOWN

INFINITE PEBBLES
Pause the game and press Down, Down, Left, Up, Up, Right, Up, Down.

INFINITE ENERGY
Pause the game and press Down, Left, Right, Down, Down, Right, Left, Down.

INFINITE HEALTH
Pause the game and press Up, Right, Down, Up, Left, Down, Right, Left.

INDIANA JONES AND THE STAFF OF KINGS

FATE OF ATLANTIS GAME

At the main menu, hold Z and press A, Up, Up, B, Down, Down, Left, Right, Left, B.

IRON MAN

ARMOR SELECTION

Iron Man's different armor suits are unlocked by completing certain missions. Refer to the following tables for when each is unlocked. After selecting a mission to play, you get the opportunity to pick the armor you wish to use.

COMPLETE MISSION	SUIT UNLOCKED
1: Escape	Mark I
2: First Flight	Mark II
3: Fight Back	Mark III
6: Flying Fortress	Comic Tin Can
9: Home Front	Classic
13: Showdown	Silver Centurion

CONCEPT ART

Concept Art is unlocked after finding certain numbers of Weapon Crates.

CONCEPT ART UNLOCKED	NUMBER OF WEAPON CRATES FOUND
Environments Set 1	6
Environments Set 2	12
Iron Man	18
Environments Set 3	24
Enemies	30
Environments Set 4	36
Villains	42
Vehicles	48
Covers	50

IVY THE KIWI?

BONUS MODE AND PICTURE BOOK

Finish the main game.

DOG COSTUME

Collect 100 red feathers—50 from the main game and 50 from Bonus Mode.

KUNG FU PANDA

INFINITE CHI

Select Cheats from the Extra menu and press Down, Right, Left, Up, Down.

INVINCIBILITY

Select Cheats from the Extra menu and press Down, Down, Right, Up, Left.

4X DAMAGE MULTIPLYER

Select Cheats from the Extra menu and press Up, Down, Up, Right, Left.

ALL MULTIPLAYER CHARACTERS

Select Cheats from the Extra menu and press Left, Down, Left, Right, Down.

DRAGON WARRIOR OUTFIT IN MULTIPLAYER

Select Cheats from the Extra menu and press Left, Down, Right, Left, Up.

THE LEGEND OF SPYRO: DAWN OF THE DRAGON

INFINITE HEALTH
Pause the game, hold Z and move the Nunchuk Right, Right, Down, Down, Left.

INFINITE MANA
Pause the game, hold Z and move the Nunchuk Up, Right, Up, Left, Down.

MAX XP
Pause the game, hold Z and move the Nunchuk Up, Left, Left, Down, Up.

ALL ELEMENTAL UPGRADES
Pause the game, hold Z and move the Nunchuk Left, Up, Down, Up, Right.

LEGO BATMAN

BATCAVE CODES
Using the computer in the Batcave, select Enter Code and enter the following codes.

CHARACTERS

CHARACTER	CODE	CHARACTER	CODE
Alfred	ZAQ637	Penguin Henchman	BJH782
Batgirl	JKR331	Penguin Minion	KJP748
Bruce Wayne	BDJ327	Poison Ivy Goon	GTB899
Catwoman (Classic)	M1AAWW	Police Marksman	HKG984
Clown Goon	HJK327	Police Officer	JRY983
Commissioner Gordon	DDP967	Riddler Goon	CRY928
Fishmonger	HGV748	Riddler Henchman	XEU824
Freeze Girl	XVK541	S.W.A.T.	HTF114
Joker Goon	UTF782	Sailor	NAV592
Joker Henchman	YUN924	Scientist	JFL786
Mad Hatter	JCA283	Security Guard	PLB946
Man-Bat	NYU942	The Joker (Tropical)	CCB199
Military Policeman	MKL382	Yeti	NJL412
Nightwing	MVY759	Zoo Sweeper	DWR243
Penguin Goon	NKA238		

VEHICLES

VEHICLE	CODE	VEHICLE	CODE
Bat-Tank	KNTT4B	Mr. Freeze's Kart	BCT229
Bruce Wayne's Private Jet	LEA664	Penguin Goon Submarine	BTN248
Catwoman's Motorcycle	HPL826	Police Bike	LJP234
Garbage Truck	DUS483	Police Boat	PLC999
Goon Helicopter	GCH328	Police Car	KJL832
Harbor Helicopter	CHP735	Police Helicopter	CWR732
Harley Quinn's Hammer Truck	RDT637	Police Van	MAC788
Mad Hatter's Glider	HS000W	Police Watercraft	VJD328
Mad Hatter's Steamboat	M4DM4N	Riddler's Jet	HAHAHA
Mr. Freeze's Iceberg	ICYICE	Robin's Submarine	TTF453
The Joker's Van	JUK657	Two-Face's Armored Truck	EFE933

CHEATS

CHEAT	CODE	CHEAT	CODE
Always Score Multiply	9LRGNB	More Batarang Targets	XWP645
Fast Batarangs	JRBDCB	Piece Detector	KHJ554
Fast Walk	ZOLM6N	Power Brick Detector	MMN786
Flame Batarang	D8NYWH	Regenerate Hearts	HJH7HJ
Freeze Batarang	XPN4NG	Score x2	N4NR3E
Extra Hearts	ML3KHP	Score x4	CX9MAT
Fast Build	EVG26J	Score x6	MLVNF2
Immune to Freeze	JXUDY6	Score x8	WCCDB9
Invincibility	WYD5CP	Score x10	18HW07
Minikit Detector	ZXGH9J		

LEGO HARRY POTTER: YEARS 1-4

RED BRICK EXTRAS

Once you have access to The Leaky Cauldron, enter Wiseacre's Wizarding Supplies from Diagon Alley. Go upstairs to enter the following. Pause the game and select Extras to toggle the cheats on/off.

CHEAT	CODE
Carrot Wands	AUC8EH
Character Studs	H27KGC
Character Token Detector	HA79V8
Christmas	T7PVVN
Disguise	4DMK2R
Fall Rescue	ZEX7MV
Extra Hearts	J9U6Z9
Fast Dig	Z9BFAD
Fast Magic	FA3GQA
Gold Brick Detector	84QNQN
Hogwarts Crest Detector	TTMC6D
Ice Rink	F88VUW

CHEAT	CODE
Invincibility	QQWC6B
Red Brick Detector	7AD7HE
Regenerate Hearts	89ML2W
Score x2	74YKR7
Score x4	J3WHNK
Score x6	XK9ANE
Score x8	HUFV2H
Score x10	H8X69Y
Silhouettes	HZBVX7
Singing Mandrake	BMEU6X
Stud Magnet	67FKWZ

WISEACRE SPELLS

Once you have access to The Leaky Cauldron, enter Wiseacre's Wizarding Supplies from Diagon Alley. Go upstairs to enter the following. You need to learn Wingardium Leviosa before you can use these cheats.

SPELL	CODE
Accio	VE9VV7
Anteoculatia	QFB6NR
Calvorio	6DNR6L
Colovaria	9GJ442
Engorgio Skullus	CD4JLX
Entomorphis	MYN3NB
Flipendo	ND2L7W
Glacius	ERA9DR

HERBIFORS	H8FTHL
Incarcerous	YEB9Q9
Locomotor Mortis	2M2XJ6
Multicorfors	JK6QRM
Redactum Skullus	UW8LRH
Rictusempra	2UCA3M
Slugulus Eructo	U6EE8X
Stupefy	UWDJ4Y
Tarantallegra	KWWQ44
Trip Jinx	YZNRF6

EEYLOPS GOLD BRICKS

Once you have access to The Leaky Cauldron, enter Wiseacre's Wizarding Supplies from Diagon Alley. Go upstairs to enter the following. To access the LEGO Builder, visit Gringott's Bank at the end of Diagon Alley.

GOLD BRICK	CODE	GOLD BRICK	CODE
1	QE4VC7	7	XY6VYZ
2	FY8H97	8	TUNC4W
3	3MQT4P	9	EJ42Q6
4	PQPM7Z	10	GFJCV9
5	ZY2CPA	11	DZCY6G
6	3GMTP6		

LEGO INDIANA JONES: THE ORIGINAL ADVENTURES

CHARACTERS

Approach the blackboard in the Classsroom and enter the following codes.

CHARACTER	CODE	CHARACTER	CODE
Bandit	12N68W	Fedora	V75YSP
Bandit Swordsman	1MK4RT	First Mate	0GIN24
Barranca	04EM94	Grail Knight	NE6THI
Bazooka Trooper (Crusade)	MK83R7	Hovitos Tribesman	H0V1SS
Bazooka Trooper (Raiders)	S93Y5R	Indiana Jones (Desert Disguise)	4J8S4M
Belloq	CHN3YU	Indiana Jones (Officer)	VJ850S
Belloq (Jungle)	TDR197	Jungle Guide	24PF34
Belloq (Robes)	VEO29L	Kao Kan	WM046L
British Commander	B73EUA	Kazim	NRH23J
British Officer	VJ5TI9	Kazim (Desert)	3M29TJ
British Soldier	DJ5I2W	Lao Che	2NK479
Captain Katanga	VJ3TT3	Maharajah	NFK5N2
Chatter Lal	ENW936	Major Toht	13NS01
Chatter Lal (Thuggee)	CNH4RY	Masked Bandit	N48SF0
Chen	3NK48T	Mola Ram	FJUR31
Colonel Dietrich	2K9RKS	Monkey Man	3RF6YJ
Colonel Vogel	8EAL4H	Pankot Assassin	2NKT72
Dancing Girl	C7EJ21	Pankot Guard	VN28RH
Donovan	3NFTU8	Sherpa Brawler	VJ37WJ
Elsa (Desert)	JSNRT9	Sherpa Gunner	ND762W
Elsa (Officer)	VMJ5US	Slave Child	OE3ENW
Enemy Boxer	8246RB	Thuggee	VM683E
Enemy Butler	VJ48W3	Thuggee Acolyte	T2R3F9
Enemy Guard	VJ7R51	Thuggee Slave Driver	VBS7GW
Enemy Guard (Mountains)	YR47WM	Village Dignitary	KD48TN
Enemy Officer	572E61	Village Elder	4682E1
Enemy Officer (Desert)	2MK450	Willie (Dinner Suit)	VK93R7
Enemy Pilot	B84ELP	Willie (Pajamas)	MEN4IP
Enemy Radio Operator	1MF94R	Wu Han	3NSLT8
Enemy Soldier (Desert)	4NSU7Q		

EXTRAS

Approach the blackboard in the Classsroom and enter the following codes. Some cheats need to be enabled by selecting Extras from the pause menu.

CHEAT	CODE	CHEAT	CODE
Artifact Detector	VIKED7	Disguises	4ID1N6
Beep Beep	VNF59Q	Fast Build	V83SL0
Character Treasure	VIES2R	Fast Dig	378RS6
Disarm Enemies	VKRNS9	Fast Fix	FJ59WS

CHEAT	CODE
Fertilizer	B1GW1F
Ice Rink	33GM7J
Parcel Detector	VUT673
Poo Treasure	WWQ1SA
Regenerate Hearts	MDLP69
Secret Characters	3X44AA
Silhouettes	3HE85H
Super Scream	VN3R7S

CHEAT	CODE
Super Slap	OP1TA5
Treasure Magnet	H86LA2
Treasure x10	VI3PS8
Treasure x2	VM4TS9
Treasure x4	VLWEN3
Treasure x6	V84RYS
Treasure x8	A72E1M

LEGO INDIANA JONES 2: THE ADVENTURE CONTINUES

Pause the game, select Enter Secret Code from the Extras menu, and enter the following.

CHARACTERS

CHARACTER	CODE
Belloq (Priest)	FTL48S
Dovchenko	WL4T6N
Enemy Boxer	7EQF47
Henry Jones	4CSAKH
Indiana Jones	PGWSEA
Indiana Jones: 2	FGLKYS
Indiana Jones (Collect)	DZFY9S
Indiana Jones (Desert)	M4C34K
Indiana Jones (Desert Disguise)	2W8QR3
Indiana Jones (Dinner Suit)	QUNZUT
Indiana Jones (Kali)	J2XS97
Indiana Jones (Officer)	3FQFKS
Interdimensional Being	PXT4UP
Lao Che	7AWX3J
Mannequin (Boy)	2UJQWC
Mannequin (Girl)	3PGSEL
Mannequin (Man)	QPWDMM
Mannequin (Woman)	U7SMVK
Mola Ram	82RMC2
Mutt	2GKS62
Salah	E88YRP
Willie	94RUAJ

EXTRAS

EFFECT	CODE
Beep Beep	UU3VSC
Disguise	Y9TE98
Fast Build	SNXC2F
Fast Dig	XYAN83
Fast Fix	3Z7PJX
Fearless	TUXNZF
Ice Rink	TY9P4U
Invincibility	6JBB65
Poo Money	SZFAAE
Score x3	PEHHPZ
Score x4	UXGTB3
Score X6	XWLJEY
Score x8	S5UZCP
Score x10	V7JYBU
Silhouettes	FQGPYH
Snake Whip	2U7YCV
Stud Magnet	EGSM5B

LEGO STAR WARS: THE COMPLETE SAGA

The following still need to be purchase after entering the codes.

CHARACTERS

ADMIRAL ACKBAR

At the bar in Mos Eisley Cantina, select Enter Code and enter ACK646.

BATTLE DROID (COMMANDER)

At the bar in Mos Eisley Cantina, select Enter Code and enter KPF958.

BOBA FETT (BOY)

At the bar in Mos Eisley Cantina, select Enter Code and enter GGF539.

BOSS NASS

At the bar in Mos Eisley Cantina, select Enter Code and enter HHY697.

CAPTAIN TARPALS

At the bar in Mos Eisley Cantina, select Enter Code and enter QRN714.

COUNT DOOKU
At the bar in Mos Eisley Cantina, select Enter Code and enter DDD748.

DARTH MAUL
At the bar in Mos Eisley Cantina, select Enter Code and enter EUK421.

EWOK
At the bar in Mos Eisley Cantina, select Enter Code and enter EWK785.

GENERAL GRIEVOUS
At the bar in Mos Eisley Cantina, select Enter Code and enter PMN576.

GREEDO
At the bar in Mos Eisley Cantina, select Enter Code and enter ZZR636.

IG-88
At the bar in Mos Eisley Cantina, select Enter Code and enter GIJ989.

IMPERIAL GUARD
At the bar in Mos Eisley Cantina, select Enter Code and enter GUA850.

JANGO FETT
At the bar in Mos Eisley Cantina, select Enter Code and enter KLJ897.

KI-ADI MUNDI
At the bar in Mos Eisley Cantina, select Enter Code and enter MUN486.

LUMINARA
At the bar in Mos Eisley Cantina, select Enter Code and enter LUM521.

PADMÉ
At the bar in Mos Eisley Cantina, select Enter Code and enter VBJ322.

R2-Q5
At the bar in Mos Eisley Cantina, select Enter Code and enter EVILR2.

STORMTROOPER
At the bar in Mos Eisley Cantina, select Enter Code and enter NBN431.

TAUN WE
At the bar in Mos Eisley Cantina, select Enter Code and enter PRX482.

VULTURE DROID
At the bar in Mos Eisley Cantina, select Enter Code and enter BDC866.

WATTO
At the bar in Mos Eisley Cantina, select Enter Code and enter PLL967.

ZAM WESELL
At the bar in Mos Eisley Cantina, select Enter Code and enter 584HJF.

SKILLS

DISGUISE
At the bar in Mos Eisley Cantina, select Enter Code and enter BRJ437.

FORCE GRAPPLE LEAP
At the bar in Mos Eisley Cantina, select Enter Code and enter CLZ738.

VEHICLES

DROID TRIFIGHTER
At the bar in Mos Eisley Cantina, select Enter Code and enter AAB123.

IMPERIAL SHUTTLE
At the bar in Mos Eisley Cantina, select Enter Code and enter HUT845.

TIE INTERCEPTOR
At the bar in Mos Eisley Cantina, select Enter Code and enter INT729.

TIE FIGHTER
At the bar in Mos Eisley Cantina, select Enter Code and enter DBH897.

ZAM'S AIRSPEEDER
At the bar in Mos Eisley Cantina, select Enter Code and enter UUU875.

LOST IN SHADOW

GOBLIN HAND
As your game loads, hold Z.

KNIFE
As your game loads, hold C.

MADDEN NFL 10

UNLOCK EVERYTHING
Select Enter Game Code from Extras and enter THEWORKS.

FRANCHISE MODE
Select Enter Game Code from Extras and enter TEAMPLAYER.

SITUATION MODE
Select Enter Game Code from Extras and enter YOUCALLIT.

SUPERSTAR MODE
Select Enter Game Code from Extras and enter EGOBOOST.

PRO BOWL STADIUM
Select Enter Game Code from Extras and enter ALLSTARS.

SUPER BOWL STADIUM
Select Enter Game Code from Extras and enter THEBIGSHOW.

MARIO & SONIC AT THE OLYMPIC GAMES

UNLOCK 4X100M RELAY EVENT
Medal in Mercury, Venus, Jupiter, and Saturn.

UNLOCK SINGLE SCULLS EVENT
Medal in Mercury, Venus, Jupiter, and Saturn.

UNLOCK DREAM RACE EVENT
Medal in Mercury, Venus, Jupiter, and Saturn.

UNLOCK ARCHERY EVENT
Medal in Moonlight Circuit.

UNLOCK HIGH JUMP EVENT
Medal in Stardust Circuit.

UNLOCK 400M EVENT
Medal in Planet Circuit.

UNLOCK DREAM FENCING EVENT
Medal in Comet Circuit.

UNLOCK DREAM TABLE TENNIS EVENT
Medal in Satellite Circuit.

UNLOCK 400M HURDLES EVENT
Medal in Sunlight Circuit.

UNLOCK POLE VAULT EVENT
Medal in Meteorite Circuit.

UNLOCK VAULT EVENT
Medal in Meteorite Circuit.

UNLOCK DREAM PLATFORM EVENT
Medal in Cosmos Circuit.

CROWNS
Get all gold medals in all events with a character to unlock their crown.

MARIO KART WII

CHARACTERS

CHARACTER	HOW TO UNLOCK
Baby Daisy	Earn 1 Star in 50cc for Mushroom, Flower, Star, and Special Cups
Baby Luigi	Unlock 8 Expert Staff Ghost Data in Time Trials
Birdo	Race 16 different courses in Time Trials or win 250 versus races
Bowser Jr.	Earn 1 Star in 100cc for Shell, Banana, Leaf, and Lightning Cups
Daisy	Win 150cc Special Cup
Diddy Kong	Win 50cc Lightning Cup
Dry Bones	Win 100cc Leaf Cup
Dry Bowser	Earn 1 Star in 150cc for Mushroom, Flower, Star, and Special Cups
Funky Kong	Unlock 4 Expert Staff Ghost Data in Time Trials
King Boo	Win 50cc Star Cup
Mii Outfit A	Win 100cc Special Cup

CHARACTER	HOW TO UNLOCK
Mii Outfit B	Unlock all 32 Expert Staff Ghost Data in Time Trials
Mii Outfit C	Get 15,000 points in Versus Mode
Rosalina	Have a Super Mario Galaxy save file and she is unlocked after 50 races or earn 1 Star in all Mirror Cups
Toadette	Race 32 different courses in Time Trials

KARTS

KART	HOW TO UNLOCK
Blue Falcon	Win Mirror Lightning Cup
Cheep Charger	Earn 1 Star in 50cc for Mushroom, Flower, Star, and Special Cups
Rally Romper	Unlock an Expert Staff Ghost Data in Time Trials
B Dasher Mk. 2	Unlock 24 Expert Staff Ghost Data in Time Trials
Royal Racer	Win 150cc Leaf Cup
Turbo Blooper	Win 50cc Leaf Cup
Aero Glider	Earn 1 Star in 150cc for Mushroom, Flower, Star, and Special Cups
Dragonetti	Win 150cc Lightning Cup
Piranha Prowler	Win 50cc Special Cup

BIKES

KART	HOW TO UNLOCK
Bubble Bike	Win Mirror Leaf Cup
Magikruiser	Race 8 different courses in Time Trials
Quacker	Win 150cc Star Cup
Dolphin Dasher	Win Mirror Star Cup
Nitrocycle	Earn 1 Star in 100cc for all cups
Rapide	Win 100cc Lightning Cup
Phantom	Win Mirror Special Cup
Torpedo	Unlock 12 Expert Staff Ghost Data in Time Trials
Twinkle Star	Win 100cc Star Cup

MARVEL SUPER HERO SQUAD

IRON MAN, BONUS COSTUME "WAR MACHINE"

Select Enter Code from the Options and enter 111111.

HULK, BONUS COSTUMES "GREY HULK" & "RED HULK"

Select Enter Code from the Options and enter 222222.

WOLVERINE, BONUS COSTUMES "WOLVERINE (BROWN COSTUME)" & "FERAL WOLVERINE"

Select Enter Code from the Options and enter 333333.

THOR, BONUS COSTUMES "THOR (CHAIN ARMOR)" & "LOKI-THOR"

Select Enter Code from the Options and enter 444444.

SILVER SURFER, BONUS COSTUMES "ANTI-SURFER" & "GOLD SURFER"

Select Enter Code from the Options and enter 555555.

FALCON, BONUS COSTUME "ULTIMATES FALCON"

Select Enter Code from the Options and enter 666666.

CHEAT "SUPER KNOCKBACK"

Select Enter Code from the Options and enter 777777.

CHEAT "NO BLOCK MODE"

Select Enter Code from the Options and enter 888888.

DOCTOR DOOM, BONUS COSTUMES "ULTIMATES DOCTOR DOOM" & "PROFESSOR DOOM"

Select Enter Code from the Options and enter 999999.

CAPTAIN AMERICA, BONUS COSTUME "ULTIMATE CAPTAIN AMERICA COSTUME"

Select Enter Code from the Options and enter 177674

A.I.M. AGENT, BONUS COSTUME "BLUE SUIT A.I.M."

Select Enter Code from the Options and enter 246246

CHEAT "GROUNDED"

Select Enter Code from the Options and enter 476863

CHEAT "ONE-HIT TAKEDOWN"

Select Enter Code from the Options and enter 663448

CHEAT "INFINITE SHARD DURATION"

Select Enter Code from the Options and enter 742737

CHEAT "THROWN OBJECT TAKEDOWN"

Select Enter Code from the Options and enter 847936

MARVEL ULTIMATE ALLIANCE

UNLOCK ALL SKINS

At the Team menu, press Up, Down, Left, Right, Left, Right, Plus.

UNLOCKS ALL HERO POWERS

At the Team menu, press Left, Right, Up, Down, Up, Down, Plus.

ALL HEROES TO LEVEL 99

At the Team menu, press Up, Left, Up, Left, Down, Right, Down, Right, Plus.

UNLOCK ALL HEROES

At the Team menu, press Up, Up, Down, Down, Left, Left, Left, Plus.

UNLOCK DAREDEVIL

At the Team menu, press Left, Left, Right, Right, Up, Down, Up, Down, Plus.

UNLOCK SILVER SURFER

At the Team menu, press Down, Left, Left, Up, Right, Up, Down, Left, Plus.

GOD MODE

During gameplay, press Up, Down, Up, Down, Up, Left, Down, Right, Plus.

TOUCH OF DEATH

During gameplay, press Left, Right, Down, Down, Right, Left, Plus.

SUPER SPEED

During gameplay, press Up, Left, Up, Right, Down, Right, Plus.

FILL MOMENTUM

During gameplay, press Left, Right, Right, Left, Up, Down, Down, Up, Plus.

UNLOCK ALL COMICS

At the Review menu, press Left, Right, Right, Left, Up, Up, Right, Plus.

UNLOCK ALL CONCEPT ART

At the Review menu, press Down, Down, Down, Right, Right, Left, Down, Plus.

UNLOCK ALL CINEMATICS

At the Review menu, press Up, Left, Left, Up, Right, Right, Up, Plus.

UNLOCK ALL LOAD SCREENS

At the Review menu, press Up, Down, Right, Left, Up, Up Down, Plus.

UNLOCK ALL COURSES

At the Comic Missions menu, press Up, Right, Left, Down, Up, Right, Left, Down, Plus.

MARVEL ULTIMATE ALLIANCE 2

GOD MODE

At any point during a game, press Up, Up, Down, Down, Left, Right, Down.

GIVE MONEY

At the Team Select or Hero Details screen press Up, Up, Down, Down, Up, Up, Up, Down.

UNLOCK ALL POWERS

At the Team Select or Hero Details screen press Up, Up, Down, Down, Left, Right, Right, Left.

ADVANCE ALL CHARACTERS TO L99

At the Hero Details screen press Down, Up, Left, Up, Right, Up, Left, Down.

UNLOCK ALL BONUS MISSIONS

While using the Bonus Mission Simulator, press Up, Right, Down, Left, Left, Right, Up, Up.

ADD 1 CHARACTER LEVEL
During a game, press Down, Up, Right, Up, Right, Up, Right, Down.

ADD 10 CHARACTER LEVELS
During a game, press Down, Up, Left, Up, Left, Up, Left, Down.

METROID: OTHER M

HARD MODE
Finish the game with all items.

THEATER MODE
Defeat final boss.

CHAPTERS	HOW TO UNLOCK
1-26	Defeat final boss
27-30	After the credits, finish bonus area and boss

GALLERY MODE
Defeat final boss.

GALLERY PAGES	HOW TO UNLOCK
1-4	Defeat final boss
5-7	After the credits, finish bonus area and boss
8	Finish the game with all items

MLB POWER PROS

EXTRA FORMS
At the main menu, press Right, Left, Up, Down, Down, Right, Right, Up, Up, Left, Down, Left.

VIEW MLB PLAYERS AT CUSTOM PLAYER MENU
Select View or Delete Custom Players/Password Display from My Data and press Up, Up, Down, Down, Left, Right, Left, Right, 1, 2.

MONSTER LAIR

CONTINUE
At the game over screen, press Left, Right, Down, Up, Select + Left.

UNLIMITED CONTINUES
Enter 68K as your initials.

SOUND TEST
At the title screen, hold 1 + 2 and press Run.

MYSIMS

PASSWORD SCREEN
Press the Minus button to bring up the pause screen. Then enter the following with the Wii Remote: 2, 1, Down, Up, Down, Up, Left, Left, Right, Right. Now you can enter the following passwords:

OUTFITS

Camouflage pants	N10ng5g
Diamond vest	Tglg0ca
Genie outfit	Gvsb3k1
Kimono dress	l3hkdvs
White jacket	R705aan

FURNITURE

Bunk bed	F3nevr0
Hourglass couch	Ghtymba
Modern couch	T7srhca
Racecar bed	Ahvmrva
Rickshaw bed	Itha7da

MYSIMS AGENTS

ASTRONAUT SUIT
At the Create-a-Sim screen, press Up, Down, Up, Down, Left, Right, Left, Right.

BLACK NINJA OUTFIT
At the Create-a-Sim screen, press Right, Up, Right, Up, Down, Left, Down, Left.

STEALTH SUIT
At the Create-a-Sim screen, press Left, Right, Left, Right, Up, Down, Up, Down.

69

MYSIMS KINGDOM

DETECTIVE OUTFIT
Pause the game and press Left, Right, Left, Right, Left, Right.

SWORDSMAN OUTFIT
Pause the game and press Down, Up, Down, Up, Down, Up, Down, Up.

TATTOO VEST OUTFIT
Pause the game and press C, Z, C, Z, B, A, B, A.

NARUTO SHIPPUDEN: CLASH OF NINJA REVOLUTION III

RYO BONUS
A 50,00 starting Ryo bonus is given if you have a saved data from Naruto Shippuden: Clash of Ninja Revolution 1 or 2 on your Nintendo Wii.

NASCAR KART RACING

JOEY LOGANO
Select Enter Cheat from the Profile Info menu and enter 426378.

NBA 2K10

ABA BALL
Select Codes from the Options menu. Then select Enter Code and enter payrespect.

2K CHINA TEAM
Select Codes from the Options menu. Then select Enter Code and enter 2kchina.

NBA 2K TEAM
Select Codes from the Options menu. Then select Enter Code and enter nba2k.

2K SPORTS TEAM
Select Codes from the Options menu. Then select Enter Code and enter 2ksports.

VISUAL CONCEPTS TEAM
Select Codes from the Options menu. Then select Enter Code and enter vcteam.

2010 ALL-STAR UNIFORMS
Select Codes from the Options menu. Then select Enter Code and enter otnresla.

HARDWOOD CLASSIC UNIFORMS

Select Codes from the Options menu. Then select Enter Code and enter wasshcicsl. This code gives Hardwood Classic Uniforms for the Cavaliers, Jazz, Magic, Raptors, timberwolves, Trail Blazers, and Warriors.

LATIN NIGHTS UNIFORMS

Select Codes from the Options menu. Then select Enter Code and enter aihinntslgt. This code gives Latin Nights jerseys for Bulls, Heat, Knicks, Lakers, Mavericks, Rockets, Spurs, and Suns.

NBA GREEN UNIFORMS

Select Codes from the Options menu. Then select Enter Code and enter nreogge. This code gives green uniforms for the Bobcats, Bulls, and Nuggets.

SECONDARY ROAD UNIFORMS

Select Codes from the Options menu. Then select Enter Code and enter eydonscar. This code gives Second Road Uniforms for the Grizzlies, Hawks, Mavericks, and Rockets.

ST. PATRICK'S DAY UNIFORMS

Select Codes from the Options menu. Then select Enter Code and enter riiasgerh. This code gives St. Patrick's Day jerseys for the Bulls, Celtics, Knicks, and Raptors.

BOBCATS RACING UNIFORM

Select Codes from the Options menu. Then select Enter Code and enter agsntrccai.

CAVALIERS CAVFANATICS UNIFORM

Select Codes from the Options menu. Then select Enter Code and enter aifnaatccv.

HORNETS MARDI GRAS UNIFORM

Select Codes from the Options menu. Then select Enter Code and enter asrdirmga.

TRAIL BLAZERS RIP CITY UNIFORM

Select Codes from the Options menu. Then select Enter Code and enter ycprtii.

NBA 2K11

MJ: CREATING A LEGEND

In Features, select Codes from the Extras menu. Choose Enter Code and enter icanbe23.

2K CHINA TEAM

In Features, select Codes from the Extras menu. Choose Enter Code and enter 2kchina.

2K SPORTS TEAM

In Features, select Codes from the Extras menu. Choose Enter Code and enter 2Ksports.

NBA 2K TEAM

In Features, select Codes from the Extras menu. Choose Enter Code and enter nba2k.

VC TEAM

In Features, select Codes from the Extras menu. Choose Enter Code and enter vcteam.

ABA BALL

In Features, select Codes from the Extras menu. Choose Enter Code and enter payrespect.

NEED FOR SPEED PROSTREET

$2,000

Select Career and then choose Code Entry. Enter 1MA9X99.

$4,000

Select Career and then choose Code Entry. Enter W2IOLL01.

$8,000

Select Career and then choose Code Entry. Enter L1IS97A1.

$10,000

Select Career and then choose Code Entry. Enter 1MI9K7E1.

$10,000

Select Career and then choose Code Entry. Enter CASHMONEY.

$10,000

Select Career and then choose Code Entry. Enter REGGAME.

AUDI TT
Select Career and then choose Code Entry. Enter ITSABOUTYOU.

CHEVELLE SS
Select Career and then choose Code Entry. Enter HORSEPOWER.

COKE ZERO GOLF GTI
Select Career and then choose Code Entry. Enter COKEZERO.

DODGE VIPER
Select Career and then choose Code Entry. Enter WORLDSLONGESTLASTING.

MITSUBISHI LANCER EVOLUTION
Select Career and then choose Code Entry. Enter MITSUBISHIGOFAR.

UNLOCK ALL BONUSES
Select Career and then choose Code Entry. Enter UNLOCKALLTHINGS.

5 REPAIR MARKERS
Select Career and then choose Code Entry. Enter SAFETYNET.

ENERGIZER VINYL
Select Career and then choose Code Entry. Enter ENERGIZERLITHIUM.

CASTROL SYNTEC VINYL
Select Career and then choose Code Entry. Enter CASTROLSYNTEC. This also gives you $10,000.

NERF N-STRIKE

BLACK HEART VENGEANCE
Select Codes from the main menu and enter BHDETA8.

CRUSHER SAD-G
Select Codes from the main menu and enter CRUSH14.

FIREFLY ELITE
Select Codes from the main menu and enter HELIOX6.

GOLIATHAN NITRO
Select Codes from the main menu and enter FIERO2.

HABANERO
Select Codes from the main menu and enter 24KGCON4.

HYDRA
Select Codes from the main menu and enter HRANGEL3.

LONGSHOT STREET
Select Codes from the main menu and enter LONGST5.

MAVERICK CRYSTAL
Select Codes from the main menu and enter CRISTOL10.

MAVERICK MIDNIGHT
Select Codes from the main menu and enter MAVMID7.

MERCURIO
Select Codes from the main menu and enter RSMERC9.

SEMPER FIRE ULTRA
Select Codes from the main menu and enter CROMO1.

SPARTAN NCS-12
Select Codes from the main menu and enter THISIS12.

STAMPEDE
Select Codes from the main menu and enter DOGIE15.

VULCAN MAGMA
Select Codes from the main menu and enter MAGMA3.

NERF: N-STRIKE ELITE

Select Codebook and enter the following codes.

10 CANISTERS
Enter NERF.

UNLIMITED AMMO
Enter DART. This can be toggled on and off.

CERBERUS CS-12
Enter DUDE.

CRUSHER SAD-G
Enter RUSH.

GOLITHAN UB-1
Enter ROCK.

HAMMERHEAD GL-1
Enter PONG.

HYDRA SG-7
Enter WIDE.

ICARUS HM-7
Enter DOOM.

LONGSHOT CS-6
Enter IDOL.

LONGSTRIKE CS-6
Enter PING.

RECON CS-6
Enter DIRT.

SEMPERFIRE RF-100
Enter FLEX.

SPARTAN NCS-12
Enter ICON.

VULCAN EBF-25
Enter LOTS.

NHL 2K9

3RD JERSEYS
At the codes menu enter R6y34bsH52.

NHL 2K10

THIRD JERSEYS
Select Cheats from the Extras menu and enter G8r23Bty56.

VISUAL CONCEPTS TEAM
Select Cheats from the Extras menu and enter vcteam.

NICKTOONS: ATTACK OF THE TOYBOTS

DAMAGE BOOST
Select Cheats from the Extras menu. Choose Enter Cheat Code and enter 456645.

INVULNERABILITY
Select Cheats from the Extras menu. Choose Enter Cheat Code and enter 313456.

UNLOCK EXO-HUGGLES 9000
Select Cheats from the Extras menu. Choose Enter Cheat Code and enter 691427.

UNLOCK MR. HUGGLES
Select Cheats from the Extras menu. Choose Enter Cheat Code and enter 654168.

UNLIMITED LOBBER GOO
Select Cheats from the Extras menu. Choose Enter Cheat Code and enter 118147.

UNLIMITED SCATTER GOO
Select Cheats from the Extras menu. Choose Enter Cheat Code and enter 971238.

UNLIMITED SPLITTER GOO
Select Cheats from the Extras menu. Choose Enter Cheat Code and enter 854511.

PINBALL HALL OF FAME – THE GOTTLIEB COLLECTION

UNLOCK TABLES IN FREEPLAY, EXTRA OPTIONS, AND PAYOUT MODE
Select Enter Code from the Main Menu and enter the following:

EFFECTS	CODE	EFFECTS	CODE
Aces High Freeplay	UNO	Strikes 'N Spares Freeplay	PBA
Big Shot Freeplay	UJP	Tee'd Off Freeplay	PGA
Black Hole Freeplay	LIS	Xolten Freeplay	BIG
Central Park Freeplay	NYC	Custom Balls in Options	CKF
Goin' Nuts Freeplay	PHF	Optional Tilt in Options	BZZ
Love Machine Freeplay	HOT	Payout Mode	WGR
Playboy Freeplay	HEF		

PIRATES PLUNDARRR

CHEAT MENU
Press + to pause the game. Enter Up, Up, Down, Down, Left, Right, Left, Right, 2, 1. A new Cheat option appears at the bottom of the menu.

AMAZON
Defeat Tecciztecatl, Witch Doctor.

SPECTRAL
Defeat Nanauatl, Hero of the Sun.

POKEMON RUMBLE

POKEMON PASSWORDS

Go to the recruitment building in the terminal and enter the following passwords to get the corresponding Pokemon.

POKEMON	PASSWORD
Blastoise	9580-1423
Charizard	7968-4528
Charmander	7927-6161
Cherrim Positive Forme	7540-5667
Chimchar	8109-8384
Eevee	0511-0403
Giratina (Origin Form)	8322-3706
Mew	9561-8808

POKEMON	PASSWORD
Piplup	9900-2455
Shaymin (Sky Form)	5468-6284
Shiny Bidoof	5575-2435
Shiny Rattata	9849-3731
Squirtle	6824-2045
Turtwig	8672-1076
Venusaur	1589-3955

PRESS YOUR LUCK 2010 EDITION

WARDROBE PIECES FOR AVATAR

Select the lock tab from the Wardrobe screen and enter SECRET.

THE PRICE IS RIGHT 2010 EDITION

AVATAR UPGRADES

Select the lock tab from the Wardrobe screen and enter PRIZES.

PRINCESS TOMATO IN THE SALAD KINGDOM

DEBUG BATTLE PASSWORD

Enter GG62 as a password.

PUNCH-OUT!!

REGAIN HEALTH BETWEEN ROUNDS

Press minus between rounds to regain health at the start of the next round.

DONKEY KONG IN EXHIBITION

Fight Donkey Kong in Last Stand mode.

CHAMPIONS MODE

Win 10 bouts in Mac's Last Stand.

RABBIDS GO HOME

ASSASSIN RABBID

Finish Nick of Time to unlock the Rabbid customization option. Enter this option and select a Rabbid. Go to the menu and select Manage Figurines from the Figurines screen. Hold C + Z and press 2, 2, 1, 1, A, A, 1, 1.

BEST BUY RABBID

Finish Nick of Time to unlock the Rabbid customization option. Enter this option and select a Rabbid. Go to the menu and select Manage Figurines from the Figurines screen. Hold C + Z and press B, 1, 1, B, A, 2, 2, A.

GEEK SQUAD RABBID

Finish Nick of Time to unlock the Rabbid customization option. Enter this option and select a Rabbid. Go to the menu and select Manage Figurines from the Figurines screen. Hold C + Z and press A, A, 1, 1, 1, 1, 2, 2.

KANGAROO RABBID

Finish Nick of Time to unlock the Rabbid customization option. Enter this option and select a Rabbid. Go to the menu and select Manage Figurines from the Figurines screen. Hold C + Z and press 1, 1, 1, 1, 1, 2, 1, 2.

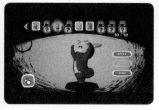

LEONARDO RABBID

Finish Nick of Time to unlock the Rabbid customization option. Enter this option and select a Rabbid. Go to the menu and select Manage Figurines from the Figurines screen. Hold C + Z and press 1, 1, 2, 2, A, A, 1, 1.

PRINCE RABBID

Finish Nick of Time to unlock the Rabbid customization option. Enter this option and select a Rabbid. Go to the menu and select Manage Figurines from the Figurines screen. Hold C + Z and press 1, 2, 1, 2, 1, 2, A, A.

SPLINTER CELL RABBID

Finish Nick of Time to unlock the Rabbid customization option. Enter this option and select a Rabbid. Go to the menu and select Manage Figurines from the Figurines screen. Hold C + Z and press B, B, B, B, A, A, A, A.

RAYMAN RAVING RABBIDS 2

FUNKYTOWN

Play each game at least once.

RABBID COSTUMES

Costumes are unlocked as you score 12,000 points in certain games and when you shoot the correct rabbid in the shooting games.

COSTUME	MINIGAME	HOW TO UNLOCK
Cossack	Chess	Earn 12,000 points
Crash Test Dummy	Shopping Cart Downhill	Earn 12,000 points
Cupid	Burgerinnii	Earn 12,000 points
Doctor	Anesthetics	Earn 12,000 points
Fireman	Paris, Pour Troujours	Shoot fireman rabbid
French Maid	Little Chemist	Earn 12,000 points
Fruit-Hat Dancer	Year of the Rabbids	Shoot rabbid wearing fruit hat
Gingerbread	Hot Cake	Earn 12,000 points
HAZE Armor	Big City Fights	Shoot rabbid with armor
Indiana Jones	Rolling Stone	Earn 12,000 points
Jet Trooper	Greatest Hits	Earn 12,000 points
Ken	RRR Xtreme Beach Volleyball	Earn 12,000 points
Martian	Bumper Cars	Earn 12,000 points
Party Girl	Paris, Mon Amour	Once inside boat, shoot girl rabbid
Raider's	American Football	Earn 12,000 points
Sam Fisher	Rabbid School	Earn 12,000 points
Samurai	The Office	Earn 12,000 points

COSTUME	MINIGAME	HOW TO UNLOCK
Space	Year of the Rabbids	Earn 12,000 points
Spider-	Spider Rabbid	Play the "Spider Rabbid" Game
TMNT, Leonardo	Usual Rabbids	Earn 12,000 points
Transformer	Plumber Rabbids	Earn 12,000 points
Vegas Showgirl	Burp	Earn 12,000 points
Voodoo	Voodoo Rabbids	Earn 12,000 points
Wrestler	Greatest Hits	Shoot rabbid in green outfit

RUBIK'S PUZZLE WORLD

ALL LEVELS AND CUBIES
At the main menu, press A, B, B, A, A.

RUGBY LEAGUE 3

$100,000,000 SALARY CAP
Go to Create a Player and enter SOMBRERO as the name.

UNLIMITED FUNDING
Go to Create a Player and enter Sugar Daddy as the name.

HUGE MUSCLES
Go to Create a Player and enter i'll be back as the name.

PRESS Z FOR MAX SPEED
Go to Create a Player and enter RSI as the name.

STRONG WIND
Go to Create a Player and enter Beans & Eggs as the name.

ONE TACKLE THEN HANDOVER
Go to Create a Player and enter Force Back as the name.

SCOOBY-DOO! AND THE SPOOKY SWAMP

BIG HEAD
Enter the clubhouse and select Codes from the Extras menu. Enter 2654.

CHIPMUNK TALK
Enter the clubhouse and select Codes from the Extras menu. Enter 3293.

DOUBLE DAMAGE
Enter the clubhouse and select Codes from the Extras menu. Enter 9991.

SLOW MOTION
Enter the clubhouse and select Codes from the Extras menu. Enter 1954.

SCOOBY-DOO! FIRST FRIGHTS

DAPHNE'S SECRET COSTUME
Select Codes from the Extras menu and enter 2839.

FRED'S SECRET COSTUME
Select Codes from the Extras menu and enter 4826.

SCOOBY DOO'S SECRET COSTUME
Select Codes from the Extras menu and enter 1585.

SHAGGY'S SECRET COSTUME
Select Codes from the Extras menu and enter 3726.

VELMA'S SECRET COSTUME
Select Codes from the Extras menu and enter 6588.

THE SECRET SATURDAYS: BEASTS OF THE 5TH SUN

ALL LEVELS
Select Enter Secret Code from the Secrets menu and enter Zon, Zon, Zon, Zon.

UNLOCK AMAROK TO BE SCANNED IN LEVEL 2
Select Enter Secret Code from the Secrets menu and enter Fiskerton, Zak, Zon, Komodo.

UNLOCK BISHOPVILLE LIZARDMAN TO BE SCANNED IN LEVEL 3
Select Enter Secret Code from the Secrets menu and enter Komodo, Zon, Zak, Komodo.

UNLOCK NAGA TO BE SCANNED IN LEVEL 7
Select Enter Secret Code from the Secrets menu and enter Zak, Zak, Zon, Fiskerton.

UNLOCK RAKSHASA TO BE SCANNED IN LEVEL 8
Select Enter Secret Code from the Secrets menu and enter Zak, Komodo, Fiskerton, Fiskerton.

UNLOCK BILOKO TO BE SCANNED IN LEVEL 9
Select Enter Secret Code from the Secrets menu and enter Zon, Zak, Zon, Fiskerton.

SHOCKMAN

REFILL ENERGY
Pause the game and press Left + Select + 2

SOUND TEST
After completing the game at the To Be Continued screen, hold Select and press Up or Down.

SHREK THE THIRD

10,000 GOLD COINS
At the gift shop, press Up, Up, Down, Up, Right, Left.

THE SIMS 2: CASTAWAY

CHEAT GNOME
During a game, press B, Z, Up, Down, B. You can now use this Gnome to get the following:

MAX ALL MOTIVES
During a game, press Minus, Plus, Z, Z, A.

MAX CURRENT INVENTORY
During a game, press Left, Right, Left, Right, A.

MAX RELATIONSHIPS
During a game, press Z, Plus, A, B, 2.

ALL RESOURCES
During a game, press A, A, Down, Down, A.

ALL CRAFTING PLANS
During a game, press Plus, Plus, Minus, Minus, Z.

ADD 1 TO SKILL
During a game, press 2, Up, Right, Z, Right.

SIMANIMALS

FERRET
Begin a game in an unlocked forest area, press 2 to pause, and select Enter Codes. Enter Ferret.

PANDA
Begin a game in an unlocked forest area, press 2 to pause, and select Enter Codes. Enter PANDA.

RED PANDA
Begin a game in an unlocked forest area, press 2 to pause, and select Enter Codes. Enter Red Panda.

SIMCITY CREATOR

EGYPTIAN BUILDING SET
Name your city Mummy's desert.

GREEK BUILDING SET
Name your city Ancient culture.

JUNGLE BUILDING SET
Name your city Become wild.

SCI-FI BUILDING SET
Name your city Future picture.

THE SIMPSONS GAME

UNLIMITED POWER FOR ALL CHARACTERS
At the Extras menu, press Plus, Left, Right, Plus, Minus, Z.

ALL MOVIES
At the Extras menu, press Minus, Left, Minus, Right, Plus, C.

ALL CLICHÉS
At the Extras menu, press Left, Minus, Right, Plus, Right, Z.

SIN AND PUNISHMENT: STAR SUCCESSOR

ISA & KACHI MODE
Defeat the game as Isa and as Kachi. Use the – button to switch between the two.

SPACE HARRIER

CONTINUE AFTER GAME OVER
At the Game Over screen, press Up, Up, Down, Down, Left, Right, Left, Right, Down, Up, Down, Up.

SPECTROBES: ORIGINS

METALIC LEO AND RYZA

At the title screen, before creating a game save, press Up, Down, Left, Right, A.

SPEED RACER

INVULNERABILITY

Select Enter Code from the Options menu and enter A, B, A, Up, Left, Down, Right.

UNLIMITED BOOST

Select Enter Code from the Options menu and enter B, A, Down, Up, B, A, Down.

LAST 3 CARS

Select Enter Code from the Options menu and enter 1, 2, 1, 2, B, A, Plus.

GRANITE CAR

Select Enter Code from the Options menu and enter B, Up, Minus, Plus, 1, Up, Plus.

MONSTER TRUCK

Select Enter Code from the Options menu and enter B, Up, Minus, 2, B, Up, Minus.

AGGRESSIVE OPPONENTS

Select Enter Code from the Options menu and enter Up, Left, Down, Right, Up, Left, Down.

PACIFIST OPPONENTS

Select Enter Code from the Options menu and enter Up, Right, Down, Left, Up, Right, Down.

TINY OPPONENTS

Select Enter Code from the Options menu and enter B, A, Left, Down, Minus, Up, Minus.

HELIUM

Select Enter Code from the Options menu and enter Minus, Up, Minus, 2, Minus, Up, Minus.

MOON GRAVITY

Select Enter Code from the Options menu and enter Up, Plus, Up, Right, Minus, Up, Minus.

OVERKILL

Select Enter Code from the Options menu and enter A, Minus, Plus, Down, Up, Plus, 1.

PSYCHEDELIC

Select Enter Code from the Options menu and enter Left, A, Right, Down, B, Up, Minus.

SPIDER-MAN: FRIEND OR FOE

NEW GREEN GOBLIN AS A SIDEKICK

While standing in the Helicarrier between levels, press Left, Down, Right, Right, Down, Left.

SANDMAN AS A SIDEKICK

While standing in the Helicarrier between levels, press Right, Right, Right, Up, Down, Left.

VENOM AS A SIDEKICK

While standing in the Helicarrier between levels, press Left, Left, Right, Up, Down, Down.

5000 TECH TOKENS

While standing in the Helicarrier between levels, press Up, Up, Down, Down, Left, Right.

SPIDER-MAN: SHATTERED DIMENSIONS

The following can be entered after completing the tutorial.

IRON SPIDER SUIT

At the main menu, press Up, Right, Right, Right, Left, Left, Left, Down, Up.

NEGATIVE ZONE SUIT

At the main menu, press Left, Right, Right, Down, Right, Down, Up, Left.

SCARLET SPIDER SUIT

At the main menu, press Right, Up, Left, Right, Up, Left, Right, Up, Left, Right.

SPONGEBOB SQUAREPANTS FEATURING NICKTOONS: GLOBS OF DOOM

When entering the following codes, the order of the characters going down is: SpongeBob SquarePants, Nicolai Technus, Danny Phantom, Dib, Zim, Tlaloc, Tak, Beautiful Gorgeous, Jimmy Neutron, Plankton. These names are shortened to the first name in the following.

ATTRACT COINS

Using the Upgrade Machine on the bottom level of the lair, select "Input cheat codes here". Enter Tlaloc, Plankton, Danny, Plankton, Tak. Coins are attracted to you making them much easier to collect.

DON'T LOSE COINS

Using the Upgrade Machine on the bottom level of the lair, select "Input cheat codes here". Enter Plankton, Jimmy, Beautiful, Jimmy, Plankton. You don't lose coins when you get knocked out.

GOO HAS NO EFFECT

Using the Upgrade Machine on the bottom level of the lair, select "Input cheat codes here". Enter Danny, Danny, Danny, Nicolai, Nicolai. Goo does not slow you down.

MORE GADGET COMBO TIME

Using the Upgrade Machine on the bottom level of the lair, select "Input cheat codes here". Enter SpongeBob, Beautiful, Danny, Plankton, Nicolai. You have more time to perform gadget combos.

PATRICK TUX IN STARFISHMAN TO THE RESCUE

Select Cheat Codes from the Extras menu and enter PATRICK. Select Activate Bonus Items to enable this bonus item.

SPONGEBOB PLANKTON IN SUPER-SIZED PATTY

Select Cheat Codes from the Extras menu and enter PANTS. Select Activate Bonus Items to enable this bonus item.

PATRICK LASER COLOR IN ROCKET RODEO

Select Cheat Codes from the Extras menu and enter ROCKET. Select Activate Bonus Items to enable this bonus item.

PATRICK ROCKET SKIN COLOR IN ROCKET RODEO

Select Cheat Codes from the Extras menu and enter SPACE. Select Activate Bonus Items to enable this bonus item.

PLANKTON ASTRONAUT SUIT IN REVENGE OF THE GIANT PLANKTON MONSTER

Select Cheat Codes from the Extras menu and enter ROBOT. Select Activate Bonus Items to enable this bonus item.

PLANKTON EYE LASER COLOR IN REVENGE OF THE GIANT PLANKTON MONSTER

Select Cheat Codes from the Extras menu and enter LASER. Select Activate Bonus Items to enable this bonus item.

PIRATE PATRICK IN ROOFTOP RUMBLE

Select Cheat Codes from the Extras menu and enter PIRATE. Select Activate Bonus Items to enable this bonus item.

HOVERCRAFT VEHICLE SKIN IN HYPNOTIC HIGHWAY—PLANKTON

Select Cheat Codes from the Extras menu and enter HOVER. Select Activate Bonus Items to enable this bonus item.

STAR WARS: THE FORCE UNLEASHED

CHEATS

Once you have accessed the Rogue Shadow, select Enter Code from the Extras menu. Now you can enter the following codes:

CHEAT	CODE
Invincibility	CORTOSIS
Unlimited Force	VERGENCE
1,000,000 Force Points	SPEEDER
All Force Powers	TYRANUS

CHEAT	CODE
Max Force Power Level	KATARN
Max Combo Level	COUNTDOOKU
Stronger Lightsaber	LIGHTSABER

COSTUMES

Once you have accessed the Rogue Shadow, select Enter Code from the Extras menu. Now you can enter the following codes:

COSTUME	CODE
All Costumes	GRANDMOFF
501st Legion	LEGION
Aayla Secura	AAYLA
Admiral Ackbar	ITSATWAP
Anakin Skywalker	CHOSENONE
Asajj Ventress	ACOLYTE
Ceremonial Jedi Robes	DANTOOINE
Chop'aa Notimo	NOTIMO
Classic stormtrooper	TK421
Count Dooku	SERENNO
Darth Desolous	PAUAN
Darth Maul	ZABRAK
Darth Phobos	HIDDENFEAR
Darth Vader	SITHLORD
Drexl Roosh	DREXLROOSH
Emperor Palpatine	PALPATINE
General Rahm Kota	MANDALORE
Han Solo	NERFHERDER
Heavy trooper	SHOCKTROOP

COSTUME	CODE
Juno Eclipse	ECLIPSE
Kento's Robe	WOOKIEE
Kleef	KLEEF
Lando Calrissian	SCOUNDREL
Luke Skywalker	T16WOMPRAT
Luke Skywalker (Yavin)	YELLOWJCKT
Mace Windu	JEDIMASTER
Mara Jade	MARAJADE
Maris Brook	MARISBROOD
Navy commando	STORMTROOP
Obi Wan Kenobi	BENKENOBI
Proxy	HOLOGRAM
Qui Gon Jinn	MAVERICK
Shaak Ti	TOGRUTA
Shadow trooper	INTHEDARK
Sith Robes	HOLOCRON
Sith Stalker Armor	KORRIBAN
Twi'lek	SECURA

STREET FIGHTER ALPHA 2

AUSTRALIA STAGE

In versus mode, highlight Sagat, hold Start, and press any button.

CHUN-LI'S HIDDEN COSTUME

At the character select, highlight Chun-li, hold Start and press any button.

SUPER MARIO GALAXY

PLAY AS LUIGI
Collect all 120 stars and fight Bowser. After the credits you will get a message that Luigi is playable.

GRAND FINALE GALAXY
Collect all 120 stars with Luigi and beat Bowser.

STAR 121
Collect 100 purple coins.

SUPER MARIO GALAXY 2

ALL LUIGI GHOSTS
Collect 9999 coins.

BANKER TOAD
Depositing star bits with Banker Toad changes his outfit as follows.

ITEM	# OF STAR BITS DEPOSITED
Glasses	1000
Spear/shield	2000
Pickaxe	4000
Scuba suit	6000
Explorer outfit	8000

GREEN STARS
Collect 120 stars to unlock 120 green stars.

WORLD S
After the game ending, you unlock World S.

GRANDMASTER GALAXY
Collect 120 stars and 120 green stars.

GRANDMASTER GALAXY COMET – THE PERFECT RUN
Deposit 9999 star bits with Banker Toad.

TEENAGE MUTANT NINJA TURTLES: SMASH-UP

NINJA RABBID AND UNDERGROUND STAGE
At the Bonus Content menu, press Up, Up, Down, Down, Down, Right, Up, Left, Right, Left.

SHREDDER AND CYBER SHREDDER OUTFIT
At the Bonus Content menu, press Up, Down, Right, Up, Down, Right, Left, Up, Right, Down.

THRILLVILLE: OFF THE RAILS

$50,000
During a game, press C, Z, B, C, Z, B, A.

500 THRILL POINTS
During a game, press Z, C, B, Z, C, B, C.

ALL MISSIONS
During a game, press C, Z, B, C, Z, B, Z.

ALL PARKS
During a game, press C, Z, B, C, Z, B, C.

ALL RIDES
During a game, press C, Z, B, C, Z, B, B.

ALL MINIGAMES
During a game, press C, Z, B, C, Z, B, Right.

TIGER WOODS PGA TOUR 09 ALL-PLAY

SPECTATORS BIG HEAD MODE
Select EA SPORTS Extras from My Tiger '09, choose Password and enter cephalus.

TIGER WOODS PGA TOUR 10

TW ITEMS IN PRO SHOP
Select Password from the Options and enter eltigre.

TONY HAWK RIDE

RYAN SHECKLER
Select Cheats from the Options menu and enter SHECKLERSIG.

QUICKSILVER 80'S LEVEL
Select Cheats from the Options menu and enter FEELINGEIGHTIES.

TONY HAWK'S PROVING GROUND

Select Cheat Codes from the Options and enter the following cheats. Some codes need to be enabled by selecting Cheats from the Options during a game.

UNLOCK	CHEAT
Unlocks Bosco	MOREMILK
Unlocks Cam	NOTACAMERA
Unlocks Cooper	THECOOP
Unlocks Eddie X	SKETCHY
Unlocks El Patinador	PILEDRIVER
Unlocks Eric	FLYAWAY
Unlocks Judy Nails	LOVEROCKNROLL
Unlocks Mad Dog	RABBIES
Unlocks MCA	INTERGALACTIC
Unlocks Mel	NOTADUDE
Unlocks Rube	LOOKSSMELLY
Unlocks Spence	DAPPER

UNLOCK	CHEAT
Unlocks Shayne	MOVERS
Unlocks TV Producer	SHAKER
Unlock FDR	THEPREZPARK
Unlock Lansdowne	THELOCALPARK
Unlock Air & Space Museum	THEINDOORPARK
Unlocks all Fun Items	OVERTHETOP
Unlock all Game Movies	WATCHTHIS
Unlock all Rigger Pieces	IMGONNABUILD
All specials unlocked and in player's special list	LOTSOFTRICKS
Full Stats	BEEFEDUP
Give player +50 skill points	NEEDSHELP

The following cheats lock you out of the Leaderboards:

Unlocks Perfect Manual	STILLAINTFALLIN
Unlocks Perfect Rail	AINTFALLIN
Unlocks Unlimited Focus	MYOPIC

You cannot use the Video Editor with the following cheats:

Invisible Man	THEMISSING
Mini Skater	TINYTATER

TRANSFORMERS: THE GAME

INFINITE HEALTH
At the Main menu, press Left, Left, Up, Left, Right, Down, Right.

INFINITE AMMO
At the Main menu, press Up, Down, Left, Right, Up, Up, Down.

NO MILITARY OR POLICE
At the Main menu, press Right, Left, Right, Left, Right, Left, Right.

ALL MISSIONS
At the Main menu, press Down, Up, Left, Right, Right, Right, Up, Down.

BONUS CYBERTRON MISSIONS
At the Main menu, press Right, Up, Up, Down, Right, Left, Left.

GENERATION 1 SKIN: JAZZ
At the Main menu, press Left, Up, Down, Down, Left, Up, Right.

GENERATION 1 SKIN: MEGATRON
At the Main menu, press Down, Left, Left, Down, Right, Right, Up.

GENERATION 1 SKIN: OPTIMUS PRIME
At the Main menu, press Down, Right, Left, Up, Down, Down, Left.

GENERATION 1 SKIN: ROBOVISION OPTIMUS PRIME
At the Main menu, press Down, Down, Up, Up, Right, Right, Right.

GENERATION 1 SKIN: STARSCREAM
At the Main menu, press Right, Down, Left, Left, Down, Up, Up.

WALL-E

The following cheats will disable saving. The five possible characters starting with Wall-E and going down are: Wall-E, Auto, EVE, M-O, GEL-A Steward.

ALL BONUS FEATURES UNLOCKED

Select Cheats from the Bonus Features menu and enter Wall-E, Auto, EVE, GEL-A Steward.

ALL GAME CONTENT UNLOCKED

Select Cheats from the Bonus Features menu and enter M-O, Auto, GEL-A Steward, EVE.

ALL SINGLE-PLAYER LEVELS UNLOCKED

Select Cheats from the Bonus Features menu and enter Auto, GEL-A Steward, M-O, Wall-E.

ALL MULTIPLAYER MAPS UNLOCKED

Select Cheats from the Bonus Features menu and enter EVE, M-O, Wall-E, Auto.

ALL HOLIDAY COSTUMES UNLOCKED

Select Cheats from the Bonus Features menu and enter Auto, Auto, GEL-A Steward, GEL-A Steward.

ALL MULTIPLAYER COSTUMES UNLOCKED

Select Cheats from the Bonus Features menu and enter GEL-A Steward, Wall-E, M-O, Auto.

UNLIMITED HEALTH UNLOCKED

Select Cheats from the Bonus Features menu and enter Wall-E, M-O, Auto, M-O.

WALL-E: MAKE ANY CUBE AT ANY TIME

Select Cheats from the Bonus Features menu and enter Auto, M-O, Auto, M-O.

WALL-EVE: MAKE ANY CUBE AT ANY TIME

Select Cheats from the Bonus Features menu and enter M-O, GEL-A Steward, EVE, EVE.

WALL-E WITH A LASER GUN AT ANY TIME

Select Cheats from the Bonus Features menu and enter Wall-E, EVE, EVE, Wall-E.

WALL-EVE WITH A LASER GUN AT ANY TIME

Select Cheats from the Bonus Features menu and enter GEL-A Steward, EVE, M-O, Wall-E.

WALL-E: PERMANENT SUPER LASER UPGRADE

Select Cheats from the Bonus Features menu and enter Wall-E, Auto, EVE, M-O.

EVE: PERMANENT SUPER LASER UPGRADE

Select Cheats from the Bonus Features menu and enter EVE, Wall-E, Wall-E, Auto.

CREDITS

Select Cheats from the Bonus Features menu and enter Auto, Wall-E, GEL-A Steward, M-O.

WII PARTY

SPOT THE SNEAK IN MINIGAMES

Play all of the 4-player minigames.

WII SPORTS

BOWLING BALL COLOR

After selecting your Mii, hold the following direction on the D-pad and press A at the warning screen:

DIRECTION	COLOR
Up	Blue
Right	Gold
Down	Green
Left	Red

NO HUD IN GOLF

Hold 2 as you select a course to disable the power meter, map, and wind speed meter.

BLUE TENNIS COURT

After selecting your Mii, hold 2 and press A at the warning screen.

WII SPORTS RESORT

MODIFY EVENTS

At the Select a Mii screen, hold 2 while pressing A while on "OK." This will make the following modifications to each event.

EVENT	MODIFICATION
Air Sports Island Flyover	No balloons or I points
Air Sports Skydiving	Play intro event
Archery	More difficult; no aiming reticule
Basketball Pickup Game	Nighttime
Frisbee Golf	No wind display or distance
Golf	No wind display or distance
Swordplay Duel	Evening
Table Tennis Match	11-point match

WIPEOUT: THE GAME

JOHN ANDERSON AND MOST LIKELY TO SUCCEED (SECOND OUTFIT)
Play a single player game.

MAD COWGIRL, VALLEY GIRL (SECOND OUTFIT) AND GRASSHOPPER
Play a multiplayer game.

CHEF MUTTEN
Defeat Wipeout Zone within 1:00.

WWE SMACKDOWN VS. RAW 2010

THE ROCK
Select Cheat Codes from the Options and enter The Great One.

VINCE'S OFFICE AND DIRT SHEET FOR BACKSTAGE BRAWL
Select Cheat Codes from the Options menu and enter BonusBrawl.

HBK/SHAWN MICHAEL'S ALTERNATE COSTUME
Select Cheat Codes from the Options menu and enter Bow Down.

JOHN CENA'S ALTERNATE COSTUME
Select Cheat Codes from the Options menu and enter CENATION.

RANDY ORTON'S ALTERNATE COSTUME
Select Cheat Codes from the Options menu and enter ViperRKO.

SANTINO MARELLA'S ALTERNATE COSTUME
Select Cheat Codes from the Options menu and enter Milan Miracle.

TRIPLE H'S ALTERNATE COSTUME
Select Cheat Codes from the Options menu and enter Suck IT!.

WWE SMACKDOWN VS. RAW 2011

JOHN CENA (ENTRANCE/CIVILIAN)
In My WWE, select Cheat Codes from the Options and enter SLURPEE.

ALL OF RANDY ORTON'S COSTUMES
In My WWE, select Cheat Codes from the Options and enter apexpredator.

TRIBUTE TO THE TROOPS ARENA
In My WWE, select Cheat Codes from the Options and enter 8thannualtribute.

Nintendo Wii™: Virtual Console

For the Virtual Console games, a Classic Controller may be needed to enter some codes.

ALTERED BEAST

LEVEL SELECT
At the Title screen, press B + Start.

BEAST SELECT
At the Title screen, hold A + B + C + Down/Left and press Start.

SOUND TEST
At the Title screen, hold A + C + Up/Right and press Start.

CHEW MAN FU

GAME COMPLETE PASSWORDS
Select Password and enter 573300 or 441300.

COMIX ZONE

STAGE SELECT
At the Jukebox menu, press C on the following numbers:
14, 15, 18, 5, 13, 1, 3, 18, 15, 6
A voice says "Oh Yeah" when entered correctly. Then, press C on 1 through 6 to warp to that stage.

INVINCIBLE
At the Jukebox menu, press C on the following numbers:
3, 12, 17, 2, 2, 10, 2, 7, 7, 11
A voice says "Oh Yeah" when entered correctly.

CREDITS
At the Options menu press A + B + C.

DR. ROBOTNIK'S MEAN BEAN MACHINE

EASY PASSWORDS

STAGE	PASSWORD
02: Frankly	Red Bean, Red Bean, Red Bean, Has Bean
03: Humpty	Clear Bean, Purple Bean, Clear Bean, Green Bean
04: Coconuts	Red Bean, Clear Bean, Has Bean, Yellow Bean
05: Davy Sprocket	Clear Bean, Blue Bean, Blue Bean, Purple Bean
06: Skweel	Clear Bean, Red Bean, Clear Bean, Purple Bean

STAGE	PASSWORD
07: Dynamight	Purple Bean, Yellow Bean, Red Bean, Blue Bean
08: Grounder	Yellow Bean, Purple Bean, Has Bean, Blue Bean
09: Spike	Yellow Bean, Purple Bean, Has Bean, Blue Bean
10: Sir Ffuzy-Logik	Red Bean, Yellow Bean, Clear Bean, Has Bean
11: Dragon Breath	Green Bean, Purple Bean, Blue Bean, Clear Bean
12: Scratch	Red Bean, Has Bean, Has Bean, Yellow Bean
13: Dr. Robotnik	Yellow Bean, Has Bean, Blue Bean, Blue Bean

NORMAL PASSWORDS

STAGE	PASSWORD
02: Frankly	Has Bean, Clear Bean, Yellow Bean, Yellow Bean
03: Humpty	Blue Bean, Clear Bean, Red Bean, Yellow Bean
04: Coconuts	Yellow Bean, Blue Bean, Clear Bean, Purple Bean
05: Davy Sprocket	Has Bean, Green Bean, Blue Bean, Yellow Bean
06: Skweel	Green Bean, Purple Bean, Purple Bean, Yellow Bean
07: Dynamight	Purple Bean, Blue Bean, Green Bean, Has Bean
08: Grounder	Green Bean, Has Bean, Clear Bean, Yellow Bean
09: Spike	Blue Bean, Purple Bean, Has Bean, Has Bean
10: Sir Ffuzy-Logik	Has Bean, Red Bean, Yellow Bean, Clear Bean
11: Dragon Breath	Clear Bean, Red Bean, Red Bean, Blue Bean
12: Scratch	Green Bean, Green Bean, Clear Bean, Yellow Bean
13: Dr. Robotnik	Purple Bean, Yellow Bean, Has Bean, Clear Bean

HARD PASSWORDS

STAGE	PASSWORD
02: Frankly	Clear Bean, Green Bean, Yellow Bean, Yellow Bean
03: Humpty	Yellow Bean, Purple Bean, Clear Bean, Purple Bean
04: Coconuts	Blue Bean, Green Bean, Clear Bean, Blue Bean
05: Davy Sprocket	Red Bean, Purple Bean, Green Bean, Green Bean
06: Skweel	Yellow Bean, Yellow Bean, Clear Bean, Green Bean
07: Dynamight	Purple Bean, Clear Bean, Blue Bean, Blue Bean
08: Grounder	Clear Bean, Yellow Bean, Has Bean, Yellow Bean
09: Spike	Purple Bean, Blue Bean, Blue Bean, Green Bean
10: Sir Ffuzy-Logik	Clear Bean, Green Bean, Red Bean, Yellow Bean
11: Dragon Breath	Blue Bean, Yellow Bean, Yellow Bean, Has Bean
12: Scratch	Green Bean, Clear Bean, Clear Bean, Blue Bean
13: Dr. Robotnik	Has Bean, Clear Bean, Purple Bean, Has Bean

HARDEST PASSWORDS

STAGE	PASSWORD
02: Frankly	Blue Bean, Blue Bean, Green Bean, Yellow Bean
03: Humpty	Green Bean, Yellow Bean, Green Bean, Clear Bean
04: Coconuts	Purple Bean, Purple Bean, RedBean, Has Bean
05: Davy Sprocket	Green Bean, Red Bean, Purple Bean, Blue Bean
06: Skweel	Purple Bean, Clear Bean, Green Bean, Yellow Bean
07: Dynamight	Blue Bean, Purple Bean, Green Bean, Has Bean
08: Grounder	Clear Bean, Purple Bean, Yellow Bean, Has Bean
09: Spike	Purple Bean, Green Bean, Has Bean, Clear Bean
10: Sir Ffuzy-Logik	Green Bean, Blue Bean, Yellow Bean, Has Bean
11: Dragon Breath	Green Bean, Purple Bean, Has Bean, Red Bean
12: Scratch	Red Bean, Green Bean, Has Bean, Blue Bean
13: Dr. Robotnik	Red Bean, Red Bean, Clear Bean, Yellow Bean

ECCO THE DOLPHIN

DEBUG MENU

Pause the game with Ecco facing the screen and press Right, B, C, B, C, Down, C, Up.

INFINITE AIR

Enter LIFEFISH as a password.

PASSWORDS

LEVEL	PASSWORD
The Undercaves	WEFIDNMP
The Vents	BQDPXJDS
The Lagoon	JNSBRIKY
Ridge Water	NTSBZTKB
Open Ocean	YWGTTJNI
Ice Zone	HZIFZBMF
Hard Water	LRFJRQLI
Cold Water	UYNFRQLC
Island Zone	LYTIOQLZ
Deep Water	MNOPOQLR
The Marble	RJNTQQLZ
The Library	RTGXQQLE

LEVEL	PASSWORD
Deep City	DDXPQQLJ
City of Forever	MSDBRQLA
Jurassic Beach	IYCBUNLB
Pteranodon Pond	DMXEUNLI
Origin Beach	EGRIUNLB
Trilobite Circle	IELMUNLB
Dark Water	RKEQUNLN
City of Forever 2	HPQIGPLA
The Tube	JUMFKMLB
The Machine	GXUBKMLF
The Last Fight	TSONLMLU

F-ZERO X

ALL TRACKS, VEHICLES, AND DIFFICULTIES

At the Mode Select screen, press Up on the D-pad, L, R, Up on the Right control stick, X, Y, ZR, Plus.

GOLDEN AXE

LEVEL SELECT

At the Character Select screen, in Arcade mode, hold Down/Left and press B + Start.

START WITH 9 CONTINUES

At the Character Select screen, in Arcade mode, hold Down/Left and then hold A + C. Release the buttons and select a character.

GRADIUS

MAX OUT WEAPONS

Pause the game and press Up, Up, Down, Down, Left, Right, Left, Right, B, A.

GRADIUS III

FULL POWER-UP

Pause the game and press Up, Up, Down, Down, L, R, L, R, B, A.

SUICIDE

Pause the game and press Up, Up, Down, Down, Left, Right, Left, Right, B, A.

MILITARY MADNESS

PASSWORDS

LEVEL	PASSWORD
01	REVOLT
02	ICARUS
03	CYRANO
04	RAMSEY
05	NEWTON

LEVEL	PASSWORD
06	SENECA
07	SABINE
08	ARATUS
09	GALIOS
10	DARWIN

LEVEL	PASSWORD	LEVEL	PASSWORD
11	PASCAL	22	ARBINE
12	HALLEY	23	RECTOS
13	BORMAN	24	YEANTA
14	APOLLO	25	MONOGA
15	KAISER	26	ATTAYA
16	NECTOR	27	DESHTA
17	MILTON	28	NEKOSE
18	IRAGAN	29	ERATIN
19	LIPTUS	30	SOLCIS
20	INAKKA	31	SAGINE
21	TETROS	32	WINNER

SOUND TEST
Enter ONGAKU as a password.

RISTAR

Select Passwords from the Options menu and enter the following:

LEVEL SELECT
ILOVEU

BOSS RUSH MODE
MUSEUM

TIME ATTACK MODE
DOFEEL

TOUGHER DIFFICULTY
SUPER

ONCHI MUSIC
MAGURO. Activate this from the Sound Test.

CLEARS PASSWORD
XXXXXX

GAME COPYRIGHT INFO
AGES

SONIC THE HEDGEHOG

LEVEL SELECT
At the Title screen, press Up, Down, Left, Right. A sound of a ring being collected plays if the code is entered correctly. Hold A and press Start to access the Level Select.

CONTROL MODE
At the Title screen, press Up, C, Down, C, Left, C, Right, C. Then, hold A and press Start.

DEBUG MODE
After entering the Control Mode, hold A and press Start. Press A to change Sonic into another sprite. Press B to change back to Sonic. Press C to place that sprite. Pause the game and press A to restart. Hold B for slow motion and press C to advance a frame.

CHANGE DEMO
During the demo, hold C and Sonic will start making mistakes.

WARIO'S WOODS

HARD BATTLES
Highlight VS. Computer Mode, hold Left and press Start.

XBOX 360™

TABLE OF CONTENTS

2010 FIFA WORLD CUP SOUTH AFRICA

ADIDAS U11 TEAM

Go to EA Extras in My 2010 FIFA World Cup. Select Unlockable Code Entry and enter WSBJPJYODFYQIIGK.

FINAL MATCH BALL

Go to EA Extras in My 2010 FIFA World Cup. Select Unlockable Code Entry and enter FGWIXGFXTNSICLSS

ADIDAS ADIPURE III TRX (BLACK/SUN)

Go to EA Extras in My 2010 FIFA World Cup. Select Unlockable Code Entry and enter HHDOPWPMIXZQOJOZ

ADIDAS F50 ADIZERO (BLACK/SUN/SUN)

Go to EA Extras in My 2010 FIFA World Cup. Select Unlockable Code Entry and enter SGFSTZPPXCHHMJMH

ADIDAS F50 ADIZERO (CHAMELEON)

Go to EA Extras in My 2010 FIFA World Cup. Select Unlockable Code Entry and enter VOKMNEZTJOQPULUT

ADIDAS F50 ADIZERO (SUN/BLACK/GOLD)

Go to EA Extras in My 2010 FIFA World Cup. Select Unlockable Code Entry and enter YOZCCVIFJGKQJWTW

ADIDAS PREDATOR X (BLACK/SUN)

Go to EA Extras in My 2010 FIFA World Cup. Select Unlockable Code Entry and enter OCEGZCUHXOBSBNFU

COCA-COLA CELEBRATIONS

Go to EA Extras in My 2010 FIFA World Cup. Select Unlockable Code Entry and enter the following:

CELEBRATION	CODE	HOW TO PERFORM
Baby Cradle	UGSIMLBHLFPUBFJY	Left Trigger + A
Dance	KBRRWKUIRSTWUJQW	Left Trigger + B
Dying Fly	DVMNJPBTLHJZGECP	Left Trigger + X
Flying Dive	DBQDUXQTRWTVXYDC	Left Trigger + Y
Prancing Bird	TWVBIXYACAOLGOWO	🆁🅱 + B
River Dance	MIKAKPUMEEWNTQVE	🆁🅱 + X
Side Slide	VNDWDUDLMGRNHDNV	🆁🅱 + Y
Speed Skating	LHEHJZTPYYQDJQXB	🆁🅱 + A

AMPED 3

ALL SLEDS

Select Cheat Codes from the Options screen and press Right Trigger, ❌, Left Trigger, Down, Right, 🅻🅱, Left Trigger, Right Trigger, 🅈, ❌.

ALL GEAR

Select Cheat Codes from the Options and press 🅈, Down, Up, Left, Right, 🅻🅱, Right, Right Trigger, Right Trigger, 🆁🅱.

ALL TRICKS

Select Cheat Codes from the Options screen and press 🅻🅱, Right Trigger, 🅈, Up, Down, ❌, Left Trigger, Left, 🆁🅱, Right Trigger.

ALL LEVELS

Select Cheat Codes from the Options screen and press ❌, 🅈, Up, Left, 🅻🅱, 🅻🅱, Right Trigger, ❌, 🅈, Left Trigger.

ALL CONFIGS

Select Cheat Codes from the Options screen and press Down, ❌, Right, 🅻🅱, Right, 🆁🅱, ❌, Right Trigger, Left Trigger, 🅈.

SUPER SPINS

Select Cheat Codes from the Options screen and press ❌(x4), 🅈(x3), ❌.

AWESOME METER ALWAYS FULL

Select Cheat Codes from the Options screen and press Up, Right Trigger, ❌, 🅈 🅻🅱, ❌, Down, 🅻🅱, Right Trigger, 🆁🅱.

ALL AWESOMENESS

Select Cheat Codes from the Options screen and press 🆁🅱, 🆁🅱, Down, Left, Up, Right Trigger, ❌, 🆁🅱, ❌, ❌.

ALL BUILD LICENSES

Select Cheat Codes from the Options screen and press Left, Right Trigger, ⓛⓑ, Right Trigger, ✗, ✗, ⓨ, Down, Up, ✗.

ALL BUILD OBJECTS

Select Cheat Codes from the Options screen and press Left Trigger, Right Trigger, Up, Up, ⓡⓑ, Left, Right, ✗, ⓨ, ⓛⓑ.

ALL CHALLENGES

Select Cheat Codes from the Options screen and press Right, ⓛⓑ, Left Trigger, ✗, Left, ⓡⓑ, Right Trigger, ⓨ, Left Trigger, ✗.

LOUD SPEAKERS

Select Cheat Codes from the Options screen and press ⓨ. Right Trigger, Right Trigger, ⓛⓑ, Down, Down, Left, Left, Right, ⓛⓑ.

LOW GRAVITY BOARDERS

Select Cheat Codes from the Options screen and press Right Trigger, Down, Down, Up, ✗, ⓛⓑ, ⓨ, Right Trigger, ⓨ, Down.

NO AI

Select Cheat Codes from the Options screen and press ✗, ✗, ⓛⓑ, Down, Right, Right, Up, ⓨ, ⓨ, Left Trigger.

ALL MUSIC

Select Cheat Codes from the Options screen and press Up, Left, Right Trigger, ⓡⓑ, Right Trigger, Up, Down, Left, ⓨ, Left Trigger.

AVATAR: THE LAST AIRBENDER – THE BURNING EARTH

UNLIMITED HEALTH
Select Code Entry from the Extras menu and enter 65049.

DOUBLE DAMAGE
Select Code Entry from the Extras menu and enter 90210.

MAXIMUM LEVEL
Select Code Entry from the Extras menu and enter 89121.

UNLIMITED SPECIALS
Select Code Entry from the Extras menu and enter 66206.

ONE-HIT DISHONOR
Select Code Entry from the Extras menu and enter 28260.

ALL BONUS GAMES
Select Code Entry from the Extras menu and enter 99801.

UNLOCKS GALLERY
Select Code Entry from the Extras menu and enter 85061.

BAJA: EDGE OF CONTROL

ALL VEHICLES AND TRACKS
Select Cheat Codes from the Options menu and enter SHOWTIME.

ALL PARTS
Select Cheat Codes from the Options menu and enter SUPERMAX.

93

BAKUGAN BATTLE BRAWLERS

1,000 BP
Enter 33204429 as your name.

5,000 BP
Enter 42348294 as your name.

10,000 BP
Enter 46836478 as your name.

100,000 BP
Enter 18499753 as your name.

500,000 BP
Enter 26037947 as your name.

BANJO-KAZOOIE

In Treasure Trove Cove, enter the Sandcastle and spell CHEAT by using your Beak Buster on the desired letter. A sound will confirm the entry of the letter. The following cheats will now be available for you. Two things to keep in mind. The first is that no sound will confirm the correct letter. Secondly, ignore the spaces in the phrases...just spell the entire phrase out.

AREA OPENING CHEATS

ACCESS CLANKER'S CAVERN
THERES NOWHERE DANKER THAN IN WITH CLANKER

ACCESS MAD MONSTER MANSION
THE JIGGYS NOW MADE WHOLE INTO THE MANSION YOU CAN STROLL

ACCESS GOBI'S VALLEY
GOBIS JIGGY IS NOW DONE TREK ON IN AND GET SOME SUN

ACCESS RUSTY BUCKET BAY
WHY NOT TAKE A TRIP INSIDE GRUNTYS RUSTY SHIP

ACCESS CLICK CLOCK WOOD
THIS ONES GOOD AS YOU CAN ENTER THE WOOD

ACCESS FREEZEEZY PEAK
THE JIGGYS DONE SO OFF YOU GO INTO FREEZEEZY PEAK AND ITS SNOW

ACCESS BUBBLEGLOOP SWAMP
NOW INTO THE SWAMP YOU CAN STOMP

HIDDEN EGG CHEATS

The Hidden Egg cheats will only work if you have been to the level previously.

REVEAL THE BLUE EGG IN GOBI'S VALLEY BEHIND THE LOCKED GATE IN THE ROCK WALL
A DESERT DOOR OPENS WIDE ANCIENT SECRETS WAIT INSIDE

REVEAL THE PURPLE EGG IN TREASURE TROVE COVE IN SHARKFOOD ISLAND
OUT OF THE SEA IT RISES TO REVEAL MORE SECRET PRIZES

REVEAL THE ICE KEY IN FREEZEEZY PEAK IN THE ICE CAVE
NOW YOU CAN SEE A NICE ICE KEY WHICH YOU CAN HAVE FOR FREE

REVEAL THE LIGHT BLUE EGG IN GRUNTILDA'S LAIR-YOU'LL FIND IT IN THE CASK MARKED WITH AN X
DONT YOU GO AND TELL HER ABOUT THE SECRET IN HER CELLAR

REVEAL THE GREEN EGG IN MAD MONSTER MANSION IN THE SAME ROOM AS LOGGO THE TOILET
AMIDST THE HAUNTED GLOOM A SECRET IN THE BATHROOM

REVEAL THE YELLOW EGG IN CLICK CLOCK WOOD IN NABNUTS' TREE HOUSE
NOW BANJO WILL BE ABLE TO SEE IT ON NABNUTS TABLE

REVEAL THE RED EGG IN RUSTY BUCKET BAY IN THE CAPTAIN'S CABIN
THIS SECRET YOULL BE GRABBIN IN THE CAPTAINS CABIN

NOTE DOOR CHEATS

These will pop those note doors open without having to find the required notes.

DOOR 2
THESE GO RIGHT ON THROUGH NOTE DOOR TWO

DOOR 3
NOTE DOOR THREE GET IN FOR FREE

DOOR 4
TAKE A TOUR THROUGH NOTE DOOR FOUR

DOOR 5
USE THIS CHEAT NOTE DOOR FIVE IS BEAT

DOOR 6
THIS TRICKS USED TO OPEN NOTE DOOR SIX

DOOR 7
THE SEVENTH NOTE DOOR IS NOW NO MORE

SWITCH AND OBSTACLE CHEATS FOR GRUNTILDA'S LAIR

These will allow you to alter certain obstacles throughout Gruntilda's Lair. Sometimes, the cheat will even remove them completely.

RAISE THE PIPES NEAR CLANKER'S CAVERN
BOTH PIPES ARE THERE TO CLANKERS LAIR

RAISE THE LARGE PIPE NEAR CLANKER'S CAVERN:
YOULL CEASE TO GRIPE WHEN UP GOES A PIPE

UNLOCK THE PATH NEAR CLANKER'S CAVERN THAT LEADS TO THE CLICK CLOCK WOOD PICTURE
ONCE IT SHONE BUT THE LONG TUNNEL GRILLE IS GONE

REVEAL THE PODIUM FOR THE CLICK CLOCK WOOD JIGGY
DONT DESPAIR THE TREE JIGGY PODIUM IS NOW THERE

UNLOCK THE PATH INSIDE THE GIANT WITCH STATUE, NEAR BUBBLEGLOOP SWAMP (OPEN THE GRILL)
SHES AN UGLY BAT SO LETS REMOVE HER GRILLE AND HAT

UNLOCK THE PATH TO THE FREEZEEZY PEAK PICTURE BEHIND THE ICE CUBE
ITS YOUR LUCKY DAY AS THE ICE BALL MELTS AWAY

UNLOCK PASSAGES BLOCKED BY COBWEBS
WEBS STOP YOUR PLAY SO TAKE THEM AWAY

REVEAL A JIGGY IN GRUNTILDA'S STATUE BY SMASHING THE EYE NEAR MAD MONSTER MANSION
GRUNTY WILL CRY NOW YOUVE SMASHED HER EYE

RAISE THE WATER LEVEL NEAR RUSTY BUCKET BAY
UP YOU GO WITHOUT A HITCH UP TO THE WATER LEVEL SWITCH

UNLOCK THE PATH TO THE CRYPT NEAR MAD MONSTER MANSION (REMOVE THE GATE)
YOU WONT HAVE TO WAIT NOW THERES NO CRYPT GATE

REMOVE THE COFFIN LID IN THE CRYPT
THIS SHOULD GET RID OF THE CRYPT COFFIN LID

CRUMBLE ALL BREAKABLE WALLS
THEY CAUSE TROUBLE BUT NOW THEYRE RUBBLE

ACTIVATE SPECIAL PADS

Skip the lesson from Bottles by entering these codes.

ACTIVATE THE FLY PAD
YOU WONT BE SAD NOW YOU CAN USE THE FLY PAD

ACTIVATE THE SHOCK JUMP PAD
YOULL BE GLAD TO SEE THE SHOCK JUMP PAD

95

EXTRA HEALTH CHEAT

Skip the note-hunt and get that extra health by entering this cheat.

AN ENERGY BAR TO GET YOU FAR

Remember, to enter a code you must first enter the word CHEAT in the Sandcastle.

BANJO-TOOIE

REGAIN ENERGY

Go to the Code Chamber in the Mayahem Temple and access the scroll on the wall. If you have been awarded this cheat by Cheato, enter HONEYBACK. If not, enter CHEATOKCABYENOH.

FALLS DON'T HURT

Go to the Code Chamber in the Mayahem Temple and access the scroll on the wall. If you have been awarded this cheat by Cheato, enter FALLPROOF. If not, enter CHEATOFOORPLLAF.

HOMING EGGS

Go to the Code Chamber in the Mayahem Temple and access the scroll on the wall. If you have been awarded this cheat, enter HOMING. If not, enter CHEATOGNIMOH.

DOUBLES MAXIMUM EGGS

Go to the Code Chamber in the Mayahem Temple and access the scroll on the wall. If you have been awarded this cheat by Cheato, enter EGGS. If not, enter CHEATOSGGE.

DOUBLES MAXIMUM FEATHERS

Go to the Code Chamber in the Mayahem Temple and access the scroll on the wall. If you have been awarded this cheat by Cheato, enter FEATHERS. If not, enter CHEATOSREHTAEF.

JOLLY ROGER LAGOON'S JUKEBOX

Go to the Code Chamber in the Mayahem Temple and access the scroll on the wall. If you have been awarded this cheat, enter JUKEBOX. If not, enter CHEATOXOBEKUJ.

SIGNS IN JIGGYWIGGY'S TEMPLE GIVE HINTS TO GET EACH JIGGY

Go to the Code Chamber in the Mayahem Temple and access the scroll on the wall. If you have been awarded this cheat, enter GETJIGGY. If not, enter CHEATOYGGIJTEG.

ALL LEVELS

Go to the Code Chamber in the Mayahem Temple and enter JIGGYWIGGYSPECIAL.

SPEED BANJO

Go to the Code Chamber in the Mayahem Temple and enter SUPERBANJO.

SPEED ENEMIES

Go to the Code Chamber in the Mayahem Temple and enter SUPERBADDY.

INFINITE EGGS AND FEATHERS

Go to the Code Chamber in the Mayahem Temple and enter NESTKING.

INFINITE HONEY

Go to the Code Chamber in the Mayahem Temple and enter HONEYKING.

BATTLESTATIONS: MIDWAY

ALL CAMPAIGN AND CHALLENGE MISSIONS

At the mission select, hold 🔘 + 🔘 + Right Trigger + Left Trigger and press ✖.

BEAT'N GROOVY

ALTERNATE CONTROLS

At the title screen, press Up, Up, Down, Down, Left, Right, Left, Right, Ⓑ, Ⓐ.

EN 10: ALIEN FORCE VILGAX ATTACKS

EVEL SKIP
Pause the game and enter Portal in the Cheats menu.

NLOCK ALL SPECIAL ATTACKS OR ALL FORMS
Pause the game and enter Everythingproof in the Cheats menu.

NLOCK ALL ALIEN FORMS
ause the game and enter Primus in the Cheats menu.

TOGGLE INVULNERABILITY ON AND OFF
Pause the game and enter Xlmrsmoothy in the Cheats menu.

GIVES PLAYER FULL HEALTH
Pause the game and enter Herotime in the Cheats menu.

QUICK ENERGY REGENERATION
Pause the game and enter Generator in the Cheats menu.

EN 10 ULTIMATE ALIEN: COSMIC DESTRUCTION

ese cheats disable Achievements. To remove the cheats, you will need to start a new game.

000,000 DNA
Pause the game, select Cheats, and enter ash.

EGENERATE HEALTH
Pause the game, select Cheats, and enter ealth.

EGENERATE ENERGY
ause the game, select Cheats, and enter nergy.

PGRADE EVERYTHING
ause the game, select Cheats, and enter pgrade.

ALL LEVELS
Pause the game, select Cheats, and enter Levels.

ENEMIES DO DOUBLE DAMAGE/ PLAYER DOES 1/2 DAMAGE
Pause the game, select Cheats, and enter Hard.

UNLOCKS RATH
Pause the game, select Cheats, and enter Primus.

IOLOGY BATTLE

CREASED CONFLICT LEVEL IN GLOBAL CHALLENGE MODE
the Global Challenge Mode lobby, press Ⓐ to access the game controls/start screen. At this creen, hold Ⓨ and press Ⓐ.

LAZING ANGELS: SQUADRONS OF WWII

L MISSIONS, MEDALS, & PLANES
the Main menu hold Left Trigger + Right Trigger and press ❌, 🅛🅑, 🆁🅑, Ⓨ, Ⓨ 🆁🅑, 🅛🅑, ❌.

D MODE
ause the game, hold Left Trigger and press ❌, Ⓨ, Ⓨ, ❌ Release Left Trigger, hold Right igger and press Ⓨ, ❌, ❌, Ⓨ. Re-enter the code to disable it.

GOD MODE

Pause the game, hold Left Trigger and press ❌, ⓨ, ⓨ, ❌ Release Left Trigger, hold Right Trigger and press ⓨ, ❌, ❌, ⓨ. Re-enter the code to disable it.

INCREASED DAMAGE

Pause the game, hold Left Trigger and press 🔵, 🔵, 🔴. Release Left Trigger, hold Right Trigger and press 🔴, 🔴, 🔵. Re-enter the code to disable it.

BLAZING ANGELS 2: SECRET MISSIONS OF WWII

Achievements are disabled when using these codes.

ALL MISSIONS AND PLANES UNLOCKED

At the Main menu, hold Left Trigger + Right Trigger, and press ❌, 🔵, 🔴, ⓨ, ⓨ, 🔴, 🔵, ❌.

GOD MODE

Pause the game, hold Left Trigger, and press ❌, ⓨ, ⓨ, ❌. Release Left Trigger, hold Right Trigger and press ⓨ, ❌, ❌, ⓨ. Re-enter the code to disable it.

INCREASED DAMAGE WITH ALL WEAPONS

Pause the game, hold Left Trigger, and press 🔵, 🔵, 🔴. Release Left Trigger, hold Right Trigger, and press 🔴, 🔴, 🔵. Re-enter the code to disable it.

BLUR

BMW CONCEPT 1 SERIES TII CHROME

In the Multiplayer Showroom, highlight the BMW Concept 1 Series tii and press Left Trigger, Right Trigger, Left Trigger, Right Trigger.

FULLY UPGRADE FORD BRONCO

In the Multiplayer Showroom, highlight the Ford Bronco and press Left Trigger, Right Trigger, Left Trigger, Right Trigger.

AVATAR AWARDS

AWARD	EARNED BY
Wreck Tee	Earn the Been there, got the T-shirt Achievement
Friend Rechallenge Tee	Defeat a friends rechallenge.
Legend Tee	Unlock first Legend Rank in multiplayer.
Showdown Tee	Complete Showdown
Sticker Tee	Complete the Sticker Book.

BURNOUT PARADISE

BEST BUY CAR

Pause the game and select Sponsor Product Code from the Under the Hood menu. Enter Bestbuy. Need A License to use this car offline.

CIRCUIT CITY CAR

Pause the game and select Sponsor Product Code from the Under the Hood menu. Enter Circuitcity. Need Burnout Paradise License to use this car offline.

GAMESTOP CAR

Pause the game and select Sponsor Product Code from the Under the Hood menu. Enter Gamestop. Need A License to use this car offline.

WALMART CAR

Pause the game and select Sponsor Product Code from the Under the Hood menu. Enter Walmart. Need Burnout Paradise License to use this car offline.

"STEEL WHEELS" GT

Pause the game and select Sponsor Product Code from the Under the Hood menu. Enter G23X 5K8Q GX2V 04B1 or E60J 8Z7T MS8L 51U6.

LICENSES

LICENSE	NUMBER OF WINS NEEDED
D	2
C	7
B	16
A	26
Burnout Paradise	45
Elite License	All events

CARS

UNLOCK EVERYTHING

Select Cheat Codes from the Options and enter IF900HP.

ALL CHARACTERS

Select Cheat Codes from the Options and enter YAYCARS.

ALL CHARACTER SKINS

Select Cheat Codes from the Options and enter R4MONE.

ALL MINI-GAMES AND COURSES

Select Cheat Codes from the Options and enter MATTL66.

FAST START

Select Cheat Codes from the Options and enter IMSPEED.

INFINITE BOOST

Select Cheat Codes from the Options and enter VROOOOM.

ART

Select Cheat Codes from the Options and enter CONC3PT.

VIDEOS

Select Cheat Codes from the Options and enter WATCHIT.

CARS MATER-NATIONAL

ALL ARCADE RACES, MINI-GAMES, AND WORLDS

Select Codes/Cheats from the options and enter PLAYALL.

ALL CARS

Select Codes/Cheats from the options and enter MATTEL07.

ALTERNATE LIGHTNING MCQUEEN COLORS

Select Codes/Cheats from the options and enter NCEDUDZ.

ALL COLORS FOR OTHERS

Select Codes/Cheats from the options and enter PAINTIT.

UNLIMITED TURBO

Select Codes/Cheats from the options and enter ZZOOOOM.

EXTREME ACCELERATION

Select Codes/Cheats from the options and enter 0TO200X.

EXPERT MODE

Select Codes/Cheats from the options and enter VRYFAST.

ALL BONUS ART

Select Codes/Cheats from the options and enter BUYTALL.

TM

CASTLEVANIA: SYMPHONY OF THE NIGHT

Before using the following codes, complete the game with 170%.

PLAY AS RICHTER BELMONT

Enter RICHTER as your name.

ALUCARD WITH AXELORD ARMOR

Enter AXEARMOR as your name.

ALUCARD WITH 99 LUCK AND OTHER STATS ARE LOW

Enter X-X!V"Q as your name.

COMIC JUMPER: THE ADVENTURES OF CAPTAIN SMILEY

AVATAR AWARDS

AWARD	EARNED BY
Captain Smiley Giant Head	Complete the whole game
Gerda T-Shirt (female only)	Complete the 1st Level
Star T-Shirt (male only)	Complete the 1st Level

COMMAND & CONQUER 3: TIBERIUM WARS

FREE NOD SHADOW SQUADS

During a NOD game, pause and press Left, Right, Up, Up, Up, Down, RB, LB, LB, B. This code does not work in Skirmish or Career.

COSTUME QUEST

AVATAR AWARDS

AWARD	EARNED BY
Pumpkin Pail	Start a new game.
Pumpkin Mask	Complete the game.

CRASH BANDICOOT: MIND OVER MUTANT

A cheat can be deactivated by re-entering the code.

FREEZE ENEMIES WITH TOUCH

Pause the game, hold Right Trigger and press Down, Down, Down, Up.

ENEMIES DROP X4 DAMAGE

Pause the game, hold Right Trigger and press Up, Up, Up, Left.

ENEMIES DROP PURPLE FRUIT

Pause the game, hold Right Trigger and press Up, Down, Down, Up.

ENEMIES DROP SUPER KICK

Pause the game, hold Right Trigger and press Up, Right, Down, Left.

ENIMIES DROP WUMPA FRUIT

Pause the game, hold Right Trigger and press Right, Right, Right, Up.

SHADOW CRASH

Pause the game, hold Right Trigger and press Left, Right, Left, Right.

DEFORMED CRASH

Pause the game, hold Right Trigger and press Left, Left, Left, Down.

CRASH OF THE TITANS

BIG HEAD CRASH
Pause the game, hold the Right Trigger, and press ❌, ❌, ❨, ❶.

SHADOW CRASH
Pause the game, hold the Right Trigger, and press ❨, ❌, ❨, ❶.

DEATHSPANK

AVATAR AWARDS

AWARD	EARNED BY
Dragon Hatchling	Complete Ms. Heybenstances quest to rescue the hatchlings.
Unicorn Poop T-shirt	Kill the twin dragons guarding the artifact.

DEFENSE GRID: THE AWAKENING

The following cheats will disable Achievements.

100,000 RESOURCES
Click and hold the Right Thumbstick and press Right, Right, Right, Right

CORES CANNOT BE TAKEN
Click and hold the Right Thumbstick and press Up, Left, Down, Right

FREE CAMERA MODE
Click and hold the Right Thumbstick and press Down, Up, Down, Down

INSTANT VICTORY
Click and hold the Right Thumbstick and press Up, Up, Up, Up

KILL ALL ALIENS
Click and hold the Right Thumbstick and press Left, Right, Left, Right

KILL ALL ALIENS CARRYING CORES
Click and hold the Right Thumbstick and press Up, Down, Down, Up

LEVEL SELECT
Click and hold the Right Thumbstick and press Up, Up, Down, Down, Left, Right, Left, Right

SELF-DESTRUCT (INSTANT DEFEAT)
Click and hold the Right Thumbstick and press Down, Down, Down, Down

TOGGLE TARGET RETICULE
Click and hold the Right Thumbstick and press Down, Up, Down, Up

UNLOCK ALL TOWER TYPES
Click and hold the Right Thumbstick and press Up, Down, Left, Right

DIRT 2

Win the given events to earn the following cars:

GET THIS CAR	BY WINNING THIS EVENT
Ford RS200 Evolution	Rally Cross World Tour
Toyota Stadium Truck	Landrush World Tour
Mitsubishi Pajero Dakar 1993	Raid World Tour
Dallenbach Special	Trailblazer World Tour
1995 Subaru Impreza WRX STi	Colin McRae Challenge
Colin McRae R4 [X Games]	X Games Europe
Mitsubishi Lancer Evolution X [X Games]	X Games Asia
Subaru Impreza WRX STi [X Games]	X Games America
Ford Escort MKII and MG Metro 6R4	All X Games events

DJ HERO

Select Cheats from Options and enter the following. Some codes will disable high scores and progress. Cheats cannot be used in tutorials and online.

UNLOCK ALL CONTENT
Enter tol0.

ALL CHARACTER ITEMS
Enter uNA2.

ALL VENUES
Enter Wv1u.

ALL DECKS
Enter LAuP.

ALL HEADPHONES
Enter 62Db.

ALL MIXES
Enter 82xl.

AUTO SCRATCH
Enter it6j.

AUTO EFFECTS DIAL
Enter ab1l.

AUTO FADER
Enter sl5d.

AUTO TAPPER
Enter zith.

AUTO WIN EUPHORIA
Enter r3a9.

BLANK PLINTHS
Enter ipr0.

HAMSTER SWITCH
Enter 7geo.

HYPER DECK MODE
Enter 76st.

SHORT DECK
Enter 51uc.

BLACK AND WHITE
Enter b!99.

EDGE EFFECT
Enter 2u4u.

INVISIBLE DJ
Enter oh5t.

MIDAS
Enter 4pe5.

PITCH BLACK OUT
Enter d4kr.

PLAY IN THE BEDROOM
Enter g7nh.

RAINBOW
Enter ?jy!.

ANY DJ, ANY SETLIST
Enter 0jj8.

DAFT PUNK'S CONTENT
Enter d1g?.

DJ AM'S CONTENT
Enter k07u.

DJ JAZZY JEFF'S CONTENT
Enter n1fz.

DJ SHADOW'S CONTENT
Enter omxv.

DJ Z-TRIP'S CONTENT
Enter 5rtg.

GRANDMASTER FLASH'S CONTENT
Enter ami8.

DJ HERO 2

ALL BONUS CONTENT
Select Cheats from the Options. Choose Retail Cheats and enter VIP Pass.

DAVID GUETTA
Select Cheats from the Options. Choose Retail Cheats and enter Guetta Blaster.

DEADMAU5
Select Cheats from the Options. Choose Retail Cheats and enter Open The Trap.

DON KING PRESENTS: PRIZEFIGHTER

Re-enter a code to disable the cheat.

INVULNERABILITY
Select Enter Unlock Code from the Extras menu and enter SHIELDOFSTEEL.

MAXIMUM STATS
Select Enter Unlock Code from the Extras menu and enter BROUSSARDMODE.

INFINITE ADRENALINE
Select Enter Unlock Code from the Extras menu and enter FISTOFTHENORTHSHIELDS.

INFINITE STAMINA
Select Enter Unlock Code from the Extras menu and enter FEELTHEBURN.

SKIP GETUP GAME
Select Enter Unlock Code from the Extras menu and enter NEVERQUIT.

PLAY AS RICARDO MAYORGA
Select Enter Unlock Code from the Extras menu and enter POTSEMAG.

GREAT MOMENTS IN BOXING VIDEO
Select Enter Unlock Code from the Extras menu and enter 1BESTBUYBEST.

EVERY EXTEND EXTRA EXTREME

FINE ADJUSTMENT MENU
At the Start screen, press **LB**, **RB**, **LB**, **RB**, **LB**, **RB**, **LB**, **RB**.

FATAL FURY SPECIAL

CHEAT MENU
During a game, hold Start and push **A** + **X** + **Y**.

FIGHT NIGHT ROUND 3

ALL VENUES
Create a champ with a first name of NEWVIEW.

FLATOUT: ULTIMATE CARNAGE

MOB CAR IN SINGLE EVENTS
Select Enter Code from Extras and enter BIGTRUCK.

PIMPSTER IN SINGLE EVENTS
Select Enter Code from Extras and enter RUTTO.

ROCKET IN SINGLE EVENTS
Select Enter Code from Extras and enter KALJAKOPPA.

FUEL

CAMO ARMY HELMET
Select Bonus Codes from the Options and enter 48992519.

ROAD ADDICT JACKET
Select Bonus Codes from the Options and enter 20061977.

SPEED ANGEL SHORTS
Select Bonus Codes from the Options and enter 91031985.

BUTTERFLY LIVERY FOR THE SLUDGERAY VEHICLE
Select Bonus Codes from the Options and enter 18021974.

LIGHTNING BOLT LIVERY FOR THE MUDHOG VEHICLE
Select Bonus Codes from the Options and enter 17121973.

WARRIOR VEHICLE
Select Bonus Codes from the Options and enter 18041851.

FULL AUTO

ALL TRACKS, VEHICLES, & WEAPONS
Create a new profile with the name magicman.

GAMERBOTS: THIRD-ROBOT SHOOTING

300,000 GP
Enter 24162444 as a gift code.

DEMON SWORD
Enter 39121412 as a gift code.

DUAL FLAME
Enter 34094035 as a gift code.

SPIKED CLUB
Enter 56095802 as a gift code.

STAR SLICER
Enter 55122302 as a gift code.

G.I. JOE: THE RISE OF COBRA

CLASSIC DUKE
At the main menu, press Left, Up, ✗, Up, Right, ✓.

CLASSIC SCARLETT
At the main menu, press Right, Up, Down, Down, ✓.

GRID

ALL DRIFT CARS
Select Bonus Codes from the Options. Then choose Enter Code and enter TUN58396.

ALL MUSCLE CARS
Select Bonus Codes from the Options. Then choose Enter Code and enter MUS59279.

BUCHBINDER EMOTIONAL ENGINEERING BMW 320SI
Select Bonus Codes from the Options. Then choose Enter Code and enter F93857372. You can use this in Race Day or in GRID World once you've started your own team.

EBAY
Select Bonus Codes from the Options. Then choose Enter Code and enter DAFJ55E01473M0. You can use this in Race Day or in GRID World once you've started your own team.

GAMESTATION BMW 320SI
Select Bonus Codes from the Options. Then choose Enter Code and enter G29782655. You can use this in Race Day or in GRID World once you've started your own team.

MICROMANIA PAGANI ZONDA R
Select Bonus Codes from the Options. Then choose Enter Code and enter M38572343. You can use this in Race Day or in GRID World once you've started your own team.

PLAY.COM ASTON MARTIN DBR9
Select Bonus Codes from the Options. Then choose Enter Code and enter P47203845. You can use this in Race Day or in GRID World once you've started your own team.

HARRY POTTER AND THE HALF-BLOOD PRINCE

BONUS TWO-PLAYER DUELING ARENA CASTLE GATES
At the Rewards menu, press Right, Right, Down, Down, Left, Right, Left, Right, Left, Right, Start.

HYDRO THUNDER HURRICANE

AVATAR AWARDS

AWARD	EARNED BY
Hydro Thunder Hurricane T-Shirt	Get 500 points.
Razorback Toy Boat	Earn 18,500 points.

IRON MAN

CLASSIC ARMOR
Clear One Man Army vs. Mercs.

EXTREMIS ARMOR
Clear One Man Army vs. Maggia.

MARK II ARMOR
Clear One Man Army vs. Ten Rings.

HULKBUSTER ARMOR
Clear One Man Army vs. AIM-X. Can also be unlocked when clear game save data from Incredible Hulk is stored on the same console.

SILVER CENTURION ARMOR
Clear Mission 13: Showdown.

CLASSIC MARK I ARMOR
Clear One Man Army vs. AIM.

TM

JUICED 2: HOT IMPORT NIGHTS

FRITO-LAY INFINITY G35 CAR
Select Cheats and Codes from the DNA Lab menu and enter MNCH.

HIDDEN CHALLENGE AND AN AUDI TT 1.8 QUATTRO
Select Cheats and Codes from the DNA Lab menu and enter YTHZ. Defeat the challenge to earn the Audi TT 1.8 Quattro.

HIDDEN CHALLENGE AND A BMW Z4
Select Cheats and Codes from the DNA Lab menu and enter GVDL. Defeat the challenge to earn the BMW Z4.

HIDDEN CHALLENGE AND A HOLDEN MONARO
Select Cheats and Codes from the DNA Lab menu and enter RBSG. Defeat the challenge to earn the Holden Monaro.

HIDDEN CHALLENGE AND A HYUNDAI COUPE 2.7 V6
Select Cheats and Codes from the DNA Lab menu and enter BSLU. Defeat the challenge to earn the Hyundai Coupe 2.7 V6.

HIDDEN CHALLENGE AND AN INFINITY G35
Select Cheats and Codes from the DNA Lab menu and enter MRHC. Defeat the challenge to earn the Infinity G35.

HIDDEN CHALLENGE AND A KOENIGSEGG CCX
Select Cheats and Codes from the DNA Lab menu and enter KDTR. Defeat the challenge to earn the Koenigsegg CCX.

HIDDEN CHALLENGE AND A MITSUBISHI PROTOTYPE X
Select Cheats and Codes from the DNA Lab menu and enter DOPX. Defeat the challenge to earn the Mitsubishi Prototype X.

HIDDEN CHALLENGE AND A NISSAN 350Z
Select Cheats and Codes from the DNA Lab menu and enter PRGN. Defeat the challenge to earn the Nissan 350Z.

HIDDEN CHALLENGE AND A NISSAN SKYLINE R34 GT-R
Select Cheats and Codes from the DNA Lab menu and enter JWRS. Defeat the challenge to earn the Nissan Skyline R34 GT-R.

HIDDEN CHALLENGE AND A SALEEN S7
Select Cheats and Codes from the DNA Lab menu and enter WIKF. Defeat the challenge to earn the Saleen S7.

HIDDEN CHALLENGE AND A SEAT LEON CUPRA R
Select Cheats and Codes from the DNA Lab menu and enter FAMQ. Defeat the challenge to earn the Seat Leon Cupra R.

KUNG FU PANDA

INFINITE CHI
Select Cheats from the Extra menu and press Down, Right, Left, Up, Down.

INVINCIBILITY
Select Cheats from the Extra menu and press Down, Down, Right, Up, Left.

FULL UPGRADES
Select Cheats from the Extra menu and press Left, Right, Down, Left, Up.

4X DAMAGE MULTIPLIER
Select Cheats from the Extra menu and press Up, Down, Up, Right, Left.

ALL MULTIPLAYER CHARACTERS
Select Cheats from the Extra menu and press Left, Down, Left, Right, Down.

DRAGON WARRIOR OUTFIT IN MULTIPLAYER
Select Cheats from the Extra menu and press Left, Down, Right, Left, Up.

ALL OUTFITS
Select Cheats from the Extra menu and press Right, Left, Down, Up, Right.

LARA CROFT AND THE GUARDIAN OF LIGHT

LARA CROFT HEAVY JUNGLE OUTFIT
Complete the game.

LARA CROFT JUNGLE OUTFIT
Score 1,410,000 points.

LARA CROFT BIKER OUTFIT
Score 1,900,000 points.

LARA CROFT LEGEND OUTFIT
Defeat Xolotl.

DOPPELGANGER OUTFIT
Score 2,400,000 points.

THE LEGEND OF SPYRO: DAWN OF THE DRAGON

UNLIMITED LIFE
Pause the game, hold **LB** and press Right, Right, Down, Down, Left with the Left Control Stick.

UNLIMITED MANA
Pause the game, hold **RB** and press Up, Right, Up, Left, Down with the Left Control Stick.

MAXIMUM XP
Pause the game, hold **RB** and press Up, Left, Left, Down, Up with the Left Control Stick.

ALL ELEMENTAL UPGRADES
Pause the game, hold **LB** and press Left, Up, Down, Up, Right with the Left Control Stick.

LEGO BATMAN

BATCAVE CODES
Using the computer in the Batcave, select Enter Code and enter the following codes.

CHARACTERS

CHARACTER	CODE	CHARACTER	CODE
Alfred	ZAQ637	Penguin Henchman	BJH782
Batgirl	JKR331	Penguin Minion	KJP748
Bruce Wayne	BDJ327	Poison Ivy Goon	GTB899
Catwoman (Classic)	M1AAWW	Police Marksman	HKG984
Clown Goon	HJK327	Police Officer	JRY983
Commissioner Gordon	DDP967	Riddler Goon	CRY928
Fishmonger	HGY748	Riddler Henchman	XEU824
Freeze Girl	XVK541	S.W.A.T.	HTF114
Joker Goon	UTF782	Sailor	NAV592
Joker Henchman	YUN924	Scientist	JFL786
Mad Hatter	JCA283	Security Guard	PLB946
Man-Bat	NYU942	The Joker (Tropical)	CCB199
Military Policeman	MKL382	Yeti	NJL412
Nightwing	MVY759	Zoo Sweeper	DWR243
Penguin Goon	NKA238		

VEHICLES

VEHICLE	CODE	VEHICLE	CODE
Bat-Tank	KNTT4B	Mr. Freeze's Kart	BCT229
Bruce Wayne's Private Jet	LEA664	Penguin Goon Submarine	BTN248
Catwoman's Motorcycle	HPL826	Police Bike	LJP234
Garbage Truck	DUS483	Police Boat	PLC999
Goon Helicopter	GCH328	Police Car	KJL832
Harbor Helicopter	CHP735	Police Helicopter	CWR732
Harley Quinn's Hammer Truck	RDT637	Police Van	MAC788
Mad Hatter's Glider	HS000W	Police Watercraft	VJD328
Mad Hatter's Steamboat	M4DM4N	Riddler's Jet	HAHAHA
Mr. Freeze's Iceberg	ICYICE	Robin's Submarine	TTF453
The Joker's Van	JUK657	Two-Face's Armored Truck	EFE933

CHEATS

CHEAT	CODE
Always Score Multiply	9LRGNB
Fast Batarangs	JRBDCB
Fast Walk	ZOLM6N
Flame Batarang	D8NYWH
Freeze Batarang	XPN4NG
Extra Hearts	ML3KHP
Fast Build	EVG26J
Immune to Freeze	JXUDY6
Invincibility	WYD5CP
Minikit Detector	ZXGH9J

CHEAT	CODE
More Batarang Targets	XWP645
Piece Detector	KHJ554
Power Brick Detector	MMN786
Regenerate Hearts	HJH7HJ
Score x2	N4NR3E
Score x4	CX9MAT
Score x6	MLVNF2
Score x8	WCCDB9
Score x10	18HW07

LEGO HARRY POTTER: YEARS 1-4

RED BRICK EXTRAS

Once you have access to The Leaky Cauldron, enter Wiseacre's Wizarding Supplies from Diagon Alley. Go upstairs to enter the following. Pause the game and select Extras to toggle the cheats on/off.

CHEAT	CODE
Carrot Wands	AUC8EH
Character Studs	H27KGC
Character Token Detector	HA79V8
Christmas	T7PVVN
Disguise	4DMK2R
Fall Rescue	ZEX7MV
Extra Hearts	J9U6Z9
Fast Dig	Z9BFAD
Fast Magic	FA3GQA
Gold Brick Detector	84QNQN
Hogwarts Crest Detector	TTMC6D
Ice Rink	F88VUW

CHEAT	CODE
Invincibility	QQWC6B
Red Brick Detector	7AD7HE
Regenerate Hearts	89ML2W
Score x2	74YKR7
Score x4	J3WHNK
Score x6	XK9ANE
Score x8	HUFV2H
Score x10	H8X69Y
Silhouettes	HZBVX7
Singing Mandrake	BMEU6X
Stud Magnet	67FKWZ

WISEACRE SPELLS

Once you have access to The Leaky Cauldron, enter Wiseacre's Wizarding Supplies from Diagon Alley. Go upstairs to enter the following. You need to learn Wingardium Leviosa before you can use these cheats.

SPELL	CODE
Accio	VE9VV7
Anteoculatia	QFB6NR
Calvorio	6DNR6L
Colovaria	9GJ442
Engorgio Skullus	CD4JLX
Entomorphis	MYN3NB
Flipendo	ND2L7W
Glacius	ERA9DR
Herbifors	H8FTHL
Incarcerous	YEB9Q9

SPELL	CODE
Locomotor Mortis	2M2XJ6
Multicorfors	JK6QRM
Redactum Skullus	UW8LRH
Rictusempra	2UCA3M
Slugulus Eructo	U6EE8X
Stupefy	UWDJ4Y
Tarantallegra	KWWQ44
Trip Jinx	YZNRF6

EEYLOPS GOLD BRICKS

Once you have access to The Leaky Cauldron, enter Wiseacre's Wizarding Supplies from Diagon Alley. Go upstairs to enter the following. To access the LEGO Builder, visit Gringott's Bank at the end of Diagon Alley.

GOLD BRICK	CODE	GOLD BRICK	CODE
1	QE4VC7	7	XY6VYZ
2	FY8H97	8	TUNC4W
3	3MQT4P	9	EJ42Q6
4	PQPM7Z	10	GFJCV9
5	ZY2CPA	11	DZCY6G
6	3GMTP6		

LEGO INDIANA JONES: THE ORIGINAL ADVENTURES

CHARACTERS

Approach the blackboard in the Classsroom and enter the following codes.

CHARACTER	CODE	CHARACTER	CODE
Bandit	12N68W	Fedora	V75YSP
Bandit Swordsman	1MK4RT	First Mate	0GIN24
Barranca	04EM94	Grail Knight	NE6THI
Bazooka Trooper (Crusade)	MK83R7	Hovitos Tribesman	H0VISS
Bazooka Trooper (Raiders)	S93Y5R	Indiana Jones (Desert Disguise)	4J8S4M
Belloq	CHN3YU	Indiana Jones (Officer)	VJ850S
Belloq (Jungle)	TDR197	Jungle Guide	24PF34
Belloq (Robes)	VEO29L	Kao Kan	WMO46L
British Commander	B73EUA	Kazim	NRH23J
British Officer	VJ5TI9	Kazim (Desert)	3M29TJ
British Soldier	DJ5I2W	Lao Che	2NK479
Captain Katanga	VJ3TT3	Maharajah	NFK5N2
Chatter Lal	ENW936	Major Toht	13NS01
Chatter Lal (Thuggee)	CNH4RY	Masked Bandit	N48SFO
Chen	3NK48T	Mola Ram	FJUR31
Colonel Dietrich	2K9RKS	Monkey Man	3RF6YJ
Colonel Vogel	8EAL4H	Pankot Assassin	2NKT72
Dancing Girl	C7EJ21	Pankot Guard	VN28RH
Donovan	3NFTU8	Sherpa Brawler	VJ37WJ
Elsa (Desert)	JSNRT9	Sherpa Gunner	ND762W
Elsa (Officer)	VMJ5US	Slave Child	OE3ENW
Enemy Boxer	8246RB	Thuggee	VM683E
Enemy Butler	VJ48W3	Thuggee Acolyte	T2R3F9
Enemy Guard	VJ7R51	Thuggee Slave Driver	VBS7GW
Enemy Guard (Mountains)	YR47WM	Village Dignitary	KD48TN
Enemy Officer	572E61	Village Elder	4682E1
Enemy Officer (Desert)	2MK450	Willie (Dinner Suit)	VK93R7
Enemy Pilot	B84ELP	Willie (Pajamas)	MEN4IP
Enemy Radio Operator	1MF94R	Wu Han	3NSLT8
Enemy Soldier (Desert)	4NSU7Q		

EXTRAS

Approach the blackboard in the Classsroom and enter the following codes. Some cheats need to be enabled by selecting Extras from the pause menu.

CHEAT	CODE	CHEAT	CODE
Artifact Detector	VIKED7	Disguises	4ID1N6
Beep Beep	VNF59Q	Fast Build	V83SLO
Character Treasure	VIES2R	Fast Dig	378RS6
Disarm Enemies	VKRNS9	Fast Fix	FJ59WS

CHEAT	CODE
Fertilizer	B1GW1F
Ice Rink	33GM7J
Parcel Detector	VUT673
Poo Treasure	WWQ1SA
Regenerate Hearts	MDLP69
Secret Characters	3X44AA
Silhouettes	3HE85H
Super Scream	VN3R7S

CHEAT	CODE
Super Slap	0P1TA5
Treasure Magnet	H86LA2
Treasure x10	VI3PS8
Treasure x2	VM4TS9
Treasure x4	VLWEN3
Treasure x6	V84RYS
Treasure x8	A72E1M

LEGO INDIANA JONES 2: THE ADVENTURE CONTINUES

Pause the game, select Enter Secret Code from the Extras menu, and enter the following.

CHARACTERS

CHARACTER	CODE
Bellog (Priest)	FTL48S
Dovchenko	WL4T6N
Enemy Boxer	7EQF47
Henry Jones	4CSAKH
Indiana Jones	PGWSEA
Indiana Jones: 2	FGLKYS
Indiana Jones (Collect)	DZFY9S
Indiana Jones (Desert)	M4C34K
Indiana Jones (Desert Disguise)	2W8QR3
Indiana Jones (Dinner Suit)	QUNZUT
Indiana Jones (Kali)	J2XS97

CHARACTER	CODE
Indiana Jones (Officer)	3FQFKS
Interdimensional Being	PXT4UP
Lao Che	7AWX3J
Mannequin (Boy)	2UJQWC
Mannequin (Girl)	3PGSEL
Mannequin (Man)	QPWDMM
Mannequin (Woman)	U7SMVK
Mola Ram	82RMC2
Mutt	2GKS62
Salah	E88YRP
Willie	94RUAJ

EXTRAS

EFFECT	CODE
Beep Beep	UU3VSC
Disguise	Y9TE98
Fast Build	SNXC2F
Fast Dig	XYAN83
Fast Fix	3Z7PJX
Fearless	TUXNZF
Ice Rink	TY9P4U
Invincibility	6JBB65
Poo Money	SZFAAE

EFFECT	CODE
Score x3	PEHHPZ
Score x4	UXGTB3
Score X6	XWLJEY
Score x8	S5UZCP
Score x10	V7JYBU
Silhouettes	FQGPYH
Snake Whip	2U7YCV
Stud Magnet	EGSM5B

LEGO STAR WARS II: THE ORIGINAL TRILOGY

BEACH TROOPER
At Mos Eisley Canteena, select Enter Code and enter UCK868. You still need to select Characters and purchase this character for 20,000 studs.

BEN KENOBI (GHOST)
At Mos Eisley Canteena, select Enter Code and enter BEN917. You still need to select Characters and purchase this character for 1,100,000 studs.

BESPIN GUARD
At Mos Eisley Canteena, select Enter Code and enter VHY832. You still need to select Characters and purchase this character for 15,000 studs.

BIB FORTUNA
At Mos Eisley Canteena, select Enter Code and enter WTY721. You still need to select Characters and purchase this character for 16,000 studs.

BOBA FETT

At Mos Eisley Canteena, select Enter Code and enter HLP221. You still need to select Characters and purchase this character for 175,000 studs.

DEATH STAR TROOPER

At Mos Eisley Canteena, select Enter Code and enter BNC332. You still need to select Characters and purchase this character for 19,000 studs.

EWOK

At Mos Eisley Canteena, select Enter Code and enter TTT289. You still need to select Characters and purchase this character for 34,000 studs.

GAMORREAN GUARD

At Mos Eisley Canteena, select Enter Code and enter YZF999. You still need to select Characters and purchase this character for 40,000 studs.

GONK DROID

At Mos Eisley Canteena, select Enter Code and enter NFX582. You still need to select Characters and purchase this character for 1,550 studs.

GRAND MOFF TARKIN

At Mos Eisley Canteena, select Enter Code and enter SMG219. You still need to select Characters and purchase this character for 38,000 studs.

GREEDO

At Mos Eisley Canteena, select Enter Code and enter NAH118. You still need to select Characters and purchase this character for 60,000 studs.

HAN SOLO (HOOD)

At Mos Eisley Canteena, select Enter Code and enter YWM840. You still need to select Characters and purchase this character for 20,000 studs.

IG-88

At Mos Eisley Canteena, select Enter Code and enter NXL973. You still need to select Characters and purchase this character for 30,000 studs.

IMPERIAL GUARD

At Mos Eisley Canteena, select Enter Code and enter MMM111. You still need to select Characters and purchase this character for 45,000 studs.

IMPERIAL OFFICER

At Mos Eisley Canteena, select Enter Code and enter BBV889. You still need to select Characters and purchase this character for 28,000 studs.

IMPERIAL SHUTTLE PILOT

At Mos Eisley Canteena, select Enter Code and enter VAP664. You still need to select Characters and purchase this character for 29,000 studs.

IMPERIAL SPY

At Mos Eisley Canteena, select Enter Code and enter CVT125. You still need to select Characters and purchase this character for 13,500 studs.

JAWA

At Mos Eisley Canteena, select Enter Code and enter JAW499. You still need to select Characters and purchase this character for 24,000 studs.

LOBOT

At Mos Eisley Canteena, select Enter Code and enter UUB319. You still need to select Characters and purchase this character for 11,000 studs.

PALACE GUARD

At Mos Eisley Canteena, select Enter Code and enter SGE549. You still need to select Characters and purchase this character for 14,000 studs.

REBEL PILOT

At Mos Eisley Canteena, select Enter Code and enter CYG336. You still need to select Characters and purchase this character for 15,000 studs.

REBEL TROOPER (HOTH)

At Mos Eisley Canteena, select Enter Code and enter EKU849. You still need to select Characters and purchase this character for 16,000 studs.

SANDTROOPER

At Mos Eisley Canteena, select Enter Code and enter YDV451. You still need to select Characters and purchase this character for 14,000 studs.

SKIFF GUARD

At Mos Eisley Canteena, select Enter Code and enter GBU888. You still need to select Characters and purchase this character for 12,000 studs.

SNOWTROOPER

At Mos Eisley Canteena, select Enter Code and enter NYU989. You still need to select Characters and purchase this character for 16,000 studs.

STROMTROOPER

At Mos Eisley Canteena, select Enter Code and enter PTR345. You still need to select Characters and purchase this character for 10,000 studs.

THE EMPEROR

At Mos Eisley Canteena, select Enter Code and enter HHY382. You still need to select Characters and purchase this character for 275,000 studs.

TIE FIGHTER

At Mos Eisley Canteena, select Enter Code and enter HDY739. You still need to select Characters and purchase this character for 60,000 studs.

TIE FIGHTER PILOT

At Mos Eisley Canteena, select Enter Code and enter NNZ316. You still need to select Characters and purchase this character for 21,000 studs.

TIE INTERCEPTOR

At Mos Eisley Canteena, select Enter Code and enter QYA828. You still need to select Characters and purchase this character for 40,000 studs.

TUSKEN RAIDER

At Mos Eisley Canteena, select Enter Code and enter PEJ821. You still need to select Characters and purchase this character for 23,000 studs.

UGNAUGHT

At Mos Eisley Canteena, select Enter Code and enter UGN694. You still need to select Characters and purchase this character for 36,000 studs.

LEGO STAR WARS: THE COMPLETE SAGA

The following still need to be purchase after entering the codes.

CHARACTERS

ADMIRAL ACKBAR

At the bar in Mos Eisley Cantina, select Enter Code and enter ACK646.

BATTLE DROID (COMMANDER)

At the bar in Mos Eisley Cantina, select Enter Code and enter KPF958.

BOBA FETT (BOY)

At the bar in Mos Eisley Cantina, select Enter Code and enter GGF539.

BOSS NASS

At the bar in Mos Eisley Cantina, select Enter Code and enter HHY697.

CAPTAIN TARPALS

At the bar in Mos Eisley Cantina, select Enter Code and enter QRN714.

COUNT DOOKU

At the bar in Mos Eisley Cantina, select Enter Code and enter DDD748.

DARTH MAUL

At the bar in Mos Eisley Cantina, select Enter Code and enter EUK421.

EWOK

At the bar in Mos Eisley Cantina, select Enter Code and enter EWK785.

GENERAL GRIEVOUS

At the bar in Mos Eisley Cantina, select Enter Code and enter PMN576.

GREEDO

At the bar in Mos Eisley Cantina, select Enter Code and enter ZZR636.

IG-88

At the bar in Mos Eisley Cantina, select Enter Code and enter GIJ989.

IMPERIAL GUARD

At the bar in Mos Eisley Cantina, select Enter Code and enter GUA850.

JANGO FETT

At the bar in Mos Eisley Cantina, select Enter Code and enter KLJ897.

KI-ADI MUNDI

At the bar in Mos Eisley Cantina, select Enter Code and enter MUN486.

LUMINARA

At the bar in Mos Eisley Cantina, select Enter Code and enter LUM521.

PADMÉ

At the bar in Mos Eisley Cantina, select Enter Code and enter VBJ322.

R2-Q5
At the bar in Mos Eisley Cantina, select Enter Code and enter EVILR2.

STORMTROOPER
At the bar in Mos Eisley Cantina, select Enter Code and enter NBN431.

TAUN WE
At the bar in Mos Eisley Cantina, select Enter Code and enter PRX482.

VULTURE DROID
At the bar in Mos Eisley Cantina, select Enter Code and enter BDC866.

WATTO
At the bar in Mos Eisley Cantina, select Enter Code and enter PLL967.

ZAM WESELL
At the bar in Mos Eisley Cantina, select Enter Code and enter 584HJF.

SKILLS

DISGUISE
At the bar in Mos Eisley Cantina, select Enter Code and enter BRJ437.

FORCE GRAPPLE LEAP
At the bar in Mos Eisley Cantina, select Enter Code and enter CLZ738.

VEHICLES

DROID TRIFIGHTER
At the bar in Mos Eisley Cantina, select Enter Code and enter AAB123.

IMPERIAL SHUTTLE
At the bar in Mos Eisley Cantina, select Enter Code and enter HUT845.

TIE INTERCEPTOR
At the bar in Mos Eisley Cantina, select Enter Code and enter INT729.

TIE FIGHTER
At the bar in Mos Eisley Cantina, select Enter Code and enter DBH897.

ZAM'S AIRSPEEDER
At the bar in Mos Eisley Cantina, select Enter Code and enter UUU875.

LOONEY TUNES: ACME ARSENAL

UNLMITED AMMO
At the cheat menu, press Down, Left, Up, Right, Down, Left, Up, Right, Down.

LOST PLANET: EXTREME CONDITION

The following codes are for Single Player Mode on Easy Difficulty only.

500 THERMAL ENERGY
Pause the game and press Up, Up, Down, Down, Left, Right, Left, Right, ❌, ⓨ, 🆁🅱 + 🅻🅱.

INFINITE AMMUNITION
Pause the game and press Right Trigger, 🆁🅱, ⓨ, ❌, Right, Down, Left, 🅻🅱, Left Trigger, Right Trigger, 🆁🅱, ⓨ, ❌, Right, Down, Left, 🅻🅱, Left Trigger, Right Trigger, Left Trigger, 🅻🅱, 🆁🅱, ⓨ, Left, Down, ❌, 🆁🅱 + 🅻🅱.

INFINITE HEALTH
Pause the game and press Down (x3), Up, ⓨ,Up, ⓨ,Up, ⓨ, Up(x3), Down, ❌, Down, ❌, Down, ❌, Left, ⓨ, Right, ❌, Left, ⓨ, Right, ❌, 🆁🅱 + 🅻🅱.

CHANGE CAMERA ANGLE IN CUT SCENES
During a cut scene, press Ⓑ, Ⓐ,❌,ⓨ, Ⓑ, Ⓐ,❌,ⓨ, Ⓑ, Ⓐ,❌, ⓨ.

113

LUCHA LIBRE AAA HEROES DEL RING

LITTLE ONES
At the character select, press Up, Up, Down, Down, Left, Right, Left, Right. Play with them to unlock the Little Ones Can Too Achievement.

MARVEL ULTIMATE ALLIANCE

UNLOCK ALL SKINS
At the Team menu, press Up, Down, Left, Right, Left, Right, Start.

UNLOCKS ALL HERO POWERS
At the Team menu, press Left, Right, Up, Down, Up, Down, Start.

ALL HEROES TO LEVEL 99
At the Team menu, press Up, Left, Up, Left, Down, Right, Down, Right, Start.

UNLOCK ALL HEROES
At the Team menu, press Up, Up, Down, Down, Left, Left, Left, Start.

UNLOCK DAREDEVIL
At the Team menu, press Left, Left, Right, Right, Up, Down, Up, Down, Start.

UNLOCK SILVER SURFER
At the Team menu, press Down, Left, Left, Up, Right, Up, Down, Left, Start.

GOD MODE
During gameplay, press Up, Down, Up, Down, Up, Left, Down, Right, Start.

TOUCH OF DEATH
During gameplay, press Left, Right, Down, Down, Right, Left, Start.

SUPER SPEED
During gameplay, press Up, Left, Up, Right, Down, Right, Start.

FILL MOMENTUM
During gameplay, press Left, Right, Right, Left, Up, Down, Down, Up, Start.

UNLOCK ALL COMICS
At the Review menu, press Left, Right, Right, Left, Up, Up, Right, Start.

UNLOCK ALL CONCEPT ART
At the Review menu, press Down, Down, Down, Right, Right, Left, Down, Start.

UNLOCK ALL CINEMATICS
At the Review menu, press Up, Left, Left, Up, Right, Right, Up, Start.

UNLOCK ALL LOAD SCREENS
At the Review menu, press Up, Down, Right, Left, Up, Up Down, Start.

UNLOCK ALL COURSES
At the Comic Missions menu, press Up, Right, Left, Down, Up, Right, Left, Down, Start.

MARVEL ULTIMATE ALLIANCE 2

These codes will disable the ability to save.

GOD MODE
During a game, press Up, Down, Up, Down, Up, Left, Down, Right, Start.

UNLIMITED FUSION
During a game, press Right, Right, Up, Down, Up, Up, Left, Start.

UNLOCK ALL POWERS
During a game, press Left, Right, Up, Down, Up, Down, Start.

UNLOCK ALL HEROES
During a game, press Up, Up, Down, Down, Left, Left, Left, Start.

UNLOCK ALL SKINS
During a game, press Up, Down, Left, Right, Left, Right, Start.

UNLOCK JEAN GREY
During a game, press Left, Left, Right, Right, Up, Down, Up, Down, Start.

UNLOCK HULK
During a game, press Down, Left, Left, Up, Right, Up, Down, Left, Start.

UNLOCK THOR
During a game, press Up, Right, Right, Down, Right, Down, Left, Right, Start.

UNLOCK ALL AUDIO LOGS
At the main menu, press Left, Right, Right, Left, Up, Up, Right, Start.

UNLOCK ALL DOSSIERS
At the main menu, press Down, Down, Down, Right, Right, Left, Down, Start.

UNLOCK ALL MOVIES
At the main menu, press Up, Left, Left, Up, Right, Right, Up, Start.

MX VS. ATV REFLEX

MX VEHICLES FOR PURCHASE
Select Enter Cheat Code from the Options and enter brapbrap.

JUSTIN BRAYTON, KTM MX BIKES AND ATVS IN ARCADE MODE
Select Enter Cheat Code from the Options and enter readytorace.

ALL EVENT LOCATIONS IN ARCADE MODE
Select Enter Cheat Code from the Options and enter whereto.

ALL AI OPPONENTS
Select Enter Cheat Code from the Options and enter allai.

ATV VEHICLES FOR PURCHASE
Select Enter Cheat Code from the Options and enter couches.

ALL AVAILABLE RIDER GEAR
Select Enter Cheat Code from the Options and enter gearedup.

ALL AVAILABLE HELMETS
Select Enter Cheat Code from the Options and enter skullcap.

ALL AVAILABLE BOOTS
Select Enter Cheat Code from the Options and enter kicks.

ALL AVAILABLE GOGGLES
Select Enter Cheat Code from the Options and enter windows.

MX VS. ATV UNTAMED

ALL RIDING GEAR
Select Cheat Codes from the Options and enter crazylikea.

ALL HANDLEBARS
Select Cheat Codes from the Options and enter nohands.

27 GRAPHICS
Select Cheat Codes from the Options and enter STICKE✪.

NARUTO: THE BROKEN BOND

NEW SASUKE
At The Character Select press Up, Down, Ⓧ, Ⓧ, Ⓧ, Ⓧ, Ⓨ, Ⓑ.

NINE TAILS NARUTO
At the Character Select press Ⓧ, Ⓧ, Ⓧ, Ⓨ, Ⓧ, Ⓨ, Ⓧ, Ⓨ, Ⓧ, Ⓧ.

UCHIHA MADARA
At the Character Select press Ⓧ, Ⓧ, Ⓧ, Ⓨ, Ⓧ, Ⓑ, Ⓑ, Ⓐ, Ⓐ, Ⓨ.

TM

NASCAR 08

ALL CHASE MODE CARS

Select Cheat Codes from the Options menu and enter checkered flag.

EA SPORTS CAR

Select Cheat Codes from the Options menu and enter ea sports car.

FANTASY DRIVERS

Select Cheat Codes from the Options menu and enter race the pack.

WALMART CAR AND TRACK

Select Cheat Codes from the Options menu and enter walmart everyday.

NASCAR 09

ALL FANTASY DRIVERS

Select EA Extras from My Nascar, choose Cheat Codes and enter CHECKERED FLAG.

WALMART TRACK AND THE WALMART CAR

Select EA Extras from My Nascar, choose Cheat Codes and enter Walmart Everyday.

NBA 2K8

2KSPORTS TEAM

Select Codes from the Features menu and enter 2ksports.

VISUAL CONCEPTS TEAM

Select Codes from the Features menu and enter Vcteam.

ABA BALL

Select Codes from the Features menu and enter Payrespect.

NBA 2K9

2K SPORTS TEAM

Select Codes from the Features menu and enter 2ksports.

NBA 2K TEAM

Select Codes from the Features menu and enter nba2k.

2K CHINA TEAM

Select Codes from the Features menu and enter 2kchina.

SUPERSTARS

Select Codes from the Features menu and enter llmohffaae.

VC TEAM

Select Codes from the Features menu and enter vcteam.

ABA BALL

Select Codes from the Features menu and enter payrespect.

2009 ALL-STAR UNIFORMS

Select Codes from the Features menu and enter llaveyfonus.

116

NBA 2K10

ABA BALL
Select Codes from Options and enter payrespect.

2K CHINA TEAM
Select Codes from Options and enter 2kchina.

NBA 2K TEAM
Select Codes from Options and enter nba2k.

2K SPORTS TEAM
Select Codes from Options and enter 2ksports.

VISUAL CONCEPTS TEAM
Select Codes from Options and enter vcteam.

CAVFANATICS JERSEY FOR THE CAVALIERS
Select Codes from the Options menu and enter aifnaatccv.

HARDWOOD CLASSIC JERSEYS
Select Codes from the Options menu and enter wasshcicsl. This code gives Hardwood Classic Jerseys for the Cavaliers, Jazz, Magic, Raptors, timberwolves, Trail Blazers, and Warriors.

LATIN NIGHTS JERSEYS
Select Codes from the Options menu and enter aihinntslgt. This code gives Latin Nights jerseys for Bulls, Heat, Knicks, Lakers, Mavericks, Rockets, Spurs, and Suns.

NBA ALL-STAR JERSEYS
Select Codes from the Options menu and enter otnresla.

NBA GREEN JERSEYS
Select Codes from the Options menu and enter nreogge. This code gives green uniforms for the Bobcats, Bulls, and Nuggets.

MARDI GRAS JERSEY FOR THE HORNETS
Select Codes from the Options menu and enter asrdirmga.

RACING JERSEY FOR THE BOBCATS
Select Codes from the Options menu and enter agsntrccai.

RIP CITY JERSEY FOR THE BLAZERS
Select Codes from the Options menu and enter ycprtii.

SECOND ROAD JERSEYS
Select Codes from the Options menu and enter eydonscar. This code gives Second Road Jerseys for the Grizzlies, Hawks, Mavericks, and Rockets.

ST. PATRICK'S DAY JERSEYS
Select Codes from the Options menu and enter riiasgerh. This code gives St. Patrick's Day jerseys for the Bulls, Celtics, Knicks, and Raptors.

NBA 2K11

MJ: CREATING A LEGEND
In Features, select Codes from the Extras menu. Choose Enter Code and enter icanbe23.

2K CHINA TEAM
In Features, select Codes from the Extras menu. Choose Enter Code and enter 2kchina.

2K SPORTS TEAM
In Features, select Codes from the Extras menu. Choose Enter Code and enter 2Ksports.

NBA 2K TEAM
In Features, select Codes from the Extras menu. Choose Enter Code and enter nba2k.

VC TEAM

In Features, select Codes from the Extras menu. Choose Enter Code and enter vcteam.

ABA BALL

In Features, select Codes from the Extras menu. Choose Enter Code and enter payrespect.

NBA LIVE 09

SUPER DUNKS MODE

Use the Sprite vending machine in the practice area and enter spriteslam.

NBA LIVE 10

CHARLOTTE BOBCATS' 2009/2010 RACE DAY ALTERNATE JERSEYS

Select Options from My NBA Live and go to Select Codes. Enter ceobdabacarstcy.

NEW ORLEANS HORNETS' 2009/2010 MARDI GRAS ALTERNATE JERSEYS

Select Options from My NBA Live and go to Select Codes. Enter nishrag1rosmad0.

ALTERNATE JERSEYS

Select Options from My NBA Live and go to Select Codes. Enter ndnba1rooaesdc0. This unlocks alternate jerseys for Atlanta Hawks, Dallas Mavericks, Houston Rockets, and Memphis Grizzlies.

MORE HARDWOOD CLASSICS NIGHTS JERSEYS

Select Options from My NBA Live and go to Select Codes. Enter hdogdrawhoticns. This unlocks Hardwood Classics Nights jerseys for Cleveland Cavaliers, Golden State Warriors, Minnesota Timberwolves, Orlando Magic, Philadelphia 76ers.

ADIDAS EQUATIONS

Select Options from My NBA Live and go to Select Codes. Enter adaodqauieints1.

ADIDAS TS CREATORS WITH ANKLE BRACES

Select Options from My NBA Live and go to Select Codes. Enter atciadsstsdhecf.

ADIDAS TS SUPERNATURAL COMMANDERS

Select Options from My NBA Live and go to Select Codes. Enter andsicdsmatdnsr.

ADIDAS TS SUPERNATURAL CREATORS

Select Options from My NBA Live and go to Select Codes. Enter ard8siscdnatstr.

AIR MAX LEBRON VII

Select Options from My NBA Live and go to Select Codes. Enter ere1nbvlaoeknii, 2ovnaebnkrielei, 3rioabeneikenvl, ri4boenanekilve, ivl5brieekaeonn, or n6ieirvalkeeobn.

KOBE V

Select Options from My NBA Live and go to Select Codes. Enter ovze1bimenkoko0, m0kveokoiebozn2, eev0nbimokk3ozo, or bmo4inozeeo0kvk.

JORDAN CP3 IIIS

Select Options from My NBA Live and go to Select Codes. Enter iaporcdian3ejis.

JORDAN MELO M6S

Select Options from My NBA Live and go to Select Codes. Enter emlarmeoo6ajdsn.

JORDAN SIXTY PLUSES

Select Options from My NBA Live and go to Select Codes. Enter aondsuilyjrspxt.

NIKE HUARACHE LEGIONS

Select Options from My NBA Live and go to Select Codes. Enter aoieuchrahelgn.

NIKE KD 2S

Select Options from My NBA Live and go to Select Codes. Enter kk2tesaosepinrd.

NIKE ZOOM FLIP'NS

Select Options from My NBA Live and go to Select Codes. Enter epfnozaeminolki.

NBA STREET HOMECOURT

ALL TEAMS
At the Main menu, hold RB + LB and press Left, Right, Left, Right.

ALL COURTS
At the Main menu, hold RB + LB and press Up, Right, Down, Left.

BLACK/RED BALL
At the Main menu, hold RB + LB and press Up, Down, Left, Right.

NEED FOR SPEED CARBON

CASTROL CASH
At the Main menu, press Down, Up, Left, Down, Right, Up, ✗, Ⓑ. This will give you 10,000 extra cash.

INFINITE CREW CHARGE
At the Main menu, press Down, Up, Up, Right, Left, Left, Right, ✗.

INFINITE NITROUS
At the Main menu, press Left, Up, Left, Down, Left, Down, Right, ✗.

INFINITE SPEEDBREAKER
At the Main menu, press Down, Right, Right, Left, Right, Up, Down, ✗.

NEED FOR SPEED CARBON LOGO VINYLS
At the Main menu, press Right, Up, Down, Up, Down, Left, Right, ✗.

NEED FOR SPEED CARBON SPECIAL LOGO VINYLS
At the Main menu, press Up, Up, Down, Down, Down, Down, Up, ✗.

NEED FOR SPEED PROSTREET

$2,000
Select Career and then choose Code Entry. Enter 1MA9X99.

$4,000
Select Career and then choose Code Entry. Enter W2IOLL01.

$8,000
Select Career and then choose Code Entry. Enter L1IS97A1.

$10,000
Select Career and then choose Code Entry. Enter 1MI9K7E1.

$10,000
Select Career and then choose Code Entry. Enter CASHMONEY.

$10,000
Select Career and then choose Code Entry. Enter REGGAME.

AUDI TT
Select Career and then choose Code Entry. Enter ITSABOUTYOU.

CHEVELLE SS
Select Career and then choose Code Entry. Enter HORSEPOWER.

COKE ZERO GOLF GTI
Select Career and then choose Code Entry. Enter COKEZERO.

DODGE VIPER
Select Career and then choose Code Entry. Enter WORLDSLONGESTLASTING.

MITSUBISHI LANCER EVOLUTION
Select Career and then choose Code Entry. Enter MITSUBISHIGOFAR.

UNLOCK ALL BONUSES
Select Career and then choose Code Entry. Enter UNLOCKALLTHINGS.

5 REPAIR MARKERS
Select Career and then choose Code Entry. Enter SAFETYNET.

ENERGIZER VINYL
Select Career and then choose Code Entry. Enter ENERGIZERLITHIUM.

CASTROL SYNTEC VINYL
Select Career and then choose Code Entry. Enter CASTROLSYNTEC. This also gives you $10,000.

NEED FOR SPEED UNDERCOVER

$10,000
Select Secret Codes from the Options menu and enter \$EDSOC.

DIE-CAST BMW M3 E92
Select Secret Codes from the Options menu and enter)B7@B=.

DIE-CAST LEXUS IS F
Select Secret Codes from the Options menu and enter 0;5M2;.

NEEDFORSPEED.COM LOTUS ELISE
Select Secret Codes from the Options menu and enter -KJ3=E.

DIE-CAST NISSAN 240SX (S13)
Select Secret Codes from the Options menu and enter ?P:COL.

DIE-CAST PORSCHE 911 TURBO
Select Secret Codes from the Options menu and enter >8P:I;.

SHELBY TERLINGUA
Select Secret Codes from the Options menu and enter NeedForSpeedShelbyTerlingua.

DIE-CAST VOLKWAGEN R32
Select Secret Codes from the Options menu and enter!2ODBJ:.

NHL 10

THIRD JERSEYS
At the EA Extras screen, enter rwyhafwh6ekyjcmr

NHL 2K8

2007-2008 NHL REEBOK EDGE JERSEYS
From the Features menu, select Unlock 2007-2008/Enter Password. Enter S6j83RMk01.

NHL 2K9

3RD JERSEYS
From the Features menu, enter R6y34bsH52 as a code.

NHL 2K10

THIRD JERSEYS
Select Cheats from the Extras menu and enter G8r23Bty56.

VISUAL CONCEPTS TEAM
Select Cheats from the Extras menu and enter vcteam.

NPPL CHAMPIONSHIP PAINTBALL 2009

TIPPMANN X-7 AK-47 SCENARIO PAINTBALL MARKER
Select Field Gear and press Up, Up, Right, Right, Down, Down, Left, Left.

PRINCE OF PERSIA

SANDS OF TIME PRINCE/FARAH SKINS
Select Skin Manager from the Extras menu. Press Y and enter 52585854. This gives you the Sands of Time skin for the Prince and Farah from Sands of Time for the Princess. Access them from the Skin Manager

PRINCE ALTAIR IBN LA-AHAD SKIN
At the main menu, press Y for Exclusive Content. Create an Ubisoft account. Then select "Altair Skin for Prince" to unlock.

RESONANCE OF FATE

Once you have reached Chapter 7, search Leanne's closet. As she speaks her first line enter the following codes to unlock more outfits.

8-BIT GIRL SHIRT
Up, Up, Down, Down, Left, Right, Left, Right, Y, ✗

CLUB FAMITSU SHIRT
Y, Y, Up, Up, ✗, ✗, Left, Left, LB, RB

GEMAGA SHIRT
Right Trigger, Left Trigger, LB, RB, Y, Y, Y, ✗, ✗, Up

HIRAKOU SHIRT
✗, Y, LB, LB, RB, RB, Click Left Thumbstick, Click Left Thumbstick, Up, Down

PLATFORM LOGO SHIRT
Left, Up, Right, Down, RB, RB, LB, LB, Y, Click Left Thumbstick

POLITAN SUIT
Click Right Thumbstick (x3), Right, Left, Y, ✗, Left Trigger, Right Trigger, LB. This requires you to have the Reindeer Suit first.

ROCKET KNIGHT

ALL CHARACTER SKINS
At the title screen, press Up, Up, Down, Down, Left, Right, Left, Right, A, B, Start.

ROCKSTAR GAMES PRESENTS TABLE TENNIS

Use of the following codes will disable achievements.

SWEATY CHARACTER VIEWER
After loading the map and before accepting the match, press Right Trigger, Up, Down, Left Trigger, Left, Right, Y, ✗, ✗, Y.

SMALL CROWD AUDIO
After loading the map and before accepting the match, press Down, Down, Down, LB, Left Trigger, LB, Left Trigger.

BIG BALL

After loading the map and before accepting the match, press Left, Right, Left, Right, Up, Up, Up, ⊗.

COLORBLIND SPINDICATOR (ONLY IN NEWER PATCH)

After loading the map and before accepting the match, press Up, Down, ⊗, ⊗, Ⓨ, Ⓨ.

SILHOUETTE MODE

After loading the map and before accepting the match, press Up, Down, Ⓨ, Ⓨ, ⒧, Left Trigger, Right Trigger, ⒭.

BIG PADDLES CHEAT (ONLY IN NEWER PATCH)

After loading the map and before accepting the match, press Up, Left, Up, Right, Up, Down, Up, Up, ⊗, ⊗.

UNLOCK ALL

After loading the map and before accepting the match, press Up, Right, Down, Left, ⒧, Right, Up, Left, Down, ⒭.

VINTAGE AUDIO

After loading the map and before accepting the match, press Up, Up, Down, Down, Left, Right, Left, Right, ⒧, ⒭.

BIG CROWD AUDIO

After loading the map and before accepting the match, press Up, Up, Up, ⒭, Right Trigger, ⒭, Right Trigger.

OFFLINE GAMERTAGS

After loading the map and before accepting the match, press ⊗, Ⓨ, ⊗, Ⓨ, ⊗, Ⓨ, Left Trigger, Right Trigger, Down, Down, Down.

SAMURAI SHODOWN 2

PLAY AS KUROKO IN 2-PLAYER

At the character select, press Up, Down, Left, Up, Down, Right + ⊗.

SCOTT PILGRIM VS. THE WORLD: THE GAME

PLAY AS SAME CHARACTER

At the title screen, press Down, ⒭, Up, ⒧, Ⓨ, Ⓑ.

HEART SWORD

At the title screen, press ⊗, ⊗, ⊗, Ⓐ, Ⓑ, Ⓐ, Ⓨ, Ⓨ.

BLOOD MODE

At the title screen, press Ⓐ, Ⓑ, Ⓐ, ⊗, Ⓐ, Ⓑ, Ⓑ.

BOSS RUSH MODE

Pause the game on the overworld and press Right, Right, Ⓑ, ⒭, Right, Right, Ⓑ, ⒭.

ZOMBIE MODE

At the title screen, press Down, Up, Right, Down, Up, Right, Down, Up, Right, Right, Right.

SOUND CHECK BONUS LEVEL

Pause the game on the overworld and press ⒧, ⒧, ⒧, ⒭, ⒭, ⒭, ⒧, ⒭.

CHANGE MONEY TO ANIMALS

At the title screen, press Up, Up, Down, Down, Up, Up, Up, Up.

SEGA SUPERSTARS TENNIS

UNLOCK CHARACTERS
Complete the following missions to unlock the corresponding character.

CHARACTER	MISSION TO COMPLETE
Alex Kidd	Mission 1 of Alex Kidd's World
Amy Rose	Mission 2 of Sonic the Hedgehog's World
Gilius	Mission 1 of Golden Axe's World
Gum	Mission 12 of Jet Grind Radio's World
Meemee	Mission 8 of Super Monkey Ball's World
Pudding	Mission 1 of Space Channel 5's World
Reala	Mission 2 of NiGHTs' World
Shadow The Hedgehog	Mission 14 of Sonic the Hedgehog's World

SHREK THE THIRD

10,000 GOLD COINS
At the gift shop, press Up, Up, Down, Up, Right, Left.

THE SIMPSONS GAME

After unlocking the following, the outfits can be changed at the downstairs closet in the Simpson's house. The Trophies can be viewed at different locations in the house: Bart's room, Lisa's room, Marge's room, and the garage.

BART'S OUTFITS AND TROPHIES (POSTER COLLECTION)
At the main menu, press Right, Left, ✗, ✗, Y, Right Thumb Stick.

HOMER'S OUTFITS AND TROPHIES (BEER BOTTLE COLLECTION)
At the main menu, press Left, Right, Y, Y, ✗, Left Thumb Stick.

LISA'S OUTFITS AND TROPHIES (DOLLS)
At the main menu, press ✗, Y, ✗, ✗, Y, Left Thumb Stick.

MARGE'S OUTFITS AND TROPHIES (HAIR PRODUCTS)
At the main menu, press Y, ✗, Y, Y, ✗, Right Thumb Stick.

THE SIMS 3

CHEATS
Load your family, press Start, and hold ▣ + Left Trigger + ▣ + Right Trigger. The game prompts you to save another file before activating the cheats. Spoot the Llama is now available in Misc Décor. Place it in your lot and click it to access the cheats. This disables Achievements and challenges.

SKATE 2

BIG BLACK
Select Enter Cheat from the Extras menu and enter letsdowork.

3D MODE
Select Enter Cheat from the Extras menu and enter strangeloops. Use glasses to view in 3D.

SKATE 3

HOVERBOARD MODE
In Free Play, select Extras from the Options. Choose Enter Cheat Code and enter mcfly.

MINI SKATER MODE
In Free Play, select Extras from the Options. Choose Enter Cheat Code and enter miniskaters.

ZOMBIE MODE
In Free Play, select Extras from the Options. Choose Enter Cheat Code and enter zombie.

ISAAC CLARK FROM DEADSPACE
In Free Play, select Extras from the Options. Choose Enter Cheat Code and enter deadspacetoo.

DEM BONES
Beat most of the Hall of Meat Challenges.

MEAT MAN
Beat all Hall of Meat Challenges.

RESETS OBJECTS TO ORIGINAL POSITIONS
In Free Play, select Extras from the Options. Choose Enter Cheat Code and enter streetsweeper.

SONIC THE HEDGEHOG 4: EPISODE I

AVATAR AWARDS

AWARD	EARNED BY
Sonic Costume (Body)	After collecting the 7 Chaos Emeralds, defeat the final boss 1 more time
Sonic Costume (Head)	Collect all rings during ending after the final stage.

SOULCASTER

PASSWORD
Select Continue and enter JUSTIN BAILEY ------ ------ as a password. This starts you midway through the game, on hard difficulty, with plenty of money. This password is a reference to a password from Metroid.

SPIDER-MAN: FRIEND OR FOE

NEW GREEN GOBLIN AS A SIDEKICK
While standing in the Helicarrier between levels, press Left, Down, Right, Right, Down, Left.

SANDMAN AS A SIDEKICK
While standing in the Helicarrier between levels, press Right, Right, Right, Up, Down, Left.

VENOM AS A SIDEKICK
While standing in the Helicarrier between levels, press Left, Left, Right, Up, Down, Down.

5000 TECH TOKENS
While standing in the Helicarrier between levels, press Up, Up, Down, Down, Left, Right.

SPIDER-MAN: SHATTERED DIMENSIONS

The following can be entered after completing the tutorial.

IRON SPIDER SUIT

At the main menu, press Up, Right, Right, Right, Left, Left, Left, Down, Up.

NEGATIVE ZONE SUIT

At the main menu, press Left, Right, Right, Down, Right, Down, Up, Left.

SCARLET SPIDER SUIT

At the main menu, press Right, Up, Left, Right, Up, Left, Right, Up, Left, Right.

SPLIT/SECOND

HANZO FX350 CX (COMPUTER SPIELE) IN QUICK PLAY

At the Options menu, press ❌, Up, ❌, Up, ❌, Up.

RYBACK COYOTE AMX IN QUICK PLAY

At the Options menu, press Left, ❌, Left, ❌, Left, ❌, Left, ❌, Left, ❌, Right.

RYBACK MOHAWK XDX (DISNEY XD) IN QUICK PLAY

At the Options menu, press ❌, Down, ❌, Down, ❌, Down.

STAR WARS THE CLONE WARS: REPUBLIC HEROES

BIG HEAD MODE

Pause the game, select Shop, and enter Up, Down, Left, Right, Left, Right, Down, Up in Cheats.

MINI-GUN

Pause the game, select Shop, and enter Down, Left, Right, Up, Right, Up, Left, Down in Cheats.

ULTIMATE LIGHTSABER

Pause the game, select Shop, and enter Right, Down, Down, Up, Left, Up, Up, Down in Cheats.

LIGHTSABER THROW UPGRADE

Pause the game, select Shop, and enter Left, Left, Right, Right, Up, Down, Down, Up in Combat Upgrades.

SPIDER DROID UPGRADE

Pause the game, select Shop, and enter Up, Left, Down, Left, Right, Left, Left, Left in Droid-Jak Upgrades.

STAR WARS: THE FORCE UNLEASHED

CHEAT CODES

Pause the game and select Input Code. Here you can enter the following codes. Activating any of the following cheat codes will disable some unlockables, and you will be unable to save your progress.

CHEAT	CODE
All Force Powers at Max Power	KATARN
All Force Push Ranks	EXARKUN
All Saber Throw Ranks	ADEGAN
All Repulse Ranks	DATHOMIR

CHEAT	CODE
All Saber Crystals	HURRIKANE
All Talents	JOCASTA
Deadly Saber	LIGHTSABER

COMBOS

Pause the game and select Input Code. Here you can enter the following codes. Activating any of the following cheat codes will disable some unlockables, and you will be unable to save your progress.

COMBO	CODE
All Combos	MOLDYCROW
Aerial Ambush	VENTRESS
Aerial Assault	EETHKOTH
Aerial Blast	YADDLE
Impale	BRUTALSTAB
Lightning Bomb	MASSASSI
Lightning Grenade	RAGNOS

COMBO	CODE
Saber Slam	PLOKOON
Saber Sling	KITFISTO
Sith Saber Flurry	LUMIYA
Sith Slash	DARAGON
Sith Throw	SAZEN
New Combo	FREEDON
New Combo	MARAJADE

ALL DATABANK ENTRIES

Pause the game and select Input Code. Enter OSSUS.

MIRRORED LEVEL

Pause the game and select Input Code. Enter MINDTRICK. Re-enter the code to return level to normal.

SITH MASTER DIFFICULTY

Pause the game and select Input Code. Enter SITHSPAWN.

COSTUMES

Pause the game and select Input Code. Here you can enter the following codes.

COSTUME	CODE
All Costumes	SOHNDANN
Bail Organa	VICEROY
Ceremonial Jedi Robes	DANTOOINE
Drunken Kota	HARDBOILED
Emperor	MASTERMIND
Incinerator Trooper	PHOENIX
Jedi Adventure Robe	HOLOCRON
Kashyyyk Trooper	TK421GREEN
Kota	MANDALORE

COSTUME	CODE
Master Kento	WOOKIEE
Proxy	PROTOTYPE
Scout Trooper	FERRAL
Shadow Trooper	BLACKHOLE
Sith Stalker Armor	KORRIBAN
Snowtrooper	SNOWMAN
Stormtrooper	TK421WHITE
Stormtrooper Commander	TK421BLUE

STAR WARS: THE FORCE UNLEASHED II

BOBA FETT COSTUME
Pause the game, select Cheat Codes from the Options, and enter MANDALORE.

DARK APPRENTICE COSTUME
Pause the game, select Cheat Codes from the Options, and enter VENTRESS.

GENERAL KOTA COSTUME
Pause the game, select Cheat Codes from the Options, and enter RAHM.

NEIMOIDIAN COSTUME
Pause the game, select Cheat Codes from the Options, and enter GUNRAY.

REBEL COMMANDO COSTUME
Pause the game, select Cheat Codes from the Options, and enter SPECFORCE.

REBEL SOLDIER COSTUME
Pause the game, select Cheat Codes from the Options, and enter REBELSCUM.

SABER GUARD COSTUME
Pause the game, select Cheat Codes from the Options, and enter MORGUKAI.

SITH ACOLYTE COSTUME
Pause the game, select Cheat Codes from the Options, and enter HAAZEN.

STORMTROOPER COSTUME
Pause the game, select Cheat Codes from the Options, and enter TK421.

TERROR TROOPER COSTUME
Pause the game, select Cheat Codes from the Options, and enter SHADOW.

TRAINING DROID COSTUME
Pause the game, select Cheat Codes from the Options, and enter HOLODROID.

REPULSE FORCE POWER
Pause the game, select Cheat Codes from the Options, and enter MAREK.

SABRE THROW
Pause the game, select Cheat Codes from the Options, and enter TRAYA.

WISDOM LIGHTSABER CRYSTALS
Pause the game, select Cheat Codes from the Options, and enter SOLARI.

TRAINING GEAR
Have a save game from Star Wars: The Force Unleashed.

CEREMONIAL ROBES
Have a save game from Star Wars: The Force Unleashed with the Light Side ending.

SITH STALKER ARMOR
Have a save game from Star Wars: The Force Unleashed with the Dark Side ending.

STUNTMAN IGNITION

3 PROPS IN STUNT CREATOR MODE
Select Cheats from Extras and enter COOLPROP.

ALL ITEMS UNLOCKED FOR CONSTRUCTION MODE
Select Cheats from Extras and enter NOBLEMAN.

MVX SPARTAN
Select Cheats from Extras and enter fastride.

ALL CHEATS
Select Cheats from Extras and enter Wearefrozen. This unlocks the following cheats: Slo-mo Cool, Thrill Cam, Vision Switcher, Nitro Addiction, Freaky Fast, and Ice Wheels.

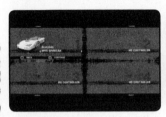 

ALL CHEATS
Select Cheats from Extras and enter Kungfoopete.

ICE WHEELS CHEAT
Select Cheats from Extras and enter IceAge.

NITRO ADDICTION CHEAT
Select Cheats from Extras and enter TheDuke.

VISION SWITCHER CHEAT
Select Cheats from Extras and enter GFXMODES.

SUPER CONTRA

UNLIMITED LIVES AND SUPER MACHINEGUN
At the Main menu, select Arcade Game, and then press Up, Up, Down, Down, Left, Right, Left, Right, **B**, **A**. Achievements and the Leaderboard are disabled with this code.

SUPER STREET FIGHTER IV

BARREL BUSTER AND CAR CRUSHER BONUS STAGES
Beat Arcade Mode in any difficulty

COLORS AND TAUNTS
Colors 1 and 2 plus the first taunt for each fighter are available from the start. For colors 11 & 12, start a game with a Street Fighter IV save game on your system. To earn the rest of the colors and taunts, you need to fight a certain number of matches with that character.

COLOR	# OF MATCHES
3	2
4	4
5	6
6	8
7	10
8	12
9	14
10	16

TAUNT	# OF MATCHES
2	1
3	3
4	5
5	7
6	9
7	11
8	13
9	15
10	16

SUPER PUZZLE FIGHTER II TURBO HD REMIX

PLAY AS AKUMA
At the Character Select screen, highlight Hsien-Ko and press Down.

PLAY AS DAN
At the Character Select screen, highlight Donovan and press Down.

PLAY AS DEVILOT
At the Character Select screen, highlight Morrigan and press Down.

PLAY AS ANITA
At the Character Select screen, hold **LB** + **RB** and choose Donovan.

PLAY AS HSIEN-KO'S TALISMAN
At the Character Select screen, hold **LB** + **RB** and choose Hsien-Ko.

PLAY AS MORRIGAN AS A BAT
At the Character Select screen, hold **LB** + **RB** and choose Morrigan.

SUPERMAN RETURNS: THE VIDEOGAME

GOD MODE
Pause the game, select Options and press Up, Up, Down, Down, Left, Right, Left, Right, **Y**, **X**.

INFINITE CITY HEALTH
Pause the game, select Options and press **Y**, Right, **Y**, Right, Up, Left, Right, **Y**.

ALL POWER-UPS
Pause the game, select Options and press Left, **Y**, Right, **X**, Down, **Y**, Up, Down, **X**, **Y**, **X**.

ALL UNLOCKABLES
Pause the game, select Options and press Left, Up, Right, Down, **Y**, **X**, **Y** Up, Right, **X**.

FREE ROAM AS BIZARRO
Pause the game, select Options and press Up, Right, Down, Right, Up, Left, Down, Right, Up.

THRILLVILLE: OFF THE RAILS

$50,000
While in a park, press **X**, **B**, **Y**, **X**, **B**, **Y**, **A**.

500 THRILL POINTS
While in a park, press **B**, **X**, **Y**, **B**, **X**, **Y**, **X**.

ALL PARKS
While in a park, press **X**, **B**, **Y**, **X**, **B**, **Y**, **X**.

ALL RIDES IN CURRENT PARK
While in a park, press **X**, **B**, **Y**, **X**, **B**, **Y**, **Y**.

MISSION UNLOCK
While in a park, press **X**, **B**, **Y**, **X**, **B**, **Y**, **B**.

ALL MINI-GAMES IN PARTY PLAY
While in a park, press **X**, **B**, **Y**, **X**, **B**, **Y**, Right.

X 360™

TIGER WOODS PGA TOUR 08

ALL COURSES
Select Password from EA Sports Extras and enter greensfees.

ALL GOLFERS
Select Password from EA Sports Extras and enter allstars.

WAYNE ROONEY
Select Password from EA Sports Extras and enter playfifa08.

INFINITE MONEY
Select Password from EA Sports Extras and enter cream.

TIGER WOODS PGA TOUR 09

SPECTATORS BIG HEAD MODE
Select EA SPORTS Extras from My Tiger '09, choose Password and enter cephalus.

TMNT

CHALLENGE MAP 2
At the Main menu, hold the **LB** and press **A**, **A**, **B**, **A**.

DON'S BIG HEAD GOODIE
At the Main menu, hold the **LB** and press **B**, **Y**, **A**, **X**.

TOMB RAIDER: LEGEND

The following codes must be unlocked in the game before using them.

BULLETPROOF
During a game, hold Left Trigger and press Ⓐ, Right Trigger, Ⓨ, Right Trigger, Ⓧ, ⓛⒷ.

DRAIN ENEMY HEALTH
During a game, hold Left Trigger and press Ⓧ, Ⓑ, Ⓐ, ⓛⒷ, Right Trigger, Ⓨ.

INFINITE ASSAULT RIFLE AMMO
During a game, hold ⓛⒷ and press Ⓐ, Ⓑ, Ⓐ, Left Trigger, Ⓧ, Ⓨ.

INFINITE GRENADE LAUNCHER AMMO
During a game, hold ⓛⒷ and press Left Trigger, Ⓨ, Right Trigger, Ⓑ, Left Trigger, Ⓧ

INFINITE SHOTGUN AMMO
During a game, hold ⓛⒷ and press Right Trigger, Ⓑ, Ⓧ, Left Trigger, Ⓧ, Ⓐ.

INFINITE SMG AMMO
During a game, hold ⓛⒷ and press Ⓑ, Ⓨ, Left Trigger, Right Trigger, Ⓐ, Ⓑ.

EXCALIBUR
During a game, hold ⓛⒷ and press Ⓨ, Ⓐ, Ⓑ, Right Trigger, Ⓨ, Left Trigger.

SOUL REAVER
During a game, hold ⓛⒷ and press Ⓐ, Right Trigger, Ⓑ, Right Trigger, Left Trigger, Ⓧ.

ONE-SHOT KILL
During a game, hold Left Trigger and press Ⓨ, Ⓐ, Ⓨ, Ⓧ, ⓛⒷ, Ⓑ.

TEXTURELESS MODE
During a game, hold Left Trigger and press ⓛⒷ, Ⓐ, Ⓑ, Ⓐ, Ⓨ, Right Trigger.

TOM CLANCY'S GHOST RECON ADVANCED WARFIGHTER

ALL MISSIONS
At the Mission Select screen, hold Back + Left Trigger + Right Trigger and press Ⓨ, ⓡⒷ, Ⓨ, ⓡⒷ, Ⓧ.

FULL HEALTH
Pause the game, hold Back + Left Trigger + Right Trigger and press ⓛⒷ, ⓛⒷ, ⓡⒷ, Ⓧ, ⓡⒷ, Ⓨ.

INVINCIBLE
Pause the game, hold Back + Left Trigger + Right Trigger and press Ⓨ, Ⓨ, Ⓧ, ⓡⒷ, Ⓧ, ⓛⒷ.

TEAM INVINCIBLE
Pause the game, hold Back + Left Trigger + Right Trigger and press Ⓧ, Ⓧ, Ⓨ, ⓡⒷ, Ⓨ, ⓛⒷ.

UNLIMITED AMMO
Pause the game, hold Back + Left Trigger + Right Trigger and press ⓡⒷ, ⓡⒷ, ⓛⒷ, Ⓧ, ⓛⒷ, Ⓨ.

TOM CLANCY'S HAWX

A-12 AVENGER II

At the hangar, hold Left Trigger and press ⊗, LB, ⊗, RB, Y, ⊗.

F-18 HARV

At the hangar, hold Left Trigger and press LB, Y, LB, Y, LB, ⊗.

FB-22 STRIKE RAPTOR

At the hangar, hold Left Trigger and press RB, ⊗, RB, ⊗, RB, Y.

TONY HAWK RIDE

RYAN SHECKLER

Select Cheats from the Options menu and enter SHECKLERSIG.

QUICKSILVER 80'S LEVEL

Select Cheats from the Options menu and enter FEELINGEIGHTIES.

TONY HAWK'S PROJECT 8

SPONSOR ITEMS

As you progress through Career mode and move up the rankings, you gain sponsors and each comes with its own Create-a-skater item.

RANK REQUIRED	CAS ITEM UNLOCKED
Rank 040	Adio Kenny V2 Shoes
Rank 050	Quiksilver Hoody 3
Rank 060	Birdhouse Tony Hawk Deck
Rank 080	Vans No Skool Gothic Shoes
Rank 100	Volcom Scallero Jacket
Rank 110	eS Square One Shoes
Rank 120	Almost Watch What You Say Deck
Rank 140	DVS Adage Shoe
Rank 150	Element Illuminate Deck
Rank 160	Etnies Sheckler White Lavender Shoes
Complete Skateshop Goal	Stereo Soundwave Deck

SKATERS

All of the skaters, except for Tony Hawk, must be unlocked by completing challenges in the Career Mode. They are useable in Free Skate and 2 Player modes.

SKATER	HOW THEY ARE UNLOCKED
Tony Hawk	Always Unloc0ked
Lyn-z Adams Hawkins	Complete Pro Challenge
Bob Burquist	Complete Pro Challenge
Dustin Dollin	Complete Pro Challenge
Nyjah Huston	Complete Pro Challenge
Bam Margera	Complete Pro Challenge
Rodney Mullen	Complete Pro Challenge
Paul Rodriguez	Complete Pro Challenge
Ryan Sheckler	Complete Pro Challenge
Daewon Song	Complete Pro Challenge
Mike Vallely	Complete Pro Challenge
Stevie Willams	Complete Pro Challenge
Travis Barker	Complete Pro Challenge
Kevin Staab	Complete Pro Challenge
Zombie	Complete Pro Challenge
Christaian Hosoi	Rank #1
Jason Lee	Complete Final Tony Hawk Goal
Photographer	Unlock Shops

SKATER	HOW THEY ARE UNLOCKED
Security Guard	Unlock School
Bum	Unlock Car Factory
Beaver Mascot	Unlock High School
Real Estate Agent	Unlock Downtown
Filmer	Unlock High School
Skate Jam Kid	Rank #4
Dad	Rank #1
Colonel	All Gaps
Nerd	Complete School Spirit Goal

CHEAT CODES

Select Cheat Codes from the Options and enter the following codes. In game you can access some codes from the Options menu.

CHEAT CODE	RESULTS
plus44	Unlocks Travis Barker
hohohosoi	Unlocks Christian Hosoi
notmono	Unlocks Jason Lee
mixitup	Unlocks Kevin Staab
strangefellows	Unlocks Dad & Skater Jam Kid
themedia	Unlocks Photog Girl & Filmer
militarymen	Unlocks Colonel & Security Guard
jammypack	Unlocks Always Special
balancegalore	Unlocks Perfect Rail
frontandback	Unlocks Perect Manual
shellshock	Unlocks Unlimited Focus
shescaresme	Unlocks Big Realtor
birdhouse	Unlocks Inkblot deck
allthebest	Full Stats
needaride	All Decks unlocked and free, except for inkblot deck and gamestop deck
yougotitall	All specials unlocked and in player's special list and set as owned in skate shop
wearelosers	Unlocks Nerd and a Bum
manineedadate	Unlocks Beaver Mascot
suckstobedead	Unlocks Officer Dick
HATEDANDPROUD	Unlocks the Vans unlockable item

TONY HAWK'S PROVING GROUND

Select Cheat Codes from the Options and enter the following cheats. Some codes need to be enabled by selecting Cheats from the Options during a game.

UNLOCK	CHEAT
Unlocks Boneman	CRAZYBONEMAN
Unlocks Bosco	MOREMILK
Unlocks Cam	NOTACAMERA
Unlocks Cooper	THECOOP
Unlocks Eddie X	SKETCHY
Unlocks El Patinador	PILEDRIVER
Unlocks Eric	FLYAWAY
Unlocks Mad Dog	RABBIES
Unlocks MCA	INTERGALACTIC
Unlocks Mel	NOTADUDE
Unlocks Rube	LOOKSSMELLY
Unlocks Spence	DAPPER
Unlocks Shayne	MOVERS
Unlocks TV Producer	SHAKER
Unlock FDR	THEPREZPARK
Unlock Lansdowne	THELOCALPARK
Unlock Air & Space Museum	THEINDOORPARK

UNLOCK	CHEAT
Unlocks all Fun Items	OVERTHETOP
Unlocks all CAS items	GIVEMESTUFF
Unlocks all Decks	LETSGOSKATE
Unlock all Game Movies	WATCHTHIS
Unlock all Lounge Bling Items	SWEETSTUFF
Unlock all Lounge Themes	LAIDBACKLOUNGE
Unlock all Rigger Pieces	IMGONNABUILD
Unlock all Video Editor Effects	TRIPPY
Unlock all Video Editor Overlays	PUTEMONTOP
All specials unlocked and in player's special list	LOTSOFTRICKS
Full Stats	BEEFEDUP
Give player +50 skill points	NEEDSHELP

The following cheats lock you out of the Leaderboards:

UNLOCK	CHEAT
Unlocks Perfect Manual	STILLAINTFALLIN
Unlocks Perfect Rail	AINTFALLIN
Unlock Super Check	BOOYAH
Unlocks Unlimited Focus	MYOPIC
Unlock Unlimited Slash Grind	SUPERSLASHIN
Unlocks 100% branch completion in NTT	FOREVERNAILED
No Bails	ANDAINTFALLIN

You can not use the Video Editor with the following cheats:

UNLOCK	CHEAT
Invisible Man	THEMISSING
Mini Skater	TINYTATER
No Board	MAGICMAN

TRANSFORMERS: THE GAME

The following cheats disable saving and achievements:

INFINITE HEALTH
At the Main menu, press Left, Left, Up, Left, Right, Down, Right.

INFINITE AMMO
At the Main menu, press Up, Down, Left, Right, Up, Up, Down.

NO MILITARY OR POLICE
At the Main menu, press Right, Left, Right, Left, Right, Left, Right.

ALL MISSIONS
At the Main menu, press Down, Up, Left, Right, Right, Right, Up, Down.

BONUS CYBERTRON MISSIONS
At the Main menu, press Right, Up, Up, Down, Right, Left, Left.

GENERATION 1 SKIN: JAZZ
At the Main menu, press Left, Up, Down, Down, Left, Up, Right.

GENERATION 1 SKIN: MEGATRON
At the Main menu, press Down, Left, Left, Down, Right, Right, Up.

GENERATION 1 SKIN: OPTIMUS PRIME
At the Main menu, press Down, Right, Left, Up, Down, Down, Left.

GENERATION 1 SKIN: ROBOVISION OPTIMUS PRIME
At the Main menu, press Down, Down, Up, Up, Right, Right, Right.

GENERATION 1 SKIN: STARSCREAM
At the Main menu, press Right, Down, Left, Left, Down, Up, Up.

TRANSFORMERS REVENGE OF THE FALLEN

LOW GRAVITY MODE
Select Cheat Code and enter Ⓐ, Ⓧ, Ⓨ, ⓔ, Ⓨ, ⓔ.

NO WEAPON OVERHEAT
Select Cheat Code and enter ⓔ, Ⓧ, Ⓐ, ⓔ, Ⓨ, ⓛⒷ.

ALWAYS IN OVERDRIVE MODE
Select Cheat Code and enter ⓛⒷ, Ⓑ, ⓛⒷ, Ⓐ, Ⓧ, ⓡ.

UNLIMITED TURBO
Select Cheat Code and enter Ⓑ, ⓔ, Ⓧ, ⓡ, Ⓐ, Ⓨ.

NO SPECIAL COOLDOWN TIME
Select Cheat Code and enter ⓡ, Ⓧ, ⓡ, ⓡ, Ⓧ, Ⓐ.

INVINCIBILITY
Select Cheat Code and enter ⓡ, Ⓐ, Ⓧ, ⓔ, Ⓧ, Ⓧ.

4X ENERGON FROM DEFEATED ENEMIES
Select Cheat Code and enter Ⓨ, Ⓧ, Ⓑ, ⓡ, Ⓐ, Ⓨ.

INCREASED WEAPON DAMAGE IN ROBOT FORM
Select Cheat Code and enter Ⓨ, Ⓨ, ⓡ, Ⓐ, ⓛⒷ, Ⓨ.

INCREASED WEAPON DAMAGE IN VEHICLE FORM
Select Cheat Code and enter Ⓨ, Ⓑ, ⓡⒷ, Ⓧ, ⓡ, ⓔ.

MELEE INSTANT KILLS
Select Cheat Code and enter ⓡ, Ⓐ, ⓛⒷ, Ⓑ, ⓡ, ⓛⒷ.

LOWER ENEMY ACCURACY
Select Cheat Code and enter Ⓧ, ⓔ, ⓡ, ⓔ, ⓡ, ⓡⒷ.

INCREASED ENEMY HEALTH
Select Cheat Code and enter Ⓑ, Ⓧ, ⓛⒷ, Ⓑ, ⓡ, Ⓨ.

INCREASED ENEMY DAMAGE
Select Cheat Code and enter ⓛⒷ, Ⓨ, Ⓐ, Ⓨ, ⓡ, ⓡ.

INCREASED ENEMY ACCURACY
Select Cheat Code and enter Ⓨ, Ⓨ, Ⓑ, Ⓐ, Ⓧ, ⓛⒷ.

SPECIAL KILLS ONLY MODE
Select Cheat Code and enter Ⓑ, Ⓑ, ⓡⒷ, Ⓑ, Ⓐ, ⓔ.

UNLOCK ALL SHANGHAI MISSIONS AND ZONES
Select Cheat Code and enter Ⓨ, ⓔ, ⓡ, ⓛⒷ, Ⓨ, Ⓐ.

UNLOCK ALL WEST COAST MISSIONS AND ZONES
Select Cheat Code and enter ⓛⒷ, ⓡⒷ, ⓡ, Ⓨ, ⓡ, Ⓑ.

UNLOCK ALL DEEP SIX MISSIONS AND ZONES
Select Cheat Code and enter Ⓧ, ⓡⒷ, Ⓨ, Ⓑ, Ⓐ, ⓛⒷ.

UNLOCK ALL EAST COAST MISSIONS AND ZONES
Select Cheat Code and enter ⓡ, ⓔ, ⓡⒷ, Ⓐ, Ⓑ, Ⓧ.

UNLOCK ALL CAIRO MISSIONS AND ZONES
Select Cheat Code and enter ⓡ, Ⓨ, Ⓐ, Ⓨ, ⓔ, ⓛⒷ.

UNLOCK AND ACTIVATE ALL UPGRADES
Select Cheat Code and enter ⓛⒷ, Ⓨ, ⓛⒷ, Ⓑ, Ⓧ, Ⓧ.

TROPICO 3

CHEAT MENU
During a game, click the Left Thumbstick and Right Thumbstick and hold them down. Add Back + Start to open the cheat menu. Activating any cheats disables achievements.

VIRTUA TENNIS 3

KING & DUKE
At the Main menu, press Up, Up, Down, Down, Left, Right, Left, Left, LB, RB.

ALL GEAR
At the Main menu, press Left, Right, Ⓑ, Left, Right, Ⓑ, Up, Down.

ALL COURTS
At the Main menu, press Up, Up, Down, Down, Left, Right, Left, Right.

WIN ONE MATCH TO WIN TOURNAMENT
At the Main menu, press Ⓑ, Left, Ⓑ, Right, Ⓑ, Up, Ⓑ, Down.

VIVA PINATA

NEW ITEMS IN PET STORE
Select New Garden and enter chewnicorn as the name.

NEW ITEMS IN PET STORE
Select New Garden and enter bullseye as the name.

NEW ITEMS IN PET STORE
Select New Garden and enter goobaa as the name.

NEW ITEMS IN PET STORE
Select New Garden and enter kittyfloss as the name.

VIVA PINATA: PARTY ANIMALS

CLASSIC GAMER AWARD ACHIEVEMENT
At the START screen, press Up, Up, Down, Down, Left, Right, Left, Right, Ⓑ, Ⓐ. This earns you 10 points toward your Gamerscore.

VIVA PINATA: TROUBLE IN PARADISE

CREDITS
Select Play Garden and name your garden Piñata People. This unlocks the ability to view the credits on the main menu.

WORLD OF OUTLAWS: SPRINT CARS

$5,000,000
Enter your name as CHICMCHIM.

ALL DRIVERS
Enter your name as MITYMASTA.

ALL TRACKS
Enter your name as JOEYJOEJOE.

WWE SMACKDOWN! VS. RAW 2008

HBK AND HHH'S DX OUTFIT
Select Cheat Codes from the Options and enter DXCostume69K2.

KELLY KELLY'S ALTERNATE OUTFIT
Select Cheat Codes from the Options and enter KellyKG12R.

BRET HART
Complete the March 31, 1996 Hall of Fame challenge by defeating Bret Hart with Shawn Michaels in a One-On-One 30-Minute Iron Man Match on Legend difficulty. Purchase from WWE Shop for $210,000.

MICK FOLEY
Complete the June 28, 1998 Hall of Fame challenge by defeating Mick Foley with The Undertaker in a H*** In a Cell Match on Legend difficulty. Purchase from WWE Shop for $210,000.

MR. MCMAHON
Win or successfully defend a championship (WWE or World Heavyweight) at WrestleMania in WWE 24/7 GM Mode. Purchase from WWE Shop for $110,000.

THE ROCK
Complete the April 1, 2001 Hall of Fame challenge by defeating The Rock with Steve Austin in a Single Match on Legend Difficulty. Purchase from WWE Shop for $210,000.

STEVE AUSTIN
Complete the March 23, 1997 Hall of Fame challenge by defeating Steve Austin with Bret Hart in a Submission Match on Legend Difficulty. Purchase from WWE Shop for $210,000.

TERRY FUNK
Complete the April 13, 1997 Hall of Fame challenge by defeating Tommy Dreamer, Sabu and Sandman with any Superstar in an ECW Extreme Rules 4-Way Match on Legend difficulty. Purchase from WWE Shop for $210,000.

MR. MCMAHON BALD
Must unlock Mr. McMahon as a playable character first. Purchase from WWE Shop for $60,000.

WWE SMACKDOWN VS. RAW 2009

BOOGEYMAN
Select Cheat Codes from My WWE and enter BoogeymanEatsWorms!!.

GENE SNITSKY
Select Cheat Codes from My WWE and enter UnlockSnitskySvR2009.

HAWKINS & RYDER
Select Cheat Codes from My WWE and enter Ryder&HawkinsTagTeam.

JILLIAN HALL
Select Cheat Codes from My WWE and enter PlayAsJillianHallSvR.

LAYLA
Select Cheat Codes from My WWE and enter UnlockECWDivaLayla09.

RIC FLAIR
Select Cheat Codes from My WWE and enter FlairWooooooooooooooo.

TAZZ
Select Cheat Codes from My WWE and enter UnlockECWTazzSvR2009.

VINCENT MCMAHON
Select Cheat Codes from My WWE and enter VinceMcMahonNoChance.

HORNSWOGGLE AS MANAGER
Select Cheat Codes from My WWE and enter HornswoggleAsManager.

CHRIS JERICHO COSTUME B
Select Cheat Codes from My WWE and enter AltJerichoModelSvR09.

CM PUNK COSTUME B
Select Cheat Codes from My WWE and enter CMPunkAltCostumeSvR!.

REY MYSTERIO COSTUME B
Select Cheat Codes from My WWE and enter BooyakaBooyaka619SvR.

SATURDAY NIGHT'S MAIN EVENT ARENA
Select Cheat Codes from My WWE and enter SatNightMainEventSvR.

WWE SMACKDOWN VS. RAW 2010

THE ROCK
Select Cheat Codes from the Options menu and enter The Great One.

DIRT SHEET BRAWL AND OFFICE STAGE BRAWL
Select Cheat Codes from the Options menu and enter BonusBrawl.

JOHN CENA'S NEW COSTUME
Select Cheat Codes from the Options menu and enter CENATION.

RANDY ORTON'S NEW COSTUME
Select Cheat Codes from the Options menu and enter ViperRKO.

SANTINO MARELLA'S NEW COSTUME
Select Cheat Codes from the Options menu and enter Milan Miracle.

SHAWN MICHAELS' NEW COSTUME
Select Cheat Codes from the Options menu and enter Bow Down.

TRIPLE H'S NEW COSTUME
Select Cheat Codes from the Options menu and enter Suck IT!.

WWE SMACKDOWN VS. RAW 2011

JOHN CENA (ENTRANCE/CIVILIAN)
In My WWE, select Cheat Codes from the Options and enter SLURPEE.

ALL OF RANDY ORTON'S COSTUMES
In My WWE, select Cheat Codes from the Options and enter apexpredator.

TRIBUTE TO THE TROOPS ARENA
In My WWE, select Cheat Codes from the Options and enter 8thannualtribute.

PLAYSTATION® 2

CONTENTS

ASTRO BOY: THE VIDEO GAME

INVULNERABLE
Pause the game and press Up, Down, Down, Up, **L1**, **R1**.

MAX STATS
Pause the game and press Left, Left, **R1**, Down, Down, **L1**.

INFINITE SUPERS
Pause the game and press Left, **L1**, Right, **L1**, Up, Down.

INFINITE DASHES
Pause the game and press **R1**, **R1**, **L1**, **R1**, Left, Up.

DISABLE SUPERS
Pause the game and press **L1**, **L1**, **R1**, **R1**, **L1**, Left.

COSTUME SWAP (ARENA AND CLASSIC COSTUMES)
Pause the game and press **R1**, Up, **L1**, Up, Down, **R1**.

UNLOCK LEVELS
Pause the game and press Up, **L1**, Right, **L1**, Down, **L1**. This allows you to travel to any level from the Story menu.

AVATAR: THE LAST AIRBENDER-THE BURNING EARTH

1 HIT DISHONOR
At the Main menu, press **L1** and select Code Entry. Enter 28260.

ALL BONUS GAME
At the Main menu, press **L1** and select Code Entry. Enter 99801.

ALL GALLERY ITEMS
At the Main menu, press **L1** and select Code Entry. Enter 85061.

DOUBLE DAMAGE
At the Main menu, press **L1** and select Code Entry. Enter 90210.

INFINITE HEALTH
At the Main menu, press **L1** and select Code Entry. Enter 65049.

MAX LEVEL
At the Main menu, press **L1** and select Code Entry. Enter 89121.

UNLIMITED SPECIAL ATTACKS
At the Main menu, press **L1** and select Code Entry. Enter 66206.

AVATAR – THE LAST AIRBENDER: INTO THE INFERNO

ALL CHAPTERS
Select Game Secrets at Ember Islands and enter 52993833.

MAX COINS
Select Game Secrets at Ember Islands and enter 66639224.

ALL ITEMS AVAILABLE AT SHOP
Select Game Secrets at Ember Islands and enter 34737253.

ALL CONCEPT ART
Select Game Secrets at Ember Islands and enter 27858343.

BAKUGAN BATTLE BRAWLERS

1,000 BP
Enter 33204429 as your name.

5,000 BP
Enter 42348294 as your name.

10,000 BP
Enter 46836478 as your name.

100,000 BP
Enter 18499753 as your name.

500,000 BP
Enter 26037947 as your name.

BEN 10: ALIEN FORCE THE GAME

LEVEL LORD
Enter Gwen, Kevin, Big Chill, Gwen as a code.

INVINCIBILITY
Enter Kevin, Big Chill, Swampfire, Kevin as a code.

ALL COMBOS
Enter Swampfire, Gwen, Kevin, Ben as a code.

INFINITE ALIENS
Enter Ben, Swampfire, Gwen, Big Chill as a code.

BEN 10: ALIEN FORCE VILGAX ATTACKS

LEVEL SKIP
Pause the game and enter Portal in the Cheats menu.

UNLOCK ALL SPECKAL ATTACKS FOR ALL FORMS
Pause the game and enter Everythingproof in the Cheats menu.

UNLOCK ALL ALIEN FORMS
Pause the game and enter Primus in the Cheats menu.

TOGGLE INVULNERABILITY ON AND OFF
Pause the game and enter Xlmrsmoothy in the Cheats menu.

GIVES PLAYER FULL HEALTH
Pause the game and enter Herotime in the Cheats menu.

QUICK ENERGY REGENERATION
Pause the game and enter Generator in the Cheats menu.

BEN 10: PROTECTOR OF EARTH

INVINCIBILITY
Select a game from the Continue option. Go to the Map Selection screen, press Start and choose Extras. Select Enter Secret Code and enter XLR8, Heatblast, Wildvine, Fourarms.

ALL COMBOS
Select a game from the Continue option. Go to the Map Selection screen, press Start and choose Extras. Select Enter Secret Code and enter Cannonblot, Heatblast, Fourarms, Heatblast.

ALL LOCATIONS
Select a game from the Continue option. Go to the Map Selection screen, press Start and choose Extras. Select Enter Secret Code and enter Heatblast, XLR8, XLR8, Cannonblot.

DNA FORCE SKINS
Select a game from the Continue option. Go to the Map Selection screen, press Start and choose Extras. Select Enter Secret Code and enter Wildvine, Fourarms, Heatblast, Cannonbolt.

DARK HEROES SKINS
Select a game from the Continue option. Go to the Map Selection screen, press Start and choose Extras. Select Enter Secret Code and enter Cannonbolt, Cannonbolt, Fourarms, Heatblast.

ALL ALIEN FORMS
Select a game from the Continue option. Go to the Map Selection screen, press Start and choose Extras. Select Enter Secret Code and enter Wildvine, Fourarms, Heatblast, Wildvine.

MASTER CONTROL
Select a game from the Continue option. Go to the Map Selection screen, press Start and choose Extras. Select Enter Secret Code and enter Cannonbolt, Heatblast, Wildvine, Fourarms.

BEN 10 ULTIMATE ALIEN: COSMIC DESTRUCTION

To remove the cheats, you will need to start a new game.

1,000,000 DNA
Pause the game, select Cheats, and enter Cash.

REGENERATE HEALTH
Pause the game, select Cheats, and enter Health.

REGENERATE ENERGY
Pause the game, select Cheats, and enter Energy.

UPGRADE EVERYTHING
Pause the game, select Cheats, and enter Upgrade.

ALL LEVELS
Pause the game, select Cheats, and enter Levels.

ENEMIES DO DOUBLE DAMAGE/ PLAYER DOES ½ DAMAGE
Pause the game, select Cheats, and enter Hard.

BOLT

Some of the following cheats can be toggled on/off by selecting Cheats from the pause menu.

ALL GAME LEVELS
Select Cheats from the Extras menu and enter Right, Up, Left, Right, Up, Right.

ALL MINI GAMES
Select Cheats from the Extras menu and enter Right, Up, Right, Right.

ENCHANCED VISION
Select Cheats from the Extras menu and enter Left, Right, Up, Down.

UNLIMITED GAS MINES
Select Cheats from the Extras menu and enter Right, Left, Left, Up, Down, Right.

UNLIMITED GROUND POUND
Select Cheats from the Extras menu and enter Right, Up, Right, Up, Left, Down.

UNLIMITED INVULNERABILITY
Select Cheats from the Extras menu and enter Down, Down, Up, Left.

UNLIMITED LASER EYES
Select Cheats from the Extras menu and enter Left, Left, Up, Right.

UNLIMITED STEALTH CAMO
Select Cheats from the Extras menu and enter Left, Down, Down, Down.

UNLIMITED SUPERBARK
Select Cheats from the Extras menu and enter Right, Left -Left, Up, Down, Up.

BRATZ: THE MOVIE

FEELIN' PRETTY CLOTHING LINE
In the Bratz office at the laptop computer, enter PRETTY.

HIGH SCHOOL CLOTHING LINE
In the Bratz office at the laptop computer, enter SCHOOL.

PASSION 4 FASHION CLOTHING

LINE
In the Bratz office at the laptop computer, enter ANGELZ.

SWEETZ CLOTHING LINE
In the Bratz office at the laptop computer, enter SWEETZ.

CAPCOM CLASSICS COLLECTION VOL. 2

UNLOCK EVERYTHING
At the Title screen, press Left, Right, Up, Down, L1, R1, L1, R1. This code unlocks Cheats, Tips, Art, and Sound Tests.

CARS

UNLOCK EVERYTHING
Select Cheat Codes from the Options and enter IF900HP.

ALL CHARACTERS
Select Cheat Codes from the Options and enter YAYCARS.

ALL CHARACTER SKINS
Select Cheat Codes from the Options and enter R4MONE.

ALL MINI-GAMES AND COURSES
Select Cheat Codes from the Options and enter MATTL66.

MATER'S COUNTDOWN CLEAN-UP MINI-GAME AND MATER'S SPEEDY CIRCUIT
Select Cheat Codes from the Options and enter TRGTEXC.

FAST START
Select Cheat Codes from the Options and enter IMSPEED.

INFINITE BOOST
Select Cheat Codes from the Options and enter VROOOOM.

ART
Select Cheat Codes from the Options and enter CONC3PT.

VIDEOS
Select Cheat Codes from the Options and enter WATCHIT.

CARS MATER-NATIONAL

ALL ARCADE RACES, MINI-GAMES, AND WORLDS
Select Codes/Cheats from the options and enter PLAYALL.

ALL CARS
Select Codes/Cheats from the options and enter MATTEL07.

ALTERNATE LIGHTNING MCQUEEN COLORS
Select Codes/Cheats from the options and enter NCEDUDZ.

ALL COLORS FOR OTHERS
Select Codes/Cheats from the options and enter PAINTIT.

UNLIMITED TURBO
Select Codes/Cheats from the options and enter ZZOOOOM.

EXTREME ACCELERATION
Select Codes/Cheats from the options and enter OTO200X.

EXPERT MODE
Select Codes/Cheats from the options and enter VRYFAST.

ALL BONUS ART
Select Codes/Cheats from the options and enter BUYTALL.

CARS RACE-O-RAMA

ALL ARCADE MODE EVENTS
Select Cheats from the Options menu and enter SLVRKEY.

ALL STORY MODE EVENTS
Select Cheats from the Options menu and enter GOLDKEY.

ALL OF LIGHTNING MCQUEEN'S FRIENDS
Select Cheats from the Options menu and enter EVRYBDY.

ALL LIGHTNING MCQUEEN CUSTOM KIT PARTS
Select Cheats from the Options menu and enter GR8MODS.

ALL PAINT JOBS FOR ALL NON-LIGHTNING MCQUEEN CHARACTERS
Select Cheats from the Options menu and enter CARSHOW.

CORALINE

BUTTON EYE CORALINE
Select Cheats from Options and enter Cheese.

CRASH OF THE TITANS

BIG HEAD CRASH
Pause the game, hold **R1**, and press ●, ●, ▲, ✖. Re-enter the code to disable.

SHADOW CRASH
Pause the game, hold **R1**, and press ▲, ●, ▲, ●. Re-enter the code to disable.

THE DA VINCI CODE

GOD MODE
Select Codes from the Options and enter VITRUVIAN MAN.

EXTRA HEALTH
Select Codes from the Options and enter SACRED FEMININE.

MISSION SELECT
Select Codes from the Options and enter CLOS LUCE 1519.

ONE-HIT WEAPON KILL
Select Codes from the Options and enter ROYAL HOLLOWAY.

ALL VISUAL DATABASE
Select Codes from the Options and enter APOCRYPHA.

ALL VISUAL DATABASE AND CONCEPT ART
Select Codes from the Options and enter ET IN ARCADIA EGO.

ONE-HIT FIST KILL
Select Codes from the Options and enter PHILLIPS EXETER.

DISNEY PRINCESS: ENCHANTED JOURNEY

BELLE'S KINGDOM
Select Secrets and enter GASTON.

GOLDEN SET
Select Secrets and enter BLUEBIRD.

FLOWER WAND
Select Secrets and enter SLEEPY.

HEART WAND
Select Secrets and enter BASHFUL.

SHELL WAND
Select Secrets and enter RAJAH.

SHIELD WAND
Select Secrets and enter CHIP.

STAR WAND
Select Secrets and enter SNEEZY.

DJ HERO

Select Cheats from Options and enter the following. Some codes will disable high scores and progress. Cheats cannot be used in tutorials and online.

UNLOCK ALL CONTENT
Enter tol0.

ALL CHARACTER ITEMS
Enter uNA2.

ALL VENUES
Enter Wv1u.

ALL DECKS
Enter LAuP.

ALL HEADPHONES
Enter 62Db.

ALL MIXES
Enter 82xl.

AUTO SCRATCH
Enter IT6j.

AUTO EFFECTS DIAL
Enter ab1L.

AUTO FADER
Enter SL5d.

AUTO TAPPER
Enter ZitH.

AUTO WIN EUPHORIA
Enter r3a9.

BLANK PLINTHS
Enter ipr0.

HAMSTER SWITCH
Enter 7geo.

HYPER DECK MODE
Enter 76st.

SHORT DECK
Enter 51uC.

INVISIBLE DJ
Enter oh5T.

PITCH BLACK OUT
Enter d4kR.

PLAY IN THE BEDROOM
Enter g7nH.

ANY DJ, ANY SETLIST
Enter 0jj8.

DAFT PUNK'S CONTENT
Enter d1g?.

DJ AM'S CONTENT
Enter k07u.

DJ JAZZY JEFF'S CONTENT
Enter n1fz.

DJ SHADOW'S CONTENT
Enter oMxV.

DJ Z-TRIP'S CONTENT
Enter 5rtg.

GRANDMASTER FLASH'S CONTENT
Enter ami8.

FLATOUT 2

ALL CARS AND 1,000,000 CREDITS
Select Enter Code from the Extras and enter GIEVEPIX.

1,000,000 CREDITS
Select Enter Code from the Extras and enter GIVECASH.

PIMPSTER CAR
Select Enter Code from the Extras and enter RUTTO.

FLATMOBILE CAR
Select Enter Code from the Extras and enter WOTKINS.

MOB CAR
Select Enter Code from the Extras and enter BIGTRUCK.

SCHOOL BUS
Select Enter Code from the Extras and enter GIEVCARPLZ.

ROCKET CAR
Select Enter Code from the Extras and enter KALJAKOPPA.

TRUCK
Select Enter Code from the Extras and enter ELPUEBLO.

FUNKMASTER FLEX'S DIGITAL HITZ FACTORY

EXTRA SKIN 1
At the main menu, press Select, Left, Right, Left, Right, Left, Right, Left, Right, Left, Right, Left, Right.

EXTRA SKIN 2
At the main menu, press Select, Left, Left, Right, Right, Left, Left, Right, Right, Left, Left, Right, Right.

EXTRA SKIN 3
At the main menu, press Select, Left, Left, Left, Right, Right, Right, Left, Left, Left, Right, Right, Right.

EXTRA SKIN 4
At the main menu, press Select, Left, Left, Left, Left, Right, Right, Right, Right, Left, Left, Left, Left.

EXTRA SONG – MUDDY BY MOTLEY
At the main menu, press Select, Up, Down, Left, Right, Up, Down, Left, Right, Up, Down, Left, Right.

G.I. JOE: THE RISE OF COBRA

CLASSIC DUKE
At the main menu, press Left, Up, ✖, Up, Right, ▲.

CLASSIC SCARLETT
At the main menu, press Right, Up, Down, Down, ▲.

THE GOLDEN COMPASS

The following codes are entered in the order of top/left, bottom/left, top/right. The Featurettes can then be accessed through the Extras menu.

VOICE SESSION 1 FETUREETE

In Extras, select Enter Code from the Game Secrets menu and enter Compass, Sun, Madonna.

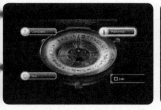 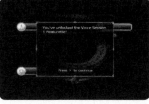

VOICE SESSION 2 FEATURETTE

In Extras, select Enter Code from the Game Secrets menu and enter Compass, Moon, Wild Man.

BEHIND THE SCENES FEATURETTE

In Extras, select Enter Code from the Game Secrets menu and enter Alpha/Omega, Alpha/Omega, Compass.

WILDLIFE WAYSTATION FEATURETTE

In Extras, select Enter Code from the Game Secrets menu and enter Griffin, Elephant, Owl.

POLAR BEARS IN MOTION FEATURETTE

In Extras, select Enter Code from the Game Secrets menu and enter Sun, Moon, Wild Man.

HARRY POTTER AND THE HALF-BLOOD PRINCE

BONUS TWO-PLAYER DUELING ARENA CASTLE GATES

At the Rewards menu, press Right, Right, Down, Down, Left, Right, Left, Right, Left, Right, Start.

ICE AGE 2: THE MELTDOWN

INFINITE PEBBLES

Pause the game and press Down, Down, Left, Up, Up, Right, Up, Down.

INFINITE ENERGY

Pause the game and press Down, Left, Right, Down, Down, Right, Left, Down.

INFINITE HEALTH

Pause the game and press Up, Right, Down, Up, Left, Down, Right, Left.

IRON MAN

ARMOR SELECTION

Iron Man's different armor suits are unlocked by completing certain missions. Refer to the following tables for when each is unlocked. After selecting a mission to play, you can pick the armor you wish to use.

COMPLETE MISSION	SUIT UNLOCKED
1: Escape	Mark I
2: First Flight	Mark II
3: Fight Back	Mark III
6: Flying Fortress	Comic Tin Can
9: Home Front	Classic
13: Showdown	Silver Centurion

CONCEPT ART

Concept Art is unlocked after finding certain numbers of Weapon Crates.

CONCEPT ART UNLOCKED	NUMBER OF WEAPON CRATES FOUND
Environments Set 1	6
Environments Set 2	12
Iron Man	18
Environments Set 3	24
Enemies	30
Environments Set 4	36
Villains	42
Vehicles	48
Covers	50

JUICED 2: HOT IMPORT NIGHTS

ASCARI KZ1
Select Cheats and Codes from the DNA Lab menu and enter KNOX. Defeat the challenge to earn the car.

NISSAN SKYLINE R34 GT-R
Select Cheats and Codes from the DNA Lab menu and enter JWRS. Defeat the challenge to earn the car.

KUNG FU PANDA

INVULNERABILITY
Select Cheats from the Extras menu and enter Down, Down, Right, Up, Left.

INFINITE CHI
Select Cheats from the Extras menu and enter Down, Right, Left, Up, Down.

BIG HEAD MODE
Select Cheats from the Extras menu and enter Down, Up, Left, Right, Right.

ALL MULTIPLAYER CHARACTERS
Select Cheats from the Extras menu and enter Left, Down, Left, Right, Down.

DRAGON WARRIOR OUTFIT IN MULTIPLAYER
Select Cheats from the Extras menu and enter Left, Down, Right, Left, Up.

THE LEGEND OF SPYRO: THE ETERNAL NIGHT

INFINITE MAGIC
Pause the game and press Up, Up, Down, Down, Left, Right, Left, Right, L1, R1, L1, R1.

THE LEGEND OF SPYRO: DAWN OF THE DRAGON

INFINITE HEALTH
Pause the game, hold L1 and press Right, Right, Down, Down, Left with the Left Analog Stick.

INFINITE MANA
Pause the game, hold L1 and press Up, Right, Up, Left, Down with the Left Analog Stick.

MAX XP
Pause the game, hold L1 and press Up, Left, Left, Down, Up with the Left Analog Stick.

ALL ELEMENTAL UPGRADES
Pause the game, hold L1 and press Left, Up, Down, Up, Right with the Left Analog Stick.

LEGO BATMAN

BATCAVE CODES

Using the computer in the Batcave, select Enter Code and enter the following codes.

CHARACTERS

CHARACTER	CODE	CHARACTER	CODE
Alfred	ZAQ637	Penguin Henchman	BJH782
Batgirl	JKR331	Penguin Minion	KJP748
Bruce Wayne	BDJ327	Poison Ivy Goon	GTB899
Catwoman (Classic)	M1AAWW	Police Marksman	HKG984
Clown Goon	HJK327	Police Officer	JRY983
Commissioner Gordon	DDP967	Riddler Goon	CRY928
Fishmonger	HGY748	Riddler Henchman	XEU824
Freeze Girl	XVK541	S.W.A.T.	HTF114
Joker Goon	UTF782	Sailor	NAV592
Joker Henchman	YUN924	Scientist	JFL786
Mad Hatter	JCA283	Security Guard	PLB946
Man-Bat	NYU942	The Joker (Tropical)	CCB199
Military Policeman	MKL382	Yeti	NJL412
Nightwing	MVY759	Zoo Sweeper	DWR243
Penguin Goon	NKA238		

VEHICLES

VEHICLE	CODE	VEHICLE	CODE
Bat-Tank	KNTT4B	Mr. Freeze's Kart	BCT229
Bruce Wayne's Private Jet	LEA664	Penguin Goon Submarine	BTN248
Catwoman's Motorcycle	HPL826	Police Bike	LJP234
Garbage Truck	DUS483	Police Boat	PLC999
Goon Helicopter	GCH328	Police Car	KJL832
Harbor Helicopter	CHP735	Police Helicopter	CWR732
Harley Quinn's Hammer Truck	RDT637	Police Van	MAC788
Mad Hatter's Glider	HS000W	Police Watercraft	VJD328
Mad Hatter's Steamboat	M4DM4N	Riddler's Jet	HAHAHA
Mr. Freeze's Iceberg	ICYICE	Robin's Submarine	TTF453
The Joker's Van	JUK657	Two-Face's Armored Truck	EFE933

CHEATS

CHEAT	CODE	CHEAT	CODE
Always Score Multiply	9LRGNB	More Batarang Targets	XWP645
Fast Batarangs	JRBDCB	Piece Detector	KHJ554
Fast Walk	ZOLM6N	Power Brick Detector	MMN786
Flame Batarang	D8NYWH	Regenerate Hearts	HJH7HJ
Freeze Batarang	XPN4NG	Score x2	N4NR3E
Extra Hearts	ML3KHP	Score x4	CX9MAT
Fast Build	EVG26J	Score x6	MLVNF2
Immune to Freeze	JXUDY6	Score x8	WCCDB9
Invincibility	WYD5CP	Score x10	18HW07
Minikit Detector	ZXGH9J		

LEGO STAR WARS II: THE ORIGINAL TRILOGY

BEACH TROOPER

At Mos Eisley Canteena, select Enter Code and enter UCK868. You still need to select Characters and purchase this character for 20,000 studs.

BEN KENOBI (GHOST)

At Mos Eisley Canteena, select Enter Code and enter BEN917. You still need to select Characters and purchase this character for 1,100,000 studs.

BESPIN GUARD

At Mos Eisley Canteena, select Enter Code and enter VHY832. You still need to select Characters and purchase this character for 15,000 studs.

BIB FORTUNA

At Mos Eisley Canteena, select Enter Code and enter WTY721. You still need to select Characters and purchase this character for 16,000 studs.

BOBA FETT

At Mos Eisley Canteena, select Enter Code and enter HLP221. You still need to select Characters and purchase this character for 175,000 studs.

DEATH STAR TROOPER

At Mos Eisley Canteena, select Enter Code and enter BNC332. You still need to select Characters and purchase this character for 19,000 studs.

EWOK

At Mos Eisley Canteena, select Enter Code and enter TTT289. You still need to select Characters and purchase this character for 34,000 studs.

GAMORREAN GUARD

At Mos Eisley Canteena, select Enter Code and enter YZF999. You still need to select Characters and purchase this character for 40,000 studs.

GONK DROID

At Mos Eisley Canteena, select Enter Code and enter NFX582. You still need to select Characters and purchase this character for 1,550 studs.

GRAND MOFF TARKIN

At Mos Eisley Canteena, select Enter Code and enter SMG219. You still need to select Characters and purchase this character for 38,000 studs.

GREEDO

At Mos Eisley Canteena, select Enter Code and enter NAH118. You still need to select Characters and purchase this character for 60,000 studs.

HAN SOLO (HOOD)

At Mos Eisley Canteena, select Enter Code and enter YWM840. You still need to select Characters and purchase this character for 20,000 studs.

IG-88

At Mos Eisley Canteena, select Enter Code and enter NXL973. You still need to select Characters and purchase this character for 30,000 studs.

IMPERIAL GUARD

At Mos Eisley Canteena, select Enter Code and enter MMM111. You still need to select Characters and purchase this character for 45,000 studs.

IMPERIAL OFFICER

At Mos Eisley Canteena, select Enter Code and enter BBV889. You still need to select Characters and purchase this character for 28,000 studs.

IMPERIAL SHUTTLE PILOT

At Mos Eisley Canteena, select Enter Code and enter VAP664. You still need to select Characters and purchase this character for 29,000 studs.

IMPERIAL SPY

At Mos Eisley Canteena, select Enter Code and enter CVT125. You still need to select Characters and purchase this character for 13,500 studs.

JAWA

At Mos Eisley Canteena, select Enter Code and enter JAW499. You still need to select Characters and purchase this character for 24,000 studs.

LOBOT

At Mos Eisley Canteena, select Enter Code and enter UUB319. You still need to select Characters and purchase this character for 11,000 studs.

PALACE GUARD

At Mos Eisley Canteena, select Enter Code and enter SGE549. You still need to select Characters and purchase this character for 14,000 studs.

REBEL PILOT

At Mos Eisley Canteena, select Enter Code and enter CYG336. You still need to select Characters and purchase this character for 15,000 studs.

REBEL TROOPER (HOTH)

At Mos Eisley Canteena, select Enter Code and enter EKU849. You still need to select Characters and purchase this character for 16,000 studs.

SANDTROOPER

At Mos Eisley Canteena, select Enter Code and enter YDV451. You still need to select Characters and purchase this character for 14,000 studs.

SKIFF GUARD

At Mos Eisley Canteena, select Enter Code and enter GBU888. You still need to select Characters and purchase this character for 12,000 studs.

SNOWTROOPER

At Mos Eisley Canteena, select Enter Code and enter NYU989. You still need to select Characters and purchase this character for 16,000 studs.

STROMTROOPER

At Mos Eisley Canteena, select Enter Code and enter PTR345. You still need to select Characters and purchase this character for 10,000 studs.

THE EMPEROR

At Mos Eisley Canteena, select Enter Code and enter HHY382. You still need to select Characters and purchase this character for 275,000 studs.

TIE FIGHTER

At Mos Eisley Canteena, select Enter Code and enter HDY739. You still need to select Characters and purchase this character for 60,000 studs.

TIE FIGHTER PILOT

At Mos Eisley Canteena, select Enter Code and enter NNZ316. You still need to select Characters and purchase this character for 21,000 studs.

TIE INTERCEPTOR

At Mos Eisley Canteena, select Enter Code and enter QYA828. You still need to select Characters and purchase this character for 40,000 studs.

TUSKEN RAIDER

At Mos Eisley Canteena, select Enter Code and enter PEJ821. You still need to select Characters and purchase this character for 23,000 studs.

UGNAUGHT

At Mos Eisley Canteena, select Enter Code and enter UGN694. You still need to select Characters and purchase this character for 36,000 studs.

LOONEY TUNES: ACME ARSENAL

UNLIMITED AMMUNITION

At the cheats menu, enter Down, Left, Up, Right, Down, Left, Up, Right, Down.

MAJOR LEAGUE BASEBALL 2K8

BIG HEAD MODE

Select Enter Cheat Code from the My 2K8 menu and enter Black Sox. This unlocks the Smart Choice cheat. Go to My Cheats to toggle the cheat on and off.

MAJOR LEAGUE BASEBALL 2K9

BIG HEADS

At the cheats menu, enter Black Sox.

MARVEL SUPER HERO SQUAD

IRON MAN, BONUS COSTUME "WAR MACHINE"

Select Enter Code from the Options and enter 111111.

HULK, BONUS COSTUMES "GREY HULK" & "RED HULK"

Select Enter Code from the Options and enter 222222.

WOLVERINE, BONUS COSTUMES "WOLVERINE (BROWN COSTUME)" & "FERAL WOLVERINE"

Select Enter Code from the Options and enter 333333.

THOR, BONUS COSTUMES "THOR (CHAIN ARMOR)" & "LOKI-THOR"

Select Enter Code from the Options and enter 444444.

SILVER SURFER, BONUS COSTUMES "ANTI-SURFER" & "GOLD SURFER"

Select Enter Code from the Options and enter 555555.

FALCON, BONUS COSTUME "ULTIMATES FALCON"

Select Enter Code from the Options and enter 666666.

CHEAT "SUPER KNOCKBACK"

Select Enter Code from the Options and enter 777777.

CHEAT "NO BLOCK MODE"

Select Enter Code from the Options and enter 888888.

DOCTOR DOOM, BONUS COSTUMES "ULTIMATES DOCTOR DOOM" & "PROFESSOR DOOM"

Select Enter Code from the Options and enter 999999.

CAPTAIN AMERICA, BONUS COSTUME "ULTIMATE CAPTAIN AMERICA COSTUME"

Select Enter Code from the Options and enter 177674

A.I.M. AGENT, BONUS COSTUME "BLUE SUIT A.I.M."

Select Enter Code from the Options and enter 246246

CHEAT "GROUNDED"

Select Enter Code from the Options and enter 476863

CHEAT "ONE-HIT TAKEDOWN"

Select Enter Code from the Options and enter 663448

MARVEL ULTIMATE ALLIANCE

UNLOCK ALL SKINS
At the Team Menu, press Up, Down, Left, Right, Left, Right, Start.

UNLOCKS ALL HERO POWERS
At the Team Menu, press Left, Right, Up, Down, Up, Down, Start.

UNLOCK ALL HEROES
At the Team Menu, press Up, Up, Down, Down, Left, Left, Left, Start.

UNLOCK DAREDEVIL
At the Team Menu, press Left, Left, Right, Right, Up, Down, Up, Down, Start.

UNLOCK SILVER SURFER
At the Team Menu, press Down, Left, Left, Up, Right, Up, Down, Left, Start.

GOD MODE
During gameplay, press Up, Down, Up, Down, Up, Left, Down, Right, Start.

TOUCH OF DEATH
During gameplay, press Left, Right, Down, Down, Right, Left, Start.

SUPER SPEED
During gameplay, press Up, Left, Up, Right, Down, Right, Start.

FILL MOMENTUM
During gameplay, press Left, Right, Right, Left, Up, Down, Down, Up, Start.

UNLOCK ALL COMICS
At the Review menu, press Left, Right, Right, Left, Up, Up, Right, Start.

UNLOCK ALL CONCEPT ART
At the Review menu, press Down, Down, Down, Right, Right, Left, Down, Start.

UNLOCK ALL MOVIES
At the Review menu, press Up, Left, Left, Up, Right, Right, Up, Start.

UNLOCK ALL LOAD SCREENS
At the Review menu, press Up, Down, Right, Left, Up, Up Down, Start.

UNLOCK ALL COURSES
At the Comic Missions menu, press Up, Right, Left, Down, Up, Right, Left, Down, Start.

MARVEL ULTIMATE ALLIANCE 2

GOD MODE
At any point during a game, press Up, Up, Down, Down, Left, Right, Down.

GIVE MONEY
At the Team Select or Hero Details screen press Up, Up, Down, Down, Up, Up, Up, Down.

UNLOCK ALL POWERS
At the Team Select or Hero Details screen press Up, Up, Down, Down, Left, Right, Right, Left.

ADVANCE ALL CHARACTERS TO L99
At the Hero Details screen press Down, Up, Left, Up, Right, Up, Left, Down.

UNLOCK ALL BONUS MISSIONS
While using the Bonus Mission Simulator, press Up, Right, Down, Left, Left, Right, Up, Up.

ADD 1 CHARACTER LEVEL
During a game, press Down, Up, Right, Up, Right, Up, Right, Down.

ADD 10 CHARACTER LEVELS
During a game, press Down, Up, Left, Up, Left, Up, Left, Down.

MLB 08: THE SHOW

ALL CLASSIC STADIUMS
At the main menu, press Down, Right, ●, ●, Left, ▲, Up, L1. The controller will vibrate if entered correctly.

ALL GOLDEN & SILVER ERA PLAYERS IN EXHIBITION
At the main menu, press L1, L2, ●, ●, ▲, ●, Down. The controller will vibrate if entered correctly.

MLB POWER PROS

VIEW MLB PLAYERS AT CREATED PLAYERS MENU
Select View or Delete Custom Players/Password Display from the My Data menu. Press Up, Up, Down, Down, Left, Right, Left Right, L1, R1.

ALVIN LOCKHART'S BATTING STANCE AND PITCHING FORM
At the main menu, press Right, Left, Up, Down, Down, Right, Right, Up, Up, Left, Down, Left. These will be available at the shop.

MX VS. ATV UNTAMED

EVERYTHING
Select Cheat Codes from the options menu and enter YOUGOTIT.

1,000,000 STORE POINTS
Select Cheat Codes from the options menu and enter MANYZEROS.

50CC BIKE CLASS
Select Cheat Codes from the options menu and enter LITTLEGUY.

ALL BIKES
Select Cheat Codes from the options menu and enter ONRAILS.

ALL CHALLENGES
Select Cheat Codes from the options menu and enter MORESTUFF.

ALL FREESTYLE TRACKS
Select Cheat Codes from the options menu and enter ALLSTYLE.

ALL GEAR
Select Cheat Codes from the options menu and enter WELLDRESSED.

ALL MACHINES

Select Cheat Codes from the options menu and enter MCREWHEELS.

ALL RIDERS

Select Cheat Codes from the options menu and enter WHOSTHAT.

ALL TRACKS

Select Cheat Codes from the options menu and enter FREETICKET.

MONSTER TRUCK

Select Cheat Codes from the options menu and enter PWNAGE.

NARUTO: ULTIMATE NINJA 2

In Naruto's house, select Input Password. This is where you can enter an element, then three signs. Enter the following here:

1,000 RYO

Water, Hare, Monkey, Monkey
Water, Ram, Horse, Dog
Water, Horse, Horse, Horse
Water, Rat, Rooster, Boar
Water, Rat, Monkey, Rooster
Fire, Rat, Dragon, Dog

5,000 RYO

Water, Tiger, Dragon, Tiger
Water, Snake, Rooster, Horse

10,000 RYO

Fire, Tiger, Tiger, Rooster
Fire, Tiger, Dragon, Hare

NASCAR 08

ALL CHASE MODE CARS

Select Cheat Codes from the Options menu and enter checkered flag.

EA SPORTS CAR

Select Cheat Codes from the Options menu and enter ea sports car.

FANTASY DRIVERS

Select Cheat Codes from the Options menu and enter race the pack.

WALMART CAR AND TRACK

Select Cheat Codes from the Options menu and enter walmart everyday.

NASCAR 09

WALMART TRACK AND THE WALMART CAR

In Chase for the Sprint Cup, enter the driver's name as WalMart EveryDay.

NBA 09 THE INSIDE

ALL-STAR 09 EAST

Select Trophy Room from the Options. Press L1, then ⦿, and enter SHPNV2K699.

ALL-STAR 09 WEST

Select Trophy Room from the Options. Press L1, then ⦿, and enter K8AV6YMLNF.

ALL TROPHIES

Select Trophy Room from the Options. Press L1, then ⦿, and enter K@ZZ@@M!.

LA LAKERS LATIN NIGHTS

Select Trophy Room from the Options. Press L1, then ⦿, and enter NMTWCTC84S.

MIAMI HEAT LATIN NIGHTS

Select Trophy Room from the Options. Press L1, then ⦿, and enter WCTGSA8SPD.

PHOENIX SUNS LATIN NIGHTS

Select Trophy Room from the Options. Press L1, then ⦿, and enter LKUTSENFJH.

SAN ANTONIO LATIN NIGHTS

Select Trophy Room from the Options. Press L1, then ⦿, and enter JFHSY73MYD.

NBA 2K10

ABA BALL
Select Codes from Options and enter payrespect.

NBA 2K TEAM
Select Codes from Options and enter nba2k.

2K SPORTS TEAM
Select Codes from Options and enter 2ksports.

VISUAL CONCEPTS TEAM
Select Codes from Options and enter vcteam.

NBA 2K11

2K CHINA TEAM
In Features, select Codes from the Extras menu. Choose Enter Code and enter 2kchina.

2K SPORTS TEAM
In Features, select Codes from the Extras menu. Choose Enter Code and enter 2Ksports.

NBA 2K TEAM
In Features, select Codes from the Extras menu. Choose Enter Code and enter nba2k.

VC TEAM
In Features, select Codes from the Extras menu. Choose Enter Code and enter vcteam.

ABA BALL
In Features, select Codes from the Extras menu. Choose Enter Code and enter payrespect.

NBA LIVE 08

ADIDAS GIL II ZERO SHOE CODES
Select NBA Codes from My NBA Live and enter the following:

SHOES	CODE
Agent Zero	ADGILLIT6BE
Black President	ADGILLIT7BF
Cuba	ADGILLIT4BC
CustOmize Shoe	ADGILLIT5BD
GilWood	ADGILLIT1B9
TS Lightswitch Away	ADGILLIT0B8
TS Lightswitch Home	ADGILLIT2BA

NCAA FOOTBALL 08

PENNANT CODES
Go to My Shrine and select Pennants. Press Select and enter the following:

PENNANT	CODE	PENNANT	CODE
#200 1st & 15 Cheat	Thanks	#212 Molasses Cheat	Game Time
#201 Blink Cheat	For	#213 Nike Free Cheat	Break Free
#202 Boing Cheat	Registering	#214 Nike Magnigrip Cheat	Hand Picked
#204 Butter Fingers Cheat	With EA	#215 Nike Pro Cheat	No Sweat
#205 Crossed The Line Cheat	Tiburon	#219 QB Dud Cheat	Elite 11
#206 Cuffed Cheat	EA Sports	#221 Steel Toe Cheat	Gridiron
#207 Extra Credit Cheat	Touchdown	#222 Stiffed Cheat	NCAA
#208 Helium Cheat	In The Zone	#223 Super Dive Cheat	Upset
#209 Hurricane Cheat	Turnover	#226 Tough As Nail Cheat	Offense
#210 Instant FrePlay Cheat	Impact	#228 What A Hit Cheat	Blitz
#211 Jumbalaya Cheat	Heisman	#229 Kicker Hex Cheat	Sideline

PENNANT	CODE
#273 2004 All-American Team	Fumble
#274 All-Alabama Team	Roll Tide
#276 All-Arkansas Team	Woopigsooie
#277 All-Auburn Team	War Eagle
#278 All-Clemson Team	Death Valley
#279 All-Colorado Team	Glory
#281 All-FSU Team	Uprising
#282 All-Georgia Team	Hunker Down
#283 All-Iowa Team	On Iowa
#285 All-LSU Team	Geaux Tigers
#287 All-Michigan Team	Go Blue
#288 All-Mississippi State Team	Hail State
#289 All-Nebraska Team	Go Big Red
#291 All-Notre Dame Team	Golden Domer
#292 All-Ohio State Team	Killer Nuts

PENNANT	CODE
#293 All-Oklahoma Team	Boomer
#294 All-Oklahoma State Team	Go Pokes
#296 All-Penn State Team	We Are
#298 All-Purdue Team	Boiler Up
#300 All-Tennessee Team	Big Orange
#301 All-Texas Team	Hook Em
#302 All-Texas A&M Team	Gig Em
#303 All-UCLA Team	Mighty
#304 All-USC Team	Fight On
#305 All-Virginia Team	Wahoos
#307 All-Washington Team	Bow Down
#308 All-Wisconsin Team	U Rah Rah
#344 MSU Mascot Team	Mizzou Rah
#385 Wyo Mascot	All Hail
#386 Zips Mascot	Hail WV

NEED FOR SPEED PROSTREET

$2,000
Select Career and then choose Code Entry. Enter 1MA9X99.

$4,000
Select Career and then choose Code Entry. Enter W2IOLL01.

$8,000
Select Career and then choose Code Entry. Enter L1IS97A1.

$10,000
Select Career and then choose Code Entry. Enter 1MI9K7E1.

$10,000
Select Career and then choose Code Entry. Enter CASHMONEY.

$10,000
Select Career and then choose Code Entry. Enter REGGAME.

AUDI TT
Select Career and then choose Code Entry. Enter ITSABOUTYOU.

CHEVELLE SS
Select Career and then choose Code Entry. Enter HORSEPOWER.

COKE ZERO GOLF GTI
Select Career and then choose Code Entry. Enter COKEZERO.

DODGE VIPER
Select Career and then choose Code Entry. Enter WORLDSLONGESTLASTING.

MITSUBISHI LANCER EVOLUTION
Select Career and then choose Code Entry. Enter MITSUBISHIGOFAR.

UNLOCK ALL BONUSES
Select Career and then choose Code Entry. Enter UNLOCKALLTHINGS.

5 REPAIR MARKERS
Select Career and then choose Code Entry. Enter SAFETYNET.

ENERGIZER VINYL
Select Career and then choose Code Entry. Enter ENERGIZERLITHIUM.

CASTROL SYNTEC VINYL
Select Career and then choose Code Entry. Enter CASTROLSYNTEC. This also gives you $10,000.

NHL 08

ALL RBK EDGE JERSEYS
At the RBK Edge Code option, enter h3oyxpwksf8ibcgt.

NHL 09

UNLOCK 3RD JERSEYS

At the cheat menu, enter xe6377uyrwm48frf.

NICKTOONS: ATTACK OF THE TOYBOTS

DAMAGE BOOST

Select Cheats from the Extras menu. Choose Enter Cheat Code and enter 456645.

INVULNERABILITY

Select Cheats from the Extras menu. Choose Enter Cheat Code and enter 313456.

UNLOCK EXO-HUGGLES 9000

Select Cheats from the Extras menu. Choose Enter Cheat Code and enter 691427.

UNLOCK MR. HUGGLES

Select Cheats from the Extras menu. Choose Enter Cheat Code and enter 654168.

UNLIMITED LOBBER GOO

Select Cheats from the Extras menu. Choose Enter Cheat Code and enter 118147.

UNLIMITED SCATTER GOO

Select Cheats from the Extras menu. Choose Enter Cheat Code and enter 971238.

UNLIMITED SPLITTER GOO

Select Cheats from the Extras menu. Choose Enter Cheat Code and enter 854511.

RATATOUILLE

Select Gusteau's Shop from the Extras menu. Choose Secrets, select the appropriate code number, and then enter the code. Once the code is entered, select the cheat you want to activate it.

CODE NUMBER	CODE	EFFECT
1	Pieceocake	Very Easy difficulty mode
2	Myhero	No impact and no damage from enemies
3	Asobo	Plays the Asobo logo
4	Shielded	No damage from enemies
5	Spyagent	Move undetected by any enemy
6	Ilikeonions	Release air every time Remy jumps
7	Hardfeelings	Head butt when attacking instead of tailswipe
8	Slumberparty	Multiplayer mode
9	Gusteauart	All Concept Art
10	Gusteauship	All four championship modes
11	Mattelme	All single player and multiplayer mini-games
12	Gusteauvid	All Videos
13	Gusteaures	All Bonus Artworks
14	Gusteaudream	All Dream Worlds in Gusteau's Shop
15	Gusteauslide	All Slides in Gusteau's Shop
16	Gusteaulevel	All single player mini-games
17	Gusteaucombo	All items in Gusteau's Shop
18	Gusteaupot	5,000 Gusteau points
19	Gusteaujack	10,000 Gusteau points
20	Gusteauomni	50,000 Gusteau points

SCOOBY-DOO! FIRST FRIGHTS

DAPHNE'S SECRET COSTUME
Select Codes from the Extras menu and enter 2839.

FRED'S SECRET COSTUME
Select Codes from the Extras menu and enter 4826.

SCOOBY DOO'S SECRET COSTUME
Select Codes from the Extras menu and enter 1585.

SHAGGY'S SECRET COSTUME
Select Codes from the Extras menu and enter 3726.

VELMA'S SECRET COSTUME
Select Codes from the Extras menu and enter 6588.

THE SECRET SATURDAYS: BEASTS OF THE 5TH SUN

ALL LEVELS
Select Enter Secret Code from the Secrets menu and enter Zon, Zon, Zon, Zon.

UNLOCK AMAROK TO BE SCANNED IN LEVEL 2
Select Enter Secret Code from the Secrets menu and enter Fiskerton, Zak, Zon, Komodo.

UNLOCK BISHOPVILLE LIZARDMAN TO BE SCANNED IN LEVEL 3
Select Enter Secret Code from the Secrets menu and enter Komodo, Zon, Zak, Komodo.

UNLOCK NAGA TO BE SCANNED IN LEVEL 7
Select Enter Secret Code from the Secrets menu and enter Zak, Zak, Zon, Fiskerton.

UNLOCK RAKSHASA TO BE SCANNED IN LEVEL 8
Select Enter Secret Code from the Secrets menu and enter Zak, Komodo, Fiskerton, Fiskerton.

UNLOCK BILOKO TO BE SCANNED IN LEVEL 9
Select Enter Secret Code from the Secrets menu and enter Zon, Zak, Zon, Fiskerton.

SEGA SUPERSTARS TENNIS

UNLOCK CHARACTERS
Complete the following missions to unlock the corresponding character.

CHARACTER	MISSION TO COMPLETE
Alex Kidd	Mission 1 of Alex Kidd's World
Amy Rose	Mission 2 of Sonic the Hedgehog's World
Gilius	Mission 1 of Golden Axe's World
Gum	Mission 12 of Jet Grind Radio's World
Meemee	Mission 8 of Super Monkey Ball's World
Pudding	Mission 1 of Space Channel 5's World
Reala	Mission 2 of NiGHTs' World
Shadow The Hedgehog	Mission 14 of Sonic the Hedgehog's World

SHREK THE THIRD

10,000 GOLD COINS
At the gift shop, press Up, Up, Down, Up, Right, Left.

THE SIMPSONS GAME

UNLIMITED POWER FOR ALL CHARACTERS
At the Extras menu, press ●, Left, Right, ●, ●, L1.

ALL CLICHÉS.
At the Extras menu, press Left, ●, Right, ●, Right, L1.

ALL MOVIES
At the Extras menu, press ●, Left, ●, Right, ●, R1.

THE SIMS 2: CASTAWAY

CHEAT GNOME
During a game, press R1, L1, Down, ●, R2. You can now use this Gnome to get the following:

MAX ALL MOTIVES
During a game, press R2, Up, ✖, ●, L1.

MAX CURRENT INVENTORY
During a game, press Left, Right, ●, R2, ●.

MAX RELATIONSHIPS
During a game, press L1, Up, R2, Left, ▲.

ALL RESOURCES
During a game, press ●, ▲, Down, ✖, Left.

ALL CRAFTING PLANS
During a game, press ✖, ▲, L2, ●, R1.

ADD 1 TO SKILL
During a game, press ▲, L1, L1, Left, ▲.

EXCLUSIVE VEST AND TANKTOP
Pause the game and go to Fashion and Grooming. Press ●, R2, R2, ▲, Down.

THE SIMS 2: PETS

CHEAT GNOME
During a game, press L1, L1, R1, ✖, ✖, Up.

GIVE SIM PET POINTS
After activating the Cheat Gnome, press ▲, ●, ✖, ●, L1, R1 during a game. Select the Gnome to access the cheat.

ADVANCE 6 HOURS
After activating the Cheat Gnome, press Up, Left, Down, Right, R1 during a game. Select the Gnome to access the cheat.

GIVE SIM SIMOLEONS
After activating the Cheat Gnome, enter the Advance 6 Hours cheat. Access the Gnome and exit. Enter the cheat again. Now, Give Sim Simoleons should be available from the Gnome.

CAT AND DOG CODES

When creating a family, press ● to Enter Unlock Code. Enter the following for new fur patterns.

FUR PATTERN/CAT OR DOG	UNLOCK CODE
Bandit Mask Cats	EEGJ2YRQZZAIZ9QHA64
Bandit Mask Dogs	EEGJ2YRQZQARQ9QHA64
Black Dot Cats	EEGJ2YRQZQ11Q9QHA64
Black Dot Dogs	EEGJ2YRQZZ11Q9QHA64
Black Smiley Cats	EEGJ2YRQQZ1RQ9QHA64
Black Smiley Dogs	EEGJ2YRZQQARQ9QHA64
Blue Bones Cats	EEGJ2YRQZZARQ9QHA64
Blue Bones Dogs	EEGJ2YRZZZ11Z9QHA64
Blue Camouflage Cats	EEGJ2YRZZQ11Q9QHA64
Blue Camouflage Dogs	EEGJ2YRZZZ1RQ9QHA64
Blue Cats	EEGJ2YRQZZAIQ9QHA64
Blue Dogs	EEGJ2YRQQQ11Z9QHA64
Blue Star Cats	EEGJ2YRQQZ11Z9QHA64
Blue Star Dogs	EEGJ2YRQZQ11Q9QHA64
Deep Red Cats	EEGJ2YRQQQAIQ9QHA64
Deep Red Dogs	EEGJ2YRQZQ1RQ9QHA64
Goofy Cats	EEGJ2YRQZQ11Z9QHA64
Goofy Dogs	EEGJ2YRZZZARQ9QHA64
Green Cats	EEGJ2YRZQQAIZ9QHA64
Green Dogs	EEGJ2YRQZQAIQ9QHA64
Green Flower Cats	EEGJ2YRQZQZAIQ9QHA64
Green Flower Dogs	EEGJ2YRQZZ1RQ9QHA64
Light Green Cats	EEGJ2YRZZQ1RQ9QHA64
Light Green Dogs	EEGJ2YRZQQ1RQ9QHA64
Navy Hearts Cats	EEGJ2YRZQZ11Q9QHA64
Navy Hearts Dogs	EEGJ2YRQQZ11Q9QHA64
Neon Green Cats	EEGJ2YRZZQAIQ9QHA64
Neon Green Dogs	EEGJ2YRZQQAIQ9QHA64
Neon Yellow Cats	EEGJ2YRZZZARQ9QHA64
Neon Yellow Dogs	EEGJ2YRQQQAIZ9QHA64
Orange Diagonal Cats	EEGJ2YRQQZAIQ9QHA64
Orange Diagonal Dogs	EEGJ2YRZQZ11Z9QHA64
Panda Cats	EEGJ2YRQZQAIZ9QHA64
Pink Cats	EEGJ2YRQZZ11Z9QHA64
Pink Dogs	EEGJ2YRZQZ1RQ9QHA64
Pink Vertical Strip Cats	EEGJ2YRQQQARQ9QHA64
Pink Vertical Strip Dogs	EEGJ2YRZZZAIQ9QHA64
Purple Cats	EEGJ2YRQQZARQ9QHA64
Purple Dogs	EEGJ2YRQQZAIQ9QHA64
Star Cats	EEGJ2YRZQZARQ9QHA64
Star Dogs	EEGJ2YRZQZAIZ9QHA64
White Paws Cats	EEGJ2YRQQQ1RQ9QHA64
White Paws Dogs	EEGJ2YRZQQ11Z9QHA64
White Zebra Stripe Cats	EEGJ2YRZZQ11Z9QHA64
White Zebra Stripe Dogs	EEGJ2YRZZZ11Q9QHA64
Zebra Stripes Dogs	EEGJ2YRZZQAIZ9QHA64

SLY 3: HONOR AMONG THIEVES

TOONAMI PLANE

While flying the regular plane, pause the game and press **R1**, **R1**, Right, Down, Down, Right.

RESTART EPISODES

Pause the game during the Episode and enter the following codes to restart that Episode. You must first complete that part of the Episode to use the code.

EPISODE	CODE
Episode 1, Day 1	Left, **R2**, Right, **L1**, **R2**, **L1**
Episode 1, Day 2	Down, **L2**, Up, Left, **R2**, **L2**
Episode 2, Day 1	Right, **L2**, Left, Up, Right, Down
Episode 2, Day 2	Down, Up, **R1**, Up, **R2**, **L2**
Episode 3, Day 1	**R2**, **R1**, **L1**, Left, **L1**, Down
Episode 3, Day 2	**L2**, **R1**, **R2**, **L2**, **L1**, Up
Episode 4, Day 1	Left, Right, **L1**, **R2**, Right, **R2**
Episode 4, Day 2	**L1**, Left, **L2**, Left, Up, **L1**
Episode 5, Day 1	Left, **R2**, Right, Up, **L1**, **R2**
Episode 5, Day 2	**R2**, **R1**, **L1**, **R1**, **R2**, **R1**
Operation Laptop Retrieval	**L2**, Left, **R1**, **L2**, **L1**, Down
Operation Moon Crash	**L2**, Up, Left, **L1**, **L2**, **L1**
Operation Reverse Double Cross	Right, Left, Up, Left, **R2**, Left
Operation Tar Be-Gone	Down, **L2**, **R1**, **L2**, **R1**, Right
Operation Turbo Dominant Eagle	Down, Right, Left, **L2**, **R1**, Right
Operation Wedding Crasher	**L2**, **R2**, Right, Down, **L1**, **R2**

SPIDER-MAN: FRIEND OR FOE

NEW GREEN GOBLIN AS A SIDEKICK

While standing in the Helicarrier between levels, press Left, Down, Right, Right, Down, Left.

SANDMAN AS A SIDEKICK

While standing in the Helicarrier between levels, press Right, Right, Right, Up, Down, Left.

VENOM AS A SIDEKICK

While standing in the Helicarrier between levels, press Left, Left, Right, Up, Down, Down.

5000 TECH TOKENS

While standing in the Helicarrier between levels, press Up, Up, Down, Down, Left, Right.

THE SPIDERWICK CHRONICLES

INVULNERABILITY

During the game, hold **L1** + **R1** and press ▲, ▲, ▲, ▲, ✕, ✕, ▲, ▲.

HEAL

During the game, hold **L1** + **R1** and press ▲, ■, ✕, ●, ▲, ■, ✕, ●.

COMBAT LOADOUT

During the game, hold **L1** + **R1** and press ▲, ▲, ✕, ✕, ■, ●, ■, ●.

INFINITE AMMO

During the game, hold **L1** + **R1** and press ■, ■, ■, ●, ✕, ✕, ✕, ▲.

FIELD GUIDE UNLOCKED

During the game, hold **L1** + **R1** and press ●, ●, ●, ■, ▲, ▲, ▲, ✕.

SPRITE A

During the game, hold **L2** + **R2** and press ▲, ✕, ●, ■, ✕, ▲, ■, ●.

SPRITE B

During the game, hold **L2** + **R2** and press ✕, ✕, ▲, ■, ●, ■, ▲, ✕.

SPRITE C

During the game, hold **L2** + **R2** and press ●, ▲, ■, ✕, ●, ▲, ■, ✕.

SPONGEBOB SQUAREPANTS FEATURING NICKTOONS: GLOBS OF DOOM

When entering the following codes, the order of the characters going down is: SpongeBob SquarePants, Nicolai Technus, Danny Phantom, Dib, Zim, Tlaloc, Tak, Beautiful Gorgeous, Jimmy Neutron, Plankton. These names are shortened to the first name in the following.

ATTRACT COINS

Using the Upgrade Machine on the bottom level of the lair, select "Input cheat codes here". Enter Tlaloc, Plankton, Danny, Plankton, Tak. Coins are attracted to you making them much easier to collect.

DON'T LOSE COINS

Using the Upgrade Machine on the bottom level of the lair, select "Input cheat codes here". Enter Plankton, Jimmy, Beautiful, Jimmy, Plankton. You don't lose coins when you get knocked out.

GOO HAS NO EFFECT

Using the Upgrade Machine on the bottom level of the lair, select "Input cheat codes here". Enter Danny, Danny, Danny, Nicolai, Nicolai. Goo does not slow you down.

MORE GADGET COMBO TIME

Using the Upgrade Machine on the bottom level of the lair, select "Input cheat codes here". Enter SpongeBob, Beautiful, Danny, Plankton, Nicolai. You have more time to perform gadget combos.

STAR WARS THE CLONE WARS: REPUBLIC HEROES

BIG HEAD MODE

Pause the game, select Shop, and enter Up, Down, Left, Right, Left, Right, Down, Up in Cheats.

MINI-GUN

Pause the game, select Shop, and enter Down, Left, Right, Up, Right, Up, Left, Down in Cheats.

ULTIMATE LIGHTSABER

Pause the game, select Shop, and enter Right, Down, Down, Up, Left, Up, Up, Down in Cheats.

LIGHTSABER THROW UPGRADE

Pause the game, select Shop, and enter Left, Left, Right, Right, Up, Down, Down, Up in Combat Upgrades.

SPIDER DROID UPGRADE

Pause the game, select Shop, and enter Up, Left, Down, Left, Right, Left, Left, Left in Droid-Jak Upgrades.

STAR WARS: THE FORCE UNLEASHED

CHEATS

Once you have accessed the Rogue Shadow, select Enter Code from the Extras menu. Now you can enter the following codes:

CHEAT	CODE	CHEAT	CODE
Invincibility	CORTOSIS	Max Force Power Level	KATARN
Unlimited Force	VERGENCE	Max Combo Level	COUNTDOOKU
1,000,000 Force Points	SPEEDER	Stronger Lightsaber	LIGHTSABER
All Force Powers	TYRANUS		

COSTUMES

Once you have accessed the Rogue Shadow, select Enter Code from the Extras menu. Now you can enter the following codes:

COSTUME	CODE	COSTUME	CODE
All Costumes	GRANDMOFF	Juno Eclipse	ECLIPSE
501st Legion	LEGION	Kento's Robe	WOOKIEE
Aayla Secura	AAYLA	Kleef	KLEEF
Admiral Ackbar	ITSATWAP	Lando Calrissian	SCOUNDREL
Anakin Skywalker	CHOSENONE	Luke Skywalker	T16WOMPRAT
Asajj Ventress	ACOLYTE	Luke Skywalker (Yavin)	YELLOWJCKT
Ceremonial Jedi Robes	DANTOOINE	Mace Windu	JEDIMASTER
Chop'aa Notimo	NOTIMO	Mara Jade	MARAJADE
Classic stormtrooper	TK421	Maris Brook	MARISBROOD
Count Dooku	SERENNO	Navy commando	STORMTROOP
Darth Desolous	PAUAN	Obi Wan Kenobi	BENKENOBI
Darth Maul	ZABRAK	Proxy	HOLOGRAM
Darth Phobos	HIDDENFEAR	Qui Gon Jinn	MAVERICK
Darth Vader	SITHLORD	Shaak Ti	TOGRUTA
Drexl Roosh	DREXLROOSH	Shadow trooper	INTHEDARK
Emperor Palpatine	PALPATINE	Sith Robes	HOLOCRON
General Rahm Kota	MANDALORE	Sith Stalker Armor	KORRIBAN
Han Solo	NERFHERDER	Twi'lek	SECURA
Heavy trooper	SHOCKTROOP		

STREET FIGHTER ALPHA ANTHOLOGY

STREET FIGHTER ALPHA

PLAY AS DAN

At the Character Select screen in Arcade Mode, hold the Start button and place the cursor on the Random Select space then input one of the following commands within 1 second:

LP LK MK HK HP MP

HP HK MK LK LP MP

LK LP MP HP HK MK

HK HP MP LP LK HK

PLAY AS M.BISON

At the Character Select screen, hold the Start button, place the cursor on the random select box, and input:

1P side: Down, Down, Back, Back, Down, Back, Back + LP + HP

2P side: Down, Down, Forward, Forward, Down, Forward, Forward + LP + HP

PLAY AS AKUMA

At the Character Select screen, hold the Start button, place the cursor on the random select box, and input:

1P side: Down, Down, Down, Back, Back, Back + LP + HP

2P side: Down, Down, Down, Forward, Forward, Forward + LP + HP

AKUMA MODE

Select your character in Arcade mode, then press and hold Start + MP + MK as the Character Selection screen ends.

RYU AND KEN VS. M.BISON

On both the 1p and 2p side in Arcade mode, press and hold Start, then:

1P side: place the cursor on Ryu and input Up, Up, release Start, Up, Up + LP

2P side: place the cursor on Ken and input Up, Up, release Start, Up, Up + HP

LAST BOSS MODE
Select Arcade mode while holding ●, ✕, and **R1**.

DRAMATIC BATTLE MODE
Select Dramatic Battle mode while holding ●, ✕, and **R2**.

RANDOM BATTLE MODE
Select Versus mode while holding ●, ✕, and **R2**.

STREET FIGHTER ALPHA 2

PLAY AS ORIGINAL CHUN-LI
Highlight Chun-Li on the Character Select screen, hold the Start button for 3 seconds, then select Chun-Li normally.

PLAY AS SHIN AKUMA
Highlight Akuma on the Character Select screen, hold the Start button for 3 seconds, then select Akuma normally.

PLAY AS EVIL RYU
Highlight Ryu on the Character Select screen, hold the Start button, input Forward, Up, Down, Back, then select Ryu normally.

PLAY AS EX DHALSIM
Highlight Dhalsim on the Character Select screen, hold the Start button, input Back, Down, Forward, Up, then select Dhalsim normally.

PLAY AS EX ZANGIEF
Highlight Zangief on the Character Select screen, hold the Start button, input Down, Back, Back, Back, Back, Up, Up, Forward, Forward, Forward, Forward, Down, then select Zangief normally.

LAST BOSS MODE
Select Arcade mode while holding the ●, ●, and **R1** buttons.

DRAMATIC BATTLE MODE
Select Dramatic Battle mode while holding the ● + ✕ + **R2**.

SELECT SPECIAL ROUTE IN SURVIVAL MODE
Select Survival Battle while holding the **R1** or **R2**.

RANDOM BATTLE MODE
Select Versus mode while holding the ● + ✕ + **R2**.

STREET FIGHTER ALPHA 2 GOLD

PLAY AS EX RYU
Highlight Ryu and press the Start button once before selecting normally.

PLAY AS EVIL RYU
Highlight Ryu and press the Start button twice before selecting normally.

PLAY AS ORIGINAL CHUN-LI
Highlight Chun-Li and press the Start button once before selecting normally.

PLAY AS EX CHUN-LI
Highlight Chun-Li and press the Start button twice before selecting normally.

PLAY AS EX KEN
Highlight Ken and press the Start button once before selecting normally.

PLAY AS EX DHALSIM
Highlight Dhalsim and press the Start button once before selecting normally.

PLAY AS EX ZANGIEF
Highlight Zangief and press the Start button once before selecting normally.

PLAY AS EX SAGAT

Highlight Sagat and press the Start button once before selecting normally.

PLAY AS EX M.BISON

Highlight M.Bison and press the Start button once before selecting normally.

PLAY USING SAKURA'S ALTERNATE COLORS

Highlight Sakura and press the Start button five times before selecting normally.

PLAY AS SHIN AKUMA

Highlight Akuma and press the Start button five times before selecting normally.

PLAY AS CAMMY

Highlight M.Bison and press the Start button twice before selecting normally.

LAST BOSS MODE

Select Arcade mode while holding ⬤ + ⬤ + R1.

SELECT SPECIAL ROUTE IN SURVIVAL MODE

Select Survival Battle while holding the R1 or R2.

DRAMATIC BATTLE MODE

Select Dramatic Battle mode while holding ⬤ + ✖ + R2.

RANDOM BATTLE MODE

Select Versus mode while holding ⬤ + ✖ + R2.

STREET FIGHTER ALPHA 3

PLAY AS BALROG

Highlight Karin for one second, then move the cursor to the random select box and hold Start before selecting normally.

PLAY AS JULI

Highlight Karin for one second, then move the cursor to the random select box and press Up, or Down, while selecting normally.

PLAY AS JUNI

Highlight Karin for one second, then move the cursor to the random select box and press Back, or Forward, while selecting normally.

CLASSICAL MODE

Press and hold HP + HK while starting game.

SPIRITED MODE

Press and hold MP + MK while starting game.

SAIKYO MODE

Press and hold LP + LK while starting game.

SHADALOO MODE

Press and hold LK + MK + HK while starting game.

SELECT SPECIAL ROUTE IN SURVIVAL MODE

Select Survival mode while holding R1 or R2.

DRAMATIC BATTLE MODE

Select Dramatic Battle mode while holding ⬤ + ✖ + R2.

RANDOM BATTLE MODE

Select Versus mode while holding ⬤ + ✖ + R2.

NEED FOR SPEED CARBON: OWN THE CITY

UNLOCK EVERYTHING

At the start menu, press ✕, ✕, Right, Left, ●, Up, Down.

JET CAR

At the start menu, press Up, Down, Left, R1, L1, ●, ▲.

LAMBORGINI MERCIALAGO

At the start menu, press ✕, ✕, Up, Down, Left, Right, ●, ●.

TRANSFORMERS CAR

At the start menu, press ✕, ✕, ✕, ●, ▲, ▲, Up, Down.

NEOPETS PETPET ADVENTURE: THE WAND OF WISHING

START GAME WITH 5 CHOCOLATE TREATS

Enter treat4u as your Petpet's name. You can then rename name your character. The chocolate treats are shaped according to the character you chose.

PHANTASY STAR PORTABLE 2

VISION PHONE

Use your Vision Phone to enter the following:

EFFECT	PASSWORD	EFFECT	PASSWORD
Akahara Reisou	24932278	Miku's T. Leek Sabers	39395344
Akahara Reisou	24932279	Mr. Ekoeko Stick	55687362
Akahara Reisou	24932280	Ogi's Head	74612418
Alis Landale Poster	41325468	Pizza Shack D Box	89747981
Angry Marshmellow	32549410	Platinum Tiger	32549412
Art Javelin	72401990	Platinum Tiger	32549414
Blank Epoch	48168861	Platinum Tiger	32549411
Blank Epoch	48168862	Platinum Tiger	32549413
Bullet Lancer	32091120	Plug Suit Asuka	34336181
Clarita Visas	29888026	Plug Suit Asuka	34336182
Crutches	98443460	Plug Suit Rei	46211351
Edelweiss Figurine	54333358	Plug Suit Rei	46211352
Hanhei Tsunagin	41761771	Plug Suit Shinji	15644322
Hanhei Tsunagin	41761772	Puyo Pop Fever Gun	54186516
Hatsune Miku's Leek Wand	12344321	Puyo Pop Fists	11293398
Kansho Bayuka	46815464	Scouring Bubble	33286491
Longinus Lance	32143166	Sonic Knuckles	34819852
Lovely Feathers	72401991	Special Pizza Cutter	34162313
Lovely Feathers	72401992	Telltale Hearts	48168860
Magical Princess	55687361	The Rappy of Hope	54684698
Magical Princess	55687362	Toop Nasur	30495153
Maverick Rifle	53962481	Trauma Bandages	98443462
Miku Hatsune Dress	39395341	Trauma Bandages	98443464
Miku Hatsune Dress	39395342	Trauma Bandages	98443461
Miku's Leek Rifle	39395345	Trauma Bandages	98443463
Miku's Leek Saber	39395343	True Hash	41761770

POCKET POOL

ALL PICTURES AND VIDEOS

At the title screen, press L, R, L, L, R, R, L (x3), R (x3), L (x4), R (x4).

PRINNY: CAN I REALLY BE THE HERO?

START A NEW GAME WITH THE ALTERNATE STORYLINE

At the main menu, highlight New Game and press ⚫, ⚫, ⚫, ⚫, ⚫, ⚫, ⚫, ⚫.

ROCKET RACING

TRIGGER MODE

At the main menu or during a game, hold L and press Up, Down, Left, Right, ⚫, release L.

TRIGGER MODE (REVERSED)

At the main menu or during a game, hold L and press Up, Down, Left, Right, ⚫, release L.

STICK MODE (DEFAULT)

At the main menu or during a game, hold L and press Up, Down, Left, Right, R, release L

SECRET AGENT CLANK

ACTIVATE CHALICE OF POWER

Press Up, Up, Down, Down, Left, Right, Left, Right to regain health once per level.

THE SECRET SATURDAYS: BEASTS OF THE 5TH SUN

ALL LEVELS

Select Enter Secret Code from the Secrets menu and enter Zon, Zon, Zon, Zon.

UNLOCK AMAROK TO BE SCANNED IN LEVEL 2

Select Enter Secret Code from the Secrets menu and enter Fiskerton, Zak, Zon, Komodo.

UNLOCK BISHOPVILLE LIZARDMAN TO BE SCANNED IN LEVEL 3

Select Enter Secret Code from the Secrets menu and enter Komodo, Zon, Zak, Komodo.

UNLOCK NAGA TO BE SCANNED IN LEVEL 7

Select Enter Secret Code from the Secrets menu and enter Zak, Zak, Zon, Fiskerton.

UNLOCK RAKSHASA TO BE SCANNED IN LEVEL 8

Select Enter Secret Code from the Secrets menu and enter Zak, Komodo, Fiskerton, Fiskerton.

UNLOCK BILOKO TO BE SCANNED IN LEVEL 9

Select Enter Secret Code from the Secrets menu and enter Zon, Zak, Zon, Fiskerton.

SEGA GENESIS COLLECTION

Before using the following cheats, select the ABC Control option. This sets the controller to the following: ⚫ is A, ⚫ is B, ⚫ is C.

ALTERED BEAST

OPTIONS MENU

At the title screen, hold ⚫ and press Start.

LEVEL SELECT

After enabling the Options menu, select a level from the menu. At the title screen, hold ⚫ and press Start.

BEAST SELECT

At the title screen, hold ⚫ + ⚫ + ⚫ + Down/Left and then press Start

SOUND TEST

At the title screen, hold ⚫ + ⚫ + Up/Right and press Start.

COMIX ZONE

INVINCIBILITY

At the jukebox screen, press C on the following sounds:
3, 12, 17, 2, 2, 10, 2, 7, 7, 11

LEVEL SELECT

At the jukebox screen, press C on the following sounds:
14, 15, 18, 5, 13, 1, 3, 18, 15, 6
Press C on the desired level.

ECCO THE DOLPHIN

INVINCIBILITY

When the level name appears, hold ⬤ + Start until the level begins.

DEBUG MENU

Pause the game with Ecco facing the screen and press Right, ❌,⬤, ❌,⬤, Down,⬤, Up.

INFINITE AIR

Enter LIFEFISH as a password

PASSWORDS

LEVEL	PASSWORD	LEVEL	PASSWORD
The Undercaves	WEFIDNMP	Deep City	DDXPQQLJ
The Vents	BQDPXJDS	City of Forever	MSDBRQLA
The Lagoon	JNSBRIKY	Jurassic Beach	IYCBUNLB
Ridge Water	NTSBZTKB	Pteranodon Pond	DMXEUNLI
Open Ocean	YWGTTJNI	Origin Beach	EGRIUNLB
Ice Zone	HZIFZBMF	Trilobite Circle	IELMUNLB
Hard Water	LRFJRQLI	Dark Water	RKEQUNLN
Cold Water	UYNFRQLC	City of Forever 2	HPQIGPLA
Island Zone	LYTIOQLZ	The Tube	JUMFKMLB
Deep Water	MNOPOQLR	The Machine	GXUBKMLF
The Marble	RJNTQQLZ	The Last Fight	TSONLMLU
The Library	RTGXQQLE		

FLICKY

ROUND SELECT

Begin a new game. Before the first round appears, hold ⬤ + ⬤ + Up + Start. Press Up or Down to select a Round.

GAIN GROUND

LEVEL SELECT

At the Options screen, press ⬤, ⬤, ❌, ⬤.

GOLDEN AXE

LEVEL SELECT

Select Arcade Mode. At the character select, hold Down/Left +❌ and press Start. Press Up or Down to select a level.

RISTAR

Select Passwords from the Options menu and enter the following:

LEVEL SELECT
ILOVEU

TIME ATTACK MODE
DOFEEL

BOSS RUSH MODE
MUSEUM

TOUGHER DIFFICULTY
SUPER

ONCH! MUSIC
MAGURO. Activate this from the Sound Test.

GAME COPYRIGHT INFO
AGES

CLEARS PASSWORD
XXXXXX

SONIC THE HEDGEHOG

LEVEL SELECT
At the title screen, press Up, Down, Left, Right. Hold ● and press Start.

SONIC THE HEDGEHOG 2

LEVEL SELECT
Select Sound Test from the options. Press C on the following sounds in order: 19, 65, 09, 17.
At the title screen, hold ● and press Start.

VECTORMAN

DEBUG MODE
At the options screen, press ●, ✖, ✖, ●, Down, ●, ✖, ✖, ●.

REFILL LIFE
Pause the game and press ●, ✖, Right, ●, ●, ●, Down, ●, ✖, Right, ●.

VECTORMAN 2

LEVEL SELECT
Pause the game and press Up, Right, ●,✖, ●, Down, Left, ●, Down.

EXTRA LIFE
Pause the game and press Right, Up, ✖, ●, Down, Up, ✖, Down, Up, ✖. Repeat for more lives.

FULL ENERGY
Pause the game and press ✖, ●, ✖, ●, Left, Up, Up.

NEW WEAPON
Pause the game and press ●, ●, Left, Left, Down, ●, Down. Repeat for more weapons.

SHREK THE THIRD

10,000 BONUS COINS
Press Up, Up, Down, Up, Right, Left at the Gift Shop.

THE SIMPSONS GAME

UNLIMITED POWER FOR ALL CHARACTERS
At the Extras menu, press ▲, Left, Right, ▲, ●, L.

ALL MOVIES
At the Extras menu, press ●, Left, ●, Right, ▲, R.

ALL CLICHÉS
At the Extras menu, press Left, ●, Right, ▲, Right, L.

THE SIMS 2: CASTAWAY

CHEAT GNOME
During a game, press L, R, Up, ✪, R. You can now use this Gnome to get the following during Live mode:

ALL PLANS
During a game, press ✪, R, ✪, R, ✪.

ALL CRAFT AND RESOURCES
During a game, press ●, ▲, R, Down, Down, Up.

MAX FOOD AND RESOURCES
During a game, press ● (x4), L.

THE SIMS 2: PETS

CHEAT GNOME
During a game, press L, L, R, ✪, ✪, Up. Now you can enter the following cheats:

ADVANCE TIME 6 HOURS
During a game, press Up, Left, Down, Right, R.

GIVE SIM PET POINTS
During a game, press ▲, ●, ✪, ●, L, R.

$10,000
During a game, press ▲, Up, Left, Down, Right.

SPIDER-MAN: FRIEND OR FOE

NEW GOBLIN
At the stage complete screen, hold L + R and press ●, Down, ✪, Right, ●, Up, ▲, Left.

STAR WARS: THE FORCE UNLEASHED

CHEATS
Once you have accessed the Rogue Shadow, select Enter Code from the Extras menu. Now you can enter the following codes:

CHEAT	CODE
Invincibility	CORTOSIS
Unlimited Force	VERGENCE
1,000,000 Force Points	SPEEDER
All Force Powers	TYRANUS
Max Force Power Level	KATARN
Max Combo Level	COUNTDOOKU
Amplified Lightsaber Damage	LIGHTSABER

COSTUMES
Once you have accessed the Rogue Shadow, select Enter Code from the Extras menu. Now you can enter the following codes:

COSTUME	CODE	COSTUME	CODE
All Costumes	GRANDMOFF	Drexl Roosh	DREXLROOSH
501st Legion	LEGION	Emperor Palpatine	PALPATINE
Aayla Secura	AAYLA	General Rahm Kota	MANDALORE
Admiral Ackbar	ITSATWAP	Han Solo	NERFHERDER
Anakin Skywalker	CHOSENONE	Heavy trooper	SHOCKTROOP
Asajj Ventress	ACOLYTE	Juno Eclipse	ECLIPSE
Ceremonial Jedi Robes	DANTOOINE	Kento's Robe	WOOKIEE
Chop'aa Notimo	NOTIMO	Kleef	KLEEF
Classic stormtrooper	TK421	Lando Calrissian	SCOUNDREL
Count Dooku	SERENNO	Luke Skywalker	T16WOMPRAT
Darth Desolous	PAUAN	Luke Skywalker (Yavin)	YELLOWJCKT
Darth Maul	ZABRAK	Mace Windu	JEDIMASTER
Darth Phobos	HIDDENFEAR	Mara Jade	MARAJADE
Darth Vader	SITHLORD	Maris Brook	MARISBROOD

COSTUME	CODE
Navy commando	STORMTROOP
Obi Wan Kenobi	BENKENOBI
Proxy	HOLOGRAM
Qui Gon Jinn	MAVERICK
Shaak Ti	TOGRUTA

COSTUME	CODE
Shadow trooper	INTHEDARK
Sith Robes	HOLOCRON
Sith Stalker Armor	KORRIBAN
Twi'lek	SECURA

STAR WARS: LETHAL ALLIANCE

ALL LEVELS
Select Create Profile from the Profiles menu and enter HANSOLO.

ALL LEVELS AND REFILL HEALTH WHEN DEPLETED
Select Create Profile from the Profiles menu and enter JD1MSTR.

REFILL HEALTH WHEN DEPLETED
Select Create Profile from the Profiles menu and enter B0BAF3T.

STRIKERS 1945 PLUS PORTABLE

XP-55 ASCENDER
At the random select, press Down, Up, Down, Up, Down, Down, Down, Down, Up.

SUPER MONKEY BALL ADVENTURE

ALL CARDS
At the mode select, press ■, ▲, ●, ■, ▲, ●, ■, ▲, ●, ■, ▲, ●.

THRILLVILLE: OFF THE RAILS

$50,000
During a game, press ■, ●, ▲, ■, ●, ▲, ✕. Repeat this code as much as desired.

ALL PARKS
During a game, press ■, ●, ▲, ■, ●, ▲, ■.

ALL RIDES
During a game, press ■, ●, ▲, ■, ●, ▲, ▲. Some rides still need to be researched.

COMPLETE MISSIONS
During a game, press ■, ●, ▲, ■, ●, ▲, ●. Then, at the Missions menu, highlight a mission and press ■ to complete that mission. Some missions have Bronze, Silver, and Gold objectives. For these missions the first press of ■ earns the Bronze, the second earns the Silver, and the third earns the Gold.

TIGER WOODS PGA TOUR 09

UNLOCK PGA TOUR EVENTS
Enter BEATIT as a password.

$1,000,000
Enter JACKPOT as a password.

UNLOCK ALL CLOTHING AND EQUIPMENT
Enter SHOP2DROP as a password.

MAX SKILL POINTS AND ALL CLOTHING AND EQUIPMENT
Enter IAMRUBBISH as a password.

UNLOCK ALL COVER STORIES
Enter HEADLINER as a password.

TOMB RAIDER: LEGEND

You need to unlock the following cheats before they can be used.

BULLETPROOF

During a game, hold L and press ✕, R, △, R, ⬤, R.

DRAW ENEMY HEALTH

During a game, hold L and press ⬤, ⬤, ✕, R, R, △.

INFINITE ASSUALT RIFLE AMMO

During a game, hold L and press ✕, O, ✕, R, ⬤, △.

INFINITE GRENADE LAUNCHER

During a game, hold L and press R, △, R, ⬤, R, ⬤.

INFINITE SHOTGUN AMMO

During a game, hold L and press R, ⬤, ⬤, R, ⬤, ✕.

INFINITE SMG AMMO

During a game, hold L and press ⬤, △, R, R, ✕, ⬤.

ONE SHOT KILL

During a game, hold L and press △, ✕, △, ⬤, R, ⬤.

TEXTURELESS MODE

hold L and press R, ✕, ⬤, ✕, △, R.

WIELD EXCALIBUR

During a game, hold L and press △, ✕, ⬤, R, △, R.

TOY STORY 3

BUZZ USES LASER IN ALL STORY LEVELS

Select Cheat Codes from the Bonus menu and enter BLASER. Activate the cheat from the pause menu.

WOODY'S BANDIT OUTFIT

Select Cheat Codes from the Bonus menu and enter BANDIT. Activate the cheat from the pause menu.

TOY ALIENS WEAR 3D GLASSES

Select Cheat Codes from the Bonus menu and enter 3DGLAS. Activate the cheat from the pause menu.

OLD MOVIE EFFECT

Select Cheat Codes from the Bonus menu and enter OLDMOV. Activate the cheat from the pause menu.

VALKYRIA CHRONICLES II

TANK STICKERS

Enter the following codes in Extra Mode for the desired effect.

STICKER	CODE	STICKER	CODE
Alicia Gunther	K1C7XKLJMXUHRD8S	Isara Gunther and Isara's Dream	37LRK5D214VQVFYH
Blitz Logo	VWUYNJQ8HGSVXR7J	Prince Maximilian and Imperial Flag	H73G4L9GLJR1CHJP
Edy Nelson	R5PT1MXEY3BW8VBE	Selvaria	53K8FKGP1GHQ4SBN
Edy's Squad	CR6BG1A9LYQKB6WJ	Sonic the Hedgehog	CUP34ASEZ9WDKBYV
SEGA Logo	6RK45S59F7U2JLTD	Super Monkey Ball	7JMNHZ83TGH7XFKT
Skies of Arcadia	WVZLPTYXURS1Q8TV	Yakuza	QAKVXZTALF4TU7SK
Crazy Taxi	38WV17PK45TYAF8V	Vanquish Tank	BUNLT4EXDS74QRCR
Faldio	GWNU95RSETW1VGNQ		
Gallian Military	TXU14EUV74PCR3TE		

CHARACTERS

Enter the following codes in Extra Mode for the desired effect.

CHARACTER	CODE
Alicia Gunther	KBAFLFHICAJTKMIY
Edy's Detachment	TKBHCNBERHRKJNFG
Julius Kroze	AMNKZKYTKNBNKYMT
Lamar/Ramal	LITSGAAMEORFRCRQ
Landzaat Farudio	KNWRJRGSMLASTNSQ
Maximillian	KBFHZRJTKMKSKNKP
Mintz	CKRJWNSXTYMNGZRT
Selvaria	KSNEGA56LPY7CTQ9
Support-class Aliasse, Lancer-class Cosette and Armor-type Zeri	PZRJQM7SK4HPXTYM

VIRTUA TENNIS 3

ALL COURTS

At the Game Mode screen, press Up, Up, Down, Down, Left, Right, Left, Right.

ALL GEAR

At the Game Mode screen, press Left, Right, ◉, Left, Right, ◉, Up, Down.

KING & DUKE

At the Game Mode screen, press Up, Up, Down, Down, Left, Right, L, R.

WALL-E

KILL ALL

Select Cheats and then Secret Codes. Enter BOTOFWAR.

UNDETECTED BY ENEMIES

Select Cheats and then Secret Codes. Enter STEALTHARMOR.

LASERS CHANGE COLORS

Select Cheats and then Secret Codes. Enter RAINBOWLAZER.

CUBES ARE EXPLOSIVE

Select Cheats and then Secret Codes. Enter EXPLOSIVEWORLD.

LIGHTEN DARK AREAS

Select Cheats and then Secret Codes. Enter GLOWINTHEDARK.

GOGGLES

Select Cheats and then Secret Codes. Enter BOTOFMYSTERY.

GOLD TRACKS

Select Cheats and then Secret Codes. Enter GOLDENTRACKS.

WHAT DID I DO TO DESERVE THIS, MY LORD!? 2

WHAT DID I DO TO DESERVE THIS, MY LORD!?

At the title screen, press L, R, L, R, L, R, L, R, L, R to play the first What Did I Do to Deserve This, My Lord!?

WHAT DID I NOT DO TO DESERVE THIS, MY LORD!?

After entering the above code and the game loads, enter the same code again at the title screen. This is the Hard Mode of What Did I Do to Deserve This, My Lord!?.

PLAYSTATIO

WORLD CHAMPIONSHIP POKER 2: FEATURING HOWARD LEDERER

SKIP WEEK AND MONEY CHEATS

At the career world map, hold **R1**. Hold **L1** and release **R1**. Hold Up and release **L1**. Hold **L1** and release Up. Hold **R1** and release **L1**. While still holding **R1**, press Up/Down to skip weeks and Right/Left for money.

WRC: FIA WORLD RALLY CHAMPIONSHIP

UNLOCK EVERYTHING
Create a new profile with the name PADLOCK.

EXTRA AVATARS
Create a new profile with the name UGLYMUGS.

GHOST CAR
Create a new profile with the name SPOOKY.

SUPERCHARGER
Create a new profile with the name MAXPOWER.

TIME TRIAL GHOST CARS
Create a new profile with the name AITRIAL.

BIRD CAMERA
Create a new profile with the name dovecam.

REVERSES CONTROLS
Create a new profile with the name REVERSE.

WWE SMACKDOWN VS. RAW 2010

THE ROCK
Select Cheat Codes from the Options and enter The Great One.

VINCE'S OFFICE AND DIRT SHEET FOR BACKSTAGE BRAWL
Select Cheat Codes from the Options menu and enter BonusBrawl.

HBK/SHAWN MICHAEL'S ALTERNATE COSTUME
Select Cheat Codes from the Options menu and enter Bow Down.

JOHN CENA'S ALTERNATE COSTUME
Select Cheat Codes from the Options menu and enter CENATION.

RANDY ORTON'S ALTERNATE COSTUME
Select Cheat Codes from the Options menu and enter ViperRKO.

SANTINO MARELLA'S ALTERNATE COSTUME
Select Cheat Codes from the Options menu and enter Milan Miracle.

TRIPLE H'S ALTERNATE COSTUME
Select Cheat Codes from the Options menu and enter Suck IT!.

WWE SMACKDOWN VS. RAW 2011

JOHN CENA (ENTRANCE/CIVILIAN)
In My WWE, select Cheat Codes from the Options and enter SLURPEE.

ALL OF RANDY ORTON'S COSTUMES
In My WWE, select Cheat Codes from the Options and enter apexpredator.

TRIBUTE TO THE TROOPS ARENA
In My WWE, select Cheat Codes from the Options and enter 8thannualtribute.

X-MEN LEGENDS II: RISE OF APOCALYPSE

ALL CHARACTERS

At the Team Management screen, press Right, Left, Left, Right, Up, Up, Up, Start.

LEVEL 99 CHARACTERS

At the Team Management screen, press Up, Down, Up, Down, Left, Up, Left, Right, Start.

ALL SKILLS

At the Team Management screen, press Left, Right, Left, Right, Down, Up, Start.

SUPER SPEED

Pause the game and press Up, Up, Up, Down, Up, Down, Start.

UNLIMITED XTREME POWER

Pause the game and press Left, Down, Right, Down, Up, Up, Down, Up Start.

100,000 TECHBITS

At Forge or Beast's equipment screen, press Up, Up, Up, Down, Right, Right, Start.

ALL CINEMATICS

A the Review menu, press Left, Right, Right, Left, Down, Down, Left, Start.

ALL COMIC BOOKS

At the Review menu, press Right, Left, Left, Right, Up, Up, Right, Start.

YU-GI-OH! 5D'S TAG FORCE 4

HIGH NOON CONSTELLATION PACK

At the card shop, press Right (x5), ⬤ (x7), Select (x3).

YU-GI-OH! 5D'S TAG FORCE 5

HIGH NOON CONSTELLATION PACK

At the card shop, press Up, Up, Down, Down, L, R, L, R, ⬤, ▲.

YU-GI-OH! DUEL MONSTERS GX: TAG FORCE 3

MIDDAY CONSTELLATION BOOSTER PACK

At the store, get to the booster pack menu and press Up, Up, Down, Down, Left, Right, Left, Right, ✖, ⬤. The pack will now be available at the store.

YU-GI-OH! GX TAG FORCE

BOOSTER PACK

At the card shop, press Up, Up, Down, Down, Left, Right, Left, Right, ⊗, ◉.

YU-GI-OH! GX TAG FORCE 2

MIDDDAY CONSTELLATION BOOSTER PACK

When buying booster packs, press Up, Up, Down, Down, Left, Right, Left, Right, ⊗, ◉.

YU-GI-OH! CARD PASSWORDS

Enter the following in the Password Machine to obtain for rental:

PASSWORD	EFFECT	PASSWORD	EFFECT
4-Starred Ladybug of Doom	83994646	Ancient Gear Cannon	80045583
7 Colored Fish	23771716	Ancient Gear Castle	92001300
A Cat of Ill Omen	24140059	Ancient Gear Drill	67829249
A Deal With Dark Ruler	06850209	Ancient Gear Golem	83104731
A Feather of the Phoenix	49140998	Ancient Gear Soldier	56094445
A Feint Plan	68170903	Ancient Lamp	54912977
A Hero Emerges	21597117	Ancient Lizard Warrior	43230671
A Legendary Ocean	00295517	Andro Sphinx	15013468
A Man With Wdjat	51351302	Anteatereatingant	13250922
A Rival Appears!	05728014	Anti-Aircraft Flower	65064143
A Wingbeat of Giant Dragon	28596933	Anti-Spell	53112492
A-Team: Trap Disposal Unit	13026402	Apprentice Magician	09156135
Abare Ushioni	89718302	Appropriate	48539234
Absolute End	27744077	Aqua Madoor	85639257
Absorbing Kid From the Sky	49771608	Aqua Spirit	40916023
Abyss Soldier	18318842	Arcane Archer of the Forest	55001420
Abyssal Designator	89801755	Archfiend of Gilfer	50287060
Acid Trap Hole	41356845	Archfiend Soldier	49881766
Acrobat Monkey	47372349	Archlord Zerato	18378582
Adhesion Trap Hole	62325062	Armaill	53153481
Adhesive Explosive	53828396	Armed Changer	90374791
After the Struggle	25345186	Armed Dragon LV 3	00980973
Agido	16135253	Armed Dragon LV 5	46384672
Airknight Parshath	18036057	Armed Dragon LV 7	73879377
Aitsu	48202661	Armed Dragon LV10	59464593
Alkana Knight Joker	06150044	Armed Ninja	09076207
Alpha the Magnet Warrior	99785935	Armed Samurai - Ben Kei	84430950
Altar for Tribute	21070956	Armor Axe	07180418
Amazon Archer	91869203	Armor Break	79649195
Amazoness Archers	67987611	Armored Lizard	15480588
Amazoness Blowpiper	73574678	Armored Starfish	17535588
Amazoness Chain Master	29654737	Armored Zombie	20277860
Amazoness Paladin	47480070	Array of Revealing Light	69296555
Amazoness Swords Woman	94004268	Arsenal Bug	42364374
Amazoness Tiger	10979723	Arsenal Robber	55348096
Ambulance Rescueroid	98927491	Arsenal Summoner	85489096
Ambulanceroid	36378213	Assault on GHQ	62633180
Ameba	95174353	Astral Barrier	37053871
Amphibian Beast	67371383	Asura Priest	02134346
Amphibious Bugroth MK-3	64342551	Aswan Apparition	88236094
Amplifier	00303660	Atomic Firefly	87340664
An Owl of Luck	23927567	Attack and Receive	63689843
Ancient Elf	93221206	Attack Reflector Unit	91989718
Ancient Gear	31557782	Aussa the Earth Charmer	37970940
Ancient Gear Beast	10509340	Autonomous Action Unit	71453557

PASSWORD	EFFECT
Avatar of the Pot	99284890
Axe Dragonute	84914462
Axe of Despair	40619825
B. Skull Dragon	11901678
B.E.S. Covered Core	15317640
B.E.S. Crystal Core	22790789
B.E.S. Tetran	44954628
Baby Dragon	88819587
Back to Square One	47453433
Backfire	82705573
Backup Soldier	36280194
Bad Reaction to Simochi	40633297
Bait Doll	07165085
Ballista of Rampart Smashing	00242146
Banisher of the Light	61528025
Bark of Dark Ruler	41925941
Barrel Dragon	81480460
Basic Insect	89091579
Battery Charger	61181383
Batteryman AA	63142001
Batteryman C	19733961
Batteryman D	55401221
Battle Footballer	48094997
Battle Ox	05053103
Battle-Scarred	94463200
Bazoo The Soul-Eater	40133511
Beast Soul Swap	35149085
Beaver Warrior	32452818
Beckoning Light	16255442
Beelze Frog	49522489
Begone, Knave	20374520
Behemoth the King of All Animals	22996376
Beiige, Vanguard of Dark World	33731070
Berserk Dragon	85605684
Berserk Gorilla	39168895
Beta the Magnet Warrior	39256679
Bickuribox	25655502
Big Bang Shot	61127349
Big Burn	95472621
Big Core	14148099
Big Koala	42129512
Big Shield Gardna	65240384
Big Wave Small Wave	51562916
Big-Tusked Mammoth	59380081
Bio-Mage	58696829
Birdface	45547649
Black Illusion Ritual	41426869
Black Luster Soldier - Envoy of the Beginning	72989439
Black Pendant	65169794
Black Tyranno	38670435
Blackland Fire Dragon	87564352
Blade Knight	39507162
Blade Rabbit	58268433
Blade Skater	97023549
Bladefly	28470714
Blast Held By a Tribute	89041555
Blast Magician	21051146
Blast with Chain	98239899

PASSWORD	EFFECT
Blasting the Ruins	21466326
Blazing Inpachi	05464695
Blind Destruction	32015116
Blindly Loyal Goblin	35215622
Block Attack	25880422
Blockman	48115277
Blowback Dragon	25551951
Blue-Eyes Shining Dragon	53347303
Blue-Eyes Toon Dragon	53183600
Blue-Eyes Ultimate Dragon	23995346
Blue-Eyes White Dragon	89631139
Blue-Winged Crown	41396436
Bokoichi the Freightening Car	08715625
Bombardment Beetle	57409948
Bonding - H20	45898858
Boneheimer	98456117
Book of Life	02204140
Book of Moon	14087893
Book of Taiyou	38699854
Boss Rush	66947414
Bottom Dweller	81386177
Bottomless Shifting Sand	76532077
Bottomless Trap Hole	29401950
Bountiful Artemis	32226881
Bowganian	52090844
Bracchio-Raidus	16507828
Brain Control	87910978
Brain Jacker	40267580
Branch!	30548775
Breaker the Magical Warrior	71413901
Broww, Huntsman of Dark World	79126789
Brron, Mad King of Dark World	06214884
Bubble Blaster	53586134
Bubble Illusion	80075749
Bubble Shuffle	61968753
Bubonic Vermin	06104968
Burning Algae	41859700
Burning Beast	59364406
Burning Land	24294108
Burst Breath	80163754
Burst Return	27191436
Burst Stream of Destruction	17655904
Buster Blader	78193831
Buster Rancher	84740193
Butterfly Dagger - Elma	69243953
Byser Shock	17597059
Call of The Haunted	97077563
Call of the Mummy	04861205
Cannon Soldier	11384280
Cannonball Spear Shellfish	95614612
Card of Safe Return	57953380
Card Shuffle	12183332
Castle of Dark Illusions	00062121
Cat's Ear Tribe	95841282
Catapult Turtle	95727991
Cathedral of Nobles	29762407
Catnipped Kitty	96501677
Cave Dragon	93220472
Ceasefire	36468556

PASSWORD	EFFECT	PASSWORD	EFFECT
Celtic Guardian	91152256	Curse of Aging	41398771
Cemetery Bomb	51394546	Curse of Anubis	66742250
Centrifugal	01801154	Curse of Darkness	84970821
Ceremonial Bell	20228463	Curse of Dragon	28279543
Cetus of Dagala	28106077	Curse of the Masked Beast	94377247
Chain Burst	48276469	Curse of Vampire	34294855
Chain Destruction	01248895	Cyber Dragon	70095154
Chain Disappearance	57139487	Cyber End Dragon	01546123
Chain Energy	79323590	Cyber Twin Dragon	74157028
Chain Thrasher	88190453	Cyber-Dark Edge	77625948
Chainsaw Insect	77252217	Cyber-Stein	69015963
Change of Heart	04031928	Cyberdark Dragon	40418351
Chaos Command Magician	72630549	Cyberdark Horn	41230939
Chaos Emperor Dragon - Envoy of the End	82301904	Cyberdark Keel	03019642
Chaos End	61044390	D - Shield	62868900
Chaos Greed	97439308	D - Time	99075257
Chaos Necromancer	01434352	D. D. Assailant	70074904
Chaos Sorcerer	09596126	D. D. Borderline	60912752
Chaosrider Gutaph	47829960	D. D. Crazy Beast	48148828
Charcoal Inpachi	13179332	D. D. Dynamite	08628798
Charm of Shabti	50412166	D. D. M. - Different Dimension Master	82112775
Charubin the Fire Knight	37421579	D. D. Trainer	86498013
Chiron the Mage	16956455	D. D. Trap Hole	05606466
Chopman the Desperate Outlaw	40884383	D. D. Warrior Lady	07572887
Chorus of Sanctuary	81380218	Dancing Fairy	90925163
Chthonian Alliance	46910446	Dangerous Machine TYPE-6	76895648
Chthonian Blast	18271561	Dark Artist	72520073
Chthonian Polymer	72287557	Dark Bat	67049542
Chu-Ske the Mouse Fighter	08508055	Dark Blade	11321183
Clay Charge	22479888	Dark Blade the Dragon Knight	86805855
Cliff the Trap Remover	06967870	Dark Driceratops	65287621
Cobra Jar	86801871	Dark Dust Spirit	89111398
Cobraman Sakuzy	75109441	Dark Elf	21417692
Cold Wave	60682203	Dark Energy	04614116
Collected Power	07565547	Dark Factory of Mass Production	90928333
Combination Attack	08964854	Dark Flare Knight	13722870
Command Knight	10375182	Dark Hole	53129443
Commander Covington	22666164	Dark Magic Attack	02314238
Commencement Dance	43417563	Dark Magic Ritual	76792184
Compulsory Evacuation Device	94192409	Dark Magician	46986414
Confiscation	17375316	Dark Magician Girl	38033121
Conscription	31000575	Dark Magician of Chaos	40737112
Continuous Destruction Punch	68057622	Dark Magician's Tome of Black Magic	67227834
Contract With Exodia	33244944	Dark Master - Zorc	97642679
Contract With the Abyss	69035382	Dark Mirror Force	20522190
Contract With the Dark Master	96420087	Dark Paladin	98502113
Convulsion of Nature	62966332	Dark Room of Nightmare	85562745
Cost Down	23265313	Dark Sage	92377303
Covering Fire	74458486	Dark Snake Syndrome	47233801
Crab Turtle	91782219	Dark-Piercing Light	45895206
Crass Clown	93889755	Darkfire Dragon	17881964
Creature Swap	31036355	Darkfire Soldier #1	05388481
Creeping Doom Manta	52571838	Darkfire Soldier #2	78861134
Crimson Ninja	14618326	Darkworld Thorns	43500484
Criosphinx	18654201	De-Spell	19159413
Cross Counter	37083210	Deal of Phantom	69122763
Crush D. Gandra	64681432	Decayed Commander	10209545
Cure Mermaid	85802526		

PASSWORD	EFFECT
Dedication Through Light And Darkness	69542930
Deepsea Shark	28593363
Dekoichi the Battlechanted Locomotive	87621407
Delinquent Duo	44763025
Demotion	72575145
Des Counterblow	39131963
Des Croaking	44883830
Des Dendle	12965761
Des Feral Imp	81985784
Des Frog	84451804
Des Kangaroo	78613627
Des Koala	69579761
Des Lacooda	02326738
Des Wombat	09637706
Desert Sunlight	93747864
Destertapir	13409151
Destiny Board	94212438
Destiny Hero - Captain Tenacious	77608643
Destiny Hero - Diamond Dude	13093792
Destiny Hero - Doom Lord	41613948
Destiny Hero - Dreadmaster	40591390
Destiny Signal	35464895
Destroyer Golem	73481154
Destruction Ring	21219755
Dian Keto the Cure Master	84257639
Dice Jar	03549275
Dimension Distortion	95194279
Dimensional Warrior	37043180
Disappear	24623598
Disarmament	20727787
Disc Fighter	19612721
Dissolverock	40826495
Divine Dragon Ragnarok	62113340
Divine Wrath	49010598
DNA Surgery	74701381
DNA Transplant	56769674
Doitsu	57062206
Dokurorider	99721536
Dokuroyaiba	30325729
Don Turtle	03493978
Don Zaloog	76922029
Doriado	84916669
Doriado's Blessing	23965037
Dragon Seeker	28563545
Dragon Treasure	01435851
Dragon Zombie	66672569
Dragon's Mirror	71490127
Dragon's Rage	54178050
Dragoness the Wicked Knight	70681994
Draining Shield	43250041
Dream Clown	13215230
Drillago	99050989
Drillroid	71218746
Dunames Dark Witch	12493482
Dust Tornado	60082867
Earth Chant	59820352
Earthbound Spirit	67105242

PASSWORD	EFFECT
Earthquake	82828051
Eatgaboon	42578427
Ebon Magician Curran	46128076
Electro-Whip	37820550
Elegant Egotist	90219263
Element Dragon	30314994
Elemental Burst	61411502
Elemental Hero Avian	21844576
Elemental Hero Bladedge	59793705
Elemental Hero Bubbleman	79979666
Elemental Hero Burstinatrix	58932615
Elemental Hero Clayman	84327329
Elemental Hero Electrum/ Erekshieler	29343734
Elemental Hero Flame Wingman	35809262
Elemental Hero Mariner	14225239
Elemental Hero Necroid Shaman	81003500
Elemental Hero Neos	89943723
Elemental Hero Phoenix Enforcer	41436536
Elemental Hero Shining Flare Wingman	25366484
Elemental Hero Shining Phoenix Enforcer	88820235
Elemental Hero Sparkman	20721928
Elemental Hero Thunder Giant	61204971
Elemental Mistress Doriado	99414158
Elemental Recharge	36586443
Elf's Light	39897277
Emblem of Dragon Destroyer	06390406
Embodiment of Apophis	28649820
Emergency Provisions	53046408
Emes the Infinity	43580269
Empress Judge	15237615
Empress Mantis	58818411
Enchanted Javelin	96355986
Enchanting Mermaid	75376965
Enemy Controller	98045062
Enraged Battle Ox	76909279
Enraged Muka Muka	91862578
Eradicating Aerosol	94716515
Eternal Draught	56606928
Eternal Rest	95051344
Exhausting Spell	95451366
Exile of the Wicked	26725158
Exiled Force	74131780
Exodia Necross	12600382
Exodia the Forbidden One	33396948
Fairy Box	21598948
Fairy Dragon	20315854
Fairy King Truesdale	45425051
Fairy Meteor Crush	97687912
Faith Bird	75582395
Fatal Abacus	77910045
Fenrir	00218704
Feral Imp	41392891
Fiber Jar	78706415
Fiend Comedian	81172176
Fiend Scorpion	26566878
Fiend's Hand	52800428

PASSWORD	EFFECT	PASSWORD	EFFECT
Fiend's Mirror	31890399	Gatling Dragon	87751584
Final Countdown	95308449	Gazelle the King of Mythical Beasts	05818798
Final Destiny	18591904	Gear Golem the Moving Fortress	30190809
Final Flame	73134081	Gearfried the Iron Knight	00423705
Final Ritual of the Ancients	60369732	Gearfried the Swordmaster	57046845
Fire Darts	43061293	Gemini Elf	69140098
Fire Eye	88435542	Getsu Fuhma	21887179
Fire Kraken	46534755	Giant Axe Mummy	78266168
Fire Princess	64752646	Giant Germ	95178994
Fire Reaper	53581214	Giant Kozaky	58185394
Fire Sorcerer	27132350	Giant Orc	73698349
Firegrass	53293545	Giant Rat	97017120
Firewing Pegasus	27054370	Giant Red Seasnake	58831685
Fireyarou	71407486	Giant Soldier of Stone	13039848
Fissure	66788016	Giant Trunade	42703248
Five God Dragon (Five Headed Dragon)	99267150	Gift of the Mystical Elf	98299011
Flame Cerebrus	60862676	Giga Gagagigo	43793530
Flame Champion	42599677	Giga-Tech Wolf	08471389
Flame Dancer	12883044	Gigantes	47606319
Flame Ghost	58528964	Gigobyte	53776525
Flame Manipulator	34460851	Gil Garth	38445524
Flame Swordsman	45231177	Gilasaurus	45894482
Flame Viper	02830619	Giltia the D. Knight	51828629
Flash Assailant	96890582	Girochin Kuwagata	84620194
Flower Wolf	95952802	Goblin Attack Force	78658564
Flying Fish	31987274	Goblin Calligrapher	12057781
Flying Kamakiri #1	84834865	Goblin Elite Attack Force	85306040
Flying Kamakiri #2	03134241	Goblin Thief	45311864
Follow Wind	98252586	Goblin's Secret Remedy	11868825
Foolish Burial	81439173	Gogiga Gagagigo	39674352
Forest	87430998	Golem Sentry	82323207
Fortress Whale	62337487	Good Goblin Housekeeping	09744376
Fortress Whale's Oath	77454922	Gora Turtle	80233946
Frenzied Panda	98818516	Graceful Charity	79571449
Frozen Soul	57069605	Graceful Dice	74137509
Fruits of Kozaky's Studies	49998907	Gradius	10992251
Fuh-Rin-Ka-Zan	01781310	Gradius' Option	14291024
Fuhma Shuriken	09373534	Granadora	13944422
Fulfillment of the Contract	48206762	Grand Tiki Elder	13676474
Fushi No Tori	38538445	Granmarg the Rock Monarch	60229110
Fusion Gate	33550694	Gravedigger Ghoul	82542267
Fusion Recovery	18511384	Gravekeeper's Cannonholder	99877698
Fusion Sage	26902560	Gravekeeper's Curse	50712728
Fusion Weapon	27967615	Gravekeeper's Guard	37101832
Fusionist	01641883	Gravekeeper's Servant	16762927
Gadget Soldier	86281779	Gravekeeper's Spear Soldier	63695531
Gagagigo	49003308	Gravekeeper's Spy	24317029
Gaia Power	56594520	Gravekeeper's Vassal	99690140
Gaia the Dragon Champion	66889139	Graverobber's Retribution	33737664
Gaia the Fierce Knight	06368038	Gravity Bind	85742772
Gale Dogra	16229315	Gray Wing	29618570
Gale Lizard	77491079	Great Angus	11813953
Gamble	37313786	Great Long Nose	02356994
Gamma the Magnet Warrior	11549357	Great Mammoth of Goldfine	54622031
Garma Sword	90844184	Green Gadget	41172955
Garma Sword Oath	78577570	Gren Maju Da Eiza	36584821
Garoozis	14977074	Ground Attacker Bugroth	58314394
Garuda the Wind Spirit	12980777	Ground Collapse	90502999

PASSWORD	EFFECT
Gruesome Goo	65623423
Gryphon Wing	55608151
Gryphon's Feather Duster	34370473
Guardian Angel Joan	68007326
Guardian of the Labyrinth	89272878
Guardian of the Sea	85448931
Guardian Sphinx	40659562
Guardian Statue	75209824
Gust Fan	55321970
Gyaku-Gire Panda	09817927
Gyroid	18325492
Hade-Hane	28357177
Hamburger Recipe	80811661
Hammer Shot	26412047
Hamon	32491822
Hand of Nephthys	98446407
Hane-Hane	07089711
Hannibal Necromancer	05640330
Hard Armor	20060230
Harpie Girl	34100324
Harpie Lady 1	91932350
Harpie Lady 2	27927359
Harpie Lady 3	54415063
Harpie Lady Sisters	12206212
Harpie's Brother	30532390
Harpies' Hunting Ground	75782277
Hayabusa Knight	21015833
Headless Knight	05434080
Heart of Clear Water	64801562
Heart of the Underdog	35762283
Heavy Mech Support Platform	23265594
Heavy Storm	19613556
Helios - The Primordial Sun	54493213
Helios Duo Megistus	80887952
Helios Tris Megiste	17286057
Helping Robo for Combat	47025270
Hero Barrier	44676200
HERO Flash!!	00191749
Hero Heart	67951831
Hero Kid	32679370
Hero Ring	26647858
Hero Signal	22020907
Hidden Book of Spell	21840375
Hidden Soldier	02047519
Hieracosphinx	82260502
Hieroglyph Lithograph	10248192
High Tide Gyojin	54579801
Hiita the Fire Charmer	00759393
Hino-Kagu-Tsuchi	75745607
Hinotama Soul	96851799
Hiro's Shadow Scout	81863068
Hitotsu-Me Giant	76184692
Holy Knight Ishzark	57902462
Homunculus the Alchemic Being	40410110
Horn of Heaven	98069388
Horn of Light	38552107
Horn of the Unicorn	64047146
Horus The Black Flame Dragon LV4	75830094

PASSWORD	EFFECT
Horus The Black Flame Dragon LV6	11224103
Horus The Black Flame Dragon LV8	48229808
Hoshiningen	67629977
House of Adhesive Tape	15083728
Howling Insect	93107608
Huge Revolution	65396880
Human-Wave Tactics	30353551
Humanoid Slime	46821314
Humanoid Worm Drake	05600127
Hungry Burger	30243636
Hydrogeddon	22587018
Hyena	22873798
Hyozanryu	62397231
Hyper Hammerhead	02671330
Hysteric Fairy	21297224
Icarus Attack	53567095
Illusionist Faceless Mage	28546905
Impenetrable Formation	96631852
Imperial Order	61740673
Inaba White Rabbit	77084837
Incandescent Ordeal	33031674
Indomitable Fighter Lei Lei	84173492
Infernal Flame Emperor	19847532
Infernal Queen Archfiend	08581705
Inferno	74823665
Inferno Fire Blast	52684508
Inferno Hammer	17185260
Inferno Reckless Summon	12247206
Inferno Tempest	14391920
Infinite Cards	94163677
Infinite Dismissal	54109233
Injection Fairy Lily	79575620
Inpachi	97923414
Insect Armor with Laser Cannon	03492538
Insect Barrier	23615409
Insect Imitation	96965364
Insect Knight	35052053
Insect Princess	37957847
Insect Queen	91512835
Insect Soldiers of the Sky	07019529
Inspection	16227556
Interdimensional Matter Transporter	36261276
Invader From Another Dimension	28450915
Invader of Darkness	56647086
Invader of the Throne	03056267
Invasion of Flames	26082229
Invigoration	98374133
Iron Blacksmith Kotetsu	73431236
Island Turtle	04042268
Jack's Knight	90876561
Jade Insect Whistle	95214051
Jam Breeding Machine	21770260
Jam Defender	21558682
Jar of Greed	83968380
Jar Robber	33784505
Javelin Beetle	26932788

PASSWORD	EFFECT	PASSWORD	EFFECT
Javelin Beetle Pact	41182875	Lady of Faith	17358176
Jellyfish	14851496	Larvas	94675535
Jerry Beans Man	23635815	Laser Cannon Armor	77007920
Jetroid	43697559	Last Day of Witch	90330453
Jinzo	77585513	Last Turn	28566710
Jinzo #7	32809211	Launcher Spider	87322377
Jirai Gumo	94773007	Lava Battleguard	20394040
Jowgen the Spiritualist	41855169	Lava Golem	00102380
Jowls of Dark Demise	05257687	Layard the Liberator	67468948
Judge Man	30113682	Left Arm of the Forbidden One	07902349
Judgment of Anubis	55256016	Left Leg of the Forbidden One	44519536
Just Desserts	24068492	Legendary Black Belt	96438440
KA-2 Des Scissors	52768103	Legendary Flame Lord	60258960
Kabazauls	51934376	Legendary Jujitsu Master	25773409
Kagemusha of the Blue Flame	15401633	Legendary Sword	61854111
Kaibaman	34627841	Leghul	12472242
Kaiser Dragon	94566432	Lekunga	62543393
Kaiser Glider	52824910	Lesser Dragon	55444629
Kaiser Sea Horse	17444133	Lesser Fiend	16475472
Kaminari Attack	09653271	Level Conversion Lab	84397023
Kaminote Blow	97570038	Level Limit - Area A	54976796
Kamionwizard	41544074	Level Limit - Area B	03136426
Kangaroo Champ	95789089	Level Modulation	61850482
Karate Man	23289281	Level Up!	25290459
Karbonala Warrior	54541900	Levia-Dragon	37721209
Karma Cut	71587526	Light of Intervention	62867251
Kelbek	54878498	Light of Judgment	44595286
Keldo	80441106	Lighten the Load	37231841
Killer Needle	88979991	Lightforce Sword	49587034
Kinetic Soldier	79853073	Lightning Blade	55226821
King Dragun	13756293	Lightning Conger	27671321
King Fog	84686841	Lightning Vortex	69162969
King of the Skull Servants	36021814	Limiter Removal	23171610
King of the Swamp	79109599	Liquid Beast	93108297
King of Yamimakai	69455834	Little Chimera	68658728
King Tiger Wanghu	83986578	Little-Winguard	90790253
King's Knight	64788463	Lizard Soldier	20831168
Kiryu	84814897	Lord of D.	17985575
Kiseitai	04266839	Lord of the Lamp	99510761
Kishido Spirit	60519422	Lost Guardian	45871897
Knight's Title	87210505	Luminous Soldier	57282479
Koitsu	69456283	Luminous Spark	81777047
Kojikocy	01184620	Luster Dragon	11091375
Kotodama	19406822	Luster Dragon #2	17658803
Kozaky	99171160	M-Warrior #1	56342351
Kozaky's Self-Destruct Button	21908319	M-Warrior #2	92731455
Kryuel	82642348	Machine Conversion Factory	25769732
Kumootoko	56283725	Machine Duplication	63995093
Kurama	85705804	Machine King	46700124
Kuriboh	40640057	Machine King Prototype	89222931
Kuwagata Alpha	60802233	Machiners Defender	96384007
Kwagar Hercules	95144193	Machiners Force	58054262
Kycoo The Ghost Destroyer	88240808	Machiners Sniper	23782705
La Jinn The Mystical Genie of The Lamp	97590747	Machiners Soldier	60999392
Labyrinth of Nightmare	66526672	Mad Dog of Darkness	79182538
Labyrinth Tank	99551425	Mad Lobster	97240270
Lady Assailant of Flames	90147755	Mad Sword Beast	79870141
Lady Ninja Yae	82005435	Mage Power	83746708
		Magic Drain	59344077

PASSWORD	EFFECT	PASSWORD	EFFECT
Magic Jammer	77414722	Mazera DeVille	06133894
Magical Cylinder	62279055	Mech Mole Zombie	63545455
Magical Dimension	28553439	Mecha-Dog Marron	94667532
Magical Explosion	32723153	Mechanical Hound	22512237
Magical Hats	81210420	Mechanical Snail	34442949
Magical Labyrinth	64389297	Mechanical Spider	45688586
Magical Marionette	08034697	Mechanicalchaser	07359741
Magical Merchant	32362575	Meda Bat	76211194
Magical Plant Mandragola	07802006	Medusa Worm	02694423
Magical Scientist	34206604	Mefist the Infernal General	46820049
Magical Thorn	53119267	Mega Thunderball	21817254
Magician of Black Chaos	30208479	Mega Ton Magical Cannon	32062913
Magician of Faith	31560081	Megamorph	22046459
Magician's Circle	00050755	Megarock Dragon	71544954
Magician's Unite	36045450	Melchid the Four-Face Beast	86569121
Magician's Valkyrie	80304126	Memory Crusher	48700891
Magnet Circle	94940436	Mermaid Knight	24435369
Maha Vailo	93013676	Messenger of Peace	44656491
Maharaghi	40695128	Metal Armored Bug	65957473
Maiden of the Aqua	17214465	Metal Dragon	09293977
Maji-Gire Panda	60102563	Metallizing Parasite	07369217
Maju Garzett	08794435	Metalmorph	68540058
Makiu	27827272	Metalzoa	50705071
Makyura the Destructor	21593977	Metamorphosis	46411259
Malevolent Nuzzler	99597615	Meteor B. Dragon	90660762
Malfunction	06137095	Meteor Dragon	64271667
Malice Ascendant	14255590	Meteor of Destruction	33767325
Malice Dispersion	13626450	Meteorain	64274292
Mammoth Graveyard	40374923	Michizure	37580756
Man Eater	93553943	Micro-Ray	18190572
Man-Eater Bug	54652250	Mid Shield Gardna	75487237
Man-Eating Black Shark	80727036	Mighty Guard	62327910
Man-Eating Treasure Chest	13723605	Mikazukinoyaiba	38277918
Man-Thro' Tro'	43714890	Millennium Golem	47986555
Manga Ryu-Ran	38369349	Millennium Scorpion	82482194
Manju of the Ten Thousand Hands	95492061	Millennium Shield	32012841
Manticore of Darkness	77121851	Milus Radiant	07489323
Marauding Captain	02460565	Minar	32539892
Marie the Fallen One	57579381	Mind Control	37520316
Marine Beast	29929832	Mind Haxorz	75392615
Marshmallon	31305911	Mind on Air	66690411
Marshmallon Glasses	66865880	Mind Wipe	52718046
Maryokutai	71466592	Mine Golem	76321376
Masaki the Legendary Swordsman	44287299	Minefield Eruption	85519211
Mask of Brutality	82432018	Minor Goblin Official	01918087
Mask of Darkness	28933734	Miracle Dig	06343408
Mask of Restrict	29549364	Miracle Fusion	45906428
Mask of Weakness	57882509	Miracle Kid	55985014
Masked Dragon	39191307	Miracle Restoring	68334074
Masked of the Accursed	56948373	Mirage Dragon	15960641
Masked Sorcerer	10189126	Mirage Knight	49217579
Mass Driver	34906152	Mirage of Nightmare	41482598
Master Kyonshee	24530661	Mirror Force	44095762
Master Monk	49814180	Mirror Wall	22359980
Master of Dragon Knight	62873545	Misfortune	01036974
Master of Oz	27134689	Mispolymerization	58392024
Mataza the Zapper	22609617	Mistobody	47529357
Mavelus	59036972	Moai Interceptor Cannons	45159319
Maximum Six	30707994	Mobius the Frost Monarch	04929256

PASSWORD	EFFECT	PASSWORD	EFFECT
Moisture Creature	75285069	Neo-Space	40215635
Mokey Mokey	27288416	Neo-Spacian Aqua Dolphin	17955766
Mokey Mokey King	13803864	Newdoria	04335645
Mokey Mokey Smackdown	01965724	Next to be Lost	07076131
Molten Behemoth	17192817	Night Assailant	16226786
Molten Destruction	19384334	Nightmare Horse	59290628
Molten Zombie	04732017	Nightmare Penguin	81306586
Monk Fighter	03810071	Nightmare Wheel	54704216
Monster Egg	36121917	Nightmare's Steelcage	58775978
Monster Eye	84133008	Nimble Momonga	22567609
Monster Gate	43040603	Nin-Ken Dog	11987744
Monster Reborn	83764718	Ninja Grandmaster Sasuke	04041838
Monster Recovery	93108433	Ninjitsu Art of Decoy	89628781
Monster Reincarnation	74848038	Ninjitsu Art of Transformation	70861343
Mooyan Curry	58074572	Nitro Unit	23842445
Morale Boost	93671934	Niwatori	07805359
Morphing Jar	33508719	Nobleman of Crossout	71044499
Morphing Jar #2	79106360	Nobleman of Extermination	17449108
Mother Grizzly	57839750	Nobleman-Eater Bug	65878864
Mountain	50913601	Non Aggression Area	76848240
Mr. Volcano	31477025	Non-Fusion Area	27581098
Mudora	82108372	Non-Spellcasting Area	20065549
Muka Muka	46657337	Novox's Prayer	43694075
Multiplication of Ants	22493811	Nubian Guard	51616747
Multiply	40703222	Numinous Healer	02130625
Musician King	56907389	Nutrient Z	29389368
Mustering of the Dark Scorpions	68191243	Nuvia the Wicked	12953226
Mysterious Puppeteer	54098121	O - Oversoul	63703130
Mystic Horseman	68516705	Obnoxious Celtic Guardian	52077741
Mystic Lamp	98049915	Ocubeam	86088138
Mystic Plasma Zone	18161786	Offerings to the Doomed	19230407
Mystic Swordsman LV 2	47507260	Ojama Black	79335209
Mystic Swordsman LV 4	74591968	Ojama Delta Hurricane	08251996
Mystic Swordsman LV 6	60482781	Ojama Green	12482652
Mystic Tomato	83011277	Ojama King	90140980
Mystic Wok	80161395	Ojama Trio	29843091
Mystical Beast Serket	89194033	Ojama Yellow	42941100
Mystical Elf	15025844	Ojamagic	24643836
Mystical Knight of Jackal	98745000	Ojamuscle	98259197
Mystical Moon	36607978	Old Vindictive Magician	45141844
Mystical Sand	32751480	Ominous Fortunetelling	56995655
Mystical Sheep #2	30451366	Oni Tank T-34	66927994
Mystical Shine Ball	39552864	Opti-Camaflauge Armor	44762290
Mystical Space Typhoon	05318639	Opticlops	14531242
Mystik Wok	80161395	Option Hunter	33248692
Mythical Beast Cerberus	55424270	Orca Mega-Fortress of Darkness	63120904
Nanobreaker	70948327	Ordeal of a Traveler	39537362
Necklace of Command	48576971	Order to Charge	78986941
Necrovalley	47355498	Order to Smash	39019325
Needle Ball	94230224	Otohime	39751093
Needle Burrower	98162242	Outstanding Dog Marron	11548522
Needle Ceiling	38411870	Overdrive	02311603
Needle Wall	38299233	Oxygeddon	58071123
Needle Worm	81843628	Painful Choice	74191942
Negate Attack	14315573	Paladin of White Dragon	73398797
Nemuriko	90963488	Pale Beast	21263083
Neo Aqua Madoor	49563947	Pandemonium	94585852
Neo Bug	16587243	Pandemonium Watchbear	75375465
Neo the Magic Swordsman	50930991	Parasite Paracide	27911549

77

PASSWORD	EFFECT
Parasitic Ticky	87978805
Patrician of Darkness	19153634
Patroid	71930383
Penguin Knight	36039163
Penumbral Soldier Lady	64751286
People Running About	12143771
Perfect Machine King	18891691
Performance of Sword	04849037
Petit Angel	38142739
Petit Dragon	75356564
Petit Moth	58192742
Phantasmal Martyrs	93224848
Phantom Beast Cross-Wing	71181155
Phantom Beast Thunder-Pegasus	34961968
Phantom Beast Wild-Horn	07576264
Pharaoh's Servant	52550973
Pharonic Protector	89959682
Phoenix Wing Wind Blast	63356631
Photon Generator Unit	66607691
Pikeru's Circle of Enchantment	74270067
Pikeru's Second Sight	58015506
Pinch Hopper	26185991
Pineapple Blast	90669991
Piranha Army	50823978
Pitch-Black Power Stone	34029630
Pitch-Black Warwolf	88975532
Pitch-Dark Dragon	47415292
Poison Draw Frog	56840658
Poison Fangs	76539047
Poison Mummy	43716289
Poison of the Old Man	08842266
Polymerization	24094653
Possessed Dark Soul	52860176
Pot of Avarice	67169062
Pot of Generosity	70278545
Pot of Greed	55144522
Power Bond	37630732
Power Capsule	54289683
Precious Card from Beyond	68304813
Premature Burial	70828912
Prepare to Strike Back	04483989
Prevent Rat	00549481
Prickle Fairy	91559748
Primal Seed	23701465
Princess Curran	02316186
Princess of Tsurugi	51371017
Princess Pikeru	75917088
Protective Soul Ailin	11678191
Protector of the Sanctuary	24221739
Protector of the Throne	10071456
Proto-Cyber Dragon	26439287
Pumpking the King of Ghosts	29155212
Punished Eagle	74703140
Pyramid of Light	53569894
Pyramid Turtle	77044671
Queen's Knight	25652259
Rabid Horseman	94905343
Rafflesia Seduction	31440542
Raging Flame Sprite	90810762

PASSWORD	EFFECT
Raigeki	12580477
Raigeki Break	04178474
Rain Of Mercy	66719324
Rainbow Flower	21347810
Rallis the Star Bird	41382147
Rancer Dragonute	11125718
Rapid-Fire Magician	06337436
Rare Metalmorph	12503902
Raregold Armor	07625614
Raviel, Lord of Phantasms	69890967
Ray & Temperature	85309439
Ray of Hope	82529174
Re-Fusion	74694807
Ready For Intercepting	31785398
Really Eternal Rest	28121403
Reaper of the Cards	33066139
Reaper of the Nightmare	85684223
Reasoning	58577036
Reborn Zombie	23421244
Reckless Greed	37576645
Recycle	96316857
Red Archery Girl	65570596
Red Gadget	86445415
Red Medicine	38199696
Red Moon Baby	56387350
Red-Eyes B. Chick	36262024
Red-Eyes B. Dragon	74677422
Red-Eyes Black Metal Dragon	64335804
Red-Eyes Darkness Dragon	96561011
Reflect Bounder	02851070
Regenerating Mummy	70821187
Reinforcement of the Army	32807846
Release Restraint	75417459
Relinquished	64631466
Reload	22589918
Remove Trap	51482758
Rescue Cat	14878891
Rescueroid	24311595
Reshef the Dark Being	62420419
Respect Play	08951260
Return from the Different Dimension	27174286
Return of the Doomed	19827717
Reversal of Graves	17484499
Reversal Quiz	05990062
Revival Jam	31709826
Right Arm of the Forbidden One	70903634
Right Leg of the Forbidden One	08124921
Ring of Defense	58641905
Ring of Destruction	83555666
Ring of Magnetism	20436034
Riryoku Field	70344351
Rising Air Current	45778932
Rising Energy	78211862
Rite of Spirit	30450531
Ritual Weapon	54351224
Robbin' Goblin	88279736
Robbin' Zombie	83258273
Robolady	92421852

PASSWORD	EFFECT	PASSWORD	EFFECT
Robotic Knight	44203504	Shadow Ghoul	30778711
Roboyarou	38916461	Shadow Of Eyes	58621589
Rock Bombardment	20781762	Shadow Tamer	37620434
Rock Ogre Grotto	68846917	Shadowknight Archfiend	09603356
Rocket Jumper	53890795	Shadowslayer	20939559
Rocket Warrior	30860696	Share the Pain	56830749
Rod of the Mind's Eye	94793422	Shield & Sword	52097679
Roll Out!	91597389	Shield Crash	30683373
Root Water	39004808	Shien's Spy	07672244
Rope of Life	93382620	Shift	59560625
Rope of Spirit	37383714	Shifting Shadows	59237154
Roulette Barrel	46303688	Shinato's Ark	60365591
Royal Command	33950246	Shinato, King of a Higher Plane	86327225
Royal Decree	51452091	Shining Abyss	87303357
Royal Keeper	16509093	Shining Angel	95956346
Royal Knight	68280530	Shooting Star Bow - Ceal	95638658
Royal Magical Library	70791313	Silent Insect	40867519
Royal Surrender	56058888	Silent Magician Lv4	73665146
Royal Tribute	72405967	Silent Magician Lv8	72443568
Ruin, Queen of Oblivion	46427957	Silent Swordsman LV3	01995985
Rush Recklessly	70046172	Silent Swordsman LV5	74388798
Ryu Kokki	57281778	Silent Swordsman LV7	37267041
Ryu Senshi	49868263	Sillva, Warlord of Dark World	32619583
Ryu-Kishin Clown	42647539	Silpheed	73001017
Ryu-Kishin Powered	24611934	Silver Fang	90357090
Saber Beetle	49645921	Simorgh, Bird of Divinity	14989021
Sacred Crane	30914564	Simultaneous Loss	92219931
Sacred Phoenix of Nephthys	61441708	Sinister Serpent	08131171
Saggi the Dark Clown	66602787	Sixth Sense	03280747
Sakuretsu Armor	56120475	Skill Drain	82732705
Salamandra	32268901	Skilled Dark Magician	73752131
Salvage	96947648	Skilled White Magician	46363422
Samsara	44182827	Skull Archfiend of Lightning	61370518
Sand Gambler	50593156	Skull Descovery Knight	78700060
Sand Moth	73648243	Skull Dog Marron	86652646
Sangan	26202165	Skull Invitation	98139712
Sanwitch	53539634	Skull Lair	06733059
Sasuke Samurai	16222645	Skull Mariner	05265750
Sasuke Samurai #2	11760174	Skull Red Bird	10202894
Sasuke Samurai #3	77379481	Skull Servant	32274490
Sasuke Samurai #4	64538655	Skull Zoma	79852326
Satellite Cannon	50400231	Skull-Mark Ladybug	64306248
Scapegoat	73915051	Skyscraper	63035430
Scarr, Scout of Dark World	05498296	Slate Warrior	78636495
Science Soldier	67532912	Smashing Ground	97169186
Scroll of Bewitchment	10352095	Smoke Grenade of the Thief	63789924
Scyscraper	63035430	Snatch Steal	45986603
Sea Serpent Warrior of Darkness	42071342	Sogen	86318356
Sealmaster Meisei	02468169	Soitsu	60246171
Second Coin Toss	36562627	Solar Flare Dragon	45985838
Second Goblin	19086954	Solar Ray	44472639
Secret Barrel	27053506	Solemn Judgment	41420027
Self-Destruct Button	57585212	Solemn Wishes	35346968
Senri Eye	60391791	Solomon's Lawbook	23471572
Serial Spell	49398568	Sonic Duck	84696266
Serpent Night Dragon	66516792	Sonic Jammer	84550200
Serpentine Princess	71829750	Sorcerer of Dark Magic	88619463
Servant of Catabolism	02792265	Soul Absorption	68073522
Seven Tools of the Bandit	03819470	Soul Exchange	68005187

PASSWORD	EFFECT
Soul of Purity and Light	77527210
Soul Release	05758500
Soul Resurrection	92924317
Soul Reversal	78864369
Soul Tiger	15734813
Soul-Absorbing Bone Tower	63012333
Souleater	31242786
Souls Of The Forgotten	04920010
Space Mambo	36119641
Spark Blaster	97362768
Sparks	76103675
Spatial Collapse	20644748
Spear Cretin	58551308
Spear Dragon	31553716
Spell Canceller	84636823
Spell Economics	04259068
Spell Purification	01669772
Spell Reproduction	29228529
Spell Shield Type-8	38275183
Spell Vanishing	29735721
Spell-Stopping Statute	10069180
Spellbinding Circle	18807108
Spherous Lady	52121290
Sphinx Teleia	51402177
Spiral Spear Strike	49328340
Spirit Barrier	53239672
Spirit Caller	48659020
Spirit Message A	94772232
Spirit Message I	31893528
Spirit Message L	30170981
Spirit Message N	67287533
Spirit of Flames	13522325
Spirit of the Breeze	53530069
Spirit of the Harp	80770678
Spirit of the Pharaoh	25343280
Spirit Reaper	23205979
Spirit Ryu	67957315
Spiritual Earth Art - Kurogane	70156997
Spiritual Energy Settle Machine	99173029
Spiritual Fire Art - Kurenai	42945701
Spiritual Water Art - Aoi	06540606
Spiritual Wind Art - Miyabi	79333300
Spiritualism	15866454
St. Joan	21175632
Stamping Destruction	81385346
Star Boy	08201910
Statue of the Wicked	65810489
Staunch Defender	92854392
Stealth Bird	03510565
Steam Gyroid	05368615
Steamroid	44729197
Steel Ogre Grotto #1	29172562
Steel Ogre Grotto #2	90908427
Stim-Pack	83225447
Stop Defense	63102017
Storming Wynn	29013526
Stray Lambs	60764581
Strike Ninja	41006930
Stronghold	13955608

PASSWORD	EFFECT
Stumbling	34646691
Success Probability 0%	06859683
Summon Priest	00423585
Summoned Skull	70781052
Summoner of Illusions	14644902
Super Conductor Tyranno	85520851
Super Rejuvenation	27770341
Super Robolady	75923050
Super Roboyarou	01412158
Supply	44072894
Susa Soldier	40473581
Swarm of Locusts	41872150
Swarm of Scarabs	15383415
Swift Gaia the Fierce Knight	16589042
Sword Hunter	51345461
Sword of Deep-Seated	98495314
Sword of Dragon's Soul	61405855
Sword of the Soul Eater	05371656
Swords of Concealing Light	12923641
Swords of Revealing Light	72302403
Swordsman of Landstar	03573512
Symbol of Heritage	45305419
System Down	18895832
T.A.D.P.O.L.E.	10456559
Tactical Espionage Expert	89698120
Tailor of the Fickle	43641473
Taunt	90740329
Tenkabito Shien	41589166
Terra the Terrible	63308047
Terraforming	73628505
Terrorking Archfiend	35975813
Terrorking Salmon	78060096
Teva	16469012
The Agent of Creation - Venus	64734921
The Agent of Force - Mars	91123920
The Agent of Judgment - Saturn	91345518
The Agent of Wisdom - Mercury	38730226
The All-Seeing White Tiger	32269855
The Big March of Animals	01689516
The Bistro Butcher	71107816
The Cheerful Coffin	41142615
The Creator	61505339
The Creator Incarnate	97093037
The Dark - Hex Sealed Fusion	52101615
The Dark Door	30606547
The Dragon Dwelling in the Cave	93346024
The Dragon's Bead	92408984
The Earl of Demise	66989694
The Earth - Hex Sealed Fusion	88696724
The Emperor's Holiday	68400115
The End of Anubis	65403020
The Eye Of Truth	34694160
The Fiend Megacyber	66362965
The Flute of Summoning Dragon	43973174
The Flute of Summoning Kuriboh	20065322
The Forceful Sentry	42829885
The Forces of Darkness	29826127
The Forgiving Maiden	84080938
The Furious Sea King	18710707

PASSWORD	EFFECT
The Graveyard in the Fourth Dimension	88089103
The Gross Ghost of Fled Dreams	68049471
The Hunter With 7 Weapons	01525329
The Illusionary Gentleman	83764996
The Immortal of Thunder	84926738
The Kick Man	90407382
The Last Warrior From Another Planet	86099788
The Law of the Normal	66926224
The League of Uniform Nomenclature	55008284
The Legendary Fisherman	03643300
The Light - Hex Sealed Fusion	15717011
The Little Swordsman of Aile	25109950
The Masked Beast	49064413
The Portrait's Secret	32541773
The Regulation of Tribe	00296499
The Reliable Guardian	16430187
The Rock Spirit	76305638
The Sanctuary in the Sky	56433456
The Second Sarcophagus	04081094
The Secret of the Bandit	99351431
The Shallow Grave	43434803
The Spell Absorbing Life	99517131
The Thing in the Crater	78243409
The Third Sarcophagus	78697395
The Trojan Horse	38479725
The Unhappy Girl	27618634
The Unhappy Maiden	51275027
The Warrior Returning Alive	95281259
Theban Nightmare	51838385
Theinen the Great Sphinx	87997872
Thestalos the Firestorm Monarch	26205777
Thousand Dragon	41462083
Thousand Energy	05703682
Thousand Needles	33977496
Thousand-Eyes Idol	27125110
Thousand-Eyes Restrict	63519819
Threatening Roar	36361633
Three-Headed Geedo	78423643
Throwstone Unit	76075810
Thunder Crash	69196160
Thunder Dragon	31786629
Thunder Nyan Nyan	70797118
Thunder of Ruler	91781589
Time Seal	35316708
Time Wizard	71625222
Timeater	44913552
Timidity	40350910
Token Festevil	83675475
Token Thanksgiving	57182235
Tongyo	69572024
Toon Cannon Soldier	79875176
Toon Dark Magician Girl	90960358
Toon Defense	43509019
Toon Gemini Elf	42386471
Toon Goblin Attack Force	15270885
Toon Masked Sorcerer	16392422

PASSWORD	EFFECT
Toon Mermaid	65458948
Toon Summoned Skull	91842653
Toon Table of Contents	89997728
Toon World	15259703
Tornado Bird	71283180
Tornado Wall	18605135
Torpedo Fish	90337190
Torrential Tribute	53582587
Total Defense Shogun	75372290
Tower of Babel	94256039
Tradgedy	35686187
Transcendent Wings	25573054
Trap Dustshoot	64697231
Trap Hole	04206964
Trap Jammer	19252988
Treeborn Frog	12538374
Tremendous Fire	46918794
Tri-Horned Dragon	39111158
Triage	30888983
Trial of Nightmare	77827521
Trial of the Princesses	72709014
Triangle Ecstasy Spark	12181376
Triangle Power	32298781
Tribe-Infecting Virus	33184167
Tribute Doll	02903036
Tribute to The Doomed	79759861
Tripwire Beast	45042329
Troop Dragon	55013285
Tsukuyomi	34853266
Turtle Oath	76806714
Turtle Tiger	37313348
Twin Swords of Flashing Light	21900719
Twin-Headed Beast	82035781
Twin-Headed Behemoth	43586926
Twin-Headed Fire Dragon	78984772
Twin-Headed Thunder Dragon	54752875
Twin-Headed Wolf	88132637
Two Thousand Needles	83228073
Two-Man Cell Battle	25578802
Two-Mouth Darkruler	57305373
Two-Pronged Attack	83887306
Tyhone	72842870
Type Zero Magic Crusher	21237481
Tyranno Infinity	83235263
Tyrant Dragon	94568601
UFOroid	07602840
UFOroid Fighter	32752319
Ultimate Insect LV1	49441499
Ultimate Insect LV3	34088136
Ultimate Insect LV5	34830502
Ultimate Insect LV7	19877898
Ultimate Obedient Fiend	32240937
Ultimate Tyranno	15894048
Ultra Evolution Pill	22431243
Umi	22702055
Umiiruka	82999629
Union Attack	60399954
United Resistance	85936485
United We Stand	56747793

PASSWORD	EFFECT	PASSWORD	EFFECT
Unity	14731897	Winged Kuriboh	57116033
Unshaven Angler	92084010	Winged Kuriboh LV10	98585345
Upstart Goblin	70368879	Winged Minion	89258225
Uraby	01784619	Winged Sage Falcos	87523462
Uria, Lord of Sealing Flames	06007213	Wingweaver	31447217
V-Tiger Jet	51638941	Witch Doctor of Chaos	75946257
Valkyrion the Magna Warrior	75347539	Witch of the Black Forest	78010363
Vampire Genesis	22056710	Witch's Apprentice	80741828
Vampire Lord	53839837	Witty Phantom	36304921
Vampire Orchis	46571052	Wolf Axwielder	56369281
Vengeful Bog Spirit	95220856	Woodborg Inpachi	35322812
Victory D	44910027	Woodland Sprite	06979239
Vilepawn Archfiend	73219648	Worm Drake	73216412
VW-Tiger Catapult	58859575	Wroughtweiler	06480253
VWXYZ-Dragon Catapult Cannon	84243274	Wynn the Wind Charmer	37744402
W-Wing Catapult	96300057	X-Head Cannon	62651957
Waboku	12607053	Xing Zhen Hu	76515293
Wall of Revealing Light	17078030	XY-Dragon Cannon	02111707
Wandering Mummy	42994702	XYZ-Dragon Cannon	91998119
Warrior Dai Grepher	75953262	XZ-Tank Cannon	99724761
Warrior of Zera	66073051	Y-Dragon Head	65622692
Wasteland	23424603	Yamata Dragon	76862289
Water Dragon	85066822	Yami	59197169
Water Omotics	02483611	Yata-Garasu	03078576
Wave Motion Cannon	38992735	Yellow Gadget	13839120
Weed Out	28604635	Yellow Luster Shield	04542651
Whiptail Crow	91996584	Yomi Ship	51534754
Whirlwind Prodigy	15090429	YZ-Tank Dragon	25119460
White Dragon Ritual	09786492	Z-Metal Tank	64500000
White Horn Dragon	73891874	Zaborg the Thunder Monarch	51945556
White Magical Hat	15150365	Zero Gravity	83133491
White Magician Pikeru	81383947	Zoa	24311372
White Ninja	01571945	Zolga	16268841
Wicked-Breaking Flameberge-Baou	68427465	Zombie Tiger	47693640
Wild Nature's Release	61166988	Zombyra the Dark	88472456
Winged Dragon, Guardian of the Fortress #1	87796900	Zure, Knight of Dark World	07459013

ONLINE GAMING FOR KIDS: A PARENT'S GUIDE

There are plenty of great games for kids on the web, but which ones are best for your child, and how can you ensure they don't visit a site that's inappropriate? Well, we've compiled a list of the most impressive and trusted gaming spots for kids, then categorized them by age. Visit these sites and choose which ones your family likes most. Once you've determined your favorites, you can then make accessing them safe and easy for your child in just three easy steps:

SAFE ONLINE GAMING FOR KIDS IS AS EASY AS 1-2-3

Here's how you can create an **Internet Games Page**—a clickable document that allows your child to safely and easily visit your family's favorite online gaming sites for kids:

1. Open a new document in Microsoft Word.

2. Type in the URLs (web site addresses) listed in this section that best suit your child's age and interests. After each URL, press ENTER to automatically create a Hyperlink. The address will then appear in blue, underlined text. That means you can now immediately go directly to that web site. Just simultaneously press CTRL and click on the blue text. See our note below for an even slicker way of doing this.

3. When your list of Hyperlinks is complete, save the file as "[Your Child's Name]'s Games" on your computer's desktop.

USER FRIENDLY LINKS

If you think your child might find it difficult to visit his or her favorite gaming sites by selecting from a list of long and sometimes unwieldy internet addresses, then customize the lists on your Internet Games Page by renaming them with something more easily recognizable. It's easy. Simply type the name you wish to use (LEGO, for example) and highlight the word with your mouse. Next, right-click on the highlighted word and select Hyperlink from the window that pops up. Another window appears with your cursor blinking in the empty Address field. Type in the proper URL here (in the case of LEGO, you would type *http://play.lego. com/en-US/games/default.aspx* into this field), then click OK. The word you highlighted on your Internet Games Page is now a Hyperlink. Using our example, that means your child can simply click on (left-click + CTRL) the word "LEGO" to visit the LEGO games site!

You can even dress up this document with colorful backgrounds and clip art to make it even more personal and appealing. You now have a resource that provides a quick and easy path for your child to access safe and entertaining gaming sites that you have seen and trust.

BEST ONLINE GAMING SITES FOR KIDS

AGES 6-7

Children in this age group may not be as computer savvy and certainly won't have as strong reading skills as older kids. So, you may need to get your child started until he or she is comfortable navigating these sites and properly understands the rules to the games.

Slime Slinger Online Game

http://www.scholastic.com/goosebumps/slimeslinger/game.asp

A fun game based on the popular Goosebumps series of books.

Highlights Kids Hidden Pictures

http://www.highlightskids.com/GamesandGiggles/HiddenPics/HIddenPixFlashObjects/h8hpiArchive.asp

More than just games, these puzzle-oriented offerings really work kids' brains.

CBeebies at BBC

http://www.bbc.co.uk/cbeebies/fun/

Lots of cute games for younger kids.

Yahooligans Games

http://kids.yahoo.com/games

Loads of fun for all ages here with a wide variety of games—puzzles, arcade, sports, and more!

Pauly's Playhouse Online Games

http://www.paulysplayhouse.com/paulys_playhouse/game_page/game.html

Wow! This site has loads of games! All pretty simple and most will have your child smiling from ear to ear.

Nick.com Games Online

http://www.nick.com/games/

Lots of good stuff here, all associated with Nick programming your child likely already enjoys.

Lego Club Games

http://play.lego.com/en-US/games/default.aspx

Great interactive fun that provides exciting scenarios that simulate playing with LEGO toys.

Barbie.com Games Online

http://barbie.everythinggirl.com/activities/fun_games/

Let's face it, most girls like Barbie as much as just about anything. The games your daughter plays on this site will not disappoint her.

EDUCATIONAL FUN!

Chicken Stacker

http://pbskids.org/lions/games/stacker.html

You can never go wrong with PBS when it comes to kids, and Between the Lions is one of many great programs. This game based on the show helps kids build their word power.

Play Kids Games.com

http://www.playkidsgames.com/

Everything from simple math to word and memory games. Plenty here for the next age group, too.

AGES 8-9

Scholastic Games

http://www.scholastic.com/kids/games.htm

Solve mysteries, answer trivia, collect rare items, and more! The fun here is all based on popular books with this age group.

Monkeybar TV

http://www.hasbro.com/monkeybartv/default.cfm?page=Entertainment/OnlineGames/GameHome

This site is operated by Hasbro, so the characters and toys associated with the games are all classics known and loved by kids and adults—including Transformers, Littlest Pet Shop, Monopoly, GI Joe, Star Wars, and others!

Cartoon Network Games Online

http://www.cartoonnetwork.com/games/index.html

Kids can't read and be active all the time, and cartoons nicely fill that need to laugh and take it easy. This is the place for hilarious games from hilarious toons.

I Spy Games Online

http://www.scholastic.com/ispy/play/

Another Scholastic gem that allows kids to use their powers of observation online!

Disney Channel Games Online

http://tv.disney.go.com/disneychannel/games/index.html

Have you ever met a fourth grader who isn't into Disney? Hannah Montana, Kim Possible, Zack & Cody... what's not to like? This site has plenty of familiar faces and fun stuff.

Kidnetics Active Online Games

http://www.kidnetic.com/

Fitness focused games and projects for kids.

EDUCATIONAL FUN!

Multiplication.com

http://www.multiplication.com/interactive_games.htm

Cute and entertaining games that help make multiplication tables a breeze.

Big Brainz

http://www.bigbrainz.com/index.php

Download a free version of Timez Attack, a great looking action video game that boosts multiplication skills!

AGE 10 & UP

If you're 10 years old, there's no reason you still can't have fun playing the games we've listed in the previous two age groups, but these will definitely appeal to the big kids.

ESPN Arcade

http://arcade.espn.go.com/

ESPN offers a great online gaming site for kids who are into sports.

Zeeks Board & Card Games

http://games.zeeks.com/games.php

Tons of free games. Not just entertaining, but a little edgy, too!

Battleship

http://www.creativecalendar.com/kids/Games/games_battleship.html

Everyone loves this game. Just as much fun online!

OTHER ONLINE GAMES

We've put these games in a separate category because they're not free. They either require a subscription or the purchase of a toy to play. However, you may consider these investments worthwhile, as they do provide some intriguing gameplay and learning opportunities. Plus, if your kids are into gaming or have friends who are, they're bound to mention these sites to you sooner or later, so you may want to see what they're all about for yourself.

Webkinz

http://www.webkinz.com/

Requires you to buy a toy before "adopting" one online, but the game experience is pretty cool. Webkinz allows kids to care for their pet, including improving and furnishing its home. Earn Kinz cash by answering trivia and doing other fun activities.

Club Penguin

http://www.clubpenguin.com/

This subscription-based online game is operated by Disney. It provides a kid-friendly virtual world where children can play games, have fun, and interact with each other...but it's not free.

A NOTE TO PARENTS

This book is an exclusive Scholastic edition that has been edited to remove all Mature-rated codes, as well as games that include excessive violence, sexual content, and inappropriate codes for children.

This book includes only E, E+, and T-rated games.

In addition, this book provides a listing of the ESRB ratings for all games included inside.

 EARLY CHILDHOOD
Titles rated EC (Early Childhood) have content that may be suitable for ages 3 and older. Contains no material that parents would find inappropriate.

 TEEN
Titles rated T (Teen) have content that may be suitable for ages 13 and older. Titles in this category may contain violence, suggestive themes, crude humor, minimal blood and/or infrequent use of strong language.

 EVERYONE
Titles rated E (Everyone) have content that may be suitable for ages 6 and older. Titles in this category may contain minimal cartoon, fantasy or mild violence and/or infrequent use of mild language.

 MATURE
Titles rated M (Mature) have content that may be suitable for persons ages 17 and older. Titles in this category may contain intense violence, blood and gore, sexual content, and/or strong language.

 EVERYONE 10+
Titles rated E10+ (Everyone 10 and older) have content that may be suitable for ages 10 and older. Titles in this category may contain more cartoon, fantasy or mild violence, mild language, and/or minimal suggestive themes.

 ADULTS ONLY
Titles rated AO (Adults Only) have content that should only be played by persons 18 years and older. Titles in this category may include prolonged scenes of intense violence and/or graphic sexual content and nudity.

CHEAT CODE
CODE
EXPLOSION

◆ DANGER ◆ **FOR HANDHELDS** ◆ COMBUSTIBLE ◆

<table>
<tr><td>

**FLIP THIS BOOK OVER
FOR HOME CONSOLES**
PlayStation® 3
Nintendo Wii™
Xbox 360™
PlayStation® 2

</td><td>

**LOOK FOR
CODEY**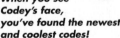

*When you see
Codey's face,
you've found the newest
and coolest codes!*

</td></tr>
</table>

CHEAT CODE EXPLOSION

EXCLUSIVE SCHOLASTIC EDITION

DK/BradyGames, a division of Penguin Group (USA) Inc.
800 East 96th Street, 3rd Floor
Indianapolis, IN 46240

PlayStation® 2, PlayStation® 3, and PSP® are registered trademarks or trademarks of Sony Computer Entertainment America, Inc. Xbox® and Xbox 360™ are registered trademarks or trademarks of Microsoft Corporation. Nintendo DS™ and Nintendo Wii™ are registered trademarks or trademarks of Nintendo of America, Inc. LEGO® is a registered trademark of the LEGO Group. Harry Potter is a trademark of Warner Bros. Entertainment. WWE, WWE Smackdown, and WWE Raw are registered trademarks of World Wrestling Entertainment, Inc. and its subsidiaries.

The ratings icon is a registered trademark of the Entertainment Software Association. All other trademarks and trade names are properties of their respective owners.

Please be advised that the ESRB ratings icons, "EC", "E", "E10+", "T", "M", "AO", and "RP" are trademarks owned by the Entertainment Software Association, and may only be used with their permission and authority. For information regarding whether a product has been rated by the ESRB, please visit www.esrb.org. For permission to use the ratings icons, please contact the ESA at esrblicenseinfo@theesa.com.

ISBN-13: 978-0-7440-1283-5

Printing Code: The rightmost double-digit number is the year of the book's printing; the rightmost single-digit number is the number of the book's printing. For example, 10-1 shows that the first printing of the book occurred in 2010.

13 12 11   4 3

Printed in the USA.

CREDITS

Title Manager
Christian Sumner

Book Designer
Doug Wilkins

Production Designer
Tracy Wehmeyer

BRADYGAMES STAFF

Global Strategy Guide Publisher
Mike Degler

Editor-In-Chief
H. Leigh Davis

Operations Manager
Stacey Beheler

Digital & Trade Category Publisher
Brian Saliba

NINTENDO DS™

TABLE OF CONTENTS

3

ADVANCE WARS: DAYS OF RUIN

UNLOCK COS

Complete the following missions to unlock the corresponding CO.

COMPLETE MISSION	CO UNLOCKED
12	Tasha
13	Gage
14	Forthsythe
20	Waylon
21	Greyfield
24	Penny
25	Tabitha
26	Caulder

ADVANCE WARS: DUAL STRIKE

ADVANCE WARS MAP

Select Map from the Design Room menu and immediately press and hold L + R. You will get a map that spells out Advance Wars. By having old versions of advance wars inserted in your DS at the same time as Dual Strike, you can unlock new buyables at the the Battle Maps Shop!

ADVANCE WARPAPER

Insert Advance Wars in the GBA slot of your Nintendo DS. Start Advance Wars: Dual Strike. Select Battle Maps and purchase Advance Warpaper. Select Display from the Design Room and choose Classic 1.

HACHI'S LAND

Insert Advance Wars in the GBA slot of your Nintendo DS. Start Advance Wars: Dual Strike. Select Battle Maps and purchase Hachi's Land for 1.

NELL'S LAND

Insert Advance Wars in the GBA slot of your Nintendo DS. Start Advance Wars: Dual Strike. Select Battle Maps and purchase Nell's Land for 1.

ADVANCE WARPAPER 2

Insert Advance Wars 2: Black Hole Rising in the GBA slot of your Nintendo DS. Start Advance Wars: Dual Strike. Select Battle Maps and purchase Advance Warpaper 2. Select Display from the Design Room and choose Classic 2.

LASH'S LAND

Insert Advance Wars 2: Black Hole Rising in the GBA slot of your Nintendo DS. Start Advance Wars: Dual Strike. Select Battle Maps and purchase Lash's Land for 1.

STRUM'S LAND

Insert Advance Wars 2: Black Hole Rising in the GBA slot of your Nintendo DS. Start Advance Wars: Dual Strike. Select Battle Maps and purchase Strum's Land for 1.

ALICE IN WONDERLAND

BIG PLAYING CARD
Enter the Bonus door, click the padlock, and enter 2273.

DORMOUSE COAT FOR DGAMER AVATAR
Enter the Bonus door, click the padlock, and enter 3676.

DORMOUSE MASK FOR DGAMER AVATAR
Enter the Bonus door, click the padlock, and enter 3675.

DRINK ME BOTTLE FOR DGAMER AVATAR
Enter the Bonus door, click the padlock, and enter 7493.

GREEN ALICE BOOK FOR DGAMER AVATAR
Enter the Bonus door, click the padlock, and enter 4625.

IMPOSSIBLE IDEAS T-SHIRT FOR DGAMER AVATAR

Enter the Bonus door, click the padlock, and enter 4332.

KEYHOLE T-SHIRT FOR DGAMER AVATAR

Enter the Bonus door, click the padlock, and enter 5398.

MAD HATTER COAT FOR DGAMER AVATAR

Enter the Bonus door, click the padlock, and enter 2628.

MAD HATTER T-SHIRT FOR DGAMER AVATAR

Enter the Bonus door, click the padlock, and enter 4288.

MARCH HARE MASK FOR DGAMER AVATAR

Enter the Bonus door, click the padlock, and enter 2675.

RED GUARD SHIELD FOR DGAMER AVATAR

Enter the Bonus door, click the padlock, and enter 7453.

RED QUEEN DRESS FOR DGAMER AVATAR

Enter the Bonus door, click the padlock, and enter 7483.

RED QUEEN MASK FOR DGAMER AVATAR

Enter the Bonus door, click the padlock, and enter 7675.

TAN ALICE BOOK FOR DGAMER AVATAR

Enter the Bonus door, click the padlock, and enter 2625.

TEA CUP FOR DGAMER AVATAR

Enter the Bonus door, click the padlock, and enter 8328.

TWEEDLE OUTFIT FOR DGAMER AVATAR

Enter the Bonus door, click the padlock, and enter 8946.

WHITE QUEEN DRESS FOR DGAMER AVATAR

Enter the Bonus door, click the padlock, and enter 9483.

WHITE RABBIT MASK FOR DGAMER AVATAR

Enter the Bonus door, click the padlock, and enter 9675.

WHITE RABBIT WATCH FOR DGAMER AVATAR

Enter the Bonus door, click the padlock, and enter 8463.

BAKUGAN BATTLE BRAWLERS

1000 BP

Start a new game and enter the name as 180978772269.

5000 BP

Start a new game and enter the name as 332044292925.

10,000 BP

Start a new game and enter the name as 423482942968.

BRONZE WARIUS

Start a new game and enter the name as 449824934071.

BATMAN: THE BRAVE AND THE BOLD – THE VIDEOGAME

BATMAN COSTUME: MEDIEVAL SUIT

In the Batcave, use the left terminal to enter 5644863.

PROTO SPARRING CHALLENGE

In the Batcave, use the left terminal to enter 6677686.

WEAPON: BARRIER

In the Batcave, use the left terminal to enter 2525655.

WEAPON: BELT SWORD

In the Batcave, use the left terminal to enter 2587973.

WEAPON: FLASHBANGS

In the Batcave, use the left terminal to enter 3527463.

WEAPON: SMOKE PELLETS

In the Batcave, use the left terminal to enter 7665336.

BATTLE OF GIANTS - DRAGONS

Select Unlock Gold Gems from the Extras Menu and enter the following passwords:

BREATH ATTACK GOLD GEMS

LEVEL	ATTACK	PASSWORD
1	NAMGILIMA	ISAM SKNF DKTD
2	NIGHHALAMA	ZNBN QOKS THGO
3	KUGDIM	AWBF CRSL HGAT
4	KUZEN	ACLC SCRS VOSK
5	SUGZAG	XSPC LLSL KJLP

CLAW ATTACK GOLD GEMS

LEVEL	ATTACK	PASSWORD
1	USUD	NAKF HLAP SDSP
2	ULUH	SAPO RLNM VUSD
3	NIGHZU	POZX MJDR GJSA
4	GHIDRU	GPGE SMEC TDTB
5	MUDRU	ABLP CGPG SGAM

HEAD ATTACK GOLD GEMS

LEVEL	ATTACK	PASSWORD
1	MEN	PQTM AONV UTNA
2	SAGHMEN	TNAP CTJS LDUF
3	KINGAL	FHSK EUFV KALP
4	DALLA	EPWB MPOR TRTA
5	AGA	GPKT BBWT SGNR

TAIL ATTACK GOLD GEMS

LEVEL	ATTACK	PASSWORD
1	A'ASH	LSSN GOAJ READ
2	ASH	FUTY HVNS LNVS
3	ASH SAR	LPAQ KOYH TGDS
4	AHS BALA	VLQL QELB IYDS
5	NAMTAGTAG	VLDB DDSL NCJA

WING ATTACK GOLD GEMS

LEVEL	ATTACK	PASSWORD
1	NIM	SGHJ VLPO QEIK
2	NIMSAHARA	QPLA OKFC NBUS
3	BARASH	IQUW ENPC SRGA
4	A'SHUM	LRYV LCJC MEBT
5	ATUKU	ALVN HRSF MSEP

BATTLE OF GIANTS: MUTANT INSECTS

ELECTICITY UPGRADE

Select Unlock Rewards from Options and enter WLUA DZCN ZNKE.

ICE UPGRADE

Select Unlock Rewards from Options and enter PLAL TALG JPZV.

TM

DS

BEN 10: PROTECTOR OF EARTH

GALACTIC ENFORCER SKINS
At the level select, press A, B, X, Y, L, R, Select.

GWEN 10 SKINS
At the level select, press Left, Right, Left, Right, L, R, Select.

ULTRA BEN SKINS
At the level select, press Up, Right, Down, Left, A, B, Select.

UPCHUCK
At the level select, press A, Left, Y, Right, X, Up, B, Down, Select.

BONUS MISSION
At the level select, press Left, L, Right, R, Up, Down, Select.

BRAIN AGE EXPRESS: ARTS & LETTERS

ELIMINATE ENEMIES IN WORD ATTACK
In Word Attack, during the Space mode, press A, Y, X, B. You can use this once each training session.

BRAIN AGE: TRAIN YOUR BRAIN IN MINUTES A DAY

BRAIN AGE CHECK SELECTION MENU
At the Daily Training Menu, hold Select while choosing Brain Age Check.

TOP 3 LISTS
At the Daily Training Menu, hold Select while choosing Graph.

BRAIN VOYAGE

ALL GOLD MEDALS
At the World Map, press A, B, Up, L, L, Y.

INFINITE COINS
At the World Tour Mode, press L, Up, X, Up, R, Y.

BUBBLE BOBBLE REVOLUTION

BONUS LEVELS IN CLASSIC MODE
At the Classic mode Title screen, press L, R, L, R, L, R, Right, Select. Touch the door at Level 20.

POWER UP! MODE IN CLASSIC VERSION
At the Classic mode Title screen, press Select, R, L, Left, Right, R, Select, Right.

SUPER BUBBLE BOBBLE IN CLASSIC VERSION
You must first defeat the boss with two players. At the Classic mode Title screen, press Left, R, Left, Select, Left, L, Left, Select.

BUILD-A-BEAR WORKSHOP

At the Select a Slot screen, press Up, Up, Down, Down, Left, Right, Left, Right, B, A. Now you can enter the following codes:

ALL LEVELS
At the level select, hold L + R.

ALL ACTIVITIES
At the workshop screen, press R.

ALL MOVES
At the garden screen, press L.

BUST-A-MOVE DS

DARK WORLD
First you must complete the game. At the Title screen, press A Left Right A.

SOUND TEST
At the Main menu, press Select, A, B, Left, Right, A, Select, Right.

CITY LIFE DS

1,000,000
Pause the game and press A, B, Y, L, R.

ALL BUILDINGS
Pause the game and hold B + Y + X + R for 2 seconds.

CLUB PENGUIN: ELITE PENGUIN FORCE

FLOWER HUNT MISSION
Change your system's date to April 1st.

APRIL ITEMS IN CATALOG
Change your system's date to April 1st.

SUMMER PARTY MISSION
Change your system's date to June 21st.

FIESTA HAT ON FROZEN POND
Change your system's date to June 21st.

JUNE ITEMS IN CATALOG
Change your system's date to June 21st.

HALLOWEEN PARTY MISSION
Change your system's date to October 31st.

FISH COSTUME IN LODGE ATTIC
Change your system's date to October 31st.

DELIVER THE PRESENTS MISSION
Change your system's date to December 25th.

ICE SKATES ON THE ICEBERG
Change your system's date to December 25th.

DINOSAUR KING

STONE CIRCLE PASSWORDS
Defeat the game to unlock the Stone Circle in South Euro. Now you can enter the following passwords to unlock dinosaurs. Find the level 1 dinosaur in a chest at the shrine.

009 DASPLETEOSARUS
Enter Grass, Water, Ligthning, Lightning, Earth, Earth, Water, Wind.

012 SIAMOTYRRANUS
Enter Fire, Wind, Fire, Water, Wind, Grass, Fire, Water.

025 JOBARIA
Enter Water, Lightning, Lightning, Earth, Fire, Earth, Fire, Wind.

029 TRICERATOPS
Enter Lightning, Fire, Lightning, Fire, Water, Lightning, Grass, Earth.

038 MONOCLONIUS
Enter Lightning, Earth, Water, Water, Grass, Fire, Earth, Wind.

046 EUOPLOCEPHALUS
Enter Earth, Earth, Grass, Water, Wind, Earth, Wind, Fire.

058 ALTIRHINUS
Enter Wind, Fire, Fire, Fire, Lightning, Earth, Water, Grass.

061 CARNOTAURUS
Enter Earth, Wind, Water, Lightning, Fire, Wind, Wind, Water.

EX ACE/EX CHOMP
Enter Lightning, Grass, Fire, Earth, Water, Water, Lightning, Fire. This gives you Ace if you are playing as Rex and Chomp as Max.

EX MINI-KING
Enter Lightning, Wind, Earth, Lightning, Grass, Wind, Fire, Water.

EX PARIS
Enter Grass, Water, Water, Earth, Wind, Grass, Lightning, Lightning.

EX SAUROPHAGANAX

Enter Fire, Water, Earth, Grass, Wind, Lightning, Fire, Water.

EX SPINY

Enter Water, Earth, Fire, Water, Fire, Grass, Wind, Earth.

EX TANK

Enter Earth, Grass, Earth, Water, Wind, Water, Grass, Fire.

EX TERRY

Enter Fire, Lightning, Wind, Wind, Water, Fire, Fire, Earth.

DISNEY FAIRIES: TINKER BELL

TINKERBELL MAGIC BOOK CODES

Talk to Queen Clarion about the Magic Book and enter the following codes.

EFFECCT	CODE
Augustus	5318 3479 7972
Baden	1199 2780 8802
Blair	6899 6003 4480
Cera	1297 0195 5747
Chipper	7980 9298 9818
Dewberry	0241 4491 0630
Elwood	3527 5660 3684
Fawn	9556 0047 1043
Idalia	2998 8832 2673
Iridessa	0724 0213 6136
Luminaria	8046 5868 5678
Magnolia	1697 4780 6430
Mariana	5138 8216 9240
Minister Autumn	2294 0281 6332
Minister Spring	2492 1155 4907
Minister Summer	2582 7972 6926
Minister Winter	2618 8587 2083
Nollie	5905 2346 9329
Olwen	7629 0545 7105
One Black Shell	1234 5678 9012
One Blue Dewdrop	0987 6543 2109
One Fairy Medal	1111 1111 1111
One Green Leaf	4444 4444 4444
One Pink Petal	2222 2222 2222
One Red Leaf	5555 5555 5555
One Snow Grain	7777 7777 7777
One Weak Thread	9999 9999 9999
One White Feather	8888 8888 8888
One Yellow Leaf	6666 6666 6666
One Yellow Petal	3333 3333 3333
Party Shoes	1390 5107 4096
Party Skirt	6572 4809 6680
Party Tiara	8469 7886 7938
Party Top	0977 4584 3869
Queen Clarion	1486 4214 8147
Rosetta	8610 2523 6122
Rune	3020 5768 5351
Silvermist	0513 4563 6800
Terence	8606 6039 6383
Tinkerbell	2495 7761 9313
Vidia	3294 3220 0349

DRAGLADE

CHARACTERS

CHARACTER	TO UNLOCK
Asuka	Defeat Daichi's story
Gyamon	Defeat Guy's story
Koki	Defeat Hibito's story
Shura	Defeat Kairu's story

HIDDEN QUEST: SHADOW OF DARKNESS

Defeat Story Mode with all of the main characters. This unlocks the hidden quest in Synethesia.

ZEKE

Complete all of the quests including Shadow of Darkness to unlock Zeke in wireless battle.

DRAGON QUEST IX: SENTINELS OF THE STARRY SKIES

MINI MEDAL REWARDS

Trade your mini medals with Cap'N Max Meddlin in Dourbridge. These are cumulative, so giving him 80 medals gets all of the rewards.

# MINI MEDALS	REWARD
4	Thief's Key
8	Mercury Bandanna
13	Bunny Suit
18	Jolly Roger Jumper
25	Transparent Tights
32	Miracle Sword
40	Sacred Armor
50	Meteorite Bracer
62	Rusty Helmet
80	Dragon Robe

After you have given him 80 mini medals, he sells items for mini medals.

# MINI MEDALS	ITEM
3	Prayer Ring
5	Elfin Elixir
8	Saint's Ashes
10	Reset Stone
15	Orichalcum
20	Pixie Boots

DOURBRIDGE SECRET SHOP

In Dourbridge, you can find a secret shop located behind the Dourbridge Item Shop. You need the Ultimate Key to access the shop.

DRAGON QUEST HEROES: ROCKET SLIME

KNIGHTRO TANK IN MULTIPLAYER

While in the church, press Y, L, L, Y, R, R, Y, Up, Down, Select.

THE NEMESIS TANK IN MULTIPLAYER

While in the church, press Y, R, R, up, L, L, Y, Down, Down, Down, Y, Select.

DRAGON QUEST MONSTERS: JOKER

CAPTAIN CROW

As you travel between the islands on the sea scooters, you are occasionally attacked by pirates. Discover the route on which the pirates are located at the bulletin board in any scoutpost den. When you face them between Infant Isle and Celeste Isle, Captain Crow makes an appearance. Defeat him and he forces himself into your team.

SOLITAIRE'S CHALLENGE

After completing the main game, load your game again for a new endeavor. The hero is in Solitaire's office, where she proposes a new nonstop challenge known as Solitaire's Challenge.

METAL KING SLIME

Acquire 100 different skills for your library and talk to the woman in Solitaire's office.

METAL KAISER SLIME

Acquire 150 different skills for your library and talk to the woman in Solitaire's office.

LEOPOLD

Acquire all of the skills for your library and talk to the woman in Solitaire's office.

LIQUID METAL SLIME

Collect 100 monsters in your library and talk to the man in Solitaire's office.

GRANDPA SLIME

Collect 200 monsters in your library and talk to the man in Solitaire's office.

EMPYREA

Collect all of the monsters in your library and talk to the man in Solitaire's office.

TRODE AND ROBBIN' HOOD

Complete both the skills and monster libraries and talk to both the man and woman in Solitaire's office.

DRAWN TO LIFE

HEAL ALL DAMAGE

During a game, press Start, hold L and press Y, X, Y, X, Y, X, A.

INVINCIBLITY

During a game, press Start, hold L and press A, X, B, B, Y.

ALIEN TEMPLATES

During a game, press Start, hold L and press X, Y, B, A, A.

ANIMAL TEMPLATES

During a game, press Start, hold L and press B, B, A, A, X.

ROBOT TEMPLATES

During a game, press Start, hold L and press Y, X, Y, X, A.

SPORTS TEMPLATES

During a game, press Start, hold L and press Y, A, B, A, X.

DRAWN TO LIFE: THE NEXT CHAPTER

TEMPLATES

At the Creation Hall, hold L and press X, Y, B, A, A to unlock the following Templates.

Astronaut Template

Knight Template

Ninja Girl Template

Spartan Template

Super Girl Template

DRAWN TO LIFE: SPONGEBOB SQUAREPANTS EDITION

EXTRA REWARD COINS

Select Cheat Entry and enter Down, Down, B, B, Down, Left, Up, Right, A.

ED, EDD N EDDY: SCAM OF THE CENTURY

INVINCIBILITY
During a game, press Select + A, Up, Select + R, Down, Up.

RESTORE HALF HEALTH
During a game, press A, A, Select + A, Down, Down, Down.

RESTORE HEALTH
During a game, press B, B, Select + X, A + R, Select.

HALF SPECIAL ATTACK GAUGE
During a game, press Down, Down, Left, Right, Select + X.

CAMERA
During a game, press Down, Up, Right, Right, Select + B.

MARSHMALLOW
During a game, press Down, Down, Left, Left, Select + A.

ELEBITS: THE ADVENTURES OF KAI & ZERO

BIG RED BONUS OMEGA
Select Download Additional Omegas from the Extra menu. Choose Download Data and press B, Y, Up, L, Right, R, Down, Left, X, A.

FINAL FANTASY FABLES: CHOCOBO TALES

OMEGA—WAVE CANNON CARD
Select Send from the Main menu and then choose Download Pop-Up Card. Press L, L, Up, B, B, Left.

GODZILLA UNLEASHED: DOUBLE SMASH

ANGUIRUS
Defeat Hedorah Terrorizes San Francisco.

DESTOROYAH
Defeat Monster Island, The Final Battle.

FIRE RODAN
Defeat Biollante Attacks Paris.

KING GHIDORAH
Defeat Mecha King Ghidorah Ravages Bangkok.

GRID

UNLOCK ALL
Select Cheat Codes from the Options and enter 233558.

INVULNERABILITY
Select Cheat Codes from the Options and enter 161650.

DRIFT MASTER
Select Cheat Codes from the Options and enter 789520.

PERFECT GRIP
Select Cheat Codes from the Options and enter 831782.

HIGH ROLLER
Select Cheat Codes from the Options and enter 401134.

GHOST CAR
Select Cheat Codes from the Options and enter 657346.

TOY CARS
Select Cheat Codes from the Options and enter 592014.

MM MODE
Select Cheat Codes from the Options and enter 800813.

INFINITE SPACE

NEW GAME+ AND EXTRA MODE

Complete the game. New Game+ gives you additional blue prints. Extra Mode is another game mode with limited resources.

IZUNA: LEGEND OF THE UNEMPLOYED NINJA

PATH OF TRAILS BONUS DUNGEON

After completing the game, touch the crystal from the beginning.

JAKE HUNTER: DETECTIVE CHRONICLES

PASSWORDS

Select Password from the main menu and enter the following:

UNLOCKABLE	PASSWORD
1 Password Info	AAAA
2 Visuals	LEET
3 Visuals	GONG
4 Visuals	CARS
5 Movies	ROSE
6 Jukebox	BIKE
7 Hints	HINT

JAKE HUNTER DETECTIVE STORY: MEMORIES OF THE PAST

JAKE HUNTER QUIZ
Select Password and enter NEET.

JAKE HUNTER SERIES
Select Password and enter MISS.

JAKE HUNTER UNLEASHED 01 BONUS
Select Password and enter NONE.

JAKE HUNTER UNLEASHED 02 BONUS
Select Password and enter ANGL.

JAKE HUNTER UNLEASHED 03 BONUS
Select Password and enter SNAP.

JAKE HUNTER UNLEASHED 04 BONUS
Select Password and enter DOOR.

JAKE HUNTER UNLEASHED 05 BONUS
Select Password and enter STOP.

JAKE HUNTER UNLEASHED DS1 BONUS
Select Password and enter KING.

JAKE HUNTER VISUALS 1
Select Password and enter LEET.

JAKE HUNTER VISUALS 2
Select Password and enter GONG.

JAKE HUNTER VISUALS 3
Select Password and enter CARS.

JAKE HUNTER VISUALS 4
Select Password and enter TREE.

JAKE HUNTER VISUALS 5
Select Password and enter PAPA.

JUKEBOX
Select Password and enter BIKE.

MOVIE GALLERY
Select Password and enter ROSE.

PASSWORD HINTS
Select Password and enter HINT.

SIDE CHARACTER'S BONUS STORY
Select Password and enter MINU.

STAFF COMMENTS 1
Select Password and enter AQUA.

STAFF COMMENTS 2
Select Password and enter MOTO.

WHAT IS A PASSWORD?
Select Password and enter AAAA.

JAM SESSIONS

BONUS SONGS
At the Free Play menu, press Up, Up, Down, Down, Left, Right, Left, Right. This unlocks I'm Gonna Miss Her by Brad Paisley, Needles and Pins by Tom Petty, and Wild Thing by Jimi Hendrix.

JUMBLE MADNESS

FEBRUARY 31 PUZZLE
For Daily Jumble and Jumble Crosswords, select the square under February 28, 2009.

KONAMI CLASSICS SERIES: ARCADE HITS
GRADIUS

ALL POWER-UPS EXCEPT SPEED
At the Gradius title screen, press Up, Up, Down, Down, Left, Right, Left, Right, B, A. After starting a game, press Start to get every power-up except Speed. This code can be entered only once.

THE LAST AIRBENDER

FOCUS UPGRADE
Select Cheats from the Options and enter Earth, Earth, Water, Earth.

HEAVY HITTER
Select Cheats from the Options and enter Water, Earth, Fire, Fire.

HEALTH UPGRADE
Select Cheats from the Options and enter Air, Water, Fire, Fire.

LEGO BATMAN

ALFRED PENNYWORTH
Use the computer in the Batcave, select Enter Code and enter ZAQ637.

BATGIRL
Use the computer in the Batcave, select Enter Code and enter JKR331.

BRUCE WAYNE
Use the computer in the Batcave, select Enter Code and enter BDJ327.

CLASSIC CATWOMAN
Use the computer in the Batcave, select Enter Code and enter M1AAWW.

CLOWN GOON
Use the computer in the Batcave, select Enter Code and enter HJK327.

COMMISSIONER GORDON
Use the computer in the Batcave, select Enter Code and enter DDP967.

FISHMONGER
Use the computer in the Batcave, select Enter Code and enter HGY748.

FREEZE GIRL
Use the computer in the Batcave, select Enter Code and enter XVK541.

FREEZE HENCHMAN
Use the computer in the Batcave, select Enter Code and enter NJL412.

JOKER GOON
Use the computer in the Batcave, select Enter Code and enter UTF782.

JOKER HENCHMAN
Use the computer in the Batcave, select Enter Code and enter YUN924.

NIGHTWING
Use the computer in the Batcave, select Enter Code and enter MVY759.

TROPICAL JOKER
Use the computer in the Batcave, select Enter Code and enter CCB199.

1 MILLION STUDS
At the main menu, press X, Y, B, B, Y, X, L, L, R, R, Up, Down, Left, Right, Start, Select.

3 MILLION STUDS
At the main menu, press Up, Up, B, Down, Down, X, Left, Left, Y, L, R, L, R, B, Y, X, Start, Select.

ALL CHARACTERS
At the main menu, press X, Up, B, Down, Y, Left, Start, Right, R, R, L, R, R, Down, Down, Up, Y, Y, Y, Start, Select.

ALL EPISODES AND FREE PLAY MODE
At the main menu, press Right, Up, R, L, X, Y, Right, Left, B, L, R, L, Down, Down, Up, Y, Y, X, X, B, B, Up, Up, L, R, Start, Select.

ALL EXTRAS
At the main menu, press Up, Down, L, R, L, R, L, Left, Right, X, X, Y, Y, B, B, L, Up, Down, L, R, L, R, Up, Up, Down, Start, Select.

LEGO BATTLES

INVINCIBLE HERO
At the Lego Store, tap the Red Brick and enter HJCRAWK.

REGENERATING HEALTH
At the Lego Store, tap the Red Brick and enter ABABLRX.

ONE HIT KILL (HEROES)
At the Lego Store, tap the Red Brick and enter AVMPWHK.

LONG RANGE MAGIC
At the Lego Store, tap the Red Brick and enter ZPWJFUQ.

SUPER MAGIC
At the Lego Store, tap the Red Brick and enter DWFTBNS.

DOUBLE LEGO BRICKS
At the Lego Store, tap the Red Brick and enter BGQOYRT.

FAST BUILDING
At the Lego Store, tap the Red Brick and enter QMSLPOE.

FAST HARVESTING
At the Lego Store, tap the Red Brick and enter PQZLJOB.

FAST MAGIC
At the Lego Store, tap the Red Brick and enter JRTPASX.

FAST MINING
At the Lego Store, tap the Red Brick and enter KVBPQRJ.

FULL UNIT CAP
At the Lego Store, tap the Red Brick and enter UMSXIRQ.

SUPER EXPLOSIONS
At the Lego Store, tap the Red Brick and enter THNBGRE.

UPGRADED TOWERS
At the Lego Store, tap the Red Brick and enter EDRFTGY.

SHOW ENEMIES
At the Lego Store, tap the Red Brick and enter IBGOFWX.

SHOW LEGO STUDS
At the Lego Store, tap the Red Brick and enter CPLYREK.

SHOW MINIKIT
At the Lego Store, tap the Red Brick and enter LJYQRAC.

SHOW RED BRICKS
At the Lego Store, tap the Red Brick and enter RTGYPKC.

REVEAL MAP
At the Lego Store, tap the Red Brick and enter SKQMXPL.

UNLOCK ISLANDER

At the Lego Store, tap the Red Brick and enter UGDRSQP.

UNLOCK NINJA MASTER

At the Lego Store, tap the Red Brick and enter SHWSDGU.

UNLOCK SPACE CRIMINAL LEADER

At the Lego Store, tap the Red Brick and enter ZVDNJSU.

UNLOCK TROLL KING

At the Lego Store, tap the Red Brick and enter XRCTVYB.

LEGO INDIANA JONES: THE ORIGINAL ADVENTURES

You should hear a confirmation sound after the following codes are entered.

ALL CHARACTERS

At the title screen, press X, Up, B, Down, Y, Left, Start, Right, R, R, L, R, R, Down, Down, Up, Y, Y, Y, Start, Select.

ALL EPISODES AND FREE PLAY MODE

Right, Up, R, L, X, Y, Right, Left, B, L, R, L, Down, Down, Up, Y, Y, X, X, B, Up, Up, L, R, Start, Select.

ALL EXTRAS

Up, Down, L, R, L, R, L, Left, Right, X, X, Y, Y, B, B, L, Up, Down, L, R, L, R, Up, Up, Down, Start, Select.

1,000,000 STUDS

At the title screen, press X, Y, B, B, Y, X, L, L, R, R, Up, Down, Left, Right, Start, Select.

3,000,000 STUDS

At the title screen, press Up, Up, B, Down, Down, X, Left, Left, Y, L, R, L, R, B, Y, X, Start, Select.

LEGO ROCK BAND

BLUR

In Tour Mode, complete Song 2.

DAVID BOWIE

In Tour Mode, complete Let's Dance.

IGGY POP

In Tour Mode, complete The Passenger.

QUEEN

In Tour Mode, complete We Are the Champions.

LEGO STAR WARS: THE COMPLETE SAGA

3,000,000 STUDS

At the main menu, press Start, Start, Down, Down, Left, Left, Up, Up, Select. This cheat can only be used once.

DEBUG MENUS

At the main menu, press Up, Left, Down, Right, Up, Left, Down, Right, Up, Left, Down, Right, R, L, Start, Select.

BONUS TOUCH GAME 1

At the main menu, press Up, Up, Down, L, L, R, R.

LEGO STAR WARS II: THE ORIGINAL TRILOGY

10 STUDS

At the Mos Eisley cantina, enter 4PR28U.

OBI WAN GHOST

At the Mos Eisley cantina, enter BEN917.

LITTLEST PET SHOP: GARDEN

GIRAFFE PET
Select Passwords from the Options and enter LPSTRU. It is available in the Meow Market.

LITTLEST PET SHOP: JUNGLE

GIRAFFE PET
Select Passwords from the Options and enter LPSTRU. It is available in the Meow Market.

LOCK'S QUEST

REPLACE CLOCKWORKS WITH KINGDOM FORCE
After completing the game, hold R and select your profile.

ENDING STORY
After completing the game, hold L and select your profile.

MARIO & LUIGI: BOWSER'S INSIDE STORY

LUMBAR NOOK ALARM
In the Lumbar Nook, when you dig into the bone, press A, B, X, Y, L, R, Y, X, B, A to set off the alarm. Otherwise, you have to wait awhile for it.

MARIO PARTY DS

BOSS BASH
Complete Story Mode.

EXPERT CPU DIFFICULTY LEVEL
Complete Story Mode.

MUSIC AND VOICE ROOM
Complete Story Mode.

SCORE SCUFFLE
Complete Story Mode.

TRIANGLE TWISTER PUZZLE MODE
Complete Story Mode.

MARVEL SUPER HERO SQUAD

APOCALYPSE MODE
Select Cheats from the Settings and enter Wolverine, Wolverine, Dr Doom, Abomination, Wolverine. This gives everyone one hit kills.

MEGA MAN STAR FORCE 3: BLACK ACE

STARS ON NEW GAME/CONTINUE SCREEN
Do the following to earn each star on the New Game/Continue screen.

STAR	HOW TO EARN
Black Ace	Defeat the game
G Comp	Collect all Giga cards
M Comp	Collect all Mega cards
S Comp	Collect all Standard cards
SS	Defeat Sirius

RANDOM SIGMA BOSSES

At the New Game/Continue screen, hold L and tap S Comp Star, G Comp Star, S Comp Star, M Comp Star, SS Star, SS Star, Black Ace Star.

FIGHT ROGUEZZ

At the New Game/Continue screen, hold L and tap G Comp Star, M Comp Star, M Comp Star, SS Star, G Comp Star, S Comp Star, Black Ace Star. RogueZZ appears in Meteor G Control CC.

MEGA MAN STAR FORCE 3: RED JOKER

STARS ON NEW GAME/CONTINUE SCREEN

DO THE FOLLOWING TO EARN EACH STAR ON THE NEW GAME/CONTINUE SCREEN.	
Star	How to earn
Red Joker	Defeat the game
G Comp	Collect all Giga cards
M Comp	Collect all Mega cards
S Comp	Collect all Standard cards
SS	Defeat Sirius

RANDOM SIGMA BOSSES

At the New Game/Continue screen, hold L and tap S Comp Star, G Comp Star, S Comp Star, M Comp Star, SS Star, SS Star, Red Joker Star.

FIGHT ROGUEZZ

At the New Game/Continue screen, hold L and tap G Comp Star, M Comp Star, M Comp Star, SS Star, G Comp Star, S Comp Star, Red Joker Star. RogueZZ appears in Meteor G Control CC.

METROID PRIME PINBALL

PHAZON MINES

Complete Omega Pirate in Multi Mission mode.

PHENDRANA DRIFTS

Complete Thardus in Multi Mission mode.

MIGHT & MAGIC: CLASH OF HEROES

UNLOCK CHARACTERS IN QUICK BATTLE AND MULTIPLAYER

Unlock new characters in Quick Battle and Multiplayer modes as you complete the chapters.

CHARACTER UNLOCKED	CHAPTER COMPLETED
Findan	1 - Anwen
Varkas	2 - Godric
Markal	3 - Fiona
Jezebeth	4 - Aidan
Cyrus	5 – Nadia

MY JAPANESE COACH

UNLOCK LESSONS

Look up the word cheat in the dictionary. Touch the V next to the verb to open the conjugation chart. Hold L + R for a few seconds. You should hear the word cheat in Japanese. Return to the main menu, go to Options, then Sound. Pressing R will advance you 1 lesson, and pressing L will advance you to the beginning of the next lesson group.

MY WORD COACH

WORD POPPERS MINIGAME

After reaching 200 word successes, at the options menu, press A, B, X, Y, A, B.

MYSIMS KINGDOM

COW COSTUME

Pause the game and press R, X, L, Y, Up, Right, Left, Down.

COW HEADGEAR

Pause the game and press L, R, Y, X, Left, Down, Left, Right.

PATCHWORK CLOTHES

Pause the game and press Right, Down, Left, Up, L, R, L, R.

PATCHWORK PANTS

Pause the game and press Down, L, Left, R, Up, Y, Right, X.

PUNK BOTTOM

Pause the game and press Left, R, L, Right, Y, Y, X, X.

PUNK TOP

Pause the game and press Up, X, Down, Y, Left, L, Right, R.

SAMURAI ARMOR

Pause the game and press Y, X, Right, Left, L, R, Down, Up.

SAMURAI HELMET

Pause the game and press X, Y, R, L, X, Y, R, L.

N+

ATARI BONUS LEVELS

Select Unlockables from the main menu, hold L + R and press A, B, A, B, A, A, B.

NAMCO MUSEUM DS

DIG-DUG 2 OLD VERSION

From the Dig Dug 2 menu, select Hardcore Options from the Settings. Change New Version to Old.

SECRET GAME: SUPER XEVIOUS

From the Xevious menu, select Hardcore Options from the Settings. Change the version to Super Xevious.

NARUTO: PATH OF THE NINJA

After defeating the game, talk to Knohamaru on the roof of the Ninja Academy. He allows you go get certain cheats by tapping four successive spots on the touch screen in order. There are 12 different spots on the screen. We have numbered them from left to right, top to bottom, as follows:

1	2	3	4
5	6	7	8
9	10	11	12

Enter the following codes by touching the four spots in the order listed.

UNLOCK	CODE
4th Hokage's Sword	4, 7, 11, 5
Fuji Fan	8, 11, 2, 5
Jiraiya	11, 3, 1, 6
Rajin's Sword	7, 6, 5, 11
Rasengan	9, 2, 12, 7

NARUTO: PATH OF THE NINJA 2

CHARACTER PASSWORDS

Talk to Konohamaru at the school to enter the following passwords. You must first complete the game for the passwords to work.

CHARACTER	PASSWORD
Gaara	D K F I A B J L
Gai	I K A G D E F L
Iruka	J G D L K A I B
Itachi Uchiha	G B E I D A L F
Jiraiya	E B J D A G F L
Kankuro	A L J K B E D G
Kyuubi Naruto	G J H L B F D E
Orochimaru	A H F B L E J G
Temari	H F I C L K B G
The Third Hokage	C G H A J B E L

MISSION PASSWORDS

Talk to Konohamaru at the school to enter the following passwords. You must first complete the game for the passwords to work.

MISSION	PASSWORD
An Extreme Battle!	H L B A K G C D
The Legendary Haze Ninja!	F G E H I D A L
The Legendary Sannin!	B C E G K F H L

NEED FOR SPEED CARBON: OWN THE CITY

INFINITE NITROUS

At the Main menu, press Up, Up, Down, Left, A, B, B, A.

NEW SUPER MARIO BROS.

PLAY AS LUIGI IN SINGLE PLAYER

At the Select a File screen, hold L + R while selecting a saved game.

SECRET CHALLENGE MODE

On the map, pause the game and press L, R, L, R, X, X, Y, Y.

THE NEW YORK TIMES CROSSWORDS

BLACK & WHITE
At the Main menu, press Up, Up, Down, Down, B, B, Y, Y.

NICKTOONS: ATTACK OF THE TOYBOTS

DANNY PHANTOM 2
Select Unlock Code from the Options and enter Tak, Jimmy, Zim, El Tigre.

SPONGEBOB 2
Select Unlock Code from the Options and enter Patrick, Jenny, Timmy, Tak.

NICKTOONS: BATTLE FOR VOLCANO ISLAND

FRUIT BECOMES TOYS IN FRUIT COLLECTING MINI-GAME
Select Unlock Codes from the Options and enter Spongebob, Danny, Timmy, Cosmo.

NIGHT AT THE MUSEUM: BATTLE OF THE SMITHSONIAN

SUPER LARRY
During a game, hold L + R, and press Left, A, Right, Right, Y.

PEGGLE: DUAL SHOT

Q LEVEL 10
Send the trial game to another DS.

PHANTASY STAR ZERO

PASSWORD MACHINE
Check out the vending machine on the far right side of the sewers. Type in special passwords here to find free items.

ITEM	PASSWORD
Selvaria's Spear	5703-8252
Selvaria's Shield	4294-2273
Blade Cannon	7839-3594
Caduceus's Rod	5139-6877
Game Master (Ge-maga)	7162-5792
CONSOLES+ (Famitsu)	9185-6189
INGame: Greg&Kiri (Nintendo Dream)	5531-0215
Nintendo Power (Dengeki DS)	3171-0109
Puyo Soul	3470-1424
Taupy Soul	9475-6843
Lassie Soul	4775-7197

PHINEAS AND FERB

STOP CANDACE
At the title screen, press X, Y, L, R, Select.

DOUBLE SPEED
At the title screen, press A, B, L, R, Select.

PHOTO DOJO

FAST FIGHTERS
At the title screen, hold Select and choose Head into Battle. Continue to hold Select and choose Vs. Mode.

PIRATES OF THE CARIBBEAN: DEAD MAN'S CHEST

10 GOLD
During a game, press Right, X, X, Right, Left.

INVINCIBILITY
During a game, press Up, Down, Left, Right (x5), Left, Right, Up, Down, Left, Right, Up (x5), Left.

UNLIMITED POWER
During a game, press Up, Up, Down, Down, Left, Right, Left, Right, L, R.

RESTORE HEALTH
During a game, press Y, Y, Select, Left, Right, Left, Right, Left.

RESTORE SAVVY
During a game, press X, X, Select, Up, Down, Up, Down, Up.

GHOST FORM MODE
During a game, press Y, X, Y, X, Y, X.

SEASICKNESS MODE
During a game, press X, X, Y, X, X, Y.

SILLY WEAPONS
During a game, press Y, Y, X, Y (x3).

AXE
During a game, press Left, L, L, Down, Down, Left, Up, Up, Down, Down.

BLUNDERBUSS
During a game, press Down, L, L, Down (x3).

CHICKEN
During a game, press Right, L, L, Up, Down, Down.

EXECUTIONER AXE
During a game, press Right, L, L, Up, Down, Up, Right, Right, Left(x2).

PIG
During a game, press Right, R, R, Down, Up, Up.

PISTOL
During a game, press Down, L, L, Down, Down, Right.

RIFLE
During a game, press Left, L, L, Up (x3).

FAST MUSIC
During a game, press Y, Select, Y (x4).

SLOW MUSIC
During a game, press Y, Select, X (x4).

DISABLE CHEATS
During a game, press X (x6).

POP CUTIE! STREET FASHION SIMULATION

LAYERED DRESS
At a phone, enter 7247.

POODLE OUTFIT
At a phone, enter 3107.

HOTEL PATAGONIA/EDDIE RETURNS
At a phone, enter 9901.

CALL GIBSONS
At a phone, enter 9801.

FASHION HOTLINE
At a phone enter 0000, 1111, 2222, 3333, 4444, 5555, 6666.

RACE DRIVER: CREATE & RACE

ALL CHALLENGES
Select Cheat Codes from Extras and enter 942785.

ALL CHAMPIONSHIPS
Select Cheat Codes from Extras and enter 761492.

ALL REWARDS
Select Cheat Codes from Extras and enter 112337.

FREE DRIVE
Select Cheat Codes from Extras and enter 171923.

NO DAMAGE
Select Cheat Codes from Extras and enter 505303.

EASY STEERING
Select Cheat Codes from Extras and enter 611334.

MINIATURE CARS
Select Cheat Codes from Extras and enter 374288.

MM VIEW
Select Cheat Codes from Extras and enter 467348.

RETRO GAME CHALLENGE

COSMIC GATE

HARD MODE
At the title screen, press Down, Down, B, B, A, A, Start.

POWERED-UP INFINITY
Pause the game and press Up, Up, A, B. This cheat can only be used once per game.

SHIP POWER-UP
Pause the game and press Up, Up, A, A, B, B.

CONTINUE GAME
At the Game Over screen, press Left + Start. You will continue the game with a score of 000.

HAGGLE MAN CODES

FULL HEALTH
Pause the game and press Down, Right, Up, Left, B, B, B, B, A, A, A, A.

SCROLLS APPEAR
Pause the game and press Up Right Down Left A A A A B B B B.

INFINITE TIME
Before a level, hold Up/Left and press A + B.

HAGGLE MAN 2

STAGE SELECT
At the title screen, hold A and press Up, Up, Right, Right, Right, Down, Down, Left, Left, Left.

FULL POWER
Pause the game and press Up, Down, Up, Down, B, B, A, A.

SCROLLS APPEAR
Pause the game and press Down, Up, Down, Up, A, A, B, B.

CONTINUE
At the Game Over scree

HAGGLE MAN 3

99 LIVES
Pause the game and press A, B, A, B, Left, Right, Left, Right.

9999 GEARS
Pause the game and press B, A, B, A, Right, Left, Right, Left.

WARP TO BOSS
Pause the game and press B, B, A, A, Left, Left, Right, Right.

RALLY KING

INVINCIBILITY
At the title screen, press Select + Left.

CARS DISAPPEAR
At the title screen, hold Select and press Down/Right.

START AT COURSE 2
At the title screen, press A, B, A, B, Up + Select.

START AT COURSE 3
At the title screen, press A, B, A, B, Left + Select.

START AT COURSE 4
At the title screen, press A, B, A, B, Down + Select.

STAR PRINCE

INVINCIBILITY
At the title screen, hold Up and press A, A, A. Then, hold Down and press B, B, B.

CONTINUE
At the Game Over screen, hold Left and press Start.

RHYTHM HEAVEN

RHYTHM TOYS – TELEPHONE NUMBERS
Enter the following numbers into the telephone in Rhythm Toys to unlock sounds from Rhythm Tengoku:
5553282338
5557325937
5557268724
5557625688

RUBIK'S PUZZLE WORLD

ALL LEVELS AND CUBIES
At the main menu, press X, Y, Y, X, X.

SCOOBY-DOO! FIRST FRIGHTS

DAPHNE'S SECRET COSTUME
Select Codes from the Extras menu and enter 2839.

FRED'S SECRET COSTUME
Select Codes from the Extras menu and enter 4826.

SCOOBY DOO'S SECRET COSTUME
Select Codes from the Extras menu and enter 1585.

SHAGGY'S SECRET COSTUME

Select Codes from the Extras menu and enter 3726.

VELMA'S SECRET COSTUME

Select Codes from the Extras menu and enter 6588.

SIMCITY CREATOR

99999999 MONEY
Enter MONEYBAGS as a password.

AMERICAN PROSPERITY AGE MAP
Enter NEWWORLD as a password.

ASIA AGE MAP
Enter SAMURAI as a password.

ASIA AGE BONUS MAP
Enter FEUDAL as a password.

DAWN OF CIVILIZATION MAP
Enter ANCIENT as a password.

GLOBAL WARMING MAP
Enter MODERN as a password.

GLOBAL WARMING BONUS MAP
Enter BEYOND as a password.

RENAISSANCE BONUS MAP
Enter HEREANDNOW as a password.

SIMCITY DS

LANDMARK BUILDINGS

Select Landmark Collection from the Museum menu. Choose Password and enter the following:

BUILDING	PASSWORD
Anglican Cathedral (UK)	kipling
Arc de Triomphe (France)	gaugin
Atomic Dome (Japan)	kawabata
Big Ben (UK)	orwell
Bowser Castle (Nintendo)	hanafuda
Brandenburg Gate (Germany)	gropius
Coit Tower	kerouac
Conciergerie (France)	rodin
Daibutsu (Japan)	mishima
Edo Castle (Japan)	shonagon
Eiffel Tower (France)	camus
Gateway Arch (USA)	twain
Grand Central Station (USA)	f.scott
Great Pyramids (Egypt)	mahfouz
Hagia Sofia (Turkey)	ataturk
Helsinki Cathedral (Finland)	kivi
Himeji Castle (Japan)	hokusai
Holstentor (Germany)	durer
Independence Hall (USA)	mlkingjr
Jefferson Memorial (USA)	thompson
Kokkai (Japan)	soseki
LA Landmark (USA)	hemingway
Lincoln Memorial (USA)	melville
Liver Building (UK)	dickens
Melbourne Cricket Ground (Australia)	damemelba
Metropolitan Cath. (UK)	austen
Moai (Chile)	allende
Mt. Fuji (Japan)	hiroshige

BUILDING	PASSWORD
National Museum (Taiwan)	yuantlee
Neuschwanstein Castle (Germany)	beethoven
Notre Dame (France)	hugo
Palace of Fine Arts (USA)	bunche
Palacio Real (Spain)	cervantes
Paris Opera (France)	daumier
Parthenon (Greece)	callas
Pharos of Alexandria (Egypt)	zewail
Rama IX Royal Park (Thailand)	phu
Reichstag (Germany)	goethe
Sagrada Familia (Spain)	dali
Shuri Castle (Japan)	basho
Smithsonian Castle (USA)	pauling
Sphinx (Egypt)	haykal
St Paul's Cathedral (UK)	defoe
St. Basil's Cathedral (Russia)	tolstoy
St. Stephen's Cathedral (Austria)	mozart
Statue of Liberty (USA)	pollack
Stockholm Palace (Sweden)	bergman
Taj Mahal (India)	tagore
Tower of London (UK)	maugham
Trafalgar Square (UK)	joyce
United Nations (UN)	amnesty
United States Capitol (USA)	poe
Washington Monument	capote
Westminster Abbey (UK)	greene
White House (USA)	Steinbeck

THE SIMS 2

MONGOO MONKEY FOR THE CASINO
Start the game with Sims 2 in the GBA slot of your Nintendo DS.

THE SIMS 2 APARTMENT PETS

$10,000
From the PDA screen, select the disk icon. Then choose Unlockable from the Options and enter Cash.

SONIC CLASSIC COLLECTION

SONIC THE HEDGEHOG

DEBUG MODE
At the title screen, press A, A, Up, Down, Left, Right, hold Y and press Start.

LEVEL SELECT
At the title screen press Up, Down, Left, Right, hold Y and press Start.

SONIC THE HEDGEHOG 2

LEVEL SELECT
At the title screen, press Up, Up, Up, Down, Down, Down, Left, Right, Left, Right, hold Y and press Start.

SONIC THE HEDGEHOG 3

LEVEL SELECT
As the SEGA logo fades, quickly press Up, Up, Down, Down, Up, Up, Up, Up. Highlight Sound Test and press Start.

SONIC KNUCKLES

LEVEL SELECT WITH SONIC THE HEDGEHOG 2
At the title screen, press Up, Up, Up, Down, Down, Down, Left, Right, Left, Right, hold A and press Start.

SOUL BUBBLES

REVEAL ALL CALABASH LOCATIONS
Pause the game and press A, L, L, R, A, Down, A, R.

ALL LEVELS
At the World Select, press L, Up, X, Up, R, Y.

ALL GALLERY ITEMS
At the Gallery, press B, Up, B, B, L, Y.

TM

SPECTROBES

CARD INPUT SYSTEM

When the Upsilon Cube is unearthed and shown to Aldous, the Card Input System feature becomes available. This will allow you to input data from Spectrobe Cards. These give you new Spectrobes and Custom Parts. If you get your hands on a Spectrobe Card and the system is unlocked, investigate the card input system in the spaceship's lower deck.

Follow the instructions on the upper screen to match the four corner points of the card to the corners of the touch screen. Touch the screen through the seven holes in the card in the order indicated on the card. If the code you input is correct, you receive Spectrobes, custom Parts, minerals or Cubes.

You can input the same card a maximum of four times. This means that you can only obtain four of the same Spectrobes from a single card. You can only input cards once. And some cards cannot be input until you have reached a certain point in the game.

The following table gives you a seven character code which refers to the spots you touch in order. The first four characters have you touching the four corners and the final three are spots among the 12 in the middle. To get Cyclone Geo, Hammer Geo, Ice Geo, Plasma Geo, or Thunder Geo, you must first beat the game.

EFFECT	CODE	EFFECT	CODE
Aobasat Apex	BACD HEP	Samurite Voltar	BACD LHM
Cyclone Geo	CDAB LGM	Sapphire Mineral	ABDC FJO
Danaphant Tuska	ABDC ELI	Segulos Propos	CDAB KIH
Danilob	DABC GLO	Seguslice	CDAB GKP
Emerald Mineral	BACD FKN	Shakor Bristle	DABC MLK
Grilden Biblad	ABDC FIH	Sigma Cube	CDAB PML
Grildragos Drafly	CDAB MHK	Tau Cube	DABC LIF
Gristar	BACD EJN	Thunder Geo	DABC MEL
Hammer Geo	ABDC ELH	Vilagrisp (Custom Part)	DABC EIN
Harumitey Lazos	DABC ILM	Vilakroma	BACD NLM
Ice Geo	CDAB HEK	Vilakroma (Custom Color 1)	CDAB LJI
Inataflare Auger	ABDC IGH	Vilakroma (Custom Color 2)	DABC EGP
Inkalade	ABDC GLP	Windora	ABDC MGP
Iota Cube	ABDC OHE	Windora (Custom Color 1)	DABC EHG
Komainu	CDAB HMJ	Windora (Custom Color 2)	CDAB JPM
Kugaster Sonara	DABC LOE	Windora Ortex	BACD IPG
Mossax Jetspa (Custom Color 1)	BACD JML	Windora Ortex (Custom Color 1)	ABDC MPH
Naglub	ABDC EJM	Windora Ortex (Custom Color 2)	DABC MGH
Plasma Geo	BACD KLE	Windora Sordina	CDAB PEO
Rho Cube	BACD PNI	Windora Sordina (Custom Color 1)	BACD MOH
Ruby Mineral	CDAB FKO	Windora Sordina (Custom Color 2)	ABDC LEN
Samukabu	ABDC OIL	Wing Geo (must beat game	DABC MNP

SPIDER-MAN 2

ALL SPECIAL MOVES

Load the game with Spider-Man: Mysterio's Menace for Game Boy Advance in the Nintendo DS.

SPONGEBOB SQUAREPANTS
FEATURING NICKTOONS: GLOBS OF DOOM

INFINITE HEALTH
Select Unlock Codes from the Options and enter Tak, Tlaloc, Jimmy Neutron, Beautiful Gorgeous.

INSTANT KO
Select Unlock Codes from the Options and enter Dib, Tak, Beautiful Gorgeous, Plankton.

EXTRA ATTACK
Select Unlock Codes from the Options and enter Dib, Plankton, Technus, Jimmy Neutron.

EXTRA DEFENSE
Select Unlock Codes from the Options and enter Zim, Danny Phantom, Plankton, Beautiful Gorgeous.

MAX DEFENSE
Select Unlock Codes from the Options and enter Plankton, Dib, Beautiful Gorgeous, Plankton.

ITEMS +
Select Unlock Codes from the Options and enter Danny Phantom, Beautiful Gorgeous, Jimmy Neutron, Technus.

ITEMS ++
Select Unlock Codes from the Options and enter SpongeBob, Tlaloc, SpongeBob, Danny Phantom.

NO HEALTH ITEMS
Select Unlock Codes from the Options and enter Tak, SpongeBob, Technus, Danny Phantom.

LOWER PRICES
Select Unlock Codes from the Options and enter Tlaloc, Zim, Beautiful Gorgeous, SpongeBob.

SUPER BEAUTIFUL GORGEOUS
Select Unlock Codes from the Options and enter Beautiful Gorgeous, Technus, Jimmy Neutron, Beautiful Gorgeous.

SUPER DANNY PHANTOM
Select Unlock Codes from the Options and enter Danny Phantom, Zim, Danny Phantom, Beautiful Gorgeous.

SUPER DIB
Select Unlock Codes from the Options and enter Zim, Plankton, Dib, Plankton.

SUPER JIMMY
Select Unlock Codes from the Options and enter Technus, Danny Phantom, Jimmy Neutron, Technus.

SUPER PLANKTON
Select Unlock Codes from the Options and enter Tak, Plankton, Dib, Technus.

SUPER SPONGEBOB
Select Unlock Codes from the Options and enter Technus, SpongeBob, Technus, Tlaloc.

SUPER TAK
Select Unlock Codes from the Options and enter Danny Phantom, Jimmy Neutron, Tak, Tlaloc.

SUPER TECHNUS
Select Unlock Codes from the Options and enter Danny Phantom, Technus, Tak, Technus.

SUPER TLALOC
Select Unlock Codes from the Options and enter Tlaloc, Beautiful Gorgeous, Dib, SpongeBob.

SUPER ZIM
Select Unlock Codes from the Options and enter Plankton, Zim, Technus, SpongeBob.

SUPER JETPACK

Select Unlock Codes from the Options and enter Beautiful Gorgeous, Tlaloc, Jimmy Neutron, Jimmy Neutron.

COLORLESS ENEMIES

Select Unlock Codes from the Options and enter Technus, Jimmy Neutron, Tlaloc, Plankton.

BLUE ENEMIES

Select Unlock Codes from the Options and enter Beautiful Gorgeous, Zim, Plankton, Technus.

RED ENEMIES

Select Unlock Codes from the Options and enter SpongeBob, Tak, Jimmy Neutron, Danny Phantom.

DIFFICULT ENEMIES

Select Unlock Codes from the Options and enter SpongeBob, Dib, Dib, Technus.

DIFFICULT BOSSES

Select Unlock Codes from the Options and enter Plankton, Beautiful Gorgeous, Technus, Tlaloc.

INVINCIBLE PARTNER

Select Unlock Codes from the Options and enter Plankton, Tak, Beautiful Gorgeous, SpongeBob.

STAR TREK: TACTICAL ASSAULT

KLINGON CAMPAIGN

At the Main menu, press Up, Down, Left, Right, Select, Start, X.

UNLOCK MISSIONS

At the Main menu, press Up, Down, Left, Right, Select, Start, Start.

EXTRA CREW UPGRADES

At the Main menu, press Up, Down, Left, Right, Select, Start, Select.

ALL SHIPS IN SKIRMISH AND MULTIPLAYER

At the Main menu, press Up, Down, Left, Right, Select, Start, Y.

ANY SHIP IN MISSIONS

At the Main menu, press Up, Down, Left, Right, Select, Start, B.

STAR WARS: THE FORCE UNLEASHED

INCREASED HEALTH

Select Unleashed Codes from the Extras menu and enter QSSPVENXO.

MAX OUT FORCE POWERS

Select Unleashed Codes from the Extras menu and enter CPLOOLKBF.

UNLIMITED FORCE ENERGY

Select Unleashed Codes from the Extras menu and enter TVENCVMJZ.

MORE POWERFUL LIGHTSABER

Select Unleashed Codes from the Extras menu and enter lightsaber.

UBER LIGHTSABER

Select Unleashed Codes from the Extras menu and enter MOMIROXIW.

ROM KOTA

Select Unleashed Codes from the Extras menu and enter mandalore.

CEREMONIAL JEDI ROBES

Select Unleashed Codes from the Extras menu and enter CURSEZRUX.

DAD'S ROBES

Select Unleashed Codes from the Extras menu and enter wookiee.

DARTH VADER'S COSTUME

Select Unleashed Codes from the Extras menu and enter HRMXRKVEN.

KENTO'S ROBE

Select Unleashed Codes from the Extras menu and enter KBVMSEVNM.

KOTA'S OUTFIT
Select Unleashed Codes from the Extras menu and enter EEDOPVENG.

SITH ROBE
Select Unleashed Codes from the Extras menu and enter ZWSFVENXA.

SITH ROBES
Select Unleashed Codes from the Extras menu and enter holocron.

SITH STALKER ARMOR
Select Unleashed Codes from the Extras menu and enter CPLZKMZTD.

STAR WARS EPISODE III: REVENGE OF THE SITH

MASTER DIFFICULTY
Defeat the game.

ANAKIN'S STARFIGHTER
Beat the Anakin bot in multiplayer.

DARTH VADER'S TIE FIGHTER
Defeat the Darth Vader bot in multiplayer.

GENERAL GREVIOUS'S STARFIGHTER
Defeat the General Grevious bot in multiplayer.

MILLENIUM FALCON
Defeat the Solo bot in multiplayer.

SLAVE I
Defeat the Fett bot in multiplayer.

X-WING
Defeat the Luke bot in multiplayer.

SUPER ROBOT TAISEN OG SAGA: ENDLESS FRONTIER

NEW GAME +
After you have finished the game and saved, load your save and start again with your items and money.

OG1 CHOKER
Start a new game or load a saved file with the GBA game Super Robot Taisen: Original Generation in the GBA slot. This item boosts your SP by 100.

OG2 PENDANT
Start a new game or load a saved file with the GBA game Super Robot Taisen 2: Original Generation in the GBA slot. This item boosts your HP by 250.

SUPER SPEED MACHINES

UNLOCK VEHICLES

WIN GRAND PRIX	UNLOCK THIS VEHICLE
1	Haima (Rally)
2	Sandstrom (4x4)
3	Striker (Sports)
4	Copperhead (Muscle)
6	Gold Digger (Custom)
7	Blue Flame (Classic)

TAMAGOTCHI CONNECTION: CORNER SHOP 3

DOUBLE LAYERED CAKE
Select Enter Code from the Special menu and enter R6194BJD6F.

TOM CLANCY'S SPLINTER CELL CHAOS THEORY

UNLIMITED AMMO/GADGETS
Defeat the game.

CHARACTER SKINS
Defeat the game.

TONY HAWK'S DOWNHILL JAM

ALWAYS SNOWSKATE
Select Buy Stuff from the Skateshop. Choose Enter Code and enter SNOWSK8T.

MIRRORED MAPS
Select Buy Stuff from the Skateshop. Choose Enter Code and enter MIRRORBALL.

ABOMINABLE SNOWMAN OUTFIT
Select Buy Stuff from the Skateshop. Choose Enter Code and enter BIGSNOWMAN.

ZOMBIE SKATER OUTFIT
Select Buy Stuff from the Skateshop. Choose Enter Code and enter ZOMBIEALIVE.

TAO'S ADVENTURE: CURSE OF THE DEMON SEAL

DEBUG MODE
During a game, press Up, Up, Down, Down, Left, Left, Right, Right, Select, Select, Start, Start, L, R, L, R, A, A, A, A, A, A, A, A, A, B.

TRANSFORMERS: WAR FOR CYBERTRON – AUTOBOTS

AUTOBOT SILVERBOLT IN STORY & ARENA
Select Cheats from the main menu and enter 10141.

DECEPTICON RAMJET IN ARENA
Select Cheats from the main menu and enter 99871.

TRANSFORMERS: WAR FOR CYBERTRON – DECEPTICONS

DECEPTICON RAMJET IN STORY & ARENA
Select Cheats from the main menu and enter 99871.

AUTOBOT SILVERBOLT IN ARENA
Select Cheats from the main menu and enter 10141.

UP

INVINCIBILITY
After completing the game, enter B, Y, B, Y, X, Y, X, Y, B, A at the title screen. This cheat disables saving.

THE URBZ: SIMS IN THE CITY

CLUB XIZZLE
Once you gain access to Club Xizzle, enter with the password "bucket."

WORLD CHAMPIONSHIP POKER

UNLOCK CASINOS

At the Title screen, press Y, X, Y, B, L, R. Then press the following direction:

DIRECTION	CASINO
Left	Amazon
Right	Nebula
Down	Renaissance

YU-GI-OH! NIGHTMARE TROUBADOUR

CREDITS

Unlock the Password Machine by defeating the Expert Cup. Enter the Duel Shop and select the Slot maching. Enter 00000375.

SOUND TEST

Unlock the Password Machine by defeating the Expert Cup. Enter the Duel Shop and select the Slot maching. Enter 57300000.

YU-GI-OH! WORLD CHAMPIONSHIP 2008

CARD PASSWORDS

Enter the following in the password machine to receive the corresponding card. You must already have the card to use the password.

PASSWORD EFFECT

CARD	PASSWORD	CARD	PASSWORD
7	67048711	Archfiend of Gilfer	50287060
7 Colored Fish	23771716	Armed Changer	90374791
7 Completed	86198326	Armed Ninja	09076207
A Feint Plan	68170903	Armored Glass	21070956
A Hero Emerges	21597117	Armored Zombie	20277860
Abyss Soldier	18318842	Array of Revealing Light	69296555
Acid Rain	21323861	Arsenal Bug	42364374
Acid Trap Hole	41356845	Arsenal Robber	55348096
Adhesive Explosive	53828196	Assault on GHQ	62633180
Agido	16135253	Asura Priest	02134346
Airknight Parshath	18036057	Attack and Receive	63689843
Aitsu	48202661	Autonomous Action Unit	71453557
Alkana Knight Joker	06150044	Axe of Despair	40619825
Alligator's Sword	64428736	Axe Raider	48305365
Alligator's Sword Dragon	03366982	B. Skull Dragon	11901678
Alpha the Magnet Warrior	99785935	Baby Dragon	88819587
Altar for Tribute	21070956	Back to Square One	47453433
Amazon Archer	91869203	Backfire	82705573
Amazoness Archers	67987611	Bad Reaction to Simochi	40633297
Amazoness Blowpiper	73574678	Bait Doll	07165085
Amazoness Chain Master	29654737	Ballista of Rampart Smashing	00242146
Amazoness Fighter	55821894	Banisher of the Light	61528025
Amazoness Paladin	47480070	Banner of Courage	10012614
Amazoness Spellcaster	81325903	Bark of The Dark Ruler	41925941
Amazoness Swords Woman	94004268	Baron of the Fiend Sword	86325596
Amazoness Tiger	10979723	Barrel Behind the Door	78783370
Amphibian Beast	67371383	Barrel Dragon	81480460
Amplifier	00303660	Battery Charger	61181383
Anti-Spell	53112492	Batteryman AA	63142001
Aqua Madoor	85639257	Batteryman C	19733961
Aqua Spirit	40916023	Batteryman D	55401221

33

CARD	PASSWORD	CARD	PASSWORD
Battle Ox	05053103	Chain Destruction	01248895
Battle Warrior	55550921	Chain Disappearance	57139487
Beast Fangs	46009906	Chain Energy	79323590
Beast Soul Swap	35149085	Chaos Command Magician	72630549
Beastking of the Swamps	99426834	Chaos End	61044390
Beautiful Headhuntress	16899564	Chaos Greed	97439308
Beckoning Light	16255442	Chimera the Flying Mythical Beast	04796100
Berfomet	77207191	Chiron the Mage	16956455
Berserk Gorilla	39168895	Chorus of Sanctuary	81380218
Beta the Magnet Warrior	39256679	Chthonian Alliance	46910446
Bickuribox	25655502	Chthonian Blast	18271561
Big Bang Shot	61127349	Chthonian Polymer	72287557
Big Eye	16768387	Clay Charge	22479888
Big Shield Gardna	65240384	Cocoon of Evolution	40240595
Birdface	45547649	Coffin Seller	65830223
Black Illusion Ritual	41426869	Cold Wave	60682203
Black Luster Ritual	55761792	Command Knight	10375182
Black Luster Soldier	72989439	Conscription	31000575
Black Magic Ritual	76792184	Continuous Destruction Punch	68057622
Black Pendant	65169794	Contract with Exodia	33244944
Bladefly	28470714	Contract with the Dark Master	96420087
Blast Held by a Tribute	89041555	Convulsion of Nature	62966332
Blast Magician	21051146	Copycat	26376390
Blast Sphere	26302522	Cosmo Queen	38999506
Blast with Chain	98239899	Covering Fire	74458486
Blasting the Ruins	21466326	Crass Clown	93889755
Blessings of the Nile	30653173	Crawling Dragon #2	38289717
Blowback Dragon	25551951	Crimson Sunbird	46696593
Blue Medicine	20871001	Crush Card Virus	57728570
Blue-Eyes Toon Dragon	53183600	Curse of Anubis	66742250
Blue-Eyes Ultimate Dragon	23995346	Curse of Darkness	84970821
Blue-Eyes White Dragon	80906030	Curse of Dragon	28279543
Blue-Eyes White Dragon	80906030	Curse of the Masked Beast	94377247
Book of Taiyou	38699854	Cursed Seal of the Forbidden Spell	58851034
Bottomless Trap Hole	29401950	Cyber Raider	39978267
Bowganian	52090844	Cyber Shield	63224564
Bracchio-Raidus	16507828	Cyber-Tech Alligator	48766543
Brain Control	87910978	D.D. Borderline	60912752
Breaker the Magical Warrior	71413901	D.D. Designator	33423043
Breath of Light	20101223	D.D. Assailant	70074904
Bright Castle	82878489	D.D. Dynamite	08628798
Burning Land	24294108	D.D. Trap Hole	05606466
Burning Spear	18937875	D.D. Warrior	37043180
Burst Return	27191436	D.D. Warrior Lady	07572887
Burst Stream of Destruction	17655904	D. Tribe	02833249
Buster Rancher	84740193	Dark Artist	72520073
Cannon Soldier	11384280	Dark Deal	65824822
Cannonball Spear Shellfish	95614612	Dark Dust Spirit	89111398
Card Destruction	72892473	Dark Elf	21417692
Card of Sanctity	04266498	Dark Energy	04614116
Card Shuffle	12183332	Dark Factory of Mass Production	90928333
Castle of Dark Illusions	00062121	Dark Jeroid	90980792
Castle Walls	44209392	Dark Magic Attack	02314238
Catapult Turtle	95727991	Dark Magic Curtain	99789342
Ceasefire	36468556	Dark Magician	46986414
Celtic Guardian	91152256	Dark Magician Girl	38033121
Cemetery Bomb	51394546	Dark Magician of Chaos	40737112
Centrifugal Field	01801154	Dark Master - Zorc	97642679
Cestus of Dagla	28106077	Dark Mimic LV1	74713516

CARD	PASSWORD	CARD	PASSWORD
Dark Mimic LV3	01102515	Eatgaboon	42578427
Dark Mirror Force	20522190	Ectoplasmer	97342942
Dark Necrofear	31829185	Ekibyo Drakmord	69954399
Dark Paladin	98502113	Electro-Whip	37820550
Dark Rabbit	99261403	Elegant Egotist	90219263
Dark Room of Nightmare	85562745	Elemental Hero Avian	21844576
Dark Sage	92377303	Elemental Hero Burstinatrix	58932615
Dark Snake Syndrome	47233801	Elemental Hero Clayman	84327329
Dark Spirit of the Silent	93599951	Elemental the Hero Flame Wingman	35809262
Dark World Lightning	93554166	Elemental Hero Rampart Blaster	47737087
Darkness Approaches	80168720	Elemental Hero Sparkman	20721928
Dark-Piercing Light	45895206	Elemental Hero Thunder Giant	61204971
Deck Devastation Virus	35027493	Embodiment of Apophis	28649820
Decoy Dragon	02732323	Emergency Provisions	53046408
Dedication through Light and Darkness	69542930	Enchanted Arrow	93260132
De-Fusion	95286165	Enchanting Fitting Room	30531525
Delta Attacker	39719977	Enemy Controller	98045062
Despair from the Dark	71200730	Energy Drain	56916805
De-Spell	19159413	Enervating Mist	26022485
Destiny Board	94212438	Enraged Battle Ox	76909279
Destruction Ring	21219755	Eradicating Aerosol	94716515
Dian Keto the Cure Master	84257639	Eternal Drought	56606928
Dice Re-Roll	83241722	Eternal Rest	95051344
Different Dimension Capsule	11961740	Exarion Universe	63749102
Different Dimension Dragon	50939127	Exchange	05556668
Different Dimension Gate	56460688	Exhausting Spell	95451366
Diffusion Wave-Motion	87880531	Exodia Necross	12600382
Dimension Fusion	23557835	Exodia the Forbidden One	33396948
Dimension Wall	67095270	Fairy Box	21598948
Dimensional Prison	70342110	Fairy King Truesdale	45425051
Dimensionhole	22959079	Fairy Meteor Crush	97687912
Disappear	24623598	Fairy's Hand Mirror	17653779
Disarmament	20727787	Fake Trap	03027001
Divine Sword - Phoenix Blade	31423101	Feather Shot	19394153
Divine Wrath	49010598	Feather Wind	71060915
DNA Surgery	74701381	Fengsheng Mirror	37406863
Doomcaliber Knight	78700060	Feral Imp	41392891
Double Coston	44436472	Fiend Comedian	81172176
Double Snare	03682106	Fiend Skull Dragon	66235877
Double Spell	24096228	Fiend's Hand Mirror	58607704
Dragged Down into the Grave	16435235	Fiend's Sanctuary	24874630
Dragon Capture Jar	50045299	Final Countdown	95308449
Dragon Seeker	28563545	Final Destiny	18591904
Dragon Treasure	01435851	Firewing Pegasus	27054370
Dragonic Attack	32437102	Fissure	66788016
Dragon's Mirror	71490127	Flame Cerebrus	60862676
Draining Shield	43250041	Flame Manipulator	34460851
Dramatic Rescue	80193355	Flame Swordsman	40502030
Dream Clown	13215230	Flying Kamakiri #1	84834865
Drill Bug	88733579	Foolish Burial	81439173
Driving Snow	00473469	Forced Ceasefire	97806240
Drop Off	55773067	Forest	87430998
Dunames Dark Witch	12493482	Fortress Whale	62337487
Dust Barrier	31476755	Fortress Whale's Oath	77454922
Dust Tornado	60082867	Frozen Soul	57069605
Earth Chant	59820352	Fulfillment of the Contract	48206762
Earthbound Spirit's Invitation	65743242	Full Salvo	70865988
Earthquake	82828051	Fusilier Dragon, the Duel-Mode Beast	51632798

CARD	PASSWORD
Fusion Gate	24094653
Fusion Sage	26902560
Fusion Sword Murasame Blade	37684215
Gaia Power	56594520
Gaia the Dragon Champion	66889139
Gaia the Fierce Knight	06368038
Gamma the Magnet Warrior	11549357
Garoozis	14977074
Garuda the Wind Spirit	12800777
Gazelle the King of Mythical Beasts	05818798
Gear Golem the Moving Fortress	30190809
Gearfried the Iron Knight	00423705
Gearfried the Swordmaster	57046845
Gemini Elf	69140098
Generation Shift	34460239
Germ Infection	24668830
Getsu Fuhma	21887179
Giant Flea	41762634
Giant Germ	95178994
Giant Rat	97017120
Giant Red Seasnake	58831685
Giant Soldier of Stone	13039848
Giant Trunade	42703248
Gigantes	47606319
Gilasaurus	45894482
Gilford the Legend	69933858
Gilford the Lightning	36354007
Gil Garth	38445524
Goblin Attack Force	78658564
Goblin Fan	04149689
Goblin King	18590133
Goblin Thief	45311864
Goblin's Secret Remedy	11868825
Goddess of Whim	67959180
Goddess with the Third Eye	53493204
Gokibore	15367030
Gorgon's Eye	52648457
Graceful Dice	74137509
Gradius' Option	14291024
Granadora	13944422
Grand Tiki Elder	13676474
Gravedigger Ghoul	82542267
Gravekeeper's Assailant	25262697
Gravekeeper's Cannonholder	99877698
Gravekeeper's Chief	62473983
Gravekeeper's Commandant	17393207
Gravekeeper's Curse	50712728
Gravekeeper's Guard	37101832
Gravekeeper's Servant	16762927
Gravekeeper's Spear Soldier	63695531
Gravekeeper's Spy	24317029
Gravekeeper's Vassal	99690140
Gravekeeper's Watcher	26084285
Gravity Axe - Grarl	32022366
Gravity Bind	85742772
Great Moth	14141448
Greed	89405199

CARD	PASSWORD
Green Baboon, Defender of the Forest	46668237
Greenkappa	61831093
Ground Collapse	90502999
Gust	73079365
Gust Fan	55321970
Gyaku-Gire Panda	09817927
Hammer Shot	26412047
Hand Collapse	74519184
Hannibal Necromancer	05640330
Harpie Lady	76812113
Harpie Lady 1	91932350
Harpie Lady 2	27927359
Harpie Lady 3	54415063
Harpie Lady Sisters	12206212
Harpies' Hunting Ground	75782277
Harpie's Pet Dragon	52040216
Headless Knight	5434080
Heart of Clear Water	64801562
Heart of the Underdog	35762283
Heavy Mech Support Platform	23265594
Heavy Slump	52417194
Heavy Storm	19613556
Helpoemer	76052811
Hercules Beetle	52584282
Hero Kid	32679370
Hero Signal	22020907
Hidden Book of Spell	21840375
Hieroglyph Lithograph	10248192
Hinotama	46130346
Hiro's Shadow Scout	81863068
Hitotsu-Me Giant	76184692
Horn Imp	69669405
Horn of Light	38552107
Horn of the Unicorn	64047146
Hoshiningen	67629977
House of Adhesive Tape	15083728
Human-Wave Tactics	30353551
Illusionist Faceless Mage	28546905
Impenetrable Formation	96631852
Inferno	74823665
Inferno Fire Blast	52684508
Infinite Cards	94163677
Infinite Dismissal	54109233
Injection Fairy Lily	79575620
Insect Armor with Laser Cannon	03492538
Insect Barrier	23615409
Insect Imitation	96965364
Insect Queen	91512835
Inspection	16227556
Interdimensional Matter Transporter	36261276
Invigoration	98374133
Jack's Knight	90876561
Jade Insect Whistle	95214051
Jam Breeding Machine	21770260
Jam Defender	21558682
Jar of Greed	83968380
Jigen Bakudan	90020065

CARD	PASSWORD
Jinzo	77585513
Jinzo #7	77585513
Jowgen the Spiritualist	41855169
Jowls of Dark Demise	05257687
Judge Man	30113682
Judgment of the Pharaoh	55948544
Just Desserts	24068492
Kabazauls	51934376
Kabazauls	51934376
Kanan the Swordsmistress	12829151
Killer Needle	88979991
Kinetic Soldier	79853073
King of the Skull Servants	36021814
King of the Swamp	79109599
King Tiger Wanghu	83986578
King's Knight	64788463
Koitsu	69456283
Krokodilus	76512652
Kryuel	82642348
Kunai with Chain	37390589
Kuriboh	40640057
Kycoo the Ghost Destroyer	88240808
Labyrinth of Nightmare	66526672
Labyrinth Tank	99551425
Larvae Moth	87756343
Laser Cannon Armor	77007920
Last Day of the Witch	90330453
Launcher Spider	87322377
Lava Battleguard	20394040
Lava Golem	00102380
Left Arm of the Forbidden One	07902349
Left Leg of the Forbidden One	44519536
Legacy of Yata-Garasu	30461781
Legendary Sword	61854111
Level Conversion Lab	84397023
Level Limit - Area A	54976796
Level Limit - Area B	03136426
Level Modulation	61850482
Level Up!	25290459
Light of Judgment	44595286
Lighten the Load	37231841
Lightforce Sword	49587034
Lightning Vortex	69162969
Little Chimera	68658728
Luminous Soldier	57482479
Luminous Spark	81777047
Luster Dragon	11091375
Machine Duplication	63995093
Machine King	46700124
Mad Sword Beast	79870141
Mage Power	83746708
Magic Cylinder	62279055
Magic Drain	59344077
Magic Formula	67227834
Magic Jammer	77414722
Magical Arm Shield	96008713
Magical Dimension	28553439
Magical Explosion	32723153
Magical Hats	81210420

CARD	PASSWORD
Magical Stone Excavation	98494543
Magical Thorn	53119267
Magician of Black Chaos	30208479
Magician of Faith	31560081
Magician's Circle	00050755
Magician's Unite	36045450
Magician's Valkyria	80304126
Maha Vailo	93013676
Maharaghi	40695128
Maiden of the Aqua	17214465
Major Riot	09074847
Malevolent Catastrophe	01224927
Malevolent Nuzzler	99597615
Malfunction	06137091
Malice Dispersion	13626450
Man-Eater Bug	54652250
Man-Eating Treasure Chest	13723605
Manga Ryu-Ran	38369349
Marauding Captain	02460565
Marie the Fallen One	57579381
Marshmallon	31305911
Marshmallon Glasses	66865880
Mask of Brutality	82432018
Mask of Darkness	28933734
Mask of Dispel	20765952
Mask of Restrict	29549364
Mask of the Accursed	56948373
Mask of Weakness	57882509
Masked Sorcerer	10189126
Mass Driver	34906152
Master Kyonshee	24530661
Mataza the Zapper	22609617
Mausoleum of the Emperor	80921533
Mechanicalchaser	07359741
Mega Ton Magical Cannon	32062913
Megamorph	22046459
Melchid the Four-Faced Beast	86569121
Meltiel, Sage of the Sky	49905576
Mesmeric Control	48642904
Messenger of Peace	44656491
Metal Detector	75646520
Metal Reflect Slime	26905245
Metalmorph	68540058
Metalzoa	50705071
Meteor Black Dragon	90660762
Meteor Dragon	64271667
Michizure	37580756
Micro Ray	18190572
Millennium Shield	32012841
Milus Radiant	07489323
Mind Control	37520316
Mind Crush	15800838
Miracle Dig	63434080
Miracle Kids	55985014
Miracle Restoring	68334074
Mirror Force	44095762
Mispolymerization	58392024
Mist body	47529357
Moisture Creature	75285069

CARD	PASSWORD
Mokey Mokey	27288416
Mokey Mokey King	13803864
Mokey Mokey Smackdown	01965724
Molten Destruction	19384334
Monster Gate	43040603
Monster Recovery	93108433
Monster Reincarnation	74848038
Mooyan Curry	58074572
Morphing Jar	33508719
Morphing Jar #2	79106360
Mother Grizzly	57839750
Mountain	50913601
Muka Muka	46657337
Multiplication of Ants	22493811
Multiply	40703222
Mushroom Man	14181608
My Body as a Shield	69279219
Mysterious Puppeteer	54098121
Mystic Box	25774450
Mystic Horseman	68516705
Mystic Probe	49251811
Mystic Swordsman LV2	47507260
Mystic Swordsman LV4	74591968
Mystic Swordsman LV6	60482781
Mystic Tomato	83011277
Mystical Elf	15025844
Mystical Moon	36607978
Mystical Refpanel	35563539
Mystical Sheep #1	30451366
Mystical Space Typhoon	05318639
Narrow Pass	40172183
Necrovalley	47355498
Needle Wall	38299233
Needle Worm	81843628
Negate Attack	14315573
Neo the Magic Swordsman	50930991
Newdoria	04335645
Next to be Lost	07076131
Nightmare Wheel	54704216
Nimble Momonga	22567609
Nitro Unit	23842445
Non Aggression Area	76848240
Non-Fusion Area	27581098
Non-Spellcasting Area	20065549
Numinous Healer	02130625
Nuvia the Wicked	12953226
Obnoxious Celtic Guard	52077741
Ojama Black	79335209
Ojama Delta Hurricane!!	08251996
Ojama Green	12482652
Ojama King	90140980
Ojama Trio	29843091
Ojama Yellow	42941100
Ojamagic	24643836
Ojamuscle	98259197
Ominous Fortunetelling	56995655
Ookazi	19523799
Opti-Camouflage Armor	44762290
Order to Charge	78986941

CARD	PASSWORD
Order to Smash	39019325
Otohime	39751093
Overpowering Eye	60577362
Panther Warrior	42035044
Paralyzing Potion	50152549
Parasite Paracide	27911549
Parrot Dragon	62762898
Patrician of Darkness	19153634
Pendulum Machine	24433920
Penguin Knight	36039163
Penguin Soldier	93920745
Perfectly Ultimate Great Moth	48579379
Petit Moth	58192742
Pharaoh's Treasure	63571750
Pigeonholing Books of Spell	96677818
Pikeru's Second Sight	58015506
Pinch Hopper	26185991
Pitch-Black Power Stone	34029630
Poison Fangs	76539047
Poison of the Old Man	08842266
Polymerization	35550694
Pot of Avarice	67169062
Premature Burial	70828912
Prepare to Strike Back	04483989
Prevent Rat	00549481
Princess of Tsurugi	51371017
Prohibition	43711255
Protector of the Sanctuary	24221739
Pumpking the King of Ghosts	29155212
Queen's Knight	25652259
Rabid Horseman	94905343
Radiant Jeral	84177693
Radiant Mirror Force	21481146
Raigeki Break	04178474
Rapid-Fire Magician	06337436
Ray of Hope	82529174
Ready for Intercepting	31785398
Really Eternal Rest	28121403
Reaper of the Cards	33066139
Reckless Greed	37576645
Recycle	96316857
Red Archery Girl	65570596
Red Medicine	38199696
Red-Eyes B. Chick	36262024
Red-Eyes Black Dragon	74677422
Red-Eyes Black Metal Dragon	64335804
Reflect Bounder	02851070
Reinforcement of the Army	32807846
Reinforcements	17814387
Release Restraint	75417459
Relieve Monster	37507488
Relinquished	64631466
Remove Trap	51482758
Respect Play	08951260
Restructer Revolution	99518961
Reversal Quiz	05990062
Reverse Trap	77622396
Revival Jam	31709826
Right Arm of the Forbidden One	70903634

CARD	PASSWORD	CARD	PASSWORD
Right Leg of the Forbidden One	08124921	Skull-Mark Ladybug	64306248
Rigorous Reaver	39180960	Skyscraper	63035430
Ring of Magnetism	20436034	Slate Warrior	78636495
Riryoku Field	70344351	Slot Machine	03797883
Rising Energy	78211862	Smashing Ground	97169186
Rite of Spirit	30450531	Smoke Grenade of the Thief	63789924
Ritual Weapon	54351224	Snake Fang	00596051
Robbin' Goblin	88279736	Sogen	86318356
Robbin' Zombie	83258273	Solar Ray	44472639
Robotic Knight	44203504	Solemn Judgment	41420027
Rock Bombardment	20781762	Solemn Wishes	35346968
Rocket Warrior	30860696	Sorcerer of the Doomed	49218300
Rod of Silence - Kay'est	95515060	Soul Absorption	68073522
Rogue Doll	91939608	Soul Demolition	76297408
Roll Out!	91597389	Soul Exchange	68005187
Royal Command	33950246	Soul of Purity and Light	77527210
Royal Decree	51452091	Soul of the Pure	47852924
Royal Magical Library	70791313	Soul Release	05758500
Royal Oppression	93016201	Soul Resurrection	92924317
Royal Surrender	56058888	Soul Reversal	78864369
Royal Tribute	72405967	Soul Taker	81510157
Rude Kaiser	26378150	Spark Blaster	97362768
Rush Recklessly	70046172	Spatial Collapse	20644748
Ryu Kokki	57281778	Special Hurricane	42598242
Ryu-Kishin	15303296	Spell Absorption	51481927
Ryu-Ran	02964201	Spell Reproduction	29228529
Sage's Stone	13604200	Spell Vanishing	29735721
Saggi the Dark Clown	66602787	Spellbinding Circle	18807108
Sakuretsu Armor	56120475	Spell-stopping Statute	10069180
Salamandra	32268901	Spiral Spear Strike	49328340
Salvage	96947648	Spirit Message "A"	94772232
Sangan	26202165	Spirit Message "I"	31893528
Sasuke Samurai #3	77379481	Spirit Message "L"	30170981
Sasuke Samurai #4	64538655	Spirit Message "N"	67287533
Satellite Cannon	50400231	Spirit of Flames	13522325
Second Coin Toss	36562627	Spirit of the Pharaoh	25343280
Sengenjin	76232340	Spirit's Invitation	92394653
Serial Spell	49398568	Spiritual Earth Art - Kurogane	70156997
Serpentine Princess	71829750	Spiritual Energy Settle Machine	99173029
Seven Tools of the Bandit	03819470	Spiritual Fire Art - Kurenai	42945701
Shadow Ghoul	30778711	Spiritual Water Art - Aoi	06540606
Shadow of Eyes	58621589	Spiritual Wind Art - Miyabi	79333300
Share the Pain	56830749	Spiritualism	15866454
Shield & Sword	52097679	St. Joan	21175632
Shield Crush	30683373	Staunch Defender	92854392
Shift	59560625	Steel Ogre Grotto #2	90908427
Shifting Shadows	59237154	Steel Scorpion	13599884
Shinato, King of a Higher Plane	86327225	Stim-Pack	83225447
Shinato's Ark	60365591	Stone Statue of the Aztecs	31812496
Shining Abyss	87303357	Stop Defense	63102017
Shining Angel	95956346	Stray Lambs	60764581
Shooting Star Bow - Ceal	95638658	Stumbling	34646691
Shrink	55713623	Swamp Battleguard	40453765
Silver Bow and Arrow	01557499	Swift Gaia the Fierce Knight	16589042
Simultaneous Loss	92219931	Sword of Deep-Seated	98495314
Skilled Dark Magician	73752131	Sword of the Soul-Eater	05371656
Skilled White Magician	46363422	Swords of Concealing Light	12923641
Skull Dice	00126218	Swords of Revealing Light	72302403
Skull Servant	32274490	Swordsman of Landstar	03573512

CARD	PASSWORD
System Down	07672244
Tailor of the Fickle	43641473
Terraforming	73628505
The A. Forces	00403847
The Agent of Force - Mars	91123920
The Agent of Judgement - Saturn	91345518
The Big March of Animals	01689516
The Bistro Butcher	71107816
The Cheerful Coffin	41142615
The Creator	61505339
The Creator Incarnate	97093037
The Dark Door	30606547
The Earl of Demise	66989694
The Fiend Megacyber	66362965
The First Sarcophagus	31076103
The Flute of Summoning Kuriboh	20065322
The Forgiving Maiden	84080938
The Gross Ghost of Fled Dreams	68049471
The Illusory Gentleman	83764996
The Inexperienced Spy	81820689
The Last Warrior from Another Planet	86099788
The Law of the Normal	66926224
The League of Uniform Nomenclature	55008284
The Little Swordsman of Aile	25109950
The Masked Beast	49064413
The Portrait's Secret	32541773
The Regulation of Tribe	00296499
The Reliable Guardian	16430187
The Rock Spirit	76305638
The Sanctuary in the Sky	56433456
The Second Sarcophagus	04081094
The Secret of the Bandit	99351431
The Shallow Grave	43434803
The Snake Hair	29491031
The Spell Absorbing Life	99517131
The Statue of Easter Island	10261698
The Third Sarcophagus	78697395
The Unhappy Girl	27618634
The Unhappy Maiden	51275027
The Warrior Returning Alive	95281259
The Wicked Worm Beast	06285791
Thestalos the Firestorm Monarch	26205777
Thousand Dragon	41462083
Thousand Energy	05703682
Thousand Knives	63391643
Thousand-Eyes Idol	27125110
Threatening Roar	36361633
Three-Headed Geedo	78423643
Thunder Crash	69196160
Thunder Dragon	31786629
Thunder Nyan Nyan	70797118
Time Machine	80987696
Time Wizard	06285791
Token Feastevil	83675475
Toon Alligator	59383041
Toon Cannon Soldier	79875176
Toon Dark Magician Girl	90960358

CARD	PASSWORD
Toon Defense	43509019
Toon Gemini Elf	42386471
Toon Goblin Attack Force	15270885
Toon Masked Sorcerer	16392422
Toon Mermaid	65458948
Toon Summoned Skull	91842653
Toon Table of Contents	89997728
Toon World	15259703
Tornado	61068510
Tornado Wall	18605135
Torpedo Fish	90337190
Tower of Babel	94256039
Tragedy	35686187
Transcendent Wings	25573054
Trap Hole	04206964
Trap Jammer	19252988
Trap Master	46461247
Tremendous Fire	46918794
Triage	30888983
Triangle Ecstasy Spark	12181376
Triangle Power	32298781
Tribute Doll	02903036
Tribute to the Doomed	79759861
Tri-Horned Dragon	39111158
Twin Swords of Flashing Light - Tryce	21900719
Twin-Headed Behemoth	43586926
Twin-Headed Thunder Dragon	54752875
Two-Headed King Rex	94119974
Two-Pronged Attack	83887306
Tyhone	72842870
Type Zero Magic Crusher	35346968
UFO Turtle	60806437
Ultimate Offering	80604091
Ultra Evolution Pill	22431243
Umiiruka	82999629
Union Attack	60399954
United We Stand	56747793
Unity	14731897
Upstart Goblin	70368879
Uraby	01784619
Valkyrion the Magna Warrior	75347539
Versago the Destroyer	50259460
Vile Germs	39774685
Vorse Raider	14898066
Waboku	12607053
Wall of Illusion	13945283
Wall of Revealing Light	17078030
Wall Shadow	63162310
Warrior Elimination	90873992
Warrior Lady of the Wasteland	05438492
Wasteland	98239899
Weapon Change	10035717
Weather Report	72053645
Weed Out	28604635
White Magical Hat	15150365
White-Horned Dragon	73891874
Wicked-Breaking Flamberge - Baou	68427465

CARD	PASSWORD
Widespread Ruin	77754944
Wild Nature's Release	61166988
Winged Dragon, Guardian of the Fortress #1	87796900
Winged Kuriboh	57116033
Winged Kuriboh LV10	98585345
Witch's Apprentice	80741828
Wolf	49417509
Wolf Axwielder	56369281
Woodland Sprite	06979239
World Suppression	12253117

CARD	PASSWORD
Xing Zhen Hu	76515293
Yamata Dragon	76862289
Yami	59197169
Yellow Luster Shield	04542651
Yu-Jo Friendship	81332143
Zaborg the Thunder Monarch	51945556
Zero Gravity	83133491
Zoa	24311372
Zolga	16268841
Zombie Warrior	31339260

ZOO KEEPER

GEKIMUZU DIFFICULTY

Earn a high score in all 4 modes.
Here are the high scores needed for each mode:

MODE	SCORE
Zoo keeper	200000
Tokoton 100	800000
Quest mode	10000
Time attack	600000

ZOO TYCOON DS

UNLOCK EVERYTHING

At the Main menu, press Up, Up, Down, Down, Left, Right, Left, Right, Up, Up, Down , Down, Left, Right, Left, Right.

PLAYSTATION® PORTABLE

CONTENTS

ASTRO BOY: THE VIDEO GAME

INVULNERABLE
Pause the game and press Up, Down, Down, Up, L1, R.

MAX STATS
Pause the game and press Left, Left, R, Down, Down, L1.

INFINITE SUPERS
Pause the game and press Left, L1, Right, L1, Up, Down.

INFINITE DASHES
Pause the game and press R, R, L1, R, Left, Up.

DISABLE SUPERS
Pause the game and press L1, L1, R, R, L1, Left.

COSTUME SWAP (ARENA AND CLASSIC COSTUMES)
Pause the game and press R, Up, L1, Up, Down, R.

UNLOCK LEVELS
Pause the game and press Up, L1, Right, L1, Down, L1. This allows you to travel to any level from the Story menu.

BEN 10: ALIEN FORCE THE GAME

LEVEL LORD
Enter Gwen, Kevin, Big Chill, Gwen as a code.

INVINCIBILITY
Enter Kevin, Big Chill, Swampfire, Kevin as a code.

ALL COMBOS
Enter Swampfire, Gwen, Kevin, Ben as a code.

INFINITE ALIENS
Enter Ben, Swampfire, Gwen, Big Chill as a code.

BEN 10: ALIEN FORCE VILGAX ATTACKS

LEVEL SKIP
Pause the game and enter Portal in the Cheats menu.

UNLOCK ALL SPECIAL ATTACKS FOR ALL FORMS
Pause the game and enter Everythingproof in the Cheats menu.

UNLOCK ALL ALIEN FORMS
Pause the game and enter Primus in the Cheats menu.

TOGGLE INVULNERABILITY ON AND OFF
Pause the game and enter Xlmrsmoothy in the Cheats menu.

GIVES PLAYER FULL HEALTH
Pause the game and enter Herotime in the Cheats menu.

QUICK ENERGY REGENERATION
Pause the game and enter Generator in the Cheats menu.

PORTABLE®

BEN 10: PROTECTOR OF EARTH

INVINCIBILITY

Select a game from the Continue option. Go to the Map Selection screen, press Start and choose Extras. Select Enter Secret Code and enter XLR8, Heatblast, Wildvine, Fourarms.

ALL COMBOS

Select a game from the Continue option. Go to the Map Selection screen, press Start and choose Extras. Select Enter Secret Code and enter Cannonblot, Heatblast, Fourarms, Heatblast.

ALL LOCATIONS

Select a game from the Continue option. Go to the Map Selection screen, press Start and choose Extras. Select Enter Secret Code and enter Heatblast, XLR8, XLR8, Cannonblot.

DNA FORCE SKINS

Select a game from the Continue option. Go to the Map Selection screen, press Start and choose Extras. Select Enter Secret Code and enter Wildvine, Fourarms, Heatblast, Cannonbolt.

DARK HEROES SKINS

Select a game from the Continue option. Go to the Map Selection screen, press Start and choose Extras. Select Enter Secret Code and enter Cannonbolt, Cannonbolt, Fourarms, Heatblast.

ALL ALIEN FORMS

Select a game from the Continue option. Go to the Map Selection screen, press Start and choose Extras. Select Enter Secret Code and enter Wildvine, Fourarms, Heatblast, Wildvine.

MASTER CONTROL

Select a game from the Continue option. Go to the Map Selection screen, press Start and choose Extras. Select Enter Secret Code and enter Cannonbolt, Heatblast, Wildvine, Fourarms.

BEN 10 ULTIMATE ALIEN: COSMIC DESTRUCTION

To remove the cheats, you will need to start a new game.

1,000,000 DNA

Pause the game, select Cheats, and enter Cash.

REGENERATE HEALTH

Pause the game, select Cheats, and enter Health.

REGENERATE ENERGY

Pause the game, select Cheats, and enter Energy.

UPGRADE EVERYTHING

Pause the game, select Cheats, and enter Upgrade.

ALL LEVELS

Pause the game, select Cheats, and enter Levels.

ENEMIES DO DOUBLE DAMAGE/PLAYER DOES 1/2 DAMAGE

Pause the game, select Cheats, and enter Hard.

CAPCOM CLASSICS COLLECTION REMIXED

UNLOCK EVERYTHING

At the title screen, press Left on D-pad, Right on D-pad, Left on Analog stick, Right on Analog stick, ●, ●, Up on D-pad, Down on D-pad.

CAPCOM PUZZLE WORLD

SUPER BUSTER BROS.

LEVEL SELECT IN TOUR MODE
At the Main menu, highlight Tour Mode, hold Down and press ❌.

SUPER PUZZLE FIGHTER

PLAY AS AKUMA
At the character select, highlight Hsien-Ko and press Down.

PLAY AS DAN
At the character select, highlight Donovan and press Down.

PLAY AS DEVILOT
At the character select, highlight Morrigan and press Down.

PLAY AS ANITA
At the character select, hold L + R and choose Donovan.

PLAY AS HSIEN-KO'S TALISMAN
At the character select, hold L + R and choose Hsien-Ko.

PLAY AS MORRIGAN AS A BAT
At the character select, hold L + R and choose Morrigan.

CARS

BONUS SPEEDWAY (REVERSED) IN CUSTOM RACE
At the Main menu hold L and press ❌, ⬛, ▲, ❌, ▲, ⬛.

ALL CARS, PAINTJOBS, TRACKS, MOVIE CLIPS AND MODES
At the main menu, hold L and press ▲, ⬛, ❌, ⬤, ▲, ❌, ⬛, ▲, ⬤, ❌.

UNLIMITED NITROUS
At the main menu, hold L and ❌, ⬛, ⬤, ⬤, ⬤, ⬤, ▲, ⬛, ❌.

CASTLEVANIA: THE DRACULA X CHRONICLES

ORIGINAL RONDO OF BLOOD

LEVEL SELECT
Enter X-X!V"Q as your player name

SYMPHONY OF THE NIGHT

PLAY AS ALUCARD WITH 99 LUCK AND LAPIS LAZULI
Start a new game with the name X-X!V"Q.

PLAY AS ALUCARD WITH AXE LORD ARMOR
After clearing the game once, start a new game with the name AXEARMOR.

PLAY AS MARIA RENARD
After clearing the game once, start a new game with the name MARIA.

PLAY AS RICHTER BELMONT
After clearing the game once, start a new game with the name RICHTER.

CRASH: MIND OVER MUTANT

A cheat can be deactivated by re-entering the code.

FREEZE ENEMIES WITH TOUCH
Pause the game, hold R and press Down, Down, Down, Up.

ENEMIES DROP X4 DAMAGE
Pause the game, hold R and press Up, Up, Up, Left.

ENEMIES DROP PURPLE FRUIT
Pause the game, hold R and press Up, Down, Down, Up.

ENEMIES DROP SUPER KICK
Pause the game, hold R and press Up, Right, Down, Left.

ENIMIES DROP WUMPA FRUIT
Pause the game, hold R and press Right, Right, Right, Up.

SHADOW CRASH
Pause the game, hold R and press Left, Right, Left, Right.

DEFORMED CRASH
Pause the game, hold R and press Left, Left, Left, Down.

CRISIS CORE—FINAL FANTASY VII

NEW GAME+

After completing the game, you'll be prompted to make a new save. Loading a game from this new save will begin a New Game+, starting the game over while allowing Zack to retain almost everything he's earned.

The following items transfer to a New Game+:

Level, Experience, SP, Gil, Playtime, Non-Key Items, Materia, and DMW Completion Rate

The following items do not transfer:

Key Items, Materia/Accessory Slot Expansion, Ability to SP Convert, DMW Images, Mission Progress, Mail, and Unlocked Shops

DESPICABLE ME: THE GAME

MINIONETTES COSTUME SET

In Gru's Lab, select cheats from the bonus menu and enter ◉, ◉, ◼, ▲, ✕.

VILLAGE FOLK COSTUME SET

In Gru's Lab, select cheats from the bonus menu and enter ▲, ✕, ✕, ◉, ✕.

TAFFY WEB GUN

In Gru's Lab, select cheats from the bonus menu and enter ✕, ◉, ◼, ✕, ▲.

DISGAEA 2: DARK HERO DAYS

AXEL MODE

Highlight New Game and press ▲, ◼, ◉, ▲, ◼, ◉, ✕.

FINAL FANTASY TACTICS: THE WAR OF THE LIONS

MUSIC TEST MODE

Enter the main character's name as PolkaPolka at the name entry screen.

FLATOUT: HEAD ON

1 MILLION CREDITS

Select Enter Code from the Extras menu and enter GIVECASH.

ALL CARS AND 1 MILLION CREDITS

Select Enter Code from the Extras menu and enter GIEVEPIX.

BIG RIG

Select Enter Code from the Extras menu and enter ELPUEBLO.

BIG RIG TRUCK
Select Enter Code from the Extras menu and enter RAIDERS.

FLATMOBILE CAR
Select Enter Code from the Extras menu and enter WOTKINS.

MOB CAR
Select Enter Code from the Extras menu and enter BIGTRUCK.

PIMPSTER CAR
Select Enter Code from the Extras menu and enter RUTTO.

ROCKET CAR
Select Enter Code from the Extras menu and enter KALJAKOPPA.

SCHOOL BUS
Select Enter Code from the Extras menu and enter GIEVCARPLZ.

G.I. JOE: THE RISE OF COBRA

CLASSIC DUKE
At the main menu, press Left, Up, Square, Up, Right, ●.

CLASSIC SCARLET
At the main menu, press Right, Up, Down, Down, ●.

GUILTY GEAR XX ACCENT CORE PLUS

FIGHT EX CHARACTERS
Highlight Arcade or M.O.M. and hold R while starting the game.

FIGHT GOLD CHARACTERS
Highlight Arcade or M.O.M. and hold L while starting the game.

FIGHT GOLD/EX CHARACTERS
Highlight Arcade or M.O.M. and hold L + R while starting the game.

HOT BRAIN

119.99 TEMPERATURE IN ALL 5 CATEGORIES
Select New Game and enter Cheat.

HOT SHOTS GOLF 2

UNLOCK EVERYTHING
Enter 2gsh as your name.

INVIZIMALS

SPECIAL INVIZIMAL
At the World Map, hold Select and press Up, Right, Down, Left. At the Big Secret select Capture Invizimals.

IRON MAN

Iron Man's different armor suits are unlocked by completing certain missions.

COMPLETE MISSION	SUIT UNLOCKED
1, Escape	Mark I
2, First Flight	Mark II
3, Fight Back	Mark III
5, Maggia Compound	Gold Tin Can
8, Frozen Ship	Classic
11, Island Meltdown	Stealth
13, Showdown	Titanium Man

PSP MINIGAMES

Minigames can be unlocked by completing the following missions. Access the minigames through the Bonus menu.

COMPLETE MISSION	PSP MINIGAME UNLOCKED
1, Escape	Tin Can Challenge 1 + 2
2, First Flight	DEATH RACE: STARK INDUSTRY
3, Fight Back	BOSS FIGHT: DREADNOUGHT
4, Weapons Transport	DEATH RACE: AFGHAN DESERT BOSS FIGHT: WHIPLASH
5, Maggia Compound	DEATH RACE: MAGGIA MANSION
6, Flying Fortress	SPEED KILL: FLYING FORTRESS SURVIVAL: FLYING FORTRESS
7, Nuclear Winter	DEATH RACE: ARTIC CIRCLE
8, Frozen Ship	SPEED KILL: FROZEN SHIP SURVIVAL: FROZEN SHIP
9, Home Front	BOSS FIGHT: TITANIUM MAN
10, Save Pepper	DEATH RACE: DAM BASSIN
11, Island Meltdown	SPEED KILL: GREEK ISLANDS SURVIVAL: GREEK ISLANDS
12, Battlesuit Factory	SPEED KILL: TINMEN FACTORY SURVIVAL: TINMEN FACTORY
13, Showdown	BOSS FIGHT: IRON MONGER

CONCEPT ART

As you progress through the game and destroy the Weapon Crates, bonuses are unlocked. You can find all of these in the Bonus menu once unlocked.

CONCEPT ART UNLOCKED	NUMBER OF WEAPON CRATES FOUND
Environments Set 1	6
Environments Set 2	12
Iron Man	18
Environments Set 3	24
Enemies	30
Environments Set 4	36
Villains	42
Vehicles	48
Covers	50

JUICED 2: HOT IMPORT NIGHTS

LAST MAN STANDING CHALLENGE AND AN ASCARI KZ1

Select Cheats and Challenges from the DNA Lab menu and enter KNOX. Defeat the challenge to earn the Ascari KZ1.

SPECIAL CHALLENGE AND AN AUDI TT 1.8 QUATTRO

Select Cheats and Challenges from the DNA Lab menu and enter YTHZ. Defeat the challenge to earn the Audi TT 1.8 Quattro.

SPECIAL CHALLENGE AND A BMW Z4

Select Cheats and Challenges from the DNA Lab menu and enter GVDL. Defeat the challenge to earn the BMW Z4.

SPECIAL CHALLENGE AND A HOLDEN MONARO
Select Cheats and Challenges from the DNA Lab menu and enter RBSG. Defeat the challenge to earn the Holden Monaro.

SPECIAL CHALLENGE AND A HYUNDAI COUPE 2.7 V6
Select Cheats and Challenges from the DNA Lab menu and enter BSLU. Defeat the challenge to earn the Hyundai Coupe 2.7 V6.

SPECIAL CHALLENGE AND AN INFINITY G35
Select Cheats and Challenges from the DNA Lab menu and enter MRHC. Defeat the challenge to earn the Infinity G35.

SPECIAL CHALLENGE AND AN INFINITY RED G35
Select Cheats and Challenges from the DNA Lab menu and enter MNCH. Defeat the challenge to earn the Infinity G35.

SPECIAL CHALLENGE AND A KOENIGSEGG CCX
Select Cheats and Challenges from the DNA Lab menu and enter KDTR. Defeat the challenge to earn the Koenigsegg CCX.

SPECIAL CHALLENGE AND A MITSUBISHI PROTOTYPE X
Select Cheats and Challenges from the DNA Lab menu and enter DOPX. Defeat the challenge to earn the Mitsubishi Prototype X.

SPECIAL CHALLENGE AND A NISSAN 350Z
Select Cheats and Challenges from the DNA Lab menu and enter PRGN. Defeat the challenge to earn the Nissan 350Z.

SPECIAL CHALLENGE AND A NISSAN SKYLINE R34 GT-R
Select Cheats and Challenges from the DNA Lab menu and enter JWRS. Defeat the challenge to earn the Nissan Skyline R34 GT-R.

SPECIAL CHALLENGE AND A SALEEN S7
Select Cheats and Challenges from the DNA Lab menu and enter WIKF. Defeat the challenge to earn the Saleen S7.

SPECIAL CHALLENGE AND A SEAT LEON CUPRA R
Select Cheats and Challenges from the DNA Lab menu and enter FAMQ. Defeat the challenge to earn the Seat Leon Cupra R.

KINGDOM HEARTS: BIRTH BY SLEEP

FINAL EPISODE
Find all of the Xehanort Reports and complete all three stories.

TRINITY ARCHIVES
Complete the story with any character.

TRINITY ARCHIVES TROPHY LIST

TROPHY	UNLOCKED BY[EL]
Power Walker	Take 99,999 steps.
Keyslinger	Defeat 9,999 Unversed.
Clockworks	Accumulate 80 hours or more of gameplay.
Arena Sweeper	Complete all arena matches.
Dairy Devotee	Activate Frozen Fortune 30 times.
In the Munny	Earn 33,333 munny.
One Down	Complete the story with any character.
Trinity	Complete all stories in at least Proud Mode.

LEGO BATMAN

BATCAVE CODES

Using the computer in the Batcave, select Enter Code and enter the following codes.

CHARACTERS

CHARACTER	CODE	CHARACTER	CODE
Alfred	ZAQ637	Penguin Henchman	BJH782
Batgirl	JKR331	Penguin Minion	KJP748
Bruce Wayne	BDJ327	Poison Ivy Goon	GTB899
Catwoman (Classic)	M1AAWW	Police Marksman	HKG984
Clown Goon	HJK327	Police Officer	JRY983
Commissioner Gordon	DDP967	Riddler Goon	CRY928
Fishmonger	HGY748	Riddler Henchman	XEU824
Freeze Girl	XVK541	S.W.A.T.	HTF114
Joker Goon	UTF782	Sailor	NAV592
Joker Henchman	YUN924	Scientist	JFL786
Mad Hatter	JCA283	Security Guard	PLB946
Man-Bat	NYU942	The Joker (Tropical)	CCB199
Military Policeman	MKL382	Yeti	NJL412
Nightwing	MVY759	Zoo Sweeper	DWR243
Penguin Goon	NKA238		

VEHICLES

VEHICLE	CODE	VEHICLE	CODE
Bat-Tank	KNTT4B	Mr. Freeze's Kart	BCT229
Bruce Wayne's Private Jet	LEA664	Penguin Goon Submarine	BTN248
Catwoman's Motorcycle	HPL826	Police Bike	LJP234
Garbage Truck	DUS483	Police Boat	PLC999
Goon Helicopter	GCH328	Police Car	KJL832
Harbor Helicopter	CHP735	Police Helicopter	CWR732
Harley Quinn's Hammer Truck	RDT637	Police Van	MAC788
Mad Hatter's Glider	HS000W	Police Watercraft	VJD328
Mad Hatter's Steamboat	M4DM4N	Riddler's Jet	HAHAHA
Mr. Freeze's Iceberg	ICYICE	Robin's Submarine	TTF453
The Joker's Van	JUK657	Two-Face's Armored Truck	EFE933

CHEATS

CHEAT	CODE	CHEAT	CODE
Always Score Multiply	9LRGNB	More Batarang Targets	XWP645
Fast Batarangs	JRBDCB	Piece Detector	KHJ554
Fast Walk	ZOLM6N	Power Brick Detector	MMN786
Flame Batarang	D8NYWH	Regenerate Hearts	HJH7HJ
Freeze Batarang	XPN4NG	Score x2	N4NR3E
Extra Hearts	ML3KHP	Score x4	CX9MAT
Fast Build	EVG26J	Score x6	MLVNF2
Immune to Freeze	JXUDY6	Score x8	WCCDB9
Invincibility	WYD5CP	Score x10	18HW07
Minikit Detector	ZXGH9J		

LEGO INDIANA JONES: THE ORIGINAL ADVENTURES

CHARACTERS

Approach the blackboard in the Classsroom and enter the following codes.

CHARACTER	CODE	CHARACTER	CODE
Bandit	12N68W	Fedora	V75YSP
Bandit Swordsman	1MK4RT	First Mate	0GIN24
Barranca	04EM94	Grail Knight	NE6THI
Bazooka Trooper (Crusade)	MK83R7	Hovitos Tribesman	HOV1SS
Bazooka Trooper (Raiders)	S93Y5R	Indiana Jones (Desert Disguise)	4J8S4M
Belloq	CHN3YU	Indiana Jones (Officer)	VJ850S
Belloq (Jungle)	TDR197	Jungle Guide	24PF34
Belloq (Robes)	VEO29L	Kao Kan	WMO46L
British Commander	B73EUA	Kazim	NRH23J
British Officer	VJ5TI9	Kazim (Desert)	3M29TJ
British Soldier	DJ5I2W	Lao Che	2NK479
Captain Katanga	VJ3TT3	Maharajah	NFK5N2
Chatter Lal	ENW936	Major Toht	13NS01
Chatter Lal (Thuggee)	CNH4RY	Masked Bandit	N48SF0
Chen	3NK48T	Mola Ram	FJUR31
Colonel Dietrich	2K9RKS	Monkey Man	3RF6YJ
Colonel Vogel	8EAL4H	Pankot Assassin	2NKT72
Dancing Girl	C7EJ21	Pankot Guard	VN28RH
Donovan	3NFTU8	Sherpa Brawler	VJ37WJ
Elsa (Desert)	JSNRT9	Sherpa Gunner	ND762W
Elsa (Officer)	VMJ5US	Slave Child	0E3ENW
Enemy Boxer	8246RB	Thuggee	VM683E
Enemy Butler	VJ48W3	Thuggee Acolyte	T2R3F9
Enemy Guard	VJ7R51	Thuggee Slave Driver	VBS7GW
Enemy Guard (Mountains)	YR47WM	Village Dignitary	KD48TN
Enemy Officer	572E61	Village Elder	4682E1
Enemy Officer (Desert)	2MK450	Willie (Dinner Suit)	VK93R7
Enemy Pilot	B84ELP	Willie (Pajamas)	MEN4IP
Enemy Radio Operator	1MF94R	Wu Han	3NSLT8
Enemy Soldier (Desert)	4NSU7Q		

EXTRAS

Approach the blackboard in the Classsroom and enter the following codes. Some cheats need to be enabled by selecting Extras from the pause menu.

CHEAT	CODE	CHEAT	CODE
Artifact Detector	VIKED7	Regenerate Hearts	MDLP69
Beep Beep	VNF59Q	Secret Characters	3X44AA
Character Treasure	VIES2R	Silhouettes	3HE85H
Disarm Enemies	VKRNS9	Super Scream	VN3R7S
Disguises	4ID1N6	Super Slap	0P1TA5
Fast Build	V83SLO	Treasure Magnet	H86LA2
Fast Dig	378RS6	Treasure x10	VI3PS8
Fast Fix	FJ59WS	Treasure x2	VM4TS9
Fertilizer	B1GW1F	Treasure x4	VLWEN3
Ice Rink	33GM7J	Treasure x6	V84RYS
Parcel Detector	VUT673	Treasure x8	A72E1M
Poo Treasure	WWQ1SA		

LEGO STAR WARS II: THE ORIGINAL TRILOGY

BEACH TROOPER
At Mos Eisley Canteena, select Enter Code and enter UCK868. You still need to select Characters and purchase this character for 20,000 studs.

BEN KENOBI (GHOST)
At Mos Eisley Canteena, select Enter Code and enter BEN917. You still need to select Characters and purchase this character for 1,100,000 studs.

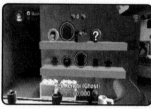

BESPIN GUARD
At Mos Eisley Canteena, select Enter Code and enter VHY832. You still need to select Characters and purchase this character for 15,000 studs.

BIB FORTUNA
At Mos Eisley Canteena, select Enter Code and enter WTY721. You still need to select Characters and purchase this character for 16,000 studs.

BOBA FETT
At Mos Eisley Canteena, select Enter Code and enter HLP221. You still need to select Characters and purchase this character for 175,000 studs.

DEATH STAR TROOPER
At Mos Eisley Canteena, select Enter Code and enter BNC332. You still need to select Characters and purchase this character for 19,000 studs.

EWOK
At Mos Eisley Canteena, select Enter Code and enter TTT289. You still need to select Characters and purchase this character for 34,000 studs.

GAMORREAN GUARD
At Mos Eisley Canteena, select Enter Code and enter YZF999. You still need to select Characters and purchase this character for 40,000 studs.

GONK DROID
At Mos Eisley Canteena, select Enter Code and enter NFX582. You still need to select Characters and purchase this character for 1,550 studs.

GRAND MOFF TARKIN
At Mos Eisley Canteena, select Enter Code and enter SMG219. You still need to select Characters and purchase this character for 38,000 studs.

GREEDO
At Mos Eisley Canteena, select Enter Code and enter NAH118. You still need to select Characters and purchase this character for 60,000 studs.

HAN SOLO (HOOD)
At Mos Eisley Canteena, select Enter Code and enter YWM840. You still need to select Characters and purchase this character for 20,000 studs.

IG-88

At Mos Eisley Canteena, select Enter Code and enter NXL973. You still need to select Characters and purchase this character for 30,000 studs.

IMPERIAL GUARD

At Mos Eisley Canteena, select Enter Code and enter MMM111. You still need to select Characters and purchase this character for 45,000 studs.

IMPERIAL OFFICER

At Mos Eisley Canteena, select Enter Code and enter BBV889. You still need to select Characters and purchase this character for 28,000 studs.

IMPERIAL SHUTTLE PILOT

At Mos Eisley Canteena, select Enter Code and enter VAP664. You still need to select Characters and purchase this character for 29,000 studs.

IMPERIAL SPY

At Mos Eisley Canteena, select Enter Code and enter CVT125. You still need to select Characters and purchase this character for 13,500 studs.

JAWA

At Mos Eisley Canteena, select Enter Code and enter JAW499. You still need to select Characters and purchase this character for 24,000 studs.

LOBOT

At Mos Eisley Canteena, select Enter Code and enter UUB319. You still need to select Characters and purchase this character for 11,000 studs.

PALACE GUARD

At Mos Eisley Canteena, select Enter Code and enter SGE549. You still need to select Characters and purchase this character for 14,000 studs.

REBEL PILOT

At Mos Eisley Canteena, select Enter Code and enter CYG336. You still need to select Characters and purchase this character for 15,000 studs.

REBEL TROOPER (HOTH)

At Mos Eisley Canteena, select Enter Code and enter EKU849. You still need to select Characters and purchase this character for 16,000 studs.

SANDTROOPER

At Mos Eisley Canteena, select Enter Code and enter YDV451. You still need to select Characters and purchase this character for 14,000 studs.

SKIFF GUARD

At Mos Eisley Canteena, select Enter Code and enter GBU888. You still need to select Characters and purchase this character for 12,000 studs.

SNOWTROOPER

At Mos Eisley Canteena, select Enter Code and enter NYU989. You still need to select Characters and purchase this character for 16,000 studs.

STORMTROOPER

At Mos Eisley Canteena, select Enter Code and enter PTR345. You still need to select Characters and purchase this character for 10,000 studs.

THE EMPEROR

At Mos Eisley Canteena, select Enter Code and enter HHY382. You still need to select Characters and purchase this character for 275,000 studs.

TIE FIGHTER

At Mos Eisley Canteena, select Enter Code and enter HDY739. You still need to select Characters and purchase this character for 60,000 studs.

TIE FIGHTER PILOT

At Mos Eisley Canteena, select Enter Code and enter NNZ316. You still need to select Characters and purchase this character for 21,000 studs.

TIE INTERCEPTOR

At Mos Eisley Canteena, select Enter Code and enter QYA828. You still need to select Characters and purchase this character for 40,000 studs.

TUSKEN RAIDER

At Mos Eisley Canteena, select Enter Code and enter PEJ821. You still need to select Characters and purchase this character for 23,000 studs.

UGNAUGHT

At Mos Eisley Canteena, select Enter Code and enter UGN694. You still need to select Characters and purchase this character for 36,000 studs.

MARVEL SUPER HERO SQUAD

IRON MAN, BONUS COSTUME "WAR MACHINE"

Select Enter Code from the Options and enter 111111.

HULK, BONUS COSTUMES "GREY HULK" & "RED HULK"

Select Enter Code from the Options and enter 222222.

WOLVERINE, BONUS COSTUMES "WOLVERINE (BROWN COSTUME)" & "FERAL WOLVERINE"

Select Enter Code from the Options and enter 333333.

THOR, BONUS COSTUMES "THOR (CHAIN ARMOR)" & "LOKI-THOR"

Select Enter Code from the Options and enter 444444.

SILVER SURFER, BONUS COSTUMES "ANTI-SURFER" & "GOLD SURFER"

Select Enter Code from the Options and enter 555555.

FALCON, BONUS COSTUME "ULTIMATES FALCON"

Select Enter Code from the Options and enter 666666.

CHEAT "SUPER KNOCKBACK"

Select Enter Code from the Options and enter 777777.

CHEAT "NO BLOCK MODE"

Select Enter Code from the Options and enter 888888.

DOCTOR DOOM, BONUS COSTUMES "ULTIMATES DOCTOR DOOM" & "PROFESSOR DOOM"

Select Enter Code from the Options and enter 999999.

CAPTAIN AMERICA, BONUS COSTUME "ULTIMATE CAPTAIN AMERICA COSTUME"

Select Enter Code from the Options and enter 177674

A.I.M. AGENT, BONUS COSTUME "BLUE SUIT A.I.M."

Select Enter Code from the Options and enter 246246

CHEAT "GROUNDED"

Select Enter Code from the Options and enter 476863

CHEAT "ONE-HIT TAKEDOWN"

Select Enter Code from the Options and enter 663448

CHEAT "INFINITE SHARD DURATION"
Select Enter Code from the Options and enter 742737

CHEAT "THROWN OBJECT TAKEDOWN"
Select Enter Code from the Options and enter 847936

MARVEL ULTIMATE ALLIANCE

UNLOCK ALL SKINS
At the Team menu, press Up, Down, Left, Right, Left, Right, Start.

UNLOCKS ALL HERO POWERS
At the Team menu, press Left, Right, Up, Down, Up, Down, Start.

ALL HEROES TO LEVEL 99
At the Team menu, press Up, Left, Up, Left, Down, Right, Down, Right, Start.

UNLOCK ALL HEROES
At the Team menu, press Up, Up, Down, Down, Left, Left, Left, Start.

UNLOCK DAREDEVIL
At the Team menu, press Left, Left, Right, Right, Up, Down, Up, Down, Start.

UNLOCK SILVER SURFER
At the Team menu, press Down, Left, Left, Up, Right, Up, Down, Left, Start.

GOD MODE
During gameplay, press Up, Down, Up, Down, Up, Left, Down, Right, Start.

TOUCH OF DEATH
During gameplay, press Left, Right, Down, Down, Right, Left, Start.

SUPER SPEED
During gameplay, press Up, Left, Up, Right, Down, Right, Start.

FILL MOMENTUM
During gameplay, press Left, Right, Right, Left, Up, Down, Down, Up, Start.

UNLOCK ALL COMICS
At the Review menu, press Left, Right, Right, Left, Up, Up, Right, Start.

UNLOCK ALL CONCEPT ART
At the Review menu, press Down, Down, Down, Right, Right, Left, Down, Start.

UNLOCK ALL CINEMATICS
At the Review menu, press Up, Left, Left, Up, Right, Right, Up, Start.

UNLOCK ALL LOAD SCREENS
At the Review menu, press Up, Down, Right, Left, Up, Up Down, Start.

UNLOCK ALL COURSES
At the Comic Missions menu, press Up, Right, Left, Down, Up, Right, Left, Down, Start.

MARVEL ULTIMATE ALLIANCE 2

GOD MODE
At any point during a game, press Up, Up, Down, Down, Left, Right, Down.

GIVE MONEY
At the Team Select or Hero Details screen press Up, Up, Down, Down, Up, Up, Up, Down.

UNLOCK ALL POWERS
At the Team Select or Hero Details screen press Up, Up, Down, Down, Left, Right, Right, Left.

ADVANCE ALL CHARACTERS TO L99
At the Hero Details screen press Down, Up, Left, Up, Right, Up, Left, Down.

UNLOCK ALL BONUS MISSIONS
While using the Bonus Mission Simulator, press Up, Right, Down, Left, Left, Right, Up, Up.

ADD 1 CHARACTER LEVEL
During a game, press Down, Up, Right, Up, Right, Up, Right, Down.

ADD 10 CHARACTER LEVELS
During a game, press Down, Up, Left, Up, Left, Up, Left, Down.

MLB 08: THE SHOW

CLASSIC FREE AGENTS AT THE PLAYER MOVEMENT MENU

At the main menu, press Left, Right, Up, Left, Right, Up, Right, Down.

SILVER ERA AND GOLDEN ERA TEAMS

At the main menu, press Right, Up, Right, Down, Down, Left, Up, Down.

BIG BALL

Pause the game and press Right, Down, Up, Left, Right, Left, Down, Up.

BIG HEAD MODE

Pause the game and press Right, Left, Down, Up, Left, Up, Down, Left.

SMALL HEAD MODE

Pause the game and press Left, Right, Down, Up, Right, Left, Down, Left.

N+

25 EXTRA LEVELS

At the main menu, hold L + R and press ✖, ●, ✖, ●, ✖, ✖, ●.

NARUTO SHIPPUDEN: ULTIMATE NINJA HEROES 3

FIGURES

At the Tree of Mettle, select Enter Password and enter the following passwords:

FIGURE	PASSWORD
Gods and Angels	Fire, Sheep, Ox, Tiger
Inheritor of the Will	Water, Dog, Snake, Ox
One Who Lurks in Darkness	Thunder, Dog, Tiger, Boar
Rivals	Earth, Sheep, Boar, Dog
Team Asuma	Fire, Dog, Rabbit, Tiger
Team Guy	Water, Dog, Rat, Rooster
Team Kurenai	Thunder, Snake, Dragon, Monkey
The Hokage's Office	Wind, Rabbit, Dragon, Ox
The Innocent Maiden	Water, Snake, Dragon, Ox
The Three Sand Siblings	Earth, Rooster, Ox, Snake

JUTSUS

At the Tree of Mettle, select Enter Password and enter the following passwords:

NINJUTSU	PASSWORD	NINJUTSU	PASSWORD
100m Punch	Thunder, Rat, Snake, Horse	Fire Style: Fire Ball Jutsu	Fire, Dragon, Rat, Monkey
Assault Blade	Wind, Rat, Rabbit, Ox	Fire Style: Yoruho'o	Fire, Horse, Rabbit, Sheep
Bring Down the House Jutsu	Thunder, Sheep, Ox, Rooster	Genjutsu: Haze	Wind, Dragon, Sheep, Rooster
Cherry Blossom Clash	Fire, Monkey, Boar, Rabbit	Genjutsu: Madder Mist	Thunder, Rooster, Boar, Dog
Dead Soul Jutsu	Thunder, Monkey, Dog, Ox	Heaven Defending Kick	Earth, Rat, Boar, Monkey
Detonation Dispersion	Wind, Dragon, Horse, Rat	Intensive Healing	Water, Rat, Tiger, Rat
Dynamic Entry	Fire, Rooster, Rabbit, Boar	Leaf Repeating Wind	Wind, Rooster, Ox, Tiger
Feather Illusion Jutsu	Water, Dragon, Boar, Dog	Lightning Blade	Thunder, Monkey, Rooster, Snake
Fire Style: Burning Ash	Fire, Rat, Rabbit, Monkey	Lightning Style: Thunderbolt Flash	Thunder, Sheep, Ox, Dog
Fire Style: Dragon Flame Bomb	Fire, Snake, Dragon, Rabbit	Slithering Snakes	Thunder, Tiger, Rooster, Dog

STUNTMAN IGNITION

3 PROPS IN STUNT CREATOR MODE
Select Cheats from Extras and enter COOLPROP.

ALL ITEMS UNLOCKED FOR CONSTRUCTION MODE
Select Cheats from Extras and enter NOBLEMAN.

MVX SPARTAN
Select Cheats from Extras and enter fastride.

ALL CHEATS
Select Cheats from Extras and enter Wearefrozen. This unlocks the following cheats: Slo-mo Cool, Thrill Cam, Vision Switcher, Nitro Addiction, Freaky Fast, and Ice Wheels.

ALL CHEATS
Select Cheats from Extras and enter Kungfoopete.

ICE WHEELS CHEAT
Select Cheats from Extras and enter IceAge.

NITRO ADDICTION CHEAT
Select Cheats from Extras and enter TheDuke.

VISION SWITCHER CHEAT
Select Cheats from Extras and enter GFXMODES.

TAK AND THE GUARDIANS OF GROSS

INVULNERABILITY
Select Cheat Codes from the Extras menu and enter KRUNKIN.

INFINITE NOVA
Select Cheat Codes from the Extras menu and enter CAKEDAY.

WEAK ENEMIES
Select Cheat Codes from the Extras menu and enter CODMODE.

ALL LEVELS
Select Cheat Codes from the Extras menu and enter GUDGEON.

ALL MINI GAMES
Select Cheat Codes from the Extras menu and enter CURLING.

ALL AWARDS
Select Cheat Codes from the Extras menu and enter SNEAKER.

ALL CONCEPT ART
Select Cheat Codes from the Extras menu and enter FRIVERS.

RAINBOW TRAIL
Select Cheat Codes from the Extras menu and enter UNICORN.

TEENAGE MUTANT NINJA TURTLES: SMASH-UP

CYBER SHREDDER
At the Bonus Content menu, press Up, Down, Right, Up, Down, Right, Left, Up, Right, Down.

4 NINJA TURTLES' ALTERNATE COSTUMES
At the Bonus Content menu, press Up, Left, Down, Right, Up, Down, Left, Up, Left, Left.

TIGER WOODS PGA TOUR 08

ALL GOLFERS
Select Passwords from the Options and enter GAMEFACE.

BRIDGESTONE ITEMS
Select Passwords from the Options and enter SHOJIRO.

COBRA ITEMS
Select Passwords from the Options and enter SNAKEKING.

GRAFALLOY ITEMS
Select Passwords from the Options and enter JUSTSHAFTS.

MACGREGOR ITEMS
Select Passwords from the Options and enter MACTEC.

MIZUNO ITEMS
Select Passwords from the Options and enter RIHACHINRIZO.

PLAYSTATION® 2

NIKE ITEMS

Select Passwords from the Options and enter JUSTDOIT.

OAKLEY ITEMS

Select Passwords from the Options and enter JANNARD.

PING ITEMS

Select Passwords from the Options and enter SOLHEIM.

PRECEPT ITEMS

Select Passwords from the Options and enter GUYSAREGOOD.

TAYLORMADE ITEMS

Select Passwords from the Options and enter MRADAMS.

TIGER WOODS PGA TOUR 09

$1,000,000

Select Passwords from the Extras menu and enter JACKPOT.

MAX SKILL POINTS

Select Passwords from the Extras menu and enter IAMRUBBISH.

ALL CLOTHING & EQUIPMENT

Select Passwords from the Extras menu and enter SHOP2DROP.

ALL PGA TOUR EVENTS

Select Passwords from the Extras menu and enter BEATIT.

ALL COVER STORIES

Select Passwords from the Extras menu and enter HEADLINER.

TONY HAWK'S PROVING GROUND

CHEAT CODES

Select Cheat Codes from the Options and enter the following cheats. Some codes need to be enabled by selecting Cheats from the Options during a game.

UNLOCK	CHEAT
Unlocks Bosco	MOREMILK
Unlocks Cam	NOTACAMERA
Unlocks Cooper	THECOOP
Unlocks Eddie X	SKETCHY
Unlocks El Patinador	PILEDRIVER
Unlocks Eric	FLYAWAY
Unlocks Judy Nails	LOVEROCKNROLL
Unlocks Mad Dog	RABBIES
Unlocks MCA	INTERGALACTIC
Unlocks Mel	NOTADUDE
Unlocks Rube	LOOKSSMELLY
Unlocks Spence	DAPPER
Unlocks Shayne	MOVERS
Unlocks TV Producer	SHAKER
Unlock FDR	THEPREZPARK
Unlock Lansdowne	THELOCALPARK
Unlock Air & Space Museum	THEINDOORPARK
Unlocks all Fun Items	OVERTHETOP
Unlock all Game Movies	WATCHTHIS
Unlock all Rigger Pieces	IMGONNABUILD
All specials unlocked and in player's special list	LOTSOFTRICKS
Full Stats	BEEFEDUP
Give player +50 skill points	NEEDSHELP
Unlocks Perfect Manual	STILLAINTFALLIN
Unlocks Perfect Rail	AINTFALLIN
Unlocks Unlimited Focus	MYOPIC
Invisible Man	THEMISSING
Mini Skater	TINYTATER

CHEAT CODE EXPLOSION FOR CONSOLES

TRANSFORMERS: THE GAME

INFINITE HEALTH
At the Main menu, press Left, Left, Up, Left, Right, Down, Right.

INFINITE AMMO
At the Main menu, press Up, Down, Left, Right, Up, Up, Down.

NO MILITARY OR POLICE
At the Main menu, press Right, Left, Right, Left, Right, Left, Right.

ALL MISSIONS
At the Main menu, press Down, Up, Left, Right, Right, Right, Up, Down.

BONUS CYBERTRON MISSIONS
At the Main menu, press Right, Up, Up, Down, Right, Left, Left.

GENERATION 1 SKIN: JAZZ
At the Main menu, press Left, Up, Down, Down, Left, Up, Right.

GENERATION 1 SKIN: MEGATRON
At the Main menu, press Down, Left, Left, Down, Right, Right, Up.

GENERATION 1 SKIN: OPTIMUS PRIME
At the Main menu, press Down, Right, Left, Up, Down, Down, Left.

GENERATION 1 SKIN: ROBOVISION OPTIMUS PRIME
At the Main menu, press Down, Down, Up, Up, Right, Right, Right.

GENERATION 1 SKIN: STARSCREAM
At the Main menu, press Right, Down, Left, Left, Down, Up, Up.

ALL COVERS
Pause the game and select Controller Setup from the Options. Press Left, Left, Right, Left, Up, Left, Left, Down.

ALL CONCEPT ART
Pause the game and select Controller Setup from the Options. Press Down, Down, Down, Up, Down, Up, Left, Left.

ALL LANDMARKS
Pause the game and select Controller Setup from the Options. Press Up, Right, Down, Left, Down, Up, Right, Left.

UP

You will need to activate the following cheats at the pause menu after entering them.

RUSSELL ATTRACTS ALL BUTTERFLIES
Select Cheats from the Bonuses menu and enter BUTTERFLY.

MUNTZ'S AVIATOR GOGGLES FOR CARL
Select Cheats from the Bonuses menu and enter AVIATORGOGGLES.

CARL JUMPS FROM TEETER TOTTER TO LIFT RUSSEL
Select Cheats from the Bonuses menu and enter CARLHEAVYWEIGHT.

BALLOONS WHEN CARL JUMPS
Select Cheats from the Bonuses menu and enter BALLOONPARTY.

WWE SMACKDOWN VS. RAW 2009

BOOGEYMAN
Select Cheat Codes from My WWE and enter BoogeymanEatsWorms!!.

GENE SNITSKY
Select Cheat Codes from My WWE and enter UnlockSnitskySvR2009.

HAWKINS & RYDER
Select Cheat Codes from My WWE and enter Ryder&HawkinsTagTeam.

JILLIAN HALL
Select Cheat Codes from My WWE and enter PlayAsJillianHallSvR.

LAYLA
Select Cheat Codes from My WWE and enter UnlockECWDivaLayla09.

RIC FLAIR
Select Cheat Codes from My WWE and enter FlairWooooooooooooo.

TAZZ
Select Cheat Codes from My WWE and enter UnlockECWTazzSvR2009.

VINCENT MCMAHON
Select Cheat Codes from My WWE and enter VinceMcMahonNoChance.

HORNSWOGGLE AS MANAGER
Select Cheat Codes from My WWE and enter HornswoggleAsManager.

CHRIS JERICHO COSTUME B
Select Cheat Codes from My WWE and enter AltJerichoModelSvR09.

CM PUNK COSTUME B
Select Cheat Codes from My WWE and enter CMPunkAltCostumeSvR!.

REY MYSTERIO COSTUME B
Select Cheat Codes from My WWE and enter BooyakaBooyaka619SvR.

SATURDAY NIGHT'S MAIN EVENT ARENA
Select Cheat Codes from My WWE and enter SatNightMainEventSvR.

WWE SMACKDOWN VS. RAW 2010

THE ROCK
Select Cheat Codes from the Options and enter The Great One.

VINCE'S OFFICE AND DIRT SHEET FOR BACKSTAGE BRAWL
Select Cheat Codes from the Options menu and enter BonusBrawl.

SHAWN MICHAELS' NEW COSTUME
Select Cheat Codes from the Options menu and enter Bow Down.

RANDY ORTON'S NEW COSTUME
Select Cheat Codes from the Options menu and enter ViperRKO.

TRIPLE H'S NEW COSTUME
Select Cheat Codes from the Options menu and enter Suck IT!.

WWE SMACKDOWN VS. RAW 2011

JOHN CENA (ENTRANCE/ CIVILIAN)
In My WWE, select Cheat Codes from the Options and enter SLURPEE.

ALL OF RANDY ORTON'S COSTUMES
In My WWE, select Cheat Codes from the Options and enter apexpredator.

TRIBUTE TO THE TROOPS ARENA
In My WWE, select Cheat Codes from the Options and enter 8thannualtribute.

X-MEN: THE OFFICIAL GAME

DANGER ROOM ICEMAN
At the Cerebro Files menu, press Right, Right, Left, Left, Down, Up, Down, Up, Start.

DANGER ROOM NIGHTCRAWLER
At the Cerebro Files menu, press Up, Up, Down, Down, Left, Right, Left, Right, Start.

DANGER ROOM WOLVERINE
At the Cerebro Files menu, press Down, Down, Up, Up, Right, Left, Right, Left, Start.

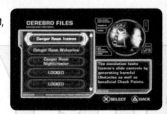